GLOBAL WARS

GLOBAL WARS

Dr. V.T. Patil

ज्ञानम् ददाति ज्ञानदा

JNANADA PRAKASHAN (P&D)

in association with

CONFEDERATION OF INDIAN UNIVERSITIES

NEW DELHI

Published by :
JNANADA PRAKASHAN (P&D)
4837/2, 24, Ansari Road, Daryaganj
New Delhi-110002
Phone : 011-23272047
Mobile : 9212137080
Email: jnanadabooksdelhi@yahoo.com
Website: www.jnanadabooks.com

Assisted by :
TEXT BOOK PROMOTION SOCIETY OF INDIA
4837/2, 24, Ansari Road, Daryaganj
New Delhi-110002
Phone : 011-23272047
Mobile : 9212137080

Edition : 2015

Global Wars

ISBN 978-81-7139-369-5

Typesetting by :
Vardhman Computers
New Delhi-110 017, India

Published by Mrs. S. Chowdhary for M/s. Jnanada Prakashan (P&D) Daryaganj, Ansari Road, New Delhi-110002, India and printed at Balaji Offset, Navin Shahdara, Delhi-110032, India.

FOREWORD

War is a reciprocated, armed conflict, between two or more non-congruous entities, aimed at reorganising a subjectively designed, geo-politically desired result.

War is an interaction in which two or more opposing forces have a "struggle of wills". The term is also used as a metaphor for non-military conflict, such as in the example of Class war.

War is not necessarily considered to be the same as occupation, murder, or genocide because of the reciprocal nature of the violent struggle, and the organised nature of the units involved.

A Civil War is either a dispute between parties within the same nation (such as in the English Civil War), or else a dispute between two nations that were created out of one formerly-united country (such as in the American Civil War). A proxy war is a war that results when two powers use third parties as substitutes for fighting each other directly.

War is also a cultural entity, and its practice is not linked to any single type of political organization or society. Rather, as discussed by John Keegan in his History Of Warfare, war is a universal phenomenon whose form and scope is defined by the society that wages it. The conduct of war extends along a continuum, from the almost universal tribal warfare that began well before recorded human history, to wars between city states, nations, or empires.

In the organised military sense, a group of combatants and their support is called an army on land, a navy at sea, and an air force in the air. Wars may be conducted simultaneously in one or more different theatres. Within each theatre, there may be one or more consecutive military campaigns.

A military campaign includes not only fighting but also intelligence, troop movements, supplies, propaganda, and other components. A period of continuous intense conflict is traditionally called a battle, although this terminology is not always applied to conflicts involving aircraft, missiles or bombs alone, in the absence of ground troops or naval forces. Also many other actions may be undertaken by military forces during a war, this could include weapons research, prison internment, assassination, occupation, and in some cases genocide may occur.

As the strategic and tactical aspects of warfare are always changing, theories and doctrines relating to warfare are often reformulated before, during, and after every major war. Carl Von Clausewitz said, 'Every age had its own kind of war, its own limiting conditions, and its own preconceptions.'

War is not limited to the human species. Ants engage in massive intra-species conflicts which might be termed warfare, and chimpanzee packs will engage each other in tribe like warfare. It is theorized that other species also engage in similar behaviour, although this is not well documented.

From late Old English (c.1050), wyrre, werre, from Old North French werre "war" (Fr. guerre), from Frankish *werra, from Proto-Germanic *werso (Compare with Old Saxon werran, Old high German werran, German verwirren "to confuse, perplex"). Cognates suggest the original sense was "to bring into confusion."

There was no common Germanic word for "war" at the dawn of historical times. Spanish, Portuguese, Italian guerra are from the same source; Romanic peoples turned to Germanic for a word to avoid Latin "bellum" because its form tended to merge with bello- "beautiful."

Before the dawn of civilization, war likely consisted of small scale raiding. One half of the people found in a Nubian cemetery dating to as early as 12,000 years ago had died of violence. Since the rise of the state some 5,000 years ago, military activity has occurred over much of the globe. The advent of gunpowder and the acceleration of technological advances led to modern warfare.

The Human Security Report 2005 documented a significant decline in the number and severity of armed conflicts since the end of the Cold War in the early 1990s. However, the evidence examined in the 2008 edition of the Center for International Development and Conflict Management's "Peace and Conflict" study indicated that the overall decline in conflicts had stalled.

Motivations for war may be different for those ordering the war than for those undertaking the war. For a state to prosecute a war it must have the support of its leadership, its military forces, and its people. For example, in the Third Punic War, Rome's leaders may have wished to make war with Carthage for the purpose of eliminating a resurgent rival, while the individual soldiers may have been motivated by a wish to make money. Since many people are involved, a war may acquire a life of its own from the confluence of many different motivations.

In Why Nations Go to War, by John G. Stoessinger, the author points out that both sides will claim that morality justifies their fight. He also states that the rationale for beginning a war depends on an overly optimistic assessment of the outcome of hostilities (casualties and costs), and on misperceptions of the enemy's intentions. In War Before Civilization, Lawrence H. Keeley, a professor at the University of Illinois, says that approximately 90-95% of known societies throughout history engaged in at least occasional warfare, and many fought constantly.

This Book will be of immense help to all those contemplating to acquire expert knowledge of the reasons of war and the related mitigation strategies.

Suggestions are welcome for improving the next edition of this important publication.

प्रियरंजन त्रिवेदी

Dr. Priya Ranjan Trivedi
President and Plenipotentiary
Confederation of Indian Universities

26 January 2010
Republic Day
New Delhi

CONTENTS

Chapter 1

WHAT IS A WAR?

War is a reciprocated, armed conflict, between two or more non-congruous entities, aimed at reorganising a subjectively designed, geo-politically desired result. In his book, On War, Prussian military theoretician Carl Von Clausewitz calls war the "continuation of political intercourse, carried on with other means." War is an interaction in which two or more opposing forces have a "struggle of wills". The term is also used as a metaphor for non-military conflict, such as in the example of Class war.

War is not necessarily considered to be the same as occupation, murder, or genocide because of the reciprocal nature of the violent struggle, and the organized nature of the units involved.

A Civil War is either a dispute between parties within the same nation (such as in the English Civil War), or else a dispute between two nations that were created out of one formerly-united country (such as in the American Civil War). A proxy war is a war that results when two powers use third parties as substitutes for fighting each other directly.

War is also a cultural entity, and its practice is not linked to any single type of political organisation or society. Rather, as discussed by John Keegan in his History Of Warfare, war is a universal phenomenon whose form and scope is defined by the society that wages it. The conduct of war extends along a continuum, from the almost universal tribal warfare that began well before recorded human history, to wars between city states, nations, or empires.

In the organised military sense, a group of combatants and their support is called an army on land, a navy at sea, and an air force in the air. Wars may be conducted simultaneously in one or more different theatres. Within each theatre, there may be one or more consecutive military campaigns.

A military campaign includes not only fighting but also intelligence, troop movements, supplies, propaganda, and other components. A period of continuous intense conflict is traditionally called a battle, although this terminology is not always applied to conflicts involving aircraft, missiles or bombs alone, in the absence of ground troops or naval forces. Also many other actions may be undertaken by military forces during a war, this could include weapons research, prison internment, assassination, occupation, and in some cases genocide may occur.

As the strategic and tactical aspects of warfare are always changing, theories and doctrines relating to warfare are often reformulated before, during, and after every major war. Carl Von Clausewitz said, 'Every age had its own kind of war, its own limiting conditions, and its own peculiar preconceptions'.

War is not limited to the human species. Ants engage in massive intra-species conflicts which might be termed warfare, and chimpanzee packs will engage each other in tribe like warfare. It is theorized that other species also engage in similar behaviour, although this is not well documented.

From late Old English (c.1050), wyrre, werre, from Old North French werre "war" (Fr. guerre), from Frankish *werra, from Proto-Germanic *werso (Compare with Old Saxon werran, Old high German werran, German verwirren "to confuse, perplex"). Cognates suggest the original sense was "to bring into confusion."

There was no common Germanic word for "war" at the dawn of historical times. Spanish, Portuguese, Italian guerra are from the same source; Romanic peoples turned to Germanic for a word to avoid Latin "bellum" because its form tended to merge with bello- "beautiful."

HISTORY OF WARFARE

Before the dawn of civilisation, war likely consisted of small-scale raiding. One half of the people found in a Nubian cemetery dating to as early as 12,000 years ago had died of violence. Since the rise of the state some 5,000 years ago, military activity has occurred over much of the globe. The advent of gunpowder and the acceleration of technological advances led to modern warfare.

Battle of White Mountain, 1620, an early battle in the Thirty Years' War.

Napoleon Bonaparte retreating from Moscow after a disastrous French invasion of Russia.

The Human Security Report 2005 documented a significant decline in the number and severity of armed conflicts since the end of the Cold War in the early 1990s. However, the evidence examined in the 2008 edition of the Center for International

Development and Conflict Management's "Peace and Conflict" study indicated that the overall decline in conflicts had stalled.

Soldiers from the U.S. Army 89th Infantry Division cross the Rhine River in assault boats, 1945.

Motivations for war may be different for those ordering the war than for those undertaking the war. For a state to prosecute a war it must have the support of its leadership, its military forces, and its people. For example, in the Third Punic War, Rome's leaders may have wished to make war with Carthage for the purpose of eliminating a resurgent rival, while the individual soldiers may have been motivated by a wish to make money. Since many people are involved, a war may acquire a life of its own from the confluence of many different motivations.

In Why Nations Go to War, by John G. Stoessinger, the author points out that both sides will claim that morality justifies their fight. He also states that the rationale for beginning a war depends on an overly optimistic assessment of the outcome of hostilities (casualties and costs), and on misperceptions of the enemy's intentions. In War Before Civilisation, Lawrence H. Keeley, a professor at the University of Illinois, says that approximately 90–95% of known societies throughout history engaged in at least occasional warfare, and many fought constantly.

In Western Europe, since the late 18th century, more than 150 conflicts and about 600 battles had taken place.

Chapter 2

MILITARY HISTORY

Military History is a humanities discipline within the scope of general historical recording of armed conflict in the history of humanity, and its impact on the societies, their cultures, economies and changing intra and international relationships.

A conflict may range from a melee between two tribal groups to conflicts between national militaries, and a world war of coalitions affecting the majority of the global human population. Military historians record and analyse the events of military history, the product of which forms an important part of how societies and their leaders formulate future plans and policies for societal development.

While human conflict has been a constant factor in the process of human social evolution over thousands of years, its historical recording only spans six millennia. There is much disagreement about when it began.

Some believe it has always been with us, derived from conflicts with other species; others stress the lack of clear evidence for it in our prehistoric past, and the fact that many peaceful, non-aggressive societies have, and still do exist. In War Before Civilisation, Lawrence H. Keeley, says that approximately 90-95% of known societies engaged in at least occasional warfare, and many fought constantly.

The essential subjects of military history study are the decision making processes of the belligerents, the society's willingness and ability to economically support war, the methods, strategic, operational and tactical used by the armed forces to achieve goals, and how these changed through the past 5,000 years of recorded history.

Through the study of history, the military command seeks to not repeat past mistakes, and improve upon its current performance by instilling an ability in commanders to perceive historical parallels during a battle, so as to capitalize on the lessons learned from the past. The main areas military history includes past conflicts, their sustainment, military command, application of doctrine known as military art and science, and the application of technology in specific military services.

The discipline of military history is dynamic, changing with development as much of the subject area as the societies and organisations that make use of it. The dynamic nature of the discipline of military history is largely related to the rapidity of change the military forces, and the art and science of managing them, as well as the frenetic pace of technological development that had taken place during the period known as the Industrial Revolution, and more recently in the nuclear and information ages.

How the change is studied, has as much to do with methods used by military historians, as the influence on these methods which are often biased towards being primarily European and technological, revolutionising how warfare is understood when compared to the previous history. This process has necessitated a periodisation of history to highlight the short spans of dramatic change between increasingly shorter periods of relative stability in development of military forces.

HISTORIOGRAPHY OF MILITARY HISTORY

Historiography is the study of the record of military conflict to gain an accurate assessment of past conflicts that may prove difficult because of bias, even in ancient times, and systematic propaganda in more modern times. For this reason military history is periodised, creating overlaying boundaries of study and analysis in which descriptions of battles by leaders may be unreliable due to the inclination to minimize mention of failures, and exaggerate when boasting of successes when viewed at a later time. This is the reason for historiographical analysis, to allow an unbiased, contemporary view of records as the participants would have perceived the events.

One military historian, Jeremy Black in a recent work raised a number of issues 21st century military historians face as an inheritance of their predecessors: Eurocentricity, a technological bias, and fascination with technology, a focus on leading military powers and dominant military systems, the separation of land from sea, and more recently air conflicts, the focus on state-to-state conflict, a lack of focus on political "tasking" in how forces are used.

If the above challenges were not sufficient for the military historians, the limitations of current methodological approaches are further complicated by the lacking of record either destroyed, or never recorded for its value as a military secret that may prevent some salient facts from being reported at all; scholars still do not know the nature of Greek fire for instance. Despite these limitations, wars are some of the most studied and detailed periods of human history.

The documentation of military history begins with the confrontation between Sumer (current Iraq) and Elam (current Iran) c.2700 BCE near the modern Basra, and includes such enduring records as the Hebrew Bible. Other prominent records in military history are the Trojan War in Homer's Iliad (though its historicity has been challenged), The Histories by Herodotus (484 BC–425 BC) who, along with Thucydides (460 BC–395 BC), is often called "father of history", the latter being regarded as the first scientific historian due to his dismissing the notions of deities taking active part in history.

His impartiality, despite being an Athenian, allowed him to take advantage of his exile to research the war from different perspectives by carefully examining documents, and interviewing eyewitnesses. The approach centered around the analysis of a leader was taken by Xenophon (430 BC–355 BC) in Anabasis, recording the expedition of Cyrus the Younger into Anatolia.

A comparative approach is made possible by the records of Julius Caesar (100 BC–44 BC), for campaigns such as Commentarii de Bello Gallico and Commentarii de Bello Civili.

Some other more recent prominent military historians include Hans Delbrück (1848-1929), Charles Oman (1860-1946), Basil Liddell Hart (1895-1970), Martin van Creveld, John Keegan, William Ledyard Rodgers, Lynn Montross, Cornelius Ryan, R. Ernest & Trevor N. Dupuy (1916-1995), George F.G. Stanley (1907-2002), John Terraine (1921-2003), Victor Davis Hanson and Jeremy Black to name a few.

Relief of Ramses II located in Abu Simbel fighting at the Battle of Kadesh on a chariot.

TECHNOLOGICAL EVOLUTION

New weapons development can dramatically alter the face of war.

In prehistoric times, fighting occurred by usage of clubs and spears, as early as 35,000 BC. Arrows, maces, and slings were developed around 12,000 BC. Chariots, pulled by animals like the onager, ox, donkey, and later the horse, originated around 2,000 BC.

The chariot was an effective, fast weapon; while one man controlled the maneuvering of the chariot, a second bowman could shoot arrows at enemy soldiers. These became crucial to the maintenance of several governments, including the New Egyptian Kingdom and the Qin dynasty.

Some of the military unit types and technologies which were developed in the ancient world are:

- Slinger
- Hoplite
- Auxiliaries
- Infantry
- Crossbowmen
- Chariots
- Cavalry

For settled agrarian civilisations, the infantry would become the core of military action. The infantry started as opposing armed groups of soldiers underneath commanders. The Greeks used rigid, heavily-armed phalanxes, but the Romans used mobile legions that were easily maneuverable.

Cavalry would become an important tool. In the Sicilian Expedition, led by Athens in an attempt to subdue Syracuse, the well-trained Syracusan cavalry became crucial to the success of the Syracusans. Macedonian Alexander the Great effectively deployed his cavalry forces to secure victories. In later battles, like the Battle of Cannae of the Second Punic War, the importance of the cavalry would be repeated.

Hannibal was able to surround the Romans on three sides and encircled them by sending the cavalry to the rear of the army. There were also horse archers, who had the ability to shoot on horseback – the Mongols were especially fearsome with this tactic. In the Middle Ages, armored cataphracts continued to fight on horseback.

Even in the First World War, cavalry was still considered important; the British mobilized 165,000 horses, the Austrians 600,000, the Germans 715,000, and the Russians more than a million.

The early Indo-Iranians developed the use of chariots in warfare. The scythed chariot was later invented in India and soon adopted by the Persian Empire. War elephants were often deployed for fighting in ancient warfare. They were first used in India and later adopted by both the Persians and Alexander the Great against one another. War elephants were also used in the Battle of the Hydaspes River, and by Hannibal in the Second Punic War against the Romans.

There were also organisational changes, made possible by better training and intercommunication. Combined arms was the concept of using infantry, cavalry, and artillery in a coordinated way. The Romans, Swiss, and others made advances with this, which arguably led to them being unbeatable for centuries.

A Greek trireme

Naval warfare was often crucial to military success. Early navies used sailing ships without cannons; often the goal was to ram the enemy ships and cause them to sink.

There was human oar power, often using slaves, built up to ramming speed. Galleys were used in the 3rd millennium BC by the Cretans. The Greeks later advanced these ships.

In 1210 BC, the first recorded naval battle was fought between Suppiluliuma II, king of the Hittites, and Cyprus, which was defeated. In the Persian Wars, the navy became of increasing importance. Triremes were involved in more complicated sea-land operations. Themistocles helped to build up a stronger Greek navy, composed of 310 ships, and defeated the Persians at the Battle of Salamis, ending the Persian invasion of Greece.

In the First Punic War, the war between Carthage and Rome started with an advantage to Carthage because of their naval experience. A Roman fleet was built in 261 BC, with the addition of the corvus that allowed Roman soldiers onboard the ships to board the enemy ships. The bridge would prove effective at the Battle of Mylae, resulting in a Roman victory.

The Vikings, in the 8th century AD, invented a ship propelled by oars with a dragon decorating the prow, hence called the Drakkar. The 12th century CE Song Dynasty invented ships with watertight bulk head compartments while the 2nd century BCE Han Dynasty invented rudders and sculled oars for their warships.

Fortifications are important in warfare. Early hill-forts were used to protect inhabitants in the Iron Age. They were primitive forts surrounded by ditches filled with water.

Forts were then built out of mud bricks, stones, wood, and other available materials. Romans used rectangular fortresses built out of wood and stone. As long as there have been fortifications, there have been contraptions to break in, dating back to the times of Romans and earlier. Siege warfare is often necessary to capture forts.

Some of the military unit types and technologies which were used in the medieval period are:

- Artillery
- Cataphract
- Condottieri
- Fyrd
- Janissary
- Knight (see also: Chivalry)
- Crossbow
- Pikeman
- Samurai
- Sipahi

Bows and arrows were often used by combatants. Egyptians shot arrows from chariots effectively. The crossbow was developed around 500 BC in China, and was used a lot in the Middle Ages. The English/Welsh longbow from the 12th century also became important in the Middle Ages. It helped to give the English a large early advantage in the Hundred Years' War, even though the English were eventually defeated. It dominated battlefields for over a century.

In the 10th century, the invention of gunpowder led to many new weapons that were improved over time. Blackpowder was used in China since the 4th century, but it was not used as a weapon until the 11th century.

Until the mid-15th century, guns were held in one hand, while the explosive charge was ignited by the other hand. Then came the matchlock, which was used widely until around the 1720s. Leonardo da Vinci made drawings of the wheel lock which made its own sparks. Eventually, the matchlock was replaced by the flintlock.

Cannons were first used in Europe in the early 14th century, and played a vital role in the Hundred Years' War. The first cannons were simply welded metal bars in the form of a cylinder, and the first cannonballs were made of stone. By 1346, at the battle of Crécy, the cannon had been used; at the Battle of Agincourt they would be used again.

A small English Civil War-era cannon

At the beginning of the 16th century, the first European fire ships were used. Ships were filled with flammable materials, set on fire, and sent to enemy lines. This tactic was successfully used by Francis Drake to scatter the Spanish Armada at the Battle of Gravelines, and would later be used by the Chinese, Russians, Greeks, and several other countries in naval battles.

Naval mines were invented in the 17th century, though they were not used in great numbers until the American Civil War. They were used heavily in the First World War and Second World War.

The first model of submarine was invented in 1624 by Cornelius Drebbel, which could go to depth of 15 feet (5 m). However, the first war submarine as we presently think of it was constructed in 1885 by Isaac Peral.

The Turtle was developed by David Bushnell during the American Revolution. Robert Fulton then improved the submarine design by creating the Nautilus (submarine).

The Howitzer, a type of field artillery, was developed in 17th century to fire high trajectory explosive shells at targets that could not be reached by flat trajectory projectiles.

A 155 mm M198 howitzer firing a shell.

Bayonets also became of wide usage to infantry soldiers. Bayonet is named after Bayonne, France where it was first manufactured in the 16th century. It is used often in infantry charges to fight in hand-to-hand combat. General Jean Martinet introduced the bayonet to the French army. They were used a lot in the American Civil War, and continued to be used in modern wars like the Invasion of Iraq.

Balloons were first used in warfare at the end of the 18th century. It was first introduced in Paris of 1783; the first balloon traveled over 5 miles (8 km). Previously military scouts could only see from high points on the ground, or from the mast of a ship. Now they could be high in the sky, signalling to troops on the ground. This made it much more difficult for troop movements to go unobserved.

At the end of the 18th century, iron-cased rockets were successfully used militarily in India against the British by Tipu Sultan of the Kingdom of Mysore during the Anglo-Mysore Wars. Rockets were generally inaccurate at that time, though William Hale, in 1844, was able to develop a better rocket. The new rocket no longer needed the rocket stick, and had a higher accuracy.

In the 1860s there were a series of advancements in rifles. The first repeating rifle was designed in 1860 by a company bought out by Winchester, which made new and improved versions. Springfield rifles arrived in the mid-19th century also. Machine guns arrived in the middle of the 19th century. Automatic rifles and light machine guns first arrived at the beginning of the 20th century.

Also in the 1860s came the first boats that would later be known as torpedo boats. These were first used in the American Civil War, but generally were not successful. Several Confederates used spar torpedoes, which were bombs on long poles designed to attach to boats. In the later part of the 19th century, the self-propelled torpedo was developed. The HNoMS Rap

At the start of the World Wars, various nations had developed weapons that were a surprise to their adversaries, leading to a need to learn from this, and alter how to combat them. Flame throwers were first used in the first world war. The French were the first to introduce the armored car in 1902. Then in 1918, the British produced the first armored troop carrier. Many early tanks were proof of concept but impractical until further development. In World War I, the British and French held a crucial advantage due to their superiority in tanks; the Germans had only a few dozen A_7V tanks, as well as 170 captured tanks. The British and French both had over several hundred each. The French tanks included the 13 ton Schnedier-Creusot, with a 75 mm gun, and the British had the Mark IV and Mark V tanks.

On December 17, 1903, the Wright Brothers performed the first controlled, powered, heavier-than-air flight; it went 39 meters (120 ft). In 1907, the first helicopter flew, but it wasn't practical for usage. Aviation became important in World War I, in which several aces gained fame. In 1911 an aircraft took off from a warship for the first time. It was a cruiser. Take-offs were soon perfected, but deck landings on a cruiser were another matter. This led to the development of an aircraft carrier with a decent unobstructed flight deck.

Chemical warfare exploded into the public consciousness in World War I but may have been used in earlier wars without as much human attention. The Germans used gas-filled shells at the Battle of Bolimov on January 3, 1915. These were not lethal, however. In April 1915, the Germans developed a chlorine gas that was highly lethal, and used it to great effect at Second Battle of Ypres.

World War II gave rise to even more technology. The worth of the aircraft carrier was proved in the battles between the United States and Japan like the Battle of Midway. Radar was independently invented by the Allies and Axis powers. It used radio waves to detect nearby objects. Molotov cocktails were invented by the Finns in 1939, during the Winter War. The atomic bomb was developed by the Manhattan Project and launched at Hiroshima and Nagasaki in 1945, ultimately ending World War II.

During the Cold War, even though fighting did not actually occur, the superpowers – the United States and Russia – engaged in a race to develop and increase the level of technology available for military purposes. In the space race, both nations attempted to launch human beings into space to the moon. Other technological advances centered around intelligence (like the spy satellite) and missiles (ballistic missiles, cruise missiles). Nuclear submarine, invented in 1955. This meant submarines no longer had to surface as often, and could run more quietly. They evolved into becoming underwater missile platforms. Cruise missiles were invented in Nazi Germany during World War II in the form of the V-1.

PERIODS OF MILITARY HISTORY

The influence of technology on military history, and evident Eurocentrism are nowhere more pronounced then in the attempt by the military historians to divide their subject area into more manageable periods of analysis. While general discipline of history subdivides history into Ancient history (Classical antiquity), Middle Ages (Europe, 4th century–15th century), Early modern period (Europe, 14th century–18th century), Modern era (Europe, 18th century–20th century), and the Post-Modern (USA, 1949–Present), the periodisation below stresses technological change in its emphasis, particularly the crucial dramatic change during the Gunpowder warfare period.

Periodisation is not uniformly applied through time and space, affirming the claims of Eurocentrism from regional historians. For example what might be described as ancient warfare is still practised in a number of parts of the world. Other eras that are distinct in European history, such as the era of Medieval warfare, may have little relevance in East Asia.

PREHISTORIC WARFARE

The beginning of prehistoric wars is a disputed issue between anthropologists and historians. In the earliest societies, such as hunter-gatherer societies, there were no social roles or divisions of labor (with the exception of age or sex differences), so every able person contributed to any raids or defense of territory.

In War Before Civilisation, Lawrence H. Keeley, a professor at the University of Illinois, calculates that 87% of tribal societies were at war more than once per year, and some 65% of them were fighting continuously. The attrition rate of numerous close-quarter clashes, which characterize warfare in tribal warrior society, produces casualty rates of up to 60%.

The introduction of agriculture brought large differences between farm workers' societies and hunter-gatherer groups. Probably, during periods of famine, hunters started to massively attack the villages of countrymen, leading to the beginning of organized warfare. In relatively advanced agricultural societies a major differentiation of roles was possible; consequently the figure of professional soldiers or militaries as distinct, organized units was born.

ANCIENT WARFARE

The first archaeological record, though disputed, of a prehistoric battle is about 14,000 years old, and is located on the Nile in Sudan, in an area known as Cemetery 117. A large number of bodies, many with arrowheads embedded in their skeletons, indicates that they may have been the casualties of a battle.

Much of what we know of ancient history is the history of militaries: their conquests, their movements, and their technological innovations. There are many reasons for this. Kingdoms and empires, the central units of control in the ancient world, could only be maintained through military force. Due to limited agricultural ability, there were relatively few areas that could support large communities, so fighting was common.

Weapons and armor, designed to be sturdy, tended to last longer than other artifacts, and thus a great deal of surviving artifacts recovered tend to fall in this category as they are more likely to survive. Weapons and armor were also mass-produced to a scale that makes them quite plentiful throughout history, and thus more likely to be found in archaeological digs.

Such items were also considered signs of posterity or virtue, and thus were likely to placed in tombs and monuments to prominent warriors. And writing, when it existed, was often used for kings to boast of military conquests or victories.

Writing, when used by the common man, also tended to record such events, as major battles and conquests constituted major events that many would have considered worthy of recording either in an epic such as the Homeric writings pertaining to the Trojan War, or even personal writings. Indeed the earliest stories center around warfare, as war was both a common and dramatic aspect of life; the witnessing of a major battle involving many thousands of soldiers would be quite a spectacle, even today, and thus considered worthy both of being recorded in song and art, but also in realistic histories, as well as being a central element in a fictional work.

Lastly, as nation states evolved and empires grew, the increased need for order and efficiency lead to an increase in the number of records and writings. Officials and armies would have good reason for keeping detailed records and accounts involving any and all things concerning a matter such as warfare that in the words of Sun Tzu was "a matter of vital importance to the state". For all these reasons, military history comprises a large part of ancient history.

Notable militaries in the ancient world included the Egyptians, Babylonians, Persians, Ancient Greeks (notably the Spartans and Macedonians), Indians (notably the Magadhas, Gangaridais and Gandharas), Early Imperial Chinese (notably the Qin and Han Dynasties), Xiongnu Confederation, Ancient Romans, and Carthaginians.

The fertile crescent of Mesopotamia was the center of several prehistoric conquests. Mesopotamia was conquered by the Sumerians, Akkadians, Babylonians, Assyrians and Persians. Iranians were the first nation who introduced cavalry into their army. Egypt began growing as an ancient power, but eventually fell to the Persians, Greeks, Romans, Byzantines and Arabs.

The earliest recorded battle in India was the Battle of the Ten Kings. The Indian epics Mahabharata and Ramayana are centred around conflicts and refer to military formations, theories of warfare and esoteric weaponry. Chanakya's Arthashastra contains a detailed study on ancient warfare, including topics on espionage and war elephants.

Alexander the Great invaded Northwestern India and defeated King Porus in the Battle of the Hydaspes River. The same region was soon conquered by Chandragupta Maurya after defeating the Macedonians and Seleucids. He also went on to conquer the Nanda Empire and unify Northern India. Most of Southern Asia was unified under his grandson Ashoka the Great after the Kalinga War, though the empire collapsed not long after his reign.

In China, the Shang Dynasty and Zhou Dynasty had risen and collapsed. This led to a Warring States Period, in which several states continued to fight with each other over territory. Philosopher-strategists such as Confucius and Sun Tzu wrote various manuscripts on ancient warfare (as well as international diplomacy).

The Warring States era philosopher Mozi (Micius) and his Mohist followers invented various siege weapons and siege crafts, including the Cloud Ladder (a four-wheeled, protractable ramp) to scale fortified walls during a siege of an enemy city. The warring states were first unified by Qin Shi Huang after a series of military conquests, creating the first empire in 'China.'

His empire was succeeded by the Han Dynasty, which expanded into Central Asia, Northern China/Manchuria, Southern China, and present day Korea and Vietnam. The Han came into conflict with settled people such as the proto-Korean Gojoseons, and proto-Vietnamese Nanyue. They also came into conflict with the Xiongnu (Huns), Yuezhi, and other steppe civilisations.

The Han defeated and drove the Xiongnus west, securing the city-states along the silk route that continued into the Parthian Empire. After the decline of central imperial authority, the Han Dynasty collapsed into an era of civil war and continuous warfare during the Three Kingdoms period in the 3rd century CE.

The Achaemenid Persian Empire was founded by Cyrus the Great after conquering the Median Empire, Neo-Babylonian Empire, Lydia and Asia Minor. His successor Cambyses went onto conquer the Egyptian Empire, much of Central Asia, and parts of Greece, India and Libya. The empire later fell to Alexander the Great after defeating Darius III. After being ruled by the Seleucid dynasty, the Persian Empire was subsequently ruled by the Parthian and Sassanid dynasties, which were the Roman Empire's greatest rivals during the Roman-Persian Wars.

In Greece, several city-states emerged to power, including Athens and Sparta. The Greeks successfully stopped two Persian invasions, the first at the Battle of Marathon, where the Persians were led by Darius the Great, and the second at the Battle of Salamis, a naval battle where the Greek ships were deployed by orders of Themistocles and the Persians were under Xerxes I, and the land engagement of the Battle of Plataea.

The Peloponnesian War then erupted between the two Greek powers Athens and Sparta. Athens built a long wall to protect its inhabitants, but the wall helped to facilitate the spread of a plague that killed about 30,000 Atheninans, including Pericles. After a disastrous campaign against Syracuse, the Athenian navy was decisively defeated by Lysander at the Battle of Aegospotami.

The Macedonians, underneath Philip II of Macedon and Alexander the Great, invaded Persia and won several major victories, establishing Macedonia as a major power. However, following Alexander's death at an early age, the empire quickly fell apart.

Meanwhile, Rome was gaining power, following a rebellion against the Etruscans. At the three Punic Wars, the Romans defeated the neighboring power of Carthage. The First Punic War centered around naval warfare. The Second Punic War started with Hannibal's invasion of Italy by crossing the Alps. He famously won the encirclement at the Battle of Cannae. However, after Scipio invaded Carthage, Hannibal was forced to follow and was defeated at the Battle of Zama, ending the role of Carthage as a power.

After defeating Carthage the Romans went on to become the Mediterranean's dominant power, successfully campaigning in Greece. (Aemilius Paulus decisive victory over Macedonia at the Battle of Pydna), in the Middle East (Lucius Licinius Lucullus, Gnaeus Pompeius Magnus), in Gaul (Gaius Julius Caesar) and defeating several Germanic tribes (Gaius Marius, Germanicus). While Roman armies suffered several major losses, their large population and ability (and will) to replace battlefield casualties, their training, organisation, tactical and technical superiority enabled Rome to stay a predominant military force for several centuries, utilising well trained and maneuverable armies to routinely overcome the much bigger "tribal" armies of their foes (see Battles of Aqua Sextiae, Vercellae, Tigranocerta, Alesia).

In 54 BCE the Roman triumvir Marcus Licinius Crassus took the offensive against the Parthian Empire in the east. In a decisive battle at Carrhae Romans were defeated and the golden Aquila (legionary battle standards) was taken as trophy to Ctesiphon. The result was one of the worst defeats suffered by the Roman Republic in its entire history.

Romans, whose armies consisted mainly of heavy infantry and only smaller cavalry contingents until then, after this defeat learnt the importance of cavalry from Iranians and eventually introduced it into their army, just as nearly a thousand year earlier the first Iranian to reached the Iranian Plateau introduced the Assyrians to a similar reform. However, the improvement of the quality of their cavalry coincided with a decline in the quality of their infantry. During the decline of the empire, the Romans relied on "barbarians" to serve in their military as federates, as well as independent "barbarian" kingdoms and their armies to defeat invaders such as the Huns.

While successfully dealing with foreign opponents, Rome experienced numerous civil wars, notably the power struggles of Roman generals such as Marius and Sulla during the end of the Republic. Caesar was also notable for his role in the civil war against the other member of the Triumvirate (Pompey) and against the Roman Senate.

The successors of Caesar–Octavian and Mark Anthony, also fought a civil war with Caesar's assassins (Senators Brutus, Crassus, etc). Octavian and Mark Anthony eventually fought another civil war between themselves to determine the sole ruler of the Rome. Octavian emerged victorious and Rome was turned into an empire with a huge standing army of professional soldiers.

By the time of Marcus Aurelius, the Romans had expanded from the Atlantic Ocean in the west to Mesopotamia in the east and controlled Northern Africa and Central Europe up to the Black Sea. However, Aurelius marked the end of the Five Good Emperors, and Rome quickly fell to decline.

The Huns, Goths, and other barbaric groups invaded Rome, which continued to suffer from inflation and other internal strifes.

Despite the attempts of Diocletian, Constantine I, and Theodosius I, western Rome collapsed and was eventually conquered in 476. The Byzantine empire continued to prosper, however.

MEDIEVAL WARFARE

When stirrups came into use some time during the dark age militaries were forever changed. This invention coupled with technological, cultural, and social developments had forced a dramatic transformation in the character of warfare from antiquity, changing military tactics and the role of cavalry and artillery.

Similar patterns of warfare existed in other parts of the world. In China around the fifth century armies moved from massed infantry to cavalry based forces, copying the steppe nomads. The Middle East and North Africa used similar, if often more advanced, technologies than Europe.

In Japan the Medieval warfare period is considered by many to have stretched into the nineteenth century. In Africa along the Sahel and Sudan states like the Kingdom of Sennar and Fulani Empire employed Medieval tactics and weapons well after they had been supplanted in Europe.

In the Medieval period, feudalism was firmly implanted, and there existed many landlords in Europe. Landlords often owned castles to protect their territory.

The Islamic Arab Empire began rapidly expanding throughout the Middle East, North Africa, and Central Asia, initially led by Khalid ibn al-Walid, and later under the Umayyads, expanded to the Iberian Peninsula in the west and the Indus Valley in the east. The Abassids then took over the Arab Empire, though the Umayyads remained in control of Islamic Spain.

At the Battle of Tours, the Franks under Charles Martel stopped short a Muslim invasion. The Abassids defeated the Tang Chinese army at the Battle of Talas, but were later defeated by the Seljuk Turks and the Mongols centuries later, until the Arab Empire eventually came to an end after the Battle of Baghdad in 1258.

In China, the Sui Dynasty had risen and conquered the Chen Dynasty of the south. They invaded Vietnam (northern Vietnam had been in Chinese control since the Han Dynasty), fighting the troops of Champa, who had cavalry mounted on elephants. After decades of economic turmoil and a failed invasion of Korea, the Sui collapsed and was followed by the Tang Dynasty, who fought with various Turkic groups, the Tibetans of Lhasa, the Tanguts, the Khitans, and collapsed due to political fragmentation of powerful regional military governors (jiedushi). The innovative Song Dynasty followed next, inventing new weapons of war that employed the use of Greek Fire and gunpowder (see section below) against enemies such as the Jurchens.

The Mongols under Genghis Khan, Ogedei Khan, Mongke Khan, and finally Kublai Khan later invaded and eventually defeated the Chinese Song Dynasty by 1279. The Mongol Empire continued to expand throughout Asia, the Middle East, and Eastern Europe, but following the death of Genghis Khan, the Mongol expansion halted and the empire was divided among his successors.

In New Zealand, prior to European discovery, oral histories, legends and whakapapa include many stories of battles and wars. Maori warriors were held in high esteem. One group of Polynesians migrated to the Chatham Islands, where they developed the largely pacifist Moriori culture. Their pacifism left the Moriori unable to defend themselves when the islands were invaded by mainland Mâori in the 1830s.

They proceeded to massacre the Moriori and enslave the survivors. Warrior culture also developed in the isolated Hawaiian Islands. During the 1780s and 1790s the chiefs and alii were constantly fighting for power. After a series of battles the Hawaiian Islands were united for the first time under a single ruler who would become known as Kamehameha I.

GUNPOWDER WARFARE

After Gunpowder weapons were first developed in Song Dynasty China (see also Technology of Song Dynasty), the technology later spread west to the Ottoman Empire, from where it spread to the Safavid Empire of Persia and the Mughal Empire of India. The arquebus was later adopted by European armies during the Italian Wars of the early 16th century.

This all brought an end to the dominance of armored cavalry on the battlefield. The simultaneous decline of the feudal system– and the absorption of the medieval city-states into larger states– allowed the creation of professional standing armies to replace the feudal levies and mercenaries that had been the standard military component of the Middle Ages.

The period spanning between the 1648 Peace of Westphalia and the 1789 French Revolution is also known as Kabinettskriege (Princes' warfare) as wars were mainly carried out by imperial or monarchics states, decided by cabinets and limited in scope and in their aims. They also involved quickly shifting alliances, and mainly used mercenaries.

Over the period of The long 19th century all military Arms and Services underwent significant developments that included a more mobile Field artillery, the transition from use of Battalion Infantry drill in close order to open order formations and the transfer of emphasis from the use of bayonets to the rifle that replaced the Musket, and virtual replacement of all types of cavalry with the universal Dragoons, or mounted infantry.

INDUSTRIAL WARFARE

As weapons—particularly small arms—became easier to use, countries began to abandon a complete reliance on professional soldiers in favor of conscription. Technological advances became increasingly important; while the armies of the previous period had usually had similar weapons, the industrial age saw encounters such as the Battle of Sadowa, in which possession of a more advanced technology played a decisive role in the outcome.

Conscription was employed in industrial warfare to increase the amount of soldiers that were available for combat. This was used by Napoleon Bonaparte in the Napoleonic Wars.

Total war was used in industrial warfare, the objective being to prevent the opposing nation to engage in war. William Tecumseh Sherman's "March to the Sea" and Philip Sheridan's burning of the Shenandoah Valley are examples of total warfare.

MODERN WARFARE

In modern times, war has evolved from an activity steeped in tradition to a scientific enterprise where success is valued above methods. The notion of total war is the extreme of this trend. Militaries have developed technological advances rivalling the scientific accomplishments of any other field of study.

However, it should be noted that modern militaries benefit in the development of these technologies under the funding of the public, the leadership of national governments, and often in cooperation with large civilian groups, such as the General Dynamics and Lockheed Martin corporations, in the United States. And as for "total war," it may be argued that it is not an exclusive practice of modern militaries, but in the tradition of genocidal conflict that marks even tribal warfare to this day.

What distinguishes modern military organisations from those previous is not their willingness to prevail in conflict by any method, but rather the technological variety of tools and methods available to modern battlefield commanders, from submarines to satellites, from knives to nuclear warheads.

Some of the military unit types and technologies which were developed in modern times are:

- Ammunition
- Armory
- Conscription
- Grenadier
- Sappers and Miners
- Marine
- Aviation

- Rifleman
- Special Forces
- Naval Combatant
- Global Information Grid
- Active Electronically Scanned Array
- Network-centric warfare
- Supercomputer
- Space warfare
- Cyberwar

World War I was sparked by the assassination of Archduke Franz Ferdinand, leading to the mobilisation of Austria and Serbia. The Germans joined the Austrians to form the Central powers; the French, British, and Russia formed the Allied powers. Following the Battle of the Marne and the outflanking attempt of both nations in the "Race to the Sea", trench warfare ensued, leaving the war in a great deadlock.

Major operations by the Germans at the Battle of Verdun and by the British and the French at the Battle of the Somme were carried out, and new technology like tanks and chlorine gas were used. Following the USA's entrance into the war, the Germans and their allies were eventually defeated.

World War II ensued after Germany's invasion of Poland, forcing Britain and France to declare war. Germany quickly defeated France and Belgium, later aided by Italy. A hasty evacuation occurred at Dunkirk to save the Allied army from complete disaster. The Germans then attacked USSR and marched to take over the Soviet resources, but were thwarted.

Meanwhile, Japan, who had already been at war with the Chinese since 1937, had launched a surprise attack on Pearl Harbor, leading the United States to join the Allied powers. In Europe, the Allies opened three fronts: in the west, after securing Normandy; in the east, aiding the Soviet Union; and in the south, through Italy. Germany eventually surrendered, upon which the Allies turned and focused troops to do island hopping. The dropping of the atom bombs on Hiroshima and Nagasaki led to the surrender of Japan and the end of the Second World War.

Worsening relationships between wartime Allies developed into the Cold War, reaching a climax during the Cuban Missile Crisis at the same time as the Sino-Indian War. Hostilities never actually occurred, though the US-backed UN forces did engage against the communist states in the Korean War and the Vietnam War.

BEHAVIOURAL THEORIES

Psychologists such as E.F.M. Durban and John Bowlby have argued that human beings are inherently violent. This aggressiveness is fueled by displacement and projection where a person transfers their grievances into bias and hatred against other races, religions, nations or ideologies. By this theory the nation state preserves order in the local society while creating an outlet for aggression through warfare. If war is innate to human nature, as is presupposed and predetermined by many psychological theories, then there is little hope of ever escaping it.

The Italian psychoanalyst Franco Fornari, a follower of Melanie Klein, thought that war was the paranoid or projective "elaboration" of mourning. Fornari thought that war and violence develop out of our "love need": our wish to preserve and defend the sacred object to which we are attached, namely our early mother and our fusion with her. For the adult, nations are the sacred objects that generate warfare. Fornari focused upon sacrifice as the essence of war: the astonishing willingness of human beings to die for their country, to give over their bodies to their nation.

While these theories may have some general explanatory value about why war exists, they do not explain when or how they occur. Nor do they explain the existence of certain human cultures completely devoid of war. If the innate psychology of the human mind is unchanging, these variations are inconsistent. A solution adapted to this problem by militarists such as Franz Alexander is that peace does not really exist. Periods that are seen as peaceful are actually periods of preparation for a later war or when war is suppressed by a state of great power, such as the Pax Britannica.

An additional problem with theories that rest on the will of the general population, is that in history only a tiny fraction of wars have originated from a desire for war from the general populace. Far more often the general population has been reluctantly drawn into war by its rulers. One psychological theory that looks at the leaders is advanced by Maurice Walsh. He argues that the general populace is more neutral towards war and that wars only occur when leaders with a psychologically abnormal disregard for human life are placed into power. War is caused by leaders that seek war such as Napoleon, Hitler, and Stalin. Such leaders most often come to power in times of crisis when the populace opts for a decisive leader, who then leads the nation to war.

EVOLUTIONARY PSYCHOLOGY

A distinct branch of the psychological theories of war are the arguments based on evolutionary psychology. This school tends to see war as an extension of animal behaviour, such as territoriality and competition. Animals are naturally aggressive, and in humans this aggression manifests itself as warfare. However, while war has a natural cause, the development of technology has accelerated human destructiveness to a level that is irrational and damaging to the species. The earliest advocate of this theory was Konrad Lorenz.

These theories have been criticized by scholars such as John G. Kennedy, who argue that the organized, sustained war of humans differs more than just technologically from the territorial fights between animals. Ashley Montagu strongly denies such universalistic instinctual arguments, pointing out that social factors and childhood socialisation are important in determining the nature and presence of warfare. Thus while human aggression may be a universal occurrence, warfare is not and would appear to have been a historical invention, associated with certain types of human societies.

SOCIOLOGICAL THEORIES

Sociology has long been very concerned with the origins of war because of its fatness, and many thousands of theories have been advanced, many of them contradictory. Sociology has thus divided into a number of schools. One, the Primat der Innenpolitik (Primacy of Domestic Politics) school based on the works of Eckart Kehr and Hans-Ulrich Wehler, sees war as the product of domestic conditions, with only the target of aggression being determined by international realities. Thus World War I was not a product of international disputes, secret treaties, or the balance of power but a product of the economic, social, and political situation within each of the states involved.

This differs from the traditional Primat der Außenpolitik (Primacy of Foreign Politics) approach of Carl von Clausewitz and Leopold von Ranke that argues it is the decisions of statesmen and the geopolitical situation that leads to peace.

DEMOGRAPHIC THEORIES

Demographic theories can be grouped into two classes, Malthusian theories and youth bulge theories.

Gari Melchers, Mural of War, 1896.

MALTHUSIAN THEORIES

Malthusian theories see expanding population and scarce resources as a source of violent conflict.

Pope Urban II in 1095, on the eve of the First Crusade, wrote, "For this land which you now inhabit, shut in on all sides by the sea and the mountain peaks, is too narrow for your large population; it scarcely furnishes food enough for its cultivators. Hence it is that you murder and devour one another, that you wage wars, and that many among you perish in civil strife. Let hatred, therefore, depart from among you; let your quarrels end. Enter upon the road to the Holy Sepulchre; wrest that land from a wicked race, and subject it to yourselves."

This is one of the earliest expressions of what has come to be called the Malthusian theory of war, in which wars are caused by expanding populations and limited resources. Thomas Malthus (1766–1834) wrote that populations always increase until they are limited by war, disease, or famine.

This theory is thought by Malthusians to account for the relative decrease in wars during the past fifty years, especially in the developed world, where advances in agriculture have made it possible to support a much larger population than was formerly the case, and where birth control has dramatically slowed the increase in population.

YOUTH BULGE THEORY

Youth bulge theory differs significantly from malthusian theories. Its adherents see a combination of large male youth cohorts–as graphically represented as a "youth bulge" in a population pyramid–with a lack of regular, peaceful employment opportunities as a risk pool for violence.

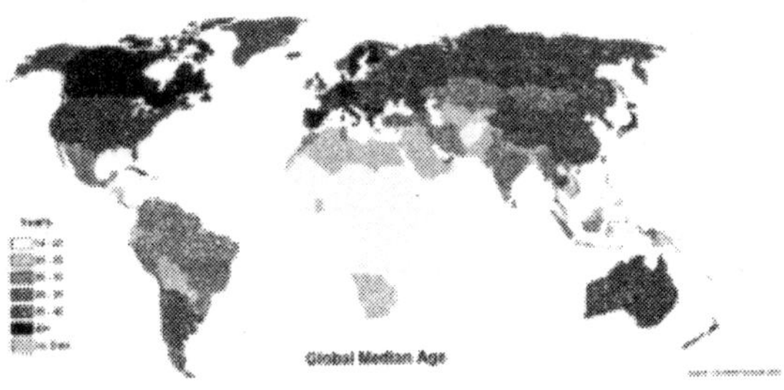

Median age by country. A youth bulge is evident for Africa, and to a lesser extent for South and Southeast Asia and Central America.

While malthusian theories focus on a disparity between a growing population and available natural resources, youth bulge theory focuses on a disparity between non-inheriting, 'excess' young males and available social positions within the existing social system of division of labour.

Contributors to the development of youth bulge theory include French sociologist Gaston Bouthoul,, U.S. sociologist Jack A. Goldstone,, U.S. political scientist Gary Fuller,, and German sociologist Gunnar Heinsohn. Samuel Huntington has modified his Clash of Civilisations theory by using youth bulge theory as its foundation:

I don't think Islam is any more violent than any other religions, and I suspect if you added it all up, more people have been slaughtered by Christians over the centuries than by Muslims. But the key factor is the demographic factor. Generally speaking, the people who go out and kill other people are males between the ages of 16 and 30. During the 1960s, 70s and 80s there were high birth rates in the Muslim world, and this has given rise to a huge youth bulge. But the bulge will fade. Muslim birth rates are going down; in fact, they have dropped dramatically in some countries. Islam did spread by the sword originally, but I don't think there is anything inherently violent in Muslim theology."

Youth Bulge theories represent a relatively recent development but seem to have become more influential in guiding U.S. foreign policy and military strategy as both Goldstone and Fuller have acted as consultants to the U.S. Government. CIA Inspector General John L. Helgerson referred to youth bulge theory in his 2002 report "The National Security Implications of Global Demographic Change".

According to Heinsohn, who has proposed youth bulge theory in its most generalized form, a youth bulge occurs when 30 to 40 per cent of the males of a nation belong to the "fighting age" cohorts from 15 to 29 years of age. It will follow periods with total fertility rates as high as 4-8 children per woman with a 15-29 year delay.

A total fertility rate of 2.1 children born by a woman during her lifetime represents a situation of in which the son will replace the father, and the daughter will replace the mother. Thus, a total fertility rate of 2.1 represents replacement level, while anything below represents a sub-replacement fertility rate leading to population decline.

Total fertility rates above 2.1 will lead to population growth and to a youth bulge. A total fertility rate of 4-8 children per mother implies 2-4 sons per mother. Consequently, one father has to leave not 1, but 2 to 4 social positions (jobs) to give all his sons a perspective for life, which is usually hard to achieve. Since respectable positions cannot be increased at the same speed as food, textbooks and vaccines, many "angry young men" find themselves in a situation that tends to escalate their adolescent anger into violence: they are

1. Demographically superfluous,
2. Might be out of work or stuck in a menial job, and
3. Often have no access to a legal sex life before a career can earn them enough to provide for a family.

The combination of these stress factors according to Heinsohn usually heads for one of six different exits:

1. Violent Crime
2. Emigration ("non violent colonisation")
3. Rebellion or putsch
4. Civil war and/or revolution
5. Genocide (to take over the positions of the slaughtered)
6. Conquest (violent colonisation, frequently including genocide abroad).

Religions and ideologies are seen as secondary factors that are being used to legitimate violence, but will not lead to violence by themselves if no youth bulge is present. Consequently, youth bulge theorists see both past "Christianist" European colonialism and imperialism and today's "Islamist" civil unrest and terrorism as results of high birth rates producing youth bulges. With the Gaza Strip now being seen as another example of youth-bulge-driven violence, especially if compared to Lebanon which is geographically close, yet remarkably more peaceful.

Among prominent historical events that have been linked to the existence of youth bulges is the role played by the historically large youth cohorts in the rebellion and revolution waves of early modern Europe, including French Revolution of 1789, and the importance of economic depression hitting the largest German youth cohorts ever in explaining the rise of Nazism in Germany in the 1930s. The 1994 Rwandan Genocide has also been analyzed as following a massive youth bulge.

While the implications of population growth have been known since the completion of the National Security Study Memorandum 200 in 1974, neither the U.S. nor the WHO have implemented the recommended measures to control population growth to avert the terrorist threat. Prominent demographer Stephen D. Mumford attributes this to the influence of the Catholic Church.

Youth Bulge theory has been subjected to statistical analysis by the World Bank, Population Action International, and the Berlin Institute for Population and Development. Detailed demographic data for most countries is available at the international database of the United States Census Bureau. Youth bulge theories have been criticized as leading to racial, gender and age discrimination.

RATIONALIST THEORIES

Rationalist theories of war assume that both sides to a potential war are rational, which is to say that each side wants to get the best possible outcome for itself for the least possible loss of life and property to its own side. Given this assumption, if both countries knew in advance how the war would turn out, it would be better for both of them to just accept the post-war outcome without having to actually pay the costs of fighting the war. This is based on the notion, generally agreed to by almost all scholars of war since Carl von Clausewitz, that wars are reciprocal, that all wars require both a decision to attack and also a decision to resist attack. Rationalist theory offers three reasons why some countries cannot find a bargain and instead resort to war: issue indivisibility, information asymmetry with incentive to deceive, and the inability to make credible commitments.

Issue indivisibility occurs when the two parties cannot avoid war by bargaining because the thing over which they are fighting cannot be shared between them, only owned entirely by one side or the other. Religious issues, such as control over the Temple Mount in Jerusalem, are more likely to be indivisible than economic issues. A bigger branch of the theory, advanced by scholars of international relations such as Geoffrey Blainey, is that both sides decide to go to war and one side may have miscalculated.

Some go further and say that there is a problem of information asymmetry with incentives to misrepresent. The two countries may not agree on who would win a war between them, or whether victory would be overwhelming or merely eked out, because each side has military secrets about its own capabilities. They will not avoid the bargaining failure by sharing their secrets, since they cannot trust each other not to lie and exaggerate their strength to extract more concessions. For example, Sweden made efforts to deceive Nazi Germany that it would resist an attack fiercely, partly by playing on the myth of Aryan superiority and by making sure that Hermann Göring only saw elite troops in action, often dressed up as regular soldiers, when he came to visit.

The American decision to enter the Vietnam War was made with the full knowledge that the communist forces would resist them, but did not believe that the guerrillas had the capability to long oppose American forces.

Thirdly, bargaining may fail due to the states' inability to make credible commitments. In this scenario, the two countries might be able to come to a bargain that would avert war if they could stick to it, but the benefits of the bargain will make one side more powerful and lead it to demand even more in the future, so that the weaker side has an incentive to make a stand now.

Rationalist explanations of war can be critiqued on a number of grounds. The assumptions of cost-benefit calculations become dubious in the most extreme genocidal cases of World War II, where the only bargain offered in some cases was infinitely bad. Rationalist theories typically assume that the state acts as a unitary individual, doing what is best for the state as a whole; this is problematic when, for example, the country's leader is beholden to a very small number of people, as in a personalistic dictatorship. Rationalist theory also assumes that the actors are rational, able to accurately assess their likelihood of success or failure, but the proponents of the psychological theories above would disagree.

Rationalist theories are usually explicated with game theory, for example, the Peace War Game, not a wargame as such, rather a simulation of economic decisions underlying war.

ECONOMIC THEORIES

Another school of thought argues that war can be seen as a growth of economic competition in a competitive international system. In this view wars begin as a pursuit of markets for natural resources and for wealth. While this theory has been applied to many conflicts. Such counter arguments become less valid as the increasing mobility of capital and information level the distributions of wealth worldwide, or when considering that it is relative, not absolute, wealth differences that may fuel wars. There are those on the extreme right of the political spectrum who provide support, fascists in particular, by asserting a natural right of the strong to whatever the weak cannot hold by force. Some centrist, capitalist, world leaders, including Presidents of the United States and US Generals, expressed support for an economic view of war.

"Is there any man, is there any woman, let me say any child here that does not know that the seed of war in the modern world is industrial and commercial rivalry?"–Woodrow Wilson, September 11, 1919, St. Louis.

"I spent 33 years and four months in active military service and during that period I spent most of my time as a high class muscle man for Big Business, for Wall Street and the bankers. In short, I was a racketeer, a gangster for capitalism."–simultaneously highest ranking and most decorated United States Marine (including two Medals of Honor) Major General Smedley Butler (and a Republican Party primary candidate for the United States Senate) 1935.

"For the corporation executives, the military metaphysic often coincides with their interest in a stable and planned flow of profit; it enables them to have their risk underwritten by public money; it enables them reasonably to expect that they can exploit for private profit now and later, the risky research developments paid for by public money. It is, in brief, a mask of the subsidized capitalism from which they extract profit and upon which their power is based." C. Wright Mills, Causes of world war 3,1960

"In the councils of government, we must guard against the acquisition of unwarranted influence, whether sought or unsought, by the military-industrial complex. The potential for disastrous rise of misplaced power exists and will persist."–Dwight Eisenhower, Farewell Address, Jan. 17, 1961. A problem with the capitalism theory is that it is difficult to point out specific major conflicts which have been caused primarily by so-called Big Business.

MARXIST THEORIES

The Marxist theory of war states that all modern wars are caused by competition for resources and markets between great (imperialist) powers. These wars are a natural progression of the free market and class system, and will only disappear once a world revolution has occurred.

POLITICAL SCIENCE THEORIES

The statistical analysis of war was pioneered by Lewis Fry Richardson following World War I. More recent databases of wars and armed conflict have been assembled by the Correlates of War Project, Peter Brecke and the Uppsala Department of Peace and Conflict Research.

There are several different international relations theory schools. Supporters of realism in international relations argue that the motivation of states is the quest for security. Which sometimes is argued to contradict the realist view, that there is much empirical evidence to support the claim that states that are democracies do not go to war with each other, an idea that has come to be known as the democratic peace theory. Other factors included are difference in moral and religious beliefs, economical and trade disagreements, declaring independence, and others.

Another major theory relating to power in international relations and machtpolitik is the Power Transition theory, which distributes the world into a hierarchy and explains major wars as part of a cycle of hegemons being destabilized by a great power which does not support the hegemons' control.

OBJECTIVIST VIEW

Ayn Rand, developer of Objectivism advocates rational individualism and laissez-faire capitalism, adduced that if men want to oppose war, it is statism that they must oppose. She maintained that so long as people hold the tribal notion that the individual is sacrificial fodder for the collective, that some men have the right to rule others by force, and that some (any) alleged "good" can justify it—there can be no peace within a nation and no peace among nations.

CONDUCT OF WARS

The war, to become known as one, must entail some degree of confrontation using weapons and other military technology and equipment by armed forces employing military tactics and Operational art within the broad military strategy subject to military logistics. War Studies by military theorists throughout military history have sought to identify the Philosophy of war, and to reduce it to a Military science.

In general, modern military science considers several factors before a National defence policy is created to allow a war to commence: the environment in the area(s) of combat operations, the posture national forces will adopt on the commencement of a war, and the type of warfare troops will be engaged in.

BEHAVIOUR AND CONDUCT IN WAR

The behaviour of troops in warfare varies considerably, both individually and as units or armies. In some circumstances, troops may engage in genocide, mass rape and ethnic cleansing. Commonly, however, the conduct of troops may be limited to posturing and sham attacks, leading to highly rule-bound and often largely symbolic combat in which casualties are much reduced from that which would be expected if soldiers were genuinely violent towards the enemy.. Situations of deliberate dampening of hostilities occurred in World War I by some accounts, e.g., a volley of gunfire being exchanged after a misplaced mortar hit the British line, after which a German soldier shouted an apology to British forces, effectively stopping a hostile exchange of gunfire.

It has been postulated that sport serves as an direct alternative to war, and may be regarded as having an equivalent social function. Sipes found war and sporting alternatives to be positively correlated.

The psychological separation between combatants, and the destructive power of modern weaponry, may act to override this effect and facilitate participation by combatants in the mass slaughter of combatants or civilians, such as in the bombing of Dresden in World War II. The unusual circumstances of warfare can incite apparently normal individuals to commit atrocities.

TYPES OF WARFARE

Conventional warfare is an attempt to reduce an opponent's military capability through open battle. It is a declared war between existing states in which nuclear, biological, or chemical weapons are not used or only see limited deployment in support of conventional military goals and maneuvers.

The opposite of conventional warfare, unconventional warfare, is an attempt to achieve military victory through acquiescence, capitulation, or clandestine support for one side of an existing conflict.

Nuclear warfare is a war in which nuclear weapons are the primary method of coercing the capitulation of the other side, as opposed to a supporting tactical or strategic role in a conventional conflict. Civil war is a war where the forces in conflict belong to the same nation or political entity and are vying for control of or independence from that nation or political entity.

Asymmetric warfare is a conflict between two populations of drastically different levels of military capability or size. Asymmetric conflicts often result in guerrilla tactics being used to overcome the sometimes vast gaps in technology and force size.

Intentional air pollution in combat is one of a collection of techniques collectively called chemical warfare. Poison gas as a chemical weapons was principally used during World War I, and resulted in an estimated 91,198 deaths and 1,205,655 injuries. Various treaties have sought to ban its further use. Non-lethal chemical weapons, such as tear gas and pepper spray, are widely used, sometimes with deadly effect.

MILITARY POSTURE

Historian Victor Davis Hanson has claimed there exists a unique "Western Way of War", in an attempt to explain the military successes of Western Europe. It originated in Ancient Greece, where, in an effort to reduce the damage that warfare has on society, the city-states developed the concept of a decisive pitched battle between heavy infantry. This would be preceded by formal declarations of war and followed by peace negotiations. In this system constant low-level skirmishing and guerrilla warfare were phased out in favour of a single, decisive contest, which in the end cost both sides less in casualties and property damage. Although it was later perverted by Alexander the Great[?], this style of war initially allowed neighbours with limited resources to coexist and prosper.

He argues that Western-style armies are characterised by an emphasis on discipline and teamwork above individual bravado.

Examples of Western victories over non-Western armies include the Battle of Marathon, the Battle of Gaugamela, the Siege of Tenochtitlan, the Battle of Plassey and the defence of Rorke's Drift.

WARFARE ENVIRONMENT

The environment in which a war is fought has a significant impact on the type of combat which takes place, and can include within its area different types of terrain. This in turn means that soldiers have to be trained to fight in a specific types of environments and terrains that generally reflects troops' mobility limitations or enablers. These include:

Conventional warfare

- Defensive warfare
- Offensive warfare
- Jungle warfare
- Border warfare a type of limited defensive warfare
- Urban warfare
- Desert warfare
- Maneuver warfare
- Trench warfare
- Mountain warfare sometimes called Alpine warfare
- Arctic warfare or Winter warfare in general
- Naval warfare or Aquatic warfare that includes Littoral, Amphibious and Riverine warfare

Unconventional warfare

- Guerilla warfare
- Psychological warfare
- Biological warfare
- Chemical warfare
- Mine warfare a type of static terrain denial warfare
- Air warfare that includes Airborne warfare and Airmobile warfare

- Sub-aquatic warfare
- Space warfare
- Electronic warfare including Radio, Radar and Network warfare
- Cyber warfare
- Directed-energy warfare
- Nuclear warfare

DEFENSIVE WARFARE

Strategic defence

A Strategic defence is a type of military planning doctrine and a set of combat activities used for the purpose of deterring, resisting and repelling a strategic offensive, conducted as either a territorial or airspace invasion, or a naval offensive to interrupt shipping lane traffic as a form of economic warfare. Strategic defensive need not be passive in nature, and often involves military deception, propaganda and psychological warfare, as well as pre-emptive strategies. All forms of military force are included in the planning, and often civil defence organisations are also included.

In terms of military theory, strategic defensive thinking seeks to understand and appreciate the theoretical and historical background to any given war and conflict scenario facing the decision-makers at the national level. The requirement of the decision makers for the strategic defence analysts is usually for providing a detailed understanding of strategic and defence issues of relevance to the national and regional relations and intentions.

Some of the more common issues encountered by strategic defence planners include:

- Problems of security and confidence-building in interstate relationships in the strategic neighbourhood
- National defence policy
- Arms proliferation and arms control in the immediate strategic region, or within reach of the weapon systems in question

- Policy advice to the higher levels of the national Defence organisation
- The strategic implications of developments in the nation's geographic region
- Reviewing security agenda, and formulating a new one if necessary

Strategic defensive is also a predominant peace-time posture of most nation-states in the world at any one time, although the national military intelligence services are always conducting operations to discover offensive threats to security to ensure adequate warning is provided to bring armed forces to a state of combat readiness.

In terms of scale of combat, the strategic defensive is considered either a war that can last from days to generations, or a military campaign as a phase of the war, involving a series of operations delimited by time and space and with specific major achievable goal allocated to a defined part of the available armed force. As a campaign, a strategic defence may consist of several battles, some of which may be offensive in nature, or may result in the conduct of withdrawals to new positions, encirclements, or sieges either by the defender or attacker as a means of securing strategic initiative. The strategic goal of a strategic defensive may require a conduct of an offensive operation far removed from the main national territory, such as the case with the 1982 Falklands campaign, which sets logistics apart as the dominant consideration in strategic defensive as a doctrine.

Chapter 3

OFFENSIVE WARFARE

An offensive is a military operation that seeks through aggressive projection of armed force to occupy territory, gain an objective or achieve some larger strategic, operational or tactical goal. Another term for an offensive often used by the media is 'invasion', or the more general 'attack'.

The offensive was considered a pre-eminent means of producing victory, although with the recognition of a defensive phase at some stage of the execution. Offensives are largely conduced as a means to secure initiative in a confrontation between opponents. They can be waged on land, at sea or in the air.

Naval offensives, such as the Japanese attack on Pearl Harbor, can have wide-ranging implications for national strategies, and require significant logistics commitment to destroy enemy military naval capabilities. It can also be used to interdict enemy shipping, such as the Battle of the Atlantic (1939–1945). Naval offensives can also be tactical in nature such as the Coronado IX operation conducted by the United States Navy's Mobile Riverine Force during the Vietnam War.

An air offensive is an operation that can describe any number of different types of operations, usually restricted to specific types of aircraft. The offensive conducted with use of fighter aircraft are predominantly concerned with establishing air superiority in a given air space, or over a given territory. A bomber offensive is sometimes also known as the strategic bombing offensive, and was prominently used by the Allies during the Second World War on a large scale. Use of ground attack aircraft in support of ground offensives can be said to be an air offensive, such as that performed in the opening phase of the Red Army's operations Kutuzov and Rumyantsev when hundreds of Il-2 aircraft were used en masse to overwhelm the Wehrmacht's ground troops.

STRATEGIC OFFENSIVE

A strategic offensive is the aggressive expression of war planning and use of strategic forces as a whole, combining all resources available for achieving defined and definitive goals that would fundamentally alter the balance of power between belligerents. However, the planning and execution of strategic offensives are always based on theoretical considerations because it is impractical, uneconomic and difficult to hide a full scale rehearsal of large scale operations.

A strategic offensive consists of simultaneous, tandem or phased operational offensives that seek to achieve specific operational objectives that eventually lead to the achievement of a strategic goal, usually a complete defeat of the opposition, but also destruction of a significant enemy force or occupation of strategically significant territory.

Any given strategic offensive is a derivative of a combination of factors such as national military doctrine, past military experience, and analysis of socio-political, economic and military circumstances.

JUNGLE WARFARE

Jungle Warfare is a term used to cover the special techniques needed for military units to survive and fight in jungle terrain.

It has been the topic of extensive study by military strategists, and was an important part of the planning for both sides in many conflicts, including World War II and the Vietnam War. The jungle environment has a variety of effects on military operations. Dense vegetation can limit lines of sight and arcs of fire, but can also provide ample opportunity for camouflage and plenty of material with which to build fortifications.

Jungle terrain, often without good roads, can be inaccessible to vehicles and so makes supply and transport difficult, which in turn places a premium on air mobility. The problems of transport make engineering resources important as they are needed to improve roads, build bridges and airfields, and improve water supplies.

Jungle environments can also be inherently unhealthy, with various tropical diseases that have to be prevented or treated by medical services. Likewise the terrain can make it difficult to deploy armoured forces, or any other kind of forces on any large scale. Successful jungle fighting emphasises effective small unit tactics and leadership.

HISTORY

World War Two

The real pioneers who methodically developed it as a specialized branch of warfare–the unconventional, low-intensity, guerrilla-style type of warfare as it is understood today–were probably the British. Examples of such early jungle-warfare forces were the Chindits, V Force and Force 136, who were small bodies of soldiers, equipped with no more than small arms and explosives, but rigorously trained in guerrilla warfare-style tactics (particularly in close-quarter combat).

Formed in the later stage of the Pacific War in support of conventional forces, these were the true jungle-warfare experts whose unconventional combat skills and tactics were specially developed for use in the jungle environment. The very beginning of it all probably traces back to immediately after the fall of Malaya and Singapore in 1942.

A few British officers, such as the legendary Freddie Spencer Chapman, eluded capture and escaped into the central Malaysian jungle where they helped organize and train bands of lightly armed local ethnic Chinese communists into a capable guerrilla force against the Japanese occupiers. What began as desperate initiatives by several determined British officers probably inspired the subsequent formation of the above-mentioned early jungle-warfare forces.

British experience in the Malayan Emergency

After the war, early skills in jungle warfare were further honed in the Malayan Emergency, when in 1948 W.W.II guerrilla fighters of the Malayan Communist Party (MCP) turned against their former British ally. Early British tactics against MCP guerrillas were unsuccessful, as W.W.II-style conventional-warfare jungle operations were ineffective against an elusive guerrilla force.

The British were quick to realize that it would take unconventional means to fight an unconventional enemy in an unconventional war, and the Special Air Service, which was created for unconventional warfare in the deserts of North Africa in W.W.II, were re-activated as the Malayan Scouts. It was the post-war SAS who pioneered the special counter insurgency tactics in the dense Malayan jungle.

By 1950 the British had a Jungle Warfare School founded by Lieutenant Colonel Walter Walker. The training given by this school was supplemented by a handbook written by Walker that was small enough to fit into a soldier's pocket and was called The Conduct of anti-Terrorist Operations in Malaya.

It included a history of Malaya, the Organisation of the British Armed Forces in Malaya, the organisation of their enemy the Malayan Communist Party, as well as the tactics and training to be used by British forces fighting in the jungles of Malaya. The first edition noted that it was not perfect, and that the GOC in Malaya welcomed criticisms and improvements.

A second edition incorporating the criticisms and improvements was issued 4 years later. A fourth edition came out in 1958. The book was not only issued to the army but to personnel in Federal Jungle Companies, the Jungle Squads, Area Security Squads and the Federal Police.

The only significant changes made in the two later editions was the inclusion on the expanded use of helicopter in operations. General Sir Gerald Templer noted in his own copy of the book that "It is largely as a result of the publication of this handbook, and its subsequent revisions, that we got militant communism in Malaya by the throat".

In addition to jungle discipline, field craft, and survival skills, special tactics such as combat tracking (first using native trackers), close-quarter fighting (tactics were developed by troopers protected only with fencing masks stalking and shooting each other in the jungle training ground with air rifles), small team operations (which led to the typical four-man special operations teams) and tree jumping (parachuting into the jungle and through the rain forest canopy) were developed to actively take the war to the Communist guerrillas instead of reacting to incidents initiated by them.

Of greater importance was the integration of the tactical jungle warfare with the strategic "winning hearts and minds" psychological, economic and political warfare as a complete counter-insurgency package. The Malayan Emergency was declared over in 1960 as the surviving Communist guerrillas were driven to the jungle near the Thai border, where they remained until they gave up their armed struggle in 1989.

AMERICAN EXPERIENCE IN VIETNAM

The British experience in counter insurgency was passed onto the Americans during their involvement in the Vietnam War, where the battlegrounds were, again, the jungle. Much of British strategic thinking on counter-insurgency tactics in a jungle environment was passed on through BRIAM (British Advisory Mission) to South Vietnam headed by Sir Robert Thompson, a former Chindit and the Permanent Secretary of Defense for Malaya during the Emergency).

The Americans further refined jungle warfare by the creation of such dedicated counter-insurgency special operations troops as the Special Forces (Green Berets), Rangers, Long Range Reconnaissance Patrols (LRRP) and Combat Tracker Teams (CTT).

Singapore Army Combat Trackers, a little known elite four-team jungle warfare unit, in Brunei during the early 1980s.

During the decade of active US combat involvement in the Vietnam War (1962-1972), jungle warfare became closely associated with counter insurgency and special operations troops.

However, although the American forces managed to have mastered jungle warfare at a tactical level in Vietnam, they were unable to install a successful strategic programme in winning a jungle-based insurgency war. Hence, the American military lost the political war in Vietnam even though U.S. forces, especially special operations troops, won almost every major military battle against the Viet Cong guerrillas and the North Vietnamese Army.

With the end of the Vietnam War, jungle warfare fell into disfavor among the major armies in the world, namely, those of the US/NATO and USSR/Warsaw Pact, which focused their attention to conventional warfare with a nuclear flavor, to be fought on the jungle-less European battlefields.

US special operations troops that were created for the purpose of fighting in the jungle environment, such as LRRP and CTT, were disbanded, while other jungle-warfare-proficient troops, such as the Special Forces and Rangers, went through a temporary period of decline, until they found their role in counter-terrorism operations in the 1980s.

The collapse of USSR in the early 1990s marked the beginning of the end of a number of proxy wars fought between the superpowers in the jungles of Africa, South America and Southeast Asia. In the euphoria at the end of the Cold War, many Western nations were quick to claim the peace dividend and reinvested resources to other priorities.

Jungle warfare was reduced in scope and priority in the regular training curriculum of most conventional Western armies. During this time, the nature of major military operations in the Middle East and Central Asia saw the need to put an emphasis upon desert warfare and urban warfare training–in both the conventional and unconventional warfare models.

BORDER WAR

Border War may refer to:

- Wars involving border disputes:
    - o List of border wars
- Border War, also referred to as Bleeding Kansas, a series of violent events, involving Free-Staters and pro-slavery elements, that took place in the Kansas Territory and the western frontier towns of the Missouri between 1854 and 1858.
- South African Border War that took place from 1966 to 1989 in South-West Africa.
- In U.S. college athletics:
    - o Border War (Kansas vs Missouri), officially known as the "Border Showdown", the rivalry between the University of Kansas and the University of Missouri

    o Border War (Colorado State vs. Wyoming), the college football game played between Colorado State University and the University of Wyoming
    o In college basketball, the term Border War typically refers to the rivalry between Indiana University and University of Kentucky. UK has the second most national championships (7) and IU the third most (5) in NCAA history. The game airs annually on CBS in December.
- Other
    o Border War: The Battle Over Illegal Immigration, a 2006 documentary about the U.S.–Mexico border

URBAN WARFARE

Urban warfare is combat conducted in urban areas such as towns and cities. Urban combat is very different from combat in the open at both the operational and tactical level. Complicating factors in urban warfare include the presence of civilians and buildings of all sorts.

Some civilians may be difficult to distinguish from combatants such as armed militias and gangs, particularly if individuals are simply trying to protect their homes from the attackers.

Tactics are complicated by a three-dimensional environment, limited fields of view and fire because of buildings, enhanced concealment and cover for defenders, below ground infrastructure, and the ease of placement of booby traps and snipers.

MILITARY TERMINOLOGY

The United States military term for urban warfare is UO an abbreviation for Urban Operations. The previously used US military term MOUT, an abbreviation for Military Operations in Urban Terrain has been replaced by UO, although the term MOUT Site is still in use.

The British military terms are OBUA (Operations in Built-Up Areas), or FIBUA (Fighting in Built-Up Areas), or sometimes

FISH (Fighting In Someone's House), or FISH and CHIPS (Fighting In Someone's House and Causing Havoc In People's Streets).

The term FOFO (Fighting in Fortified Objectives) refers to clearing enemy personnel from narrow and entrenched places like bunkers, trenches and strongholds; the dismantling of mines and wires; and the securing of footholds in enemy areas.

JGSDF soldiers from 20th Infantry Regiment practice MOUT tactics in the Ojojibara Maneuver Area of Sendai, Japan during Exercise Forest Light 2004 with American Marines.

Battle of Stalingrad fighting for a factory

URBAN OPERATIONS

Urban military operations in World War II often relied on large quantities of artillery fire and air support varying from ground attack fighters to heavy bombers. In some particularly vicious urban warfare operations such as Stalingrad and Warsaw, all weapons were used irrespective of their consequences.

Manila, the capital of the Philippines, devastated during the Battle of Manila (1945)

However, when liberating occupied territory some restraint was often applied, particularly in urban settings. For example, Canadian operations in both Ortona and Groningen avoided the use of artillery altogether to spare civilians and buildings.

Armies are bound by laws of war governing military necessity to the amount of force which can be applied when attacking an area where there are known to be civilians. Until the 1970s this was covered by customary law and IV Hague Convention "The Laws and Customs of War on Land" of 1907 and specifically articles 25-29. This has since been supplemented by the "Additional Protocols to the Geneva Conventions of 12 August 1949, and relating to the Protection of Victims of International and Non-International Armed Conflicts".

Sometimes distinction and proportionality, as in the case of the Canadians in Ortona causes the attacking force to restrain from using all the force they could when attacking a city. In other cases, such as the Battle of Stalingrad and the Battle of Berlin, both armies considered evacuating civilians only to find it impractical.

When Russian forces attacked Grozny in 1999, large amounts of artillery fire were used. The Russian Army handled the issue of civilian casualties by warning the inhabitants that they were going to launch an all-out assault on Grozny and requested that all civilians leave the city before the start of the artillery bombardment.

Fighting in an urban landscape can offer some advantages to a weaker defending force or to guerrilla fighters. The attacking army must account for three-dimensions more often, and consequently expend greater amounts of manpower in order to secure a myriad of structures, and mountains of rubble.

Ferroconcrete structures will be ruined by heavy bombardment, but it is very difficult to totally demolish such a building when it is well defended. While fighting for the Red October Steel Factory during the Battle of Stalingrad, or in 1945, Soviet forces had to fight room by room to capture the Reichstag, despite heavy bombardment with artillery at point blank range (including 203mm howtzers).

It is also difficult to destroy underground or heavily fortified structures such as bunkers and utility tunnels; during the Battle of Budapest in 1944 fighting broke out in the sewers, as both Axis and Soviet troops used them for troops movement.

URBAN WARFARE TACTICS

The characteristics of an average city include tall buildings, narrow alleys, sewage tunnels and possibly a subway system. Defenders may have the advantage of detailed local knowledge of the area, right down to the layout inside of buildings and means of travel not shown on maps.

The buildings can provide excellent sniping posts while alleys and rubble-filled streets are ideal for planting booby traps. Defenders can move from one part of the city to another undetected using underground tunnels and spring ambushes.

Meanwhile, the attackers tend to become more exposed than the defender as they must use the open streets more often, unfamiliar with the defenders' secret and hidden routes. During a house to house search the attacker is often also exposed on the streets.

Home Army soldiers assault a fortified house in downtown Warsaw during the Warsaw Uprising of 1944

BATTLE OF BERLIN

A Soviet combat group was a mixed arms unit of about eighty men, divided into assault groups of six to eight men, closely supported by field artillery. These were tactical units which were able to apply the tactics of house to house fighting that the Soviets had been forced to develop and refine at each festung stadt (fortress city) they had encountered from Stalingrad to Berlin.

The Reichstag after its capture in 1945

Berlin apartment blocks

A devastated street in Berlin city centre, 3 July, 1945.

The Germans tactics used for the urban warfare that took place in Berlin was dictated by three considerations. These were: the experience that the Germans had gained during five years of war; the physical characteristics of Berlin; and the tactics used by the Soviets.

Most of central districts of Berlin consists of city blocks with straight wide roads with several waterways, parks and large railway marshalling yards. It is predominantly flat but there are some low hills like that of Kreuzberg that is 66m above sea level.

Much of the housing stock consisted of apartments blocks built in the second half of the 19th century most of those, thanks to housing regulations, and few elevators, were five stories high built around a courtyard which could be reached from the street through a corridor large enough to take a horse and cart or the small trucks used to deliver coal.

In many places these apartment blocks were built around several courtyards one behind the other each one reached through the outer courtyards by a ground level tunnel similar to that between the first courtyard and the road. The larger more expensive flats faced the street and the smaller less expensive ones could be found around the inner courtyards.

Just as the Soviets had learned a lot about urban warfare, so had the Germans. The Waffen SS did not use the makeshift barricades erected close to street corners, because these could be raked by artillery fire from guns firing over open sights further along the straight streets.

Instead they put snipers and machine guns on the upper floors and the roofs because the Soviet tanks could not elevate their guns that high and they put men armed with panzerfausts in cellar windows to ambush tanks as they moved down the streets. These tactics were quickly adopted by the Hitler Youth and the First World War Volkssturm veterans. To counter these tactics the Soviets mounted sub-machine gunners on the tanks who sprayed every doorway and window, but this meant the tank could not traverse its turret quickly. The other solution was to rely on heavy howitzers (152mm and 203mm) firing over open sights to blast defended buildings and to use anti-aircraft guns against the German gunners on the higher floors.

Soviet combat groups started to move from house to house instead of directly down the streets. They moved through the apartments and cellars blasting holes through the walls of adjacent buildings (for which the Soviets found abandoned German panzerfausts were very effective), while others fought across the roof tops and through the attics.

These tactics took the Germans lying in ambush for tanks in the flanks. Flamethrowers and grenades were very effective, but as the Berlin civilian population had not been evacuated these tactics inevitably killed many civilians.

FIRST CHECHEN WAR

During the First Chechen War most of the Chechen fighters had been trained in the Soviet armed forces. They were divided into combat groups consisting of 15 to 20 personnel, subdivided into three or four-man fire teams.

A fire team consisted of an antitank gunner, usually armed with a Russian made RPG-7s or RPG-18s, a machine gunner and a sniper. The team would be supported by ammunition runners and assistant gunners.

To destroy Russian armoured vehicles in Grozny, five or six hunter-killer fire teams deployed at ground level, in second and third stories, and in basements. The snipers and machine gunners would pin down the supporting infantry while the antitank gunners would engage the armoured vehicle aiming at the top, rear and sides of vehicles.

Initially the Russians were taken by surprise. Their armoured columns that were supposed to take the city without difficulty as Soviet forces had taken Budapest in 1956 were decimated in fighting more reminiscent of the Battle of Budapest in late 1944.

Like their forefathers in Berlin, as a short term measure they deployed self-propelled anti-aircraft guns (ZSU-23-4 and 2K22M) to engage the Chechen combat groups, as their tank's main gun did not have the elevation and depression to engage the fire teams and an armoured vehicle's machine gun could not suppress the fire of half a dozen different fire teams simultaneously.

In the long term the Russians brought in more infantry and began a systematic advance through the city, house by house and block by block, with dismounted Russian infantry moving in support of armour. In proactive moves the Russians started to set up ambush points of their own and then move armour towards them to lure the Chechen combat groups into ambushes.

As with the Soviets tank crews in Berlin in 1945, who attached bedsprings to the outside of their turrets to reduce the damage done by German panzerfausts, some of the Russian armour was fitted quickly with a cage of wire mesh mounted some 25-30 centimetres away from the hull armor to defeat the shaped charges of the Chechen RPGs.

CLOSE-QUARTERS BATTLE

The term close-quarter battle refers to fighting methods within buildings, streets, narrow alleys and other places where visibility and maneuverability are limited.

US Marines fight in the city of Fallujah during Operation Phantom Fury/ Operation Al Fajr (New Dawn) in November 2004.

Both close-quarters-battle (CQB) and urban operations (UO) are related to urban warfare, but while UO refers mainly to the macromanagement factor (i.e. sending troops, using of heavy armoured fighting vehicles, battle management), CQB refers to the micromanagement factor—namely: how a small squad of infantry troops should fight in urban environments and/or inside buildings in order to achieve its goals with minimal casualties.

As a doctrine, CQB concerns topics such as:

- Weapons and ammunition most suitable for the mission
- Extra gear, such as bulletproof vests and night vision devices
- Accurate explosives
- Routines and drills for engaging the enemy, securing a perimeter, clearing a room, etc.
- Team maneuvers
- Methods and tactics

It should be noted that military CQB doctrine is different from police CQB doctrine, mainly because the military usually operates in hostile areas while the police operates within docile populations.

Armies that often engage in urban warfare operations may train most of their infantry in CQB doctrine.

DESERT WARFARE

Desert Warfare is combat in deserts. In desert warfare the elements can sometimes be more dangerous than the actual enemy. The desert terrain is the second most inhospitable to troops following a cold environment.

PROPERTIES AND TACTICS OF DESERT WARFARE

One of the few times desert warfare can be desirable is against foreign armies that are not familiar with the area or experienced in desert warfare. Knowing how to navigate in the desert is the desert fighter's best advantage.

Maps and intelligence personnel can not prepare a force for terrains such as small hills, rivers, and wells. There are two ways to fight in the desert, like all environments, guerrilla warfare and conventional warfare. The successful defender or attacker will need to know how to maneuver around in this environment and use it as advantage.

From a small hilltop or a hole in the ground, one man with a scoped rifle can cause heavy casualties on armies due to the lack of cover in the desert, which allows for clear vision of the enemy. A good sniper can be a major danger to an opposing army in desert terrain. The professional army is well trained and will be looking for the sniper, but one shot from a sniper is all that is needed to kill someone, and it will surprise the troops, rendering them unable to respond. However, a second shot may give away the sniper's position.

The sniper's advantage of little cover in the desert is also his disadvantage because the enemy will be looking for where a sniper would hide, and there are not many choices. Another reason to keep snipers is that they can keep an enemy from getting water as well as destroy their water supply. A small force can defeat a larger, "stronger", thirstier force.

Mobility is essential to a successful desert war. This explains the heavy use of armor in battles such as El Alamein in the Second

World War. It has been noted that mobility is so important in desert warfare, that battles can sometimes begin to resemble naval engagements, where the actual possession of territory is less important than the positions of ones tanks (or ships).

There are many enemies to the desert fighter. These include aircraft, and tanks, which can be extremely menacing to desert guerrillas because there is little way to equal such force. Additionally, there are few places to hide from such weapons in the desert environment where there is little obstruction.

Lack of water and extreme heat can also cause complications when engaging in desert warfare. Another lethal enemy is the landmine. Though not limited to desert use, it is a deadly device and underrated in its importance, as it is difficult to detect and can deny mobility.

Although many unexpected things happen in war, when two conventional armies fight, the one with the best tanks, aircraft, and tactics usually wins. A example of this would be the Gulf War and the beginning of the 2003 invasion of Iraq.

MANEUVER WARFARE

Maneuver Warfare, also spelled manoeuvre warfare, is the term used by military theorists for a concept of warfare that advocates attempting to defeat an adversary by incapacitating their decision-making through shock and disruption brought about by movement. Its concepts are reflected by a number of strategies seen throughout military history.

BACKGROUND

Methods of war stand on a continuum between maneuver warfare and attrition warfare, the focus on achieving victory through killing or capturing an adversary. Maneuver warfare advocates recognize that all warfare involves both maneuver and attrition.

Maneuver warfare concepts have historically been stressed by militaries which are smaller, more cohesive, better trained, or more technically able than attrition warfare counterparts. The term "Tactical Maneuver" is used by maneuver warfare theorists to refer to movement by forces to gain "advantageous position relative to the enemy" as opposed to its use in the phrase "maneuver warfare".

The idea of using rapid movement to keep an enemy off-balance is as old as war itself. However changing technology such as the development of cavalry and mechanized vehicles, has led to increased interest in the concepts of maneuver warfare and its role on modern battlefields.

CONCEPTS

Western (U.S.) military orthodoxy believes that with some exceptions, most battles between established armies have historically been fought based on an attrition warfare strategy. Closer examination however reveals this view is not universally held, and many military doctrines and cultures are based on replete historical examples of maneuver warfare.

The attritionalists' view of warfare involves moving masses of men and material against enemy strongpoints, with the emphasis on the destruction of the enemy's physical assets–success as measured by enemy troops killed, equipment and infrastructure destroyed, and territory taken and/or occupied. Attrition warfare tends to utilize rigidly centralised command structures that require little or no creativity or initiative from lower-level leadership (also called top-down or "command push" tactics).

This has been called "industrial war" by some since it relies on 'mass'. The semi-static, large scale battles of the American Civil War, Crimean War and World War I are classic examples of attrition warfare.

Maneuver warfare doctrine sees styles of warfare as a spectrum with attrition warfare and maneuver warfare on opposite ends. In attrition warfare the enemy is seen as a collection of targets to be found and destroyed. Attrition warfare exploits maneuver to bring to bear firepower to destroy enemy forces, maneuver warfare on the other hand, exploits firepower and attrition on key elements of opposing forces.

Maneuver warfare advocates that strategic movement can bring about the defeat of an opposing force more efficiently than by simply contacting and destroying enemy forces until they can no longer fight. Instead, in maneuver warfare, the destruction of certain enemy targets (command and control centers, logistical bases, fire support assets, etc.) is combined with isolation of enemy forces and the exploitation by movement of enemy weaknesses.

Bypassing and cutting off enemy strongpoints often results in the collapse of that strongpoint even where the physical damage is minimal (e.g. the Maginot Line). Fire power, which is used primarily to destroy as many enemy forces as possible in attrition warfare, is used to suppress or destroy enemy positions at breakthrough points during maneuver warfare. Infiltration tactics by conventional or special operations forces may be used extensively to cause chaos and confusion behind enemy lines.

Leonhard summarises maneuver warfare theory as: preempt, dislocate, and disrupt the enemy as alternatives to destruction of enemy mass through attrition warfare. Clarification of the Clausewitzian center of gravity (COG) concept in maneuver warfare terms suggests the question: is a COG the source of strength or the critical vulnerability? This issue can be resolved using the game of chess as a model: is the Queen (most powerful piece) or the King (whose loss ends the game) the opposing player's COG? Once you knock off the opposing player's King, it does not matter how many other chess pieces you take.

Since tempo and initiative are so critical to the success of maneuver warfare, command structures tend to be more decentralised, with more tactical freedom given to lower-level unit leaders. This decentralised command structure allows "on the ground" unit leaders, while still working within the guidelines of commander's overall vision, to exploit enemy weaknesses as they become evident (also called "recon-pull" tactics or directive control).

War theorist Martin VanCreveld identifies six main elements of maneuver warfare:

- Tempo: Tempo as illustrated by John Boyd's OODA loop.
- Schwerpunkt (focal point): The center of effort, or striking the enemy at the right place at the right time. According to vanCreveld, ideally, a spot that is both vital and weakly defended.
- Surprise: based on deception.
- Combined arms
- Flexibility: According to VanCreveld flexibility means a military must be well rounded, self contained and redundant.
- Decentralized command: Rapid changing situations may out pace communications. Lower levels must understand overall intent.

EARLY EXAMPLES

For the majority of history armies were limited in their speed to that of the marching soldier, about equal for everyone involved. This meant that it was possible for opposing armies to simply march around each other as long as they wished, with supply conditions often deciding where and when the battle would finally be fought. Perhaps the last and most famous example of this ended with the Battle of Agincourt in 1415, prior to which Henry V of England avoided combat while marching to Calais to resupply, allowing him to pick the battlefield.

One of most famous early maneuver tactics was the double envelopment, used by Hannibal against the Romans at the Battle of Cannae in 216 BC, and by Khalid ibn al-Walid against the Persian Empire at the Battle of Walaja in 633 AD.

In prehistoric times this began to change with the domestication of the horse, the invention of chariots and the increasing military use of the cavalry. The cavalry had two major uses: one, to attack and use its momentum to break infantry formations; and two, using the advantage of speed to cut communications and isolate formations for later defeat in detail.

NAPOLEON'S USE OF MANEUVER

Similar strategies are also possible using infantry suitably trained and in recent times it was Napoleon who showed this to great effect. He used the combination of cavalry movement and fast infantry movement to bring about the defeat of superior forces whilst they were still moving to their intended place of battle.

This allowed his forces to attack where and when he wanted, often giving him the advantage of terrain to disable effective movement by his enemy. Thus he used maneuver both strategically (when and where to fight) and tactically (how to fight the battle he chose).

Napoleon's fame as a general, and indeed his powerbase to become head of the French state, was based on a powerful and fluent campaign in Northern Italy principally against the numerically superior Austrians. He cited Frederick the Great as one of his major sources of his strategy.

He trained a normal, if rather undisciplined, French Army of Italy to be able to move faster than most thought possible, certainly likely. In part this was because his Army lived off the land and had no big logistical 'tail'. His ability to move huge armies to give battle where he wanted and in the style of his choosing became legendary and he seemed undefeatable even against larger and superior forces.

It was these and later defeats that caused the major doctrinal re-evaluation by the Prussians under Carl von Clausewitz on the revealed power of maneuver warfare. The results of this review were seen in the Franco-Prussian War.

Napoleon also arranged his forces into what we today would call 'Battle Groups' of combined arms formations to allow faster reaction time to enemy action. This is an important support measure for maneuver warfare to be most effective and was copied by von Clausewitz.

Napoleon's principal strategy was to move fast so as to engage before the enemy had time to organize, to lightly engage whilst moving to turn the flank that defended the main resupply route, to envelop and deploy blocking forces to prevent reinforcement, and to defeat in detail those contained in the envelopment. All of these activities imply faster movement than the enemy as well as faster reaction times to enemy activities. His use of fast mass marches to gain strategic advantage, cavalry probes and screens to hide his movements, and deliberate movement to gain psychological advantage by isolating forces from each other and HQ are all hallmarks of maneuver warfare. One of his major issues was the relatively slow speed of infantry movement relative to the cavalry.

MECHANISATION

As a result of the introduction of various forms of mechanized transport, starting with the steam powered trains in mid-19th century, logistics have been vastly improved and the opposing armies were no longer limited in speed by the pace of march. Some train-borne maneuvering took place during the American Civil War in the 1860s, but the sizes of the armies involved meant the system could provide only limited support. Armored trains were among the first armored fighting vehicles employed by mankind.

In the Franco-Prussian War the Prussian Army, knowing that they could field substantially larger forces than the French, devised a war plan that relied on speed by encircling and destroying/bypassing French strongpoints–the Kesselschlacht or "cauldron battle"–while the remainder of the Prussian army advanced unopposed to seize important objectives such as Paris.

If, on declaration of war, they could mobilize quickly, invade and destroy French field forces fast enough, then they would be victorious before the French army could react. This tactic was used to devastating effect in 1870, when the Prussian forces were able to rapidly encircle and defeat two large French forces before they were able to retreat. Given the success they had in 1870s, it is not surprising that the German battle plan for the First World War would be similar. The Germans attempted to repeat the "knock-out blow" against the French armies in the Schlieffen Plan.

However technology had changed considerably in the four decades, with the machine gun and considerably more powerful artillery swinging the balance of power decisively to the defense. While all combatants were desperate to get the front moving again, this proved difficult.

The introduction of the tank in a series of increasingly successful operations pointed the way out of trench warfare, but the war ended before the British plans to field thousands of them could be put into place. Germany also introduced new tactics against static warfare with infiltration and stormtrooper tactics toward the end of World War I, which bypassed resistance leaving its reduction to other means.

Between the World Wars the Germans again reviewed their doctrine and completely revised their approach again, perhaps getting back to some of the von Clausewitz ideas which were now enabled by motor transport. During the Second World War, Germany pursued its new strategy known to many as blitzkrieg, or "lightning war". Blitzkrieg is perhaps the most famous example of maneuver warfare and derived in part from the theories of many, perhaps including British officer J.F.C. Fuller, of which the British army had failed to take advantage.

The Soviets used the concept of "Deep Battle" (which they continued through the Cold War). The Western Allies were strategically attrition-oriented, though maneuver-minded comm. anders included O'Connor, Montgomery and Patton.

MANEUVER WARFARE DOCTRINE

According to the United States Marine Corps, one key concept of maneuver warfare is that maneuver is traditionally thought of as a spatial concept, that is the use of maneuver so as to gain positional advantage. The US Marine concept of maneuver however is a "warfighting philosophy that seeks to shatter the enemy's cohesion through a variety of rapid, focused, and unexpected actions which create a turbulent and rapidly deteriorating situation with which the enemy cannot cope."

THE US MARINE MANUAL GOES ON TO SAY:

"This is not to imply that firepower is unimportant. On the contrary, firepower is central to maneuver warfare. Nor do we mean to imply that we will pass up the opportunity to physically destroy the enemy. We will concentrate fires and forces at decisive points to destroy enemy elements when the opportunity presents itself and when it fits our larger purposes."

The possibility of a massive Soviet offensive in Western Europe led to the creation of the United States Army's AirLand battle doctrine. Though far from focusing on maneuver, it emphasized using combined arms to disrupt an adversary's plans by striking through their depth and was seen as moving towards maneuver warfare in comparison to the earlier Active Defense concept. The AirLand doctrine was seen by Martin van Creveld as "arguably a half way house between maneuver and attrition."

DEVELOPMENT OF MANEUVER WARFARE THEORIES

By far the most important development of manoeuvre theories took place in Germany and the USSR during the 1920s and 1930s, notably with the development of the "Deep Battle" concept that was integrated into he Red Army field regulations doctrine by Marshal Tukhachevsky.

While the Wehrmacht developed from this the operations named Blitzkrieg, in the USSR this led to the creation of the Cavalry Mechanised Groups during the Second World War, and the Operational manoeuvre groups during the Cold War.

JOHN BOYD AND US ACCEPTANCE OF MANEUVER WARFARE:

Much of the credit for acceptance of maneuver warfare in the United States military is given to fighter pilot John Boyd. None of Boyd's main ideas of maneuver warfare theory were his ideas alone or original to Boyd but were based on his research of military history. Boyd's research began during development of the close air support aircraft, the A-10.

Boyd and designer Pierre Sprey interviewed Stuka pilots and armor commanders for data regarding tactical information such as the time required to find and target a tank from the air. Boyd then broadened his research in an attempt to understand the German army's rapid successes against France in 1940. To further understand concepts used by the German military in World War II, upon which maneuver warfare is largely based, Boyd studied Clausewitz, Jomini and the Napoleonic era.

Boyd also studied tactics used by the Mongols, Byzantines and Ottomans. Boyd traced military thought back to Sun Tzu. The basic idea derived was that a combination of light troops and heavy troops seeking the enemy weak point for a decisive blow.

Boyd believed that many Western commanders focused on winning the battle while Eastern commanders fought against the enemy's mind. Boyd's critique of Clausewitz was that while Clausewitz saw the "fog of war" as producing difficulties and sought to reduce friction so as to more effectively fight the enemy, Sun Tzu actively sought to increase friction and confusion amongst opposing forces.

According to writer Grant Hammond, Boyd believed that the Battle of Marathon, Battle of Leuctra, Battle of Arbela and the Battle of Cannae were battles of maneuver warfare with "unequal distribution of forces to gain a local advantage and decisive leverage to collapse adversary resistance".

RECENT THEORISTS

Recent military theorists of a non-firepower focus include Robert Leonhard, Robert Bateman, John Boyd, Michael Wyly, and Donald Vandergriff.

LIMITATIONS IN A MODERN CONTEXT

A key requirement for success in maneuver warfare is accurate, up-to-date intelligence on the disposition of key enemy command, support and combat units. While such intelligence has been available for many of the higher profile conflicts characterising the last two decades, in operations where intelligence is either inaccurate, unavailable or unreliable, the successful implementation of strategies based on maneuver warfare can become problematic.

Furthermore, when faced with a maneuverable opponent capable of redeploying key forces quickly and discretely, or where political considerations are integral to a belligerent's definition of success, such as in asymmetrical warfare, the capacity of maneuver warfare strategies to deliver victory becomes more challenging.

An example where such shortcomings have been exposed is during the 2006 Lebanon War where, despite overwhelming firepower and complete air superiority, Israeli forces were unable to deliver a decisive blow to the command structure of Hezbollah nor effectively degrade its capacity to operate. Although inflicting heavy damage, Israel's inability to locate and destroy Hezbollah's diluted force dispositions or neutralise key command centres ultimately meant that it did not meet its war aims. Additionally, the insurgency in Iraq also demonstrates that a military victory over an opponent's conventional forces does not automatically translate into a political one.

Some military theorists such as William Lind and Colonel Thomas X. Hammes propose to overcome shortcomings of maneuver warfare with the concept of what they call fourth generation warfare. Others, for example Lieutenant-Colonel S.P. Myers writes that: "manoeuvre is more a philosophical approach to campaign design and execution than an arrangement of tactical engagements". Myers writes that maneuver warfare can evolve and that: "manoeuvrist approach in campaign design and execution remains relevant and effective as a counter-insurgency strategy at the operational level in contemporary operations".

TRENCH WARFARE

Trench Warfare was a form of warfare in which both combatants occupied static fortified fighting lines consisting largely of trenches, in which troops were largely immune to the enemy's small arms fire and were substantially sheltered from artillery. It has become a byword for stalemate in conflict, with a slow wearing down of opposing forces. Trench warfare occurred when a revolution in fire power was not matched by similar advances in mobility, resulting in a slow and grueling form of warfare in which the defence held the advantage. Both sides constructed elabourate and heavily-armed trench and dugout systems opposing each other along a front, protected from assault by barbed wire. The area between opposing trench lines (known as "no man's land") was fully exposed to small arms and artillery fire from both sides. Attacks, even if successful, often sustained severe casualties as a matter of course.

Periods of trench warfare occurred during the American Civil War, the Russo-Japanese War and the Second Anglo-Boer War, but trench warfare is mainly associated with World War I, when it lasted on the Western Front from September 1914 until the last weeks of the war. By the end of October 1914 the whole front in Belgium and France had solidified into lines of trenches, as it became clear that infantry assaults were futile in the face of rifle, machine gun and artillery fire. Both sides concentrated on breaking up enemy attacks and on protecting their own troops by digging deep into the ground. Trench warfare was also conducted on other fronts, including Italy and Gallipoli.

ORIGINS

Frontal assault became increasingly costly in the mid-19th century, due to the development of improved firearms technology. The American Civil War was the first conflict to demonstrate the bloody nature of modern mass warfare. By 1865 the war had many of the characteristics of World War I, including mass casualties, machine guns and trenches. Most of its engagements of were battles of fire and manoeuvre, though the cost of attacking across open ground was amply demonstrated, but there were two major instances of trench warfare. The Siege of Vicksburg in 1863 represented the first large-scale use of trench warfare during the war. The Battle of Petersburg, near the end of the war, lasted 10 months and had opposing trench lines stretching up to 30 miles (48 km).

American Civil War: Soldiers of the Union Army in trenches at Petersburg, 1865.

Two factors were responsible for the adoption of trench warfare. The first was the increase in the killing-power of small-arms fire. By the American Civil War rifles, manufactured in the thousands, had become ubiquitous. The adoption of the Minié ball increased the range, accuracy and rate of fire of muzzle-loading rifles. Trained troops were able to fire at a rate of three rounds per minute while maintaining accuracy up to 500 yards, though firing distances in the war were often much shorter. Effective at more than double the range of the typical smoothbore of the Napoleonic era and firing more rapidly, Civil War rifles enabled men sheltering in a trench or behind an improvised obstacle to hold a body of attackers at a much greater distance than before; attackers were unable to cross the swept zone rapidly enough to avoid prohibitive casualties, even if the defenders were heavily outnumbered. Both at Vicksburg and at Petersburg, repeated frontal assaults were bloody failures.

Secondly, the tactical situation prevented the use of manoeuvre to circumvent the defender's fortified position, for instance by turning a flank. Massed armies, moved and supplied by rail, made it possible to hold an extended front in strength. Vicksburg and

Petersburg were both essentially localised sieges, albeit conducted against trench lines rather than masonry fortifications; the siege of Petersburg was eventually broken partly by Grant's tactical manoeuvring, extending the Confederate line to breaking point. In World War I, flank marching became impossible due to the solidifying of a continuous front 475 miles (750 km) long, from frontier to sea.

The similarities between these American Civil War sieges and the titanic struggle of the Western Front can be exaggerated: they had at least as much in common with the methodical sieges of Vauban as they did with the trench warfare of World War I. Other developments appearing after the end of the American Civil War contributed greatly to the trench warfare of World War I. Barbed wire, invented in 1874, which in itself did only minor harm, could slow the progress of an attacking force and channel it into killing zones, enabling emplaced defenders to inflict crippling losses. Firepower continued to multiply, yet mobility and communications did not keep pace. In South Africa (1899–1902) the British army learned, to its cost, the effectiveness of long-range rifle fire, which could even silence artillery. Magazine-fed repeating rifles became almost universal, further increasing the firepower of the infantryman. The pre-war British army expected its infantry to fire at 12 to 15 rounds a minute. Machine guns could multiply this effect. In the American Civil War the hand-cranked Gatling guns were little more than a novelty, but by 1914 all belligerents used fully-automatic machine guns in considerable numbers: in 1912 the German army began a programme to equip each infantry battalion with a six-gun machine gun company, though it had not been completed by the outbreak of war. The British considered the Vickers machine gun to be equivalent to 40 riflemen, and they deployed two per battalion in 1914.

Firepower further increased through the improvement of artillery. The development of steel breech-loading guns by Krupp greatly increased its effectiveness, as was graphically demonstrated in the Franco-Prussian War of 1870–71. Hydraulic recoil (or QF, for Quick-Firing) mechanisms, pioneered by the French "75", greatly increased the rate of fire by avoiding the need to re-lay the gun after each shot; "fixed" munitions (shell and charge in one unit) speeded reloading. Use of high explosive shells and improved shrapnel shells amplified killing and destructive power. The introduction of telephone communication permitted artillery spotting far from the physical artillery batteries, widening artillery usefulness in indirect fire at longer ranges and speeding shifting of targets. The swept zone between attacker and defender became a no man's land, too lethal to cross.

The European powers sent observers to Manchuria in 1904–05, where they witnessed the impact of these developments in the Russo-Japanese War: they could see there the impact of machine guns, the importance of heavy artillery, indirect fire and telephone communications, and the usefulness of mortars and hand grenades. It was clear that the lethality of modern weapons would bring about a major revival in the use of obstacles and entrenchments.

A Cheshire Regiment sentry in a trench near La Boisselle during the Battle of the Somme, July 1916

IMPLEMENTATION

Although firearms, technology, and the conscript army dramatically changed the nature of warfare, most armies were completely unaware of the implications of these changes and were not prepared for their consequences. As early as 1864, the opposing armies in the American Civil War were entrenched near Petersburg, Virginia for months, and tactics which were later to be tried in Europe, such as subterranean mines, were employed to break the stalemate to little effect.

At the start of World War I, most armies prepared for a brief war whose strategy and tactics would have been familiar to Napoleon. Indeed, a number of horse cavalry units were brought to the front by train, commanded by officers who did not imagine the factors that would render them useless. Most of these units were never deployed. Infantry, armed with bolt action rifles and augmented by machine guns, needed only to dig to become nigh invulnerable. To attack frontally was to court crippling losses, so an outflanking operation was essential. After the Battle of the Aisne in September 1914, an extended series of attempted flanking moves, and matching extensions to the fortified defensive lines, soon saw the celebrated "race to the sea"; German and Allied armies produced essentially a matched pair of trench lines from the Swiss border in the south to the North Sea coast of Belgium. Trench warfare prevailed on the Western Front from September 16, 1914, until the Germans launched their "Spring Offensive", Operation Michael, on March 21, 1918.

On the Western Front, the small improvised trenches of the first few months rapidly grew deeper and more complex, gradually becoming vast areas of interlocking defensive works. Such defensive works resisted both artillery bombardments and mass infantry assaults. The space between the opposing trenches was referred to as no man's land and varied in width depending on the battlefield. On the Western Front it was typically between 100 and 300 yards (90-275 m), though only 30 yards (27 m) on Vimy Ridge. After the German withdrawal to the Hindenburg line in March 1917, it stretched to over a kilometre in places. At the infamous "Quinn's Post" in the cramped confines of the Anzac battlefield at Gallipoli, the opposing trenches were only 16 yards (15 m) apart and hand grenades were thrown constantly. On the Eastern Front and in the

Middle East, the areas to be covered were so vast, and the distances from the factories supplying shells, bullets, concrete and barbed wire so great, trench warfare in the European style often did not occur.

In the Alps, trench warfare even stretched onto vertical slopes and deep into the mountains, to heights of 3900 m (12795 ft) above sea level. The Ortler had an artillery position on its summit near the front line. The trench-line management and trench profiles had to be adapted to the rough terrain, hard rock, and harsh weather conditions. Many trench systems were constructed within glaciers like the Adamello-Presanella group or the famous city below the ice on the Marmolada in the Dolomites.

1st Lancashire Fusiliers, in communication trench near Beaumont Hamel, Somme, 1916

DEFENSIVE SYSTEM

Very early in the war, British defensive doctrine suggested a main trench system of three parallel lines, interconnected by communications trenches. The point at which a communications trench intersected the front trench was of critical importance, and it was usually heavily fortified. The front trench was lightly garrisoned and typically only occupied in force during "stand to" at dawn and dusk. Between 70 and 100 yards (64-91 m) behind the front trench was located the support (or "travel") trench, to which the garrison would retreat when the front trench was bombarded. Between 300 and 500 yards (275-460 m) further to the rear was located the third reserve trench, where the reserve troops could amass for a counter-attack if the front trenches were captured. This defensive layout was soon rendered obsolete as the power of artillery grew; however, in certain sectors of the front, the support trench was maintained as a decoy to attract the enemy bombardment away from the front and reserve lines. Fires were lit in the support line to make it appear inhabited and any damage done immediately repaired.

Temporary trenches were also built. When a major attack was planned, assembly trenches would be dug near the front trench. These were used to provide a sheltered place for the waves of attacking troops who would follow the first waves leaving from the front trench. "Saps" were temporary, unmanned, often dead-end utility trenches dug out into no-man's land. They fulfilled a variety of purposes, such as connecting the front trench to a listening post close to the enemy wire or providing an advance "jumping-off" line for a surprise attack. When one side's front line bulged towards the opposition, a salient was formed. The concave trench line facing the salient was called a "re-entrant." Large salients were perilous for their occupants because they could be assailed from three sides.

Behind the front system of trenches there were usually at least two more partially prepared trench systems, kilometres to the rear, ready to be occupied in the event of a retreat. The Germans often prepared multiple redundant trench systems; in 1916 their Somme front featured two complete trench systems, one kilometer apart, with a third partially completed system a further kilometer behind. This duplication made a decisive breakthrough virtually impossible. In the event that a section of the first trench system was captured, a "switch" trench would be dug to connect the second trench system to the still-held section of the first. The Germans made something of a science out of designing and constructing defensive

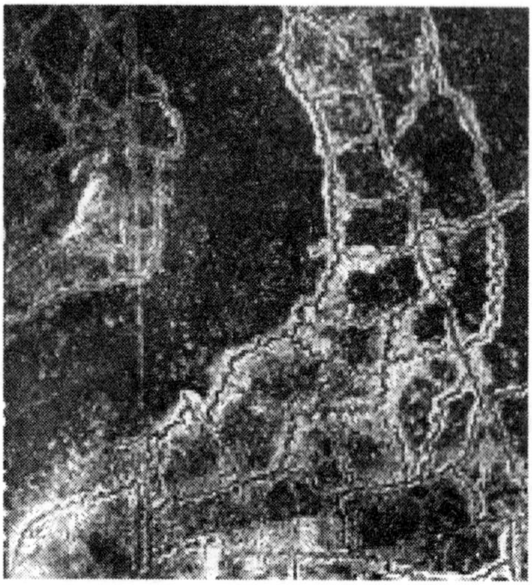

Aerial view of opposing trench lines between Loos and Hulluch, July 1917. German trenches at the right and bottom, British at the top-left.

works. They used reinforced concrete to construct deep, shell-proof, ventilated dugouts, as well as strategic strongpoints. They were more willing than their opponents to make a strategic withdrawal to a superior prepared defensive position. They were also the first to apply the concept of "defense in depth," where the front-line zone was hundreds of yards deep and contained a series of redoubts rather than a continuous trench. Each redoubt could provide supporting fire to its neighbours, and while the attackers had freedom of movement between the redoubts, they would be subjected to withering enfilade fire. The British eventually adopted a similar approach, but it was incompletely implemented when the Germans launched the 1918 Spring Offensive and proved disastrously ineffective. France, by contrast, relied on artillery and reserves, not entrenchment. The characteristic barbed wire placed before trenches, in belts 15 m (50 ft) deep or more, differed, too; the German wire was heavier gauge, and British wire cutters, designed for the thinner native product, were unable to cut it.

TRENCH CONSTRUCTION

Fighting trenches were usually about 12 feet deep. Trenches were never straight but were dug in a zigzagging or stepped pattern. Later fighting trenches broke the line into firebays connected by traverses. This meant that a soldier could never see more than 10 meters (30 ft) or so along the trench. Consequently, the entire trench could not be enfiladed if the enemy gained access at one point; or if a bomb or shell landed in the trench, the blast could not travel far. The banked earth on the lip of the trench facing the enemy was called the parapet and had a fire step. The embanked rear lip of the trench was called the parados. The parados protected the soldier's back from shells falling behind the trench. The sides of the trench were often revetted with sandbags, wooden frames and wire mesh. The floor of the trench was usually covered by wooden duckboards. In later designs the floor might be raised on a wooden frame to provide a drainage channel underneath.

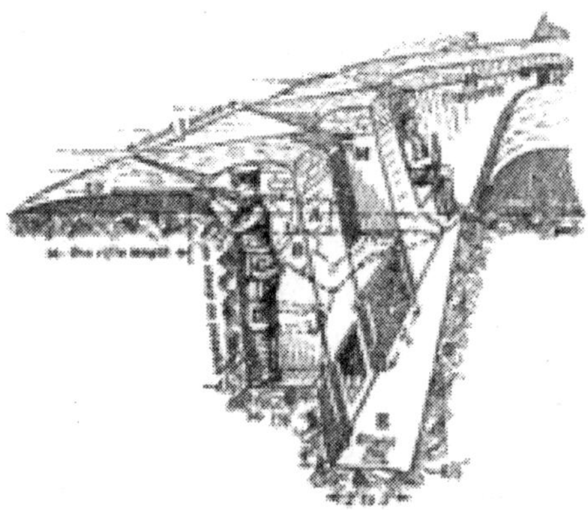

Trench construction diagram from a 1914 British infantry manual

Dugouts of varying degrees of luxury would be built in the rear of the support trench. British dugouts were usually 8 to 16 feet (2.5-5 m) deep, whereas German dugouts were typically much deeper, usually a minimum of 12 feet (3.6 m) deep and sometimes dug three stories down, with concrete staircases to reach the upper levels.

Australian light horseman using a periscope rifle, Gallipoli 1915

To allow a soldier to see out of the trench without exposing his head, a loophole could be built into the parapet. A loophole might simply be a gap in the sandbags, or it might be fitted with a steel plate. German snipers used armour-piercing bullets that allowed them to penetrate loopholes. Another means to see over the parapet was the trench periscope—in its simplest form, just a stick with two angled pieces of mirror at the top and bottom. In the Anzac trenches at Gallipoli, where the Turks held the high ground, the periscope rifle was developed to enable the Australians and New Zealanders to snipe at the enemy without exposing themselves over the parapet.

There were three standard ways to dig a trench: entrenching, sapping, and tunneling. Entrenching, where a man would stand on the surface and dig downwards, was most efficient, as it allowed a large digging party to dig the full length of the trench simultaneously. However, entrenching left the diggers exposed above ground and hence could only be carried out when free of observation, such as in a rear area or at night. Sapping involved extending the trench by digging away at the end face. The diggers were not exposed, but only one or two men could work on the trench at a time. Tunneling was like sapping except that a "roof" of soil was left in place while the trench line was established and then removed when the trench was ready to be occupied. The guidelines for British trench construction stated that it would take 450 men 6 hours at night to complete 250 m (275yd) of front-line trench system. Thereafter, the trench would require constant maintenance to prevent deterioration caused by weather or shelling.

Breastwork "trench", Armentières, 1916

The battlefield of Flanders presented numerous problems for the practice of trench warfare, especially for the Allied forces, mainly British and Canadians, who were often compelled to occupy the low ground. Heavy shelling quickly destroyed the network of ditches and water channels which had previously drained this low-lying area of Belgium. In most places, the water table was only a meter or so below the surface, meaning that any trench dug in the ground would quickly flood. Consequently, many "trenches" in Flanders were actually above ground and constructed from massive breastworks of sandbags filled with clay. Initially, both the parapet and parados of the trench were built in this way, but a later technique was to dispense with the parados for much of the trench line, thus exposing the rear of the trench to fire from the reserve line in case the front was breached.

TRENCH GEOGRAPHY

The confined, static, and subterranean nature of trench warfare resulted in it developing its own peculiar form of geography. In the forward zone, the conventional transport infrastructure of roads and rail were replaced by the network of trenches and light tramways. The critical advantage that could be gained by holding the high ground meant that minor hills and ridges gained enormous significance. Many slight hills and valleys were so subtle as to have been nameless until the front line encroached upon them. Some hills were named for their height in meters, such as Hill 60. A farmhouse, windmill, quarry, or copse of trees would become the focus of a determined struggle simply because it was the largest identifiable feature. However, it would not take the artillery long to obliterate it, so that thereafter it became just a name on a map.

German stormtroopers training with a flamethrower near Sedan, France, May 1917

Battlefield features could be given a descriptive name ("Polygon Wood" near Ypres or "Lone Pine"), a whimsical name ("Sausage Valley" and "Mash Valley" on the Somme), a unit name ("Inniskilling Inch" at Helles named for the Royal Inniskilling Fusiliers) or the name of a soldier ("Monash Valley" at Anzac named after General John Monash). Prefixing a feature with "Dead Man's" was also popular for obvious reasons, such as "Dead Man's Road" leading in to Pozières, or "Dead Man's Ridge" at Anzac.

There were numerous trench networks named "The Chessboard" or "The Gridiron" because of the pattern they described. For the Australians at Mouquet Farm, the advances were so short and the terrain so featureless that they were reduced to naming their objectives as "points" on the map, such as "Point 81" and "Point 55."

Enemy trenches, which would become objectives in an attack, needed to be named as well. Many were named for some observed event such as "German Officers' Trench" at Anzac or "Ration Trench" on the Somme. The British gave an alcoholic flavour to the German trenches in front of Ginchy: "Beer Trench," "Bitter Trench," "Hop Trench," "Ale Alley," and "Pilsen Trench." Other objectives were named according to their role in the trench system, such as the "Switch Trench" and "Intermediate Trench" on the Somme. Some sections of the British trench system read like a Monopoly board, with names such as "Park Lane" and "Bond Street". British regular divisions habitually named their trenches after units, which resulted in names such as "Munster Alley" (Royal Munster Fusiliers), "Black Watch Alley" (Black Watch Regiment) and "Border Barricade" (Border Regiment). The Anzacs tended to name features after soldiers ("Plugge's Plateau," "Walker's Ridge," "Quinn's Post," "Johnston's Jolly," "Russell's Top," "Brind's Road" and so forth).

LIFE IN THE TRENCHES

An individual unit's time in the front-line trench was usually brief; from as little as one day to as much as two weeks at a time before being relieved. The Australian 31st Battalion once spent 53 days in the line at Villers Bretonneux, but such a duration was a rare exception. The 10th Battalion, CEF, averaged front line tours of six days in 1915 and 1916.

On an individual level, a typical British soldier's year could be divided as follows:

- 15% front line
- 10% support line

- 30% reserve line
- 20% rest
- 25% other (hospital, travelling, leave, training courses, etc.)

French trench at Côte 304, Verdun, 1916

Studying French in the Trenches," The Literary Digest, October 20, 1917.

Even when in the front line, the typical battalion would only be called upon to engage in fighting a handful of times a year—making an attack, defending against an attack or participating in a raid. The frequency of combat would increase for the units of the "elite" fighting divisions—on the Allied side; the British regular divisions, the Canadian Corps, the French XX Corps and the Anzacs. Some sectors of the front saw little activity throughout the war, making life in the trenches comparatively easy. When the I Anzac Corps first arrived in France in April 1916 after the evacuation of Gallipoli, they were sent to a relatively peaceful sector south of Armentières to "acclimatise". Other sectors were in a perpetual state of violent activity. On the Western Front, Ypres was invariably hellish, especially for the British in the exposed, overlooked salient. However, quiet sectors still amassed daily casualties through sniper fire, artillery, disease, and poison gas.

In the first six months of 1916, before the launch of the Somme Offensive, the British did not engage in any significant battles on their sector of the Western Front and yet suffered 107,776 casualties. About 1 in 8 men would return alive and unwounded from the trenches.

A sector of the front would be allocated to an army corps, usually comprising three divisions. Two divisions would occupy adjacent sections of the front and the third would be in rest to the rear. This breakdown of duty would continue down through the army structure, so that within each front-line division, typically comprising three infantry brigades (regiments for the Germans), two brigades would occupy the front and the third would be in reserve. Within each front-line brigade, typically comprising four battalions, two battalions would occupy the front with two in reserve. And so on for companies and platoons. The lower down the structure this division of duty proceeded, the more frequently the units would rotate from front-line duty to support or reserve.

Chateau Wood, Ypres, 1917

During the day, snipers and artillery observers in balloons made movement perilous, so the trenches were mostly quiet. Consequently, trenches were busiest at night, when cover of darkness allowed the movement of troops and supplies, the maintenance and expansion of the barbed wire and trench system, and reconnaissance of the enemy's defenses. Sentries in listening posts out in no man's land would try to detect enemy patrols and working parties or indications that an attack was being prepared.

Pioneered by the Princess Patricia's Canadian Light Infantry in February 1915, trench raids were carried out in order to capture prisoners and "booty"—letters and other documents to provide intelligence about the unit occupying the opposing trenches. As the war progressed, raiding became part of the general British policy, the intention being to maintain the fighting spirit of the troops and to deny no man's land to the Germans. As well, they were intended to compel the enemy to reinforce, which exposed his troops to artillery fire. Such dominance was achieved at a high cost when the enemy replied with his own artillery, and a post-war British analysis concluded the benefits were probably not worth the cost. Early in the war, surprise raids would be mounted, particularly by the Canadians, but increased vigilance made achieving surprise difficult as the war progressed. By 1916, raids were carefully planned exercises in combined arms and involved close co-operation of infantry and artillery. A raid would begin with an intense artillery bombardment designed to drive off or kill the front-trench garrison and cut the barbed wire. Then the bombardment would shift to form a "box barrage", or cordon, around a section of the front line to prevent a counter-attack intercepting the raid. However, the bombardment also had the effect of notifying the enemy of the location of the planned attack, thus allowing reinforcements to be called in from wider sectors.

DEATH IN THE TRENCHES

The intensity of World War I trench warfare meant about 10% of the fighting soldiers were killed. This compared to 5% killed during the Second Boer War and 4.5% killed during World War II. For British and Dominion troops serving on the Western Front, the proportion of troops killed was 12.5%, while the total proportion of troops who became casualties (killed or wounded) was 56%.

Medical services were primitive and antibiotics had not yet been discovered. Relatively minor injuries could prove fatal through onset of infection and gangrene. The Germans recorded that 15% of leg wounds and 25% of arm wounds resulted in death, mainly through infection. The Americans recorded 44% of casualties who developed gangrene died. 50% of those wounded in the head died and 99% of those wounded in the abdomen died. 75% of wounds came from shell fire. A wound resulting from a shell fragment was usually more traumatic than a gunshot wound. A shell fragment would often introduce debris, making it more likely that the wound would become infected. These factors meant a soldier was three times more likely to die from a shell wound to the chest than from a gunshot wound. The blast from shell explosions could also kill by concussion. In addition to the physical effects of shell fire, there was the psychological damage. Men who had to endure prolonged bombardment would often suffer debilitating shell shock, a condition not well understood at the time.

Stretcher bearers, Passchendale, August 1917

As in many other wars, World War I's greatest killer was disease. Sanitary conditions in the trenches were quite poor, and common infections included dysentery, typhus, and cholera. Many soldiers suffered from parasites and related infections. Poor hygiene also led to fungal conditions, such as trench mouth and trench foot. Another common killer was exposure, since the temperature within a trench in the winter could easily fall below zero degrees Celsius (32 °F). Burial of the dead was usually a luxury that neither side could easily afford. The bodies would lie in no man's land until the front line moved, by which time the bodies were often unidentifiable. On some battlefields, such as at the Nek in Gallipoli, the bodies were not buried until after the war. On the Western Front, bodies continue to be found as fields are ploughed and building foundations dug.

At various times during the war—particularly early on—official truces were organised so that the wounded could be recovered from no man's land and the dead could be buried. Generally, senior commands disapproved of any slackening of the offensive for humanitarian reasons and so ordered their troops not to permit enemy stretcher-bearers to operate in no man's land. However, this order was almost invariably ignored by the soldiers in the trenches, who knew that it was to the mutual benefit of the fighting men of both sides to allow the wounded to be retrieved. So, as soon as hostilities ceased, parties of stretcher bearers, marked with Red Cross flags, would go out to recover the wounded, sometimes swapping enemy wounded for their own. There were occasions when this unofficial cease fire was exploited to conduct a reconnaissance or to reinforce or relieve a garrison. One famous truce was the Christmas truce between British and German soldiers in the winter of 1914 on the front near Armentieres. German soldiers began singing Christmas carols and soon soldiers left their trenches. The soldiers exchanged gifts and stories, and played several games of football. As mentioned previously, the commanders of the warring nations disapproved of this cease fire, and the British court-martialed several of their soldiers. The spirit of this truce is portrayed in the 2005 movie Merry Christmas.

WEAPONS OF WORLD WAR I TRENCH WARFARE

INFANTRY WEAPONS

The common infantry soldier had four weapons to use in the trenches: the rifle, bayonet, shotgun, and hand grenade. The standard issue British rifle was the .303 Short, Magazine, Lee-Enfield (SMLE), originally developed as a cavalry carbine, with a maximum range of 1400yd (1280 m). The Ross rifle was widely used by the Canadian Corps early in the war and was reputedly more accurate than the British SMLE. However, it proved notoriously unreliable under battlefield conditions, often jamming when dirty or fired rapidly, and was gradually discarded for routine use in favour of the SMLE, except for sniping. Early in the war, the British were able to defeat German attacks at Mons and the First Battle of Ypres with massed rifle fire, but as trench warfare developed, opportunities to assemble a line of riflemen disappeared.

The German counterpart to the Lee-Enfield was the 7.92x57mm (.323") Mauser Gewehr 98. It was less suited to rapid fire than the SMLE, due to its smaller magazine and slower rate of fire. The British soldier was equipped with a 21-inch (53 cm) sword bayonet, which was too long and unwieldy to be particularly effective in close-quarters combat. However, bayonet use was safer than firing the rifle which, in a mêlée, might strike an ally instead of an enemy. British figures recorded only 0.3% of wounds were caused by bayonets. The bayonet was also used to finish off wounded enemy soldiers during an advance, both saving ammunition and reducing the probability of being attacked from the rear. Imperial German soldiers generally carried the S98/05 "Butcher-blade" bayonet, which was an effective weapon in the open, but like the British bayonet, difficult to use in the narrow trenches when attached to a rifle.

Many soldiers preferred a short-handled spade or entrenching tool over a bayonet. They would sharpen the blade, and the shorter length made them easier to use in the confined quarters of the trenches. These tools could then be used to dig in after they had taken a trench. Since the troops were often not adequately equipped for trench warfare, improvised weapons were common in the first encounters, such as short wooden clubs and metal maces, as well as trench knives and brass knuckles. As the war progressed, better equipment was issued, and improvised arms were discarded.

Used by American soldiers in the Western front, the pump action shotgun was a formidable weapon in short range combat, enough so that Germany lodged a formal protest against their use on 14 September 1918, stating "every prisoner found to have in his possession such guns or ammunition belonging thereto forfeits his life", though this threat was apparently never carried out. The U.S. military began to issue models specially modified for combat, called "trench guns", with shorter barrels, higher capacity magazines, no choke, and often heat shields around the barrel, as well as lugs for the M1917 bayonet. Anzac and some British soldiers were also known to use sawn-off shotguns in trench raids, because of their portability, effectiveness at close range, and ease of use in the confines of a trench. This practice was not officially sanctioned, and the shotguns used were invariably modified sporting guns.

The hand grenade came to be the primary infantry weapon of trench warfare. Both sides were quick to raise specialist bombing squads. The grenade enabled a soldier to engage the enemy without exposing himself to fire, and it did not require precise accuracy to kill or maim. Another benefit is that if a soldier can get close enough to the trenches, enemies hiding in trenches can be attacked. The Germans and Turks were well equipped with grenades from the start of the war, but the British, who had ceased using grenadiers in the 1870s and did not anticipate a siege war, entered the conflict with virtually none, so soldiers had to improvise bombs with whatever was available (see Jam Tin Grenade). By late 1915, the British Mills bomb had entered wide circulation, and by the end of the war 75 million had been used.

TANKS

Tanks were first introduced by the British as a means to break the deadlock of trench warfare. They were first deployed at the Battle of Somme in limited numbers. They proved unreliable and ineffective at first, largely because of poor strategic and tactical planning, being spread too thinly on the ground. In addition, they were originally used over ground torn apart by large amounts of shell fire, which early tanks had trouble traversing. Later on, improved tanks and improved tactics allowed the tank to break through enemy lines, and become a significant element of warfare.

MACHINE GUNS

The Germans embraced the machine gun from the outset—in 1904, sixteen units were equipped with 'Maschinengewehr'—and the machine gun crews were the elite infantry units; these units were attached to Jaeger (light infantry) battalions. By 1914, British infantry units were armed with two Vickers machine guns per battalion, the Germans had six per battalion, the Russians eight. The Americans had to wait until 1917 to see every infantry unit carry at least one machine gun. After 1915, the Maschinengewehr 08 was the standard issue German machine gun; its number "08/15" entered the German language as idiomatic for "dead plain". At Gallipoli and in Palestine the Turks provided the infantry, but it was usually Germans who manned the machine guns.

The British High Command were less enthusiastic about machine guns, supposedly considering the weapon too "unsporting" and encouraging defensive fighting; and they lagged behind the Germans in adopting it. Field Marshall Sir Douglas Haig is quoted as saying in 1915, "The machine gun is a much overrated weapon; two per battalion is more than sufficient", an attitude which resulted in record numbers of British casualties. In 1915 the Machine Gun Corps was formed to train and provide sufficient heavy machine gun teams. It was the Canadians that made the best practice, pioneering area denial and indirect fire (soon adopted by all Allied armies) under the guidance of former French Army Reserve officer Major General Raymond Brutinel. Minutes before the attack on Vimy Ridge the Canadians thickened the artillery barrage by aiming machine guns at the precise angle to rain down on the Germans. They also significantly increased the amount of machine guns per battalion. To match demand, production of the Vickers machine gun was contracted to firms in the United States. By 1917, every company in the British forces were also equipped with four Lewis light machine guns, which significantly enhanced their firepower.

The heavy machine gun was a specialist weapon, and in a static trench system was employed in a scientific manner, with carefully calculated fields of fire, so that at a moment's notice an accurate burst could be fired at the enemy's parapet or a break in the wire. Equally it could be used as light artillery in bombarding distant trenches. Heavy machine guns required teams of up to eight men to move them, maintain them, and keep them supplied with ammunition. This made them impractical for offensive maneuvers, contributing to the stalemate on the Western Front.

Vickers machine gun

MORTARS

Mortars, which lobbed a shell in a high arc over a relatively short distance, were widely used in trench fighting for harassing the forward trenches, for cutting wire in preparation for a raid or attack, and for destroying dugouts, saps and other entrenchments. In 1914, the British fired a total of 545 mortar shells; in 1916, they fired over 6,500,000. Similarly, howitzers, which fire on a more direct arc than mortars, raised in number from over 1,000 shells in 1914, to over 4,500,000 in 1916. The smaller numerical difference in mortar rounds, as opposed to howitzer rounds, is presumed to be related to the expanded costs of manufacturing the larger and more resource intensive howitzer rounds.

The main British mortar was the Stokes, a precursor of the modern mortar. It was a light mortar, but was easy to use, and capable of a rapid rate of fire by virtue of the propellant cartridge being attached to the shell. To fire the Stokes mortar, the round was simply dropped into the tube, where the cartridge was ignited automatically when it struck the firing pin at the bottom. The Germans used a range of mortars. The smallest were grenade-throwers ('Granatenwerfer') which fired "pineapple" bombs. Their medium trench-mortars were called mine-throwers ('Minenwerfer'), dubbed "moaning minnies" by British Commonwealth troops. The heavy mortar was called the 'Ladungswerfer', which threw "aerial torpedoes", containing a 200lb (90 kg) charge to a range of 1000yd (914 m). The flight of the missile was so slow and leisurely men on the receiving end could make some attempt to seek shelter.

ARTILLERY

Artillery dominated the battlefields of trench warfare. An infantry attack was rarely successful if it advanced beyond the range of its supporting artillery. In addition to bombarding the enemy infantry in the trenches, the artillery could be used to precede infantry advances with a creeping barrage, or engage in counter-battery duels to try to destroy the enemy's guns. Artillery mainly fired fragmentation, high explosive, or, later in the war, gas shells. The British experimented with firing thermite incendiary shells to set trees and ruins alight.

Loading a 15-inch howitzer

Artillery pieces were of two types: guns and howitzers. Guns fired high-velocity shells over a flat trajectory and were often used to deliver fragmentation and to cut barbed wire. Howitzers lofted the shell over a high trajectory so it plunged into the ground. The largest calibers were usually howitzers. The German 420 mm howitzer weighed 20 tons and could fire a one-ton shell over 10 km. A critical feature of period artillery pieces was the hydraulic recoil mechanism, which meant the gun did not need to be re-aimed after each shot.

Initially each gun would need to register its aim on a known target, in view of an observer, in order to fire with precision during a battle. The process of gun registration would often alert the enemy an attack was being planned. Towards the end of 1917, artillery techniques were developed enabling fire to be delivered accurately without registration on the battlefield–the gun registration was done behind the lines then the pre-registered guns were brought up to the front for a surprise attack.

GAS

Early gasses were unreliable, as they could easily be blown back on the troops. There were three main types used: mustard gas, chlorine, and phosgene. This prompted the use of gas masks. Early on, improvised gas masks were made by urinating on a handkerchief and putting it over their nose and mouth so the urea would disable the poison.

Tear gas was first employed in August 1914 by the French, but this could only disable the enemy. In April 1915, chlorine was first used by Germany at the Second Battle of Ypres. A large enough dose could kill, but the gas was easy to detect by scent and sight. Those that were not killed on exposure could suffer permanent lung damage. Phosgene, first used in December 1915, was the ultimate killing gas of World War I—it was 18 times more powerful than chlorine and much more difficult to detect. However, the most effective gas was mustard gas, introduced by Germany in July 1917. Mustard gas was not as fatal as phosgene, but it was hard to detect and lingered on the surface of the battlefield and so could inflict casualties over a long period. The burns it produced were so horrific that a casualty resulting from mustard gas exposure was unlikely to be fit to fight again. Only 2% of mustard gas casualties died, mainly from secondary infections.

The first method of employing gas was by releasing it from a cylinder when the wind was favourable. Such an approach was obviously prone to miscarry if the direction of the wind was misjudged. Also, the cylinders needed to be positioned in the front trenches where they were likely to be ruptured during a bombardment. Later in the war, gas was delivered by artillery or mortar shell.

French observer with Adrian helmet in trench, Hirtzbach Woods, Haut-Rhin, France, 1917 (then Ober-Elsaß, Germany).

FLAMETHROWERS

The Germans employed 'Flammenwerfer' (flamethrowers) during the war for the first time against the French on June, 25th, 1915, then against the British on July 30 in Hooge. The technology was in its infancy, and use was not very common until the end of 1917 when portability and reliability were improved. It was used in more than 300 documented battles. In 1918, it became a weapon of choice for 'Stoßtruppen' (stormtroopers) with a team of six 'Pionieren' (pioneers) per squad.

HELMETS

During the first year of the First World War, none of the combatant nations equipped their troops with steel helmets. Soldiers went into battle wearing simple cloth or leather caps that offered virtually no protection from the damage caused by modern weapons. German troops were wearing the traditional leather 'Pickelhaube' (spiked helmet), with a covering of cloth to protect the leather from the splattering of mud. Once the war entered the static phase of trench warfare, the number of lethal head wounds that troops were receiving from fragmentation increased dramatically. The French were the first to see a need for greater protection and began to introduce steel helmets in the summer of 1915. The Adrian helmet replaced the traditional French kepi and was later adopted by the Belgian, Italian and many other armies.

At about the same time the British were developing their own helmets. The French design was rejected as not strong enough and too difficult to mass-produce. The design that was eventually approved by the British was the Brodie helmet. This had a wide brim to protect the wearer from falling objects, but offered less protection to the wearer's neck. When the Americans entered the war, this was the helmet they chose, though some units used the French Adrian helmet. The traditional German 'pickelhaube' was replaced by the 'Stahlhelm' or "steel helmet" in 1916. Some elite Italian units used a helmet derived from ancient Roman designs. None of these standard helmets could protect the face or eyes, however. Special face-covers were designed to be used by machine gunners, and the Belgians tried out goggles made of louvres to protect the eyes.

WIRE

The use of barbed wire was decisive in slowing infantry traveling across the battlefield. Without it, infantry or cavalry might cross the lines and reach the enemy machine gun posts and artillery. Slowed down by the barbed wire, they were much more likely to be shot. Liddell Hart identified barbed wire and the machine gun as the elements that had to be broken to regain a mobile battlefield. Wiring was usually done at night, to avoid casualties in no man's land. The screw picket, invented by the Germans and later adopted by the Allies during the war, was quieter than driving stakes, and thus helped decrease the amount of noise working parties would create. Methods to defeat it were rudimentary. British and Commonwealth forces relied on wire cutters, which proved unable to cope with the heavier gauge German wire. The Bangalore torpedo was adopted by many armies, and continued in use past the end of World War II.

AIRCRAFT

The fundamental purpose of the aircraft in trench warfare was reconnaissance and artillery observation. Aerial reconnaissance was so significant in exposing movements, it has been said the trench stalemate was a product of it. The role of the fighter was to protect friendly reconnaissance aircraft and destroy those of the enemy, or at least deny them the freedom of friendly airspace. This involved achieving air superiority over the battlefield by destroying the enemy's fighters as well. Spotter aircraft would monitor the fall of shells during registration of the artillery. Reconnaissance aircraft would map trench lines, first with hand-drawn diagrams, later with photography, monitor enemy troop movements, and locate enemy artillery batteries so that they could be destroyed with counter-battery fire.

NEW WEAPONS

In 1917 and 1918, new types of weapons were fielded. They changed the face of warfare tactics and were later employed during World War II.

The French introduced the CSRG 1915 Chauchat during Spring 1916 around the concept of "Walking Fire", employed in 1918 when 250,000 weapons were fielded. More than 80,000 of the best shooters received the semi-automatic RSC 1917 rifle, allowing them to rapid fire at waves of attacking soldiers. Firing ports were installed in the newly arrived FT 1917 tanks.

The French Army fielded a ground version of the Hotchkiss Canon de 37 mm used by the French Navy. It was primarily used to destroy German machine gun nests and concrete reinforced pillboxes with high explosive rounds, but an armour piercing round was designed to defeat the German tanks, making it the first anti tank gun.

A new type of machine gun was introduced in 1916. Initially an aircraft weapon, the Bergmann LMG 15 was modified for ground use, with the later dedicated ground version being the LMG 15 n.A. It was used as an infantry weapon on all European and Middle Eastern fronts until the end of World War I. It later inspired the MG 30 and the MG 34 as well as the concept of the general purpose machine gun.

German soldier with MP 18, 1918

What became known as the submachine gun had its genesis in WWI, developed around the concepts of infiltration and fire and movement, specifically to clear trenches of enemy soldiers when engagements were unlikely to occur beyond a range of a few feet. The MP 18 was the first practical submachine gun used in combat. It was fielded in 1918 by the German Army as the primary weapon of the stormtroopers, assault groups that specialized in trench combat.

MINING

The dry chalk of the Somme was especially suited to mining, but with the aid of pumps, it was also possible to mine in the sodden clay of Flanders. Specialist tunneling companies, usually made up of men who had been miners in civilian life, would dig tunnels under no man's land and beneath the enemy's trenches. These mines would then be packed with explosives and detonated, producing a large crater. The crater served two purposes: it could destroy or breach the enemy's trench and, by virtue of the raised lip that they produced, could provide a ready-made "trench" closer to the enemy's line. When a mine was detonated, both sides would race to occupy and fortify the crater.

If the miners detected an enemy tunnel in progress, they would often drive a counter-tunnel, called a counter-mine or camouflet, which would be detonated in an attempt to destroy the other tunnel prematurely. Night raids were also conducted with the sole purpose of destroying the enemy's mine workings. On occasion, mines would cross and fighting would occur underground. The mining skills could also be used to move troops unseen. On one occasion a whole British division was moved through interconnected workings and sewers without German observation. The British detonated a number of mines on July 1, 1916, the first day of the Battle of the Somme. The largest mines—the Y Sap Mine and the Lochnagar Mine—each containing 24 tons of explosives, were blown near La Boiselle, throwing earth 4,000 feet into the air.

At 3.10 AM on June 7, 1917, 19 mines were detonated by the British to launch the Battle of Messines. The average mine contained 21 tons of explosive and the largest, 125 feet beneath

Saint-Eloi, was twice the average at 42 tons. The combined force of the explosions was supposedly felt in England. As remarked by General Plumer to his staff the evening before the attack:

> "Gentlemen, we may not make history tomorrow, but we shall certainly change the geography." "Battles: The Battle of Messines, 1917".

The craters from these and many other mines on the Western Front are still visible today. Three further mines were laid for Messines but were not detonated as the tactical situation had since changed. One blew during a thunderstorm in 1955; the other two remain to this day.

TRENCH BATTLES

STRATEGY

The fundamental strategy of trench warfare was to defend one's own position strongly while trying to achieve a breakthrough into the enemy's rear. The effect was to end up in attrition; the process of progressively grinding down the opposition's resources until, ultimately, they are no longer able to wage war. This did not prevent the ambitious commander from pursuing the strategy of annihilation—the ideal of an offensive battle which produces victory in one decisive engagement. The Commander in Chief of the British forces, General Douglas Haig, was constantly seeking a "breakthrough" which could then be exploited with cavalry divisions. His major trench offensives—the Somme in 1916 and Flanders in 1917—were conceived as breakthrough battles but both degenerated into costly attrition. The Germans actively pursued a strategy of attrition in the Battle of Verdun, the sole purpose of which was to "bleed the French Army white". At the same time the Allies needed to mount offensives in order to draw attention away from other hard-pressed areas of the line.

TACTICS

The popular image of a trench assault is of a wave of soldiers, bayonets fixed, going "over the top" and marching in a line across no man's land into a hail of enemy fire. This was the standard method early in the war and successful examples are few. The more common tactic was to attack at night from an advanced post in no man's land, having cut the barbed wire beforehand. In 1917, the Germans innovated with infiltration tactics where small groups of highly trained and well-equipped troops would attack vulnerable points and bypass strong points, driving deep into the rear areas. The distance they could advance was still limited by their ability to supply and communicate.

The role of artillery in an infantry attack was twofold. The first aim of a bombardment was to prepare the ground for an infantry assault killing or demoralising the enemy garrison and destroying his defences. The duration of these initial bombardments varied, from seconds to days. The problem with artillery bombardments prior to infantry assaults was that they were often ineffective at destroying enemy defences and only served to provide the enemy with advance notice that an attack was imminent. The British bombardment that began the Battle of the Somme lasted eight days but did little damage to either the German barbed wire or their deep dug-outs where the defenders were able to see out the bombardment safely. Once the guns stopped the defenders had time to emerge and were usually ready for the attacking infantry. The second aim was to protect the attacking infantry by providing an impenetrable "barrage" or curtain of shells to prevent an enemy counter-attack. The first attempt at sophistication was the "lifting barrage" where the first objective of an attack was intensely bombarded for a period before the entire barrage "lifted" to fall on a second objective farther back. However, this usually expected too much of the infantry, and the usual outcome was that the barrage would outpace the attackers, leaving them without protection. This resulted in the use of the "creeping barrage" which would lift more frequently but in smaller steps, sweeping the ground ahead and moving so slowly that the attackers could usually follow closely behind it. This became the standard method of attack from late 1916 onward. The main benefit of the barrage was suppression of the enemy rather than to cause casualties or material damage.

Capturing the objective was half the battle, but the battle was only won if the objective was held. The attacking force would have to advance with not only the weapons required to capture a trench but also the tools—sandbags, picks and shovels, barbed wire—to fortify and defend from counter-attack. The Germans placed great emphasis on immediately counter-attacking to regain lost ground. This strategy cost them dearly in 1917 when the British started to limit their advances so as to be able to meet the anticipated counter-attack from a position of strength. Part of the British artillery was positioned close behind the original start line and took no part in the initial bombardment, being saved to support the advancing troops as they moved beyond the range of guns further back.

COMMUNICATIONS

A major difficulty faced by an attacking force in a trench battle was unreliable communications. Wireless communications were still in their infancy, so the available methods were telephone, telegraph, semaphore, signal lamps, signal flares, homing pigeons and runners. Messages frequently could not get through, or if they did, were out of date. A delay would pass when transferring news to the division, corps and army headquarters. Consequently, the outcome of many trench battles was decided by the company and platoon commanders in the thick of the fighting. Senior commanders could not influence the battle for lack of information and inability to get orders to the troops. Opportunities were frequently lost because reinforcements could not be committed at the right time or place, and supporting artillery could not react to a changing situation.

BREAKING THE DEADLOCK

Throughout World War I, the major combatants slowly groped their way towards the tactics necessary for breaking the deadlock of trench warfare, beginning with the French and Germans, with the British Empire forces also contributing to the collective learning experience. The Germans were able to reinforce their western front with additional troops from the east once Russia dropped out of the war in 1917. This allowed them to take units out of the line and train them in new methods and tactics, such as stormtroopers. The new methods involved men rushing forward in small groups using whatever cover was available and laying down covering fire for other groups in the same unit as they moved forward.

The new tactics, intended to achieve surprise by disrupting entrenched enemy positions, were to bypass strongpoints and attack the weakest parts of an enemy's line. Additionally, they acknowledged the futility of managing a grand detailed plan of operations from afar, opting instead for junior officers on the spot to exercise initiative. These infiltration tactics proved very successful during the German 1918 Spring Offensive against Allied forces.

Conceived to provide protection from fire, tanks added mobility as well. As the Allied forces perfected them, they broke the deadlock. While not effectively employed at first, tanks had tremendous effects on the morale of German troops in the closing stages of the war on the Western front. The average infantryman had no anti-tank capability, and there were no specialized anti-tank guns. Once tanks began to be used in concentrations, they easily broke through German lines and could not be dislodged through infantry counterattack.

During the last 100 days of World War I, the British forces broke through the German trench system and harried the Germans back using infantry supported by tanks and close air support. Between the two world wars these techniques were used by J.F.C. Fuller and B.H. Liddell Hart to develop theories about a new type of warfare. The ideas were picked up by the Germans, who developed them further and put them into practice as blitzkrieg.

The stunning victories by the Germans early in World War II using blitzkrieg showed fixed fortifications like the Maginot Line were worthless if there was room to circumvent them. At the Battle of Sevastopol, Red Army forces successfully held trench systems on the narrow peninsula for several months against intense German bombardment.

The Western Allies in 1944 broke through the incomplete Atlantic Wall with relative ease through a combination of amphibious landings, naval gunfire, air attack, and airborne landings. Combined arms tactics where infantry, artillery, armour and aircraft cooperate closely made trench warfare a thing of the past.

This is not to say entrenchment is redundant. It is still a valuable method for reinforcing natural obstacles to create a line of defence. For example, at the Battle of Stalingrad, soldiers on both sides dug trenches within the ruins. In addition, before the start of the Battle of Kursk, the Soviets constructed a system of defence more elaborate than any other they built during World War II. These defences succeeded in stopping the German armoured pincers meeting and enveloping the salient. Also, at the start of the Battle of Berlin, the last major assault of World War II, the Russians attacked over the river Oder against German troops dug in on the Seelow Heights, about 50 km (30 mi) east of Berlin.

Entrenchment allowed the Germans, who were massively outnumbered, to survive a bombardment from the largest concentration of artillery in history; as the Red Army attempted to cross the marshy riverside terrain, they lost tens of thousands of casualties to the entrenched Germans before breaking through.

POST-1945 TRENCH WARFARE

Trench warfare has been infrequent since the end of World War I. When two large armoured armies meet, the result has generally been mobile warfare of the type which developed in World War II. However, trench warfare reemerged in the latter stages of the Chinese Civil War (Huaihai Campaign), the Korean War, and in some locations and engagements in the Vietnam War. During the Cold War, NATO forces routinely trained to fight through extensive works called "Soviet-style trench systems", named after the Warsaw Pact's complex systems of field fortifications, an extension of Soviet field entrenching practices for which they were famous in their Great Patriotic War.

Men of the 1st Brigade, 101st Airborne Division, fire from old Viet Cong trenches.

Another example of trench warfare after World War I was the Iran–Iraq War, in which both armies had a large number of infantry with modern small arms, but very little armour, aircraft, or training in combined operations. Tactics used included trench warfare, machine gun posts, bayonet charges, use of barbed wire across trenches and on no-man's land, human wave attacks and Iraq's extensive use of chemical weapons such as mustard gas against Iranian troops and civilians as well as Iraqi Kurds. The war lasted eight years.

Although mainly a siege, it was not unusual to find an extensive trench system inside and outside the city of Sarajevo during the siege of 1992–1996. It was used mainly for transportation to the frontline or to avoid snipers inside the city. Any pre-existing structures were used as trenches, the best known example is the bobsleigh course on Trebeviæ, which was used by both Serb and Bosniak during the siege. Another example of trench stalemate was the Eritrean-Ethiopian War of 1998–2002. The front line in Korea and the front lines between Pakistan and India in Kashmir are two examples of demarcation lines which could become hot at any time. They consist of kilometers of trenches linking fortified strongpoints and in Korea surrounded by millions of land mines.

Chapter 4

MOUNTAIN WARFARE

Mountain warfare refers to warfare in the mountains or similarly rough terrain. This type of warfare is also called Alpine warfare, named after the Alps mountains. Mountain warfare is one of the most dangerous types of combat as it involves surviving not only combat with the enemy but also the extreme weather and dangerous terrain. In combat, high ground gives a great advantage in both defense and offense.

Attacking a prepared enemy position in mountain terrain requires a greater ratio of attacking soldiers to defending soldiers than would be needed on level ground. Mountains at any time of year are dangerous – lightning, strong gusts of wind, falling rocks, extreme cold, and crevasses are all additional threats to combatants. Movement, reinforcements, and medical evacuation up and down steep slopes and areas where even pack animals cannot reach involves an enormous exertion of energy.

EARLY HISTORY

The term mountain warfare is said to have come about in the Middle Ages after the monarchies of Europe found it difficult to fight the Swiss armies in the Alps. This was because the Swiss were able to fight in smaller units and took vantage points against a huge unmaneuverable army.

Similar styles of attack and defence were later employed by guerrillas, partisans and irregulars who hid in the mountains after an attack, making it challenging for an army of regulars to fight back.

WORLD WAR I

Mountain warfare came to the fore once again, during World War I, when some of the nations involved in the war had mountain divisions that had hitherto not been tested.

The Austro-Hungarian defence repelled the Italians as they took advantage of the mostly mountainous terrain, where more people succumbed to frostbite and avalanches than to bullets.

During the summer of 1918, the Battle of San Matteo took place on the Italian front, this battle was fought at the highest elevation of any in the war.

In December 1914, another offensive was launched by the Turkish supreme commander Enver Pasha with 95,000-190,000 troops against the Russians in the Caucasus. Insisting on a frontal attack against Russian positions in the mountains in the heart of winter, the end result was devastating and Enver lost 86% of his forces.

KASHMIR CONFLICT

The most dangerous and volatile of all mountain conflicts involves the ongoing one between India and Pakistan over the Kashmir region. Since the partition in 1947, both countries have been constantly locked in skirmishes and wars mainly in this Himalayan region with the highest mountains in the world.

The first hostilities between the two nations in the Indo-Pakistani War of 1947 showed that both were ill-equipped to fight in biting cold, let alone on the highest altitudes in the world.

During the Sino-Indian War of 1962, hostilities broke out between the Republic of India and People's Republic of China at some of the highest altitudes over the Himalayan mountains.

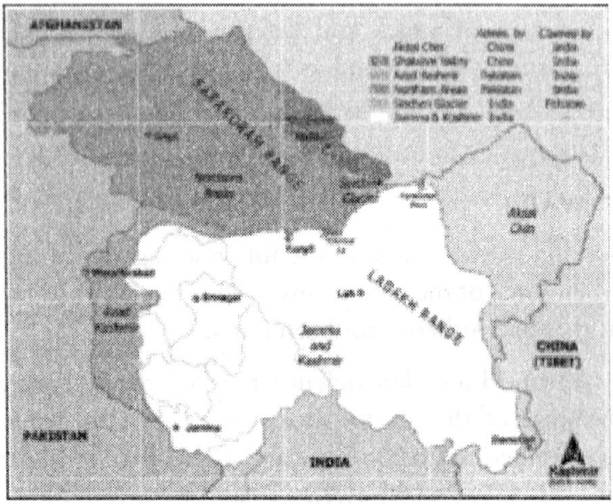

The Siachen Glacier area is the smallest orange area.

Later wars between India and Pakistan were mainly fought on the valleys rather than in the mountains, although several major mountain battles took place in all these conflicts. This changed in the Kargil War when Indian forces were faced with the huge task of flushing out Pakistani infiltrators who had captured high mountain posts.

This proxy warfare became the only modern war that was fought exclusively on mountains. Since Pakistani forces held the high ground and battles took place in peaks as high as 7,000 metres, it proved an immensely costly task for the Indian Army, supported by massed artillery and the Indian Air Force, to vacate the Pakistani troops.

As a result of its experiences in Mountain Warfare in Kargil, the Indian Army now conducts courses on specialized Artillery use in the Mountains, where ballistic projectiles have different characteristics.

On a related note, the Siachen Glacier was named the highest battleground in the world with both the countries holding their respective positions at nearly 7000 m above sea level. Over 2000 troops from both sides have died in this inhospitable terrain, with weather extremes and the natural hazards accounting for higher casualties than combat.

FALKLANDS WAR

Although most of the Falklands War took place in the Falkland Islands themselves, on hilltops in semi-Arctic conditions, during the earlier stages of the war, there was some action in the bleak mountainous island of South Georgia. South Georgia is a Peri-Antarctic Island, and since the War took place during the southern winter, Alpine conditions prevailed almost down to sea level. It was unusual, in that it combined aspects of deep water long range expeditions, Arctic Warfare and mountain warfare.

Landscape of South Georgia

Operation Paraquet was ordered by British Admiral Fieldhouse on 12 April 1982. It was to involve Mountain Troops from D Squadron SAS in Ascension, 150 Royal Marines on the tanker Tidespring, 2SBS on Plymouth and 6SBS in the submarine Conqueror. Conqueror was first on the scene and carried out a survey of key areas of the South Georgia coast. The operation was originally supposed to involve both SAS and SBS forces being infiltrated onto South Georgia by helicopters from the Tidespring and Antrim, but the plan had to be changed when the two Wessex helicopters transporting the SAS troops to an ambitious location on the west coast crashed in atrocious weather conditions on Fortuna Glacier; the troops and aircrew were rescued by Antrim's Wessex helicopter, the last remaining to the expedition.

MOUNTAIN WARFARE TRAINING

The expense of training Mountain troops precludes them from being on the order of battle of most armies except those who reasonably expect to fight in such terrain. Mountain Warfare training is one of the most difficult and arduous there is and in many countries is the exclusive purview of special forces, elite units or commandos who are as part of their remit supposed to be able to fight in difficult terrain, (for example the Royal Marines in UK) though regular units may occasionally undertake training of this nature. This is however not the case with other armies.

AUSTRIA AND GERMANY

Gebirgsjäger is the German word for mountain infantry (Gebirge meaning "mountain range", and Jäger meaning "hunter" or "ranger"). The word Jäger is the traditional German term for light infantry.

The mountain infantry of Austria have their roots in the three "Landesschützen" regiments of the Austro-Hungarian Empire. The mountain infantry of Germany carry on certain traditions of the Alpenkorps (Alpine corps) of World War I. Both countries' mountain infantry share the Edelweiss insignia. It was established in 1907 as a symbol of the Austro-Hungarian Landesschützen regiments by Emperor Franz Joseph I. These troops wore their Edelweiss on the collar of their uniforms. When the Alpenkorps came to aid the Landesschützen in defending the Austro-Hungary's southern frontier against the Italian attack in May 1915, the grateful Landesschützen honoured the men of the Alpenkorps by awarding them their own insignia: the Edelweiss.

Today the traditions of the Austrian mountain infantry (Gebirgsjäger) are maintained by the 6th Jägerbrigade in Innsbruck, subdivided in three battalions (Jägerbataillon 23, Jägerbataillon 24 and Jägerbataillon 26)

Honouring tradition, upon the creation of the Bundeswehr in 1955, the mountain infantry returned as a distinctive arm of the

German army. Until 2001, they were organized as the 1. Gebirgsdivision, but this division was disbanded in a general reform. The successor unit is Gebirgsjägerbrigade 23 which has its headquarters in Bad Reichenhall (Bavaria). Battalions of these mountain infantry are deployed in southern Bavaria.

The soldiers of the mountain infantry wear a grey cap ("Bergmütze") with an Edelweiss on its left side. This distinguishes them from all other German army soldiers who wear berets. The formal uniform, which is based on traditional skiing outfits, is also different from the standard German military uniform, and consists of ski jacket, stretch trousers and ski boots.

The "Kaiserjägermarsch" (March of the Kaiserjäger) from 1914 is the traditional military march of the German and Austrian mountain infantry.

FRANCE

Until 1859, Italy wasn't yet a unified state but a sum of kingdoms and independent republics (Kingdom of Naples, Republic of Venice, Papal States, etc.). The situation changed with the unification of Italy. France saw this geopolitical change as a possible threat from the other side of the Alps border, partially as the Italians were the first to have mountain warfare specialized troops.

The French solution was to create its own mountain corps in order to oppose a possible Italian invasion through the Alps. By December 24, 1888, a law created a troupes de montagne ("mountain troops") corps. 12 of the 31 existing Chasseurs à Pied ("Hunters on Foot") battalions were selected to be converted. These first units were named Bataillons Alpins de Chasseurs à Pied ("Hunters on Foot Alpine Battalions"), later shortened to Bataillons de Chasseurs Alpins ("Alpine Hunters Battalions").

Since 1999 they have been (with other units) part of the 27th Mountain Infantry Brigade (Brigade d'Infanterie de Montagne), and are currently organised into three battalions:

- 7th Battalion, Bourg-Saint-Maurice
- 13th Battalion, Chambéry
- 27th Battalion, Cran-Gevrier (Annecy)

All three battalions are based in cities in the French Alps, thus the name of the units.

The Chasseurs are easily recognised by their wide beret (when not in battle uniform), named tarte (= pie). The British Army adopted the the beret in the 1920s after having seen similar berets worn by the 70th Chasseurs Alpins (now disbanded).

INDIA

The Indian Army is among the most experienced in mountain warfare, having fought numerous conflicts in the Himalayas in Arunachal Pradesh and Jammu and Kashmir. Major conflicts include the 1962 Sino-Indian War and the Kargil War in 1999. Siachen Glacier is the world's highest battlefield, with about 3000 Indian troops on an around the year deployment. For over two decades, India & Pakistan have fought numerous battles in one of the most inhospitable mountain territories in the world, at altitudes over 6000 meters (20,000 feet) and the mercury dipping to -50 Celsius.

Due to the instability in the region and need for permanent deployments in the mountainous regions, the Indian Army has some of the most extensive and well developed Mountain Warfare capabilities in the world. India's mountain warfare units were vastly expanded after the 1962 war, with the creation of 6 Mountain Divisions. The Indian Army presently has 10 Army Divisions dedicated to mountain warfare (8 Mountain Divisions and 2 Mountain Strike divisions) and another infantry division earmarked for high altitude operations. Each division has a personnel strength of 10,000-13,000 troops and consists of 3 brigades with 3,000 to 4,500 men each, including support elements such as signals, provost, and intelligence units.

In 2008, the Indian Army proposed plans to raise two additional mountain divisions, with goals to be operational in five years. The two divisions will also have air assets, including Utility helicopters, Helicopter gunships and Attack helicopters.

TRAINING

The Indian Military Academy (IMA), Dehradun conducts preliminary mountaineering and mountain warfare training for all Officer Cadets. Discontinued in the late 1980s, the Bhadraj Camp was revived in 1999 after the Kargil War. The culmination is a course of a 40 km run and climbing a 5500 feet cliff with a fully loaded pack at night.

For more specialized training, the Army operates the Parvat Ghatak School at Tawang, Arunachal Pradesh. This high-altitude commando school is the highest of its kind at 15,000 feet. With the mercury dipping to minus 20 degrees providing a freezing tougher terrain to impart training in conditions similar to Siachen.

Another school, the High Altitude Warfare School (HAWS) is located near Gulmarg, Jammu and Kashmir. Set up in 1948 as the 19 Infantry Division Ski School, HAWS has over the years become the Indian Army's nodal center for "specialised training and dissemination of doctrines" in high-altitude, mountain and snow warfare. HAWS Mountain warfare courses are conducted in the Sonamarg area, and snow-craft & winter warfare training in the Gulmarg area. HAWS played an important role during the Kargil War by conducting crash courses for troops prior to their deployment.

Given the extensive experience of the Indian Army in mountain warfare, troops from other nations regularly train and conduct joint exercises at these schools. Because of its experience in fighting wars in mountain regions for over 50 years, as well as its history of recruitment of natives from the Himalayan regions of India and Nepal (such as Gurkha, Kumaon), Indian Mountain Warfare Units are considered among the best in the world. Numerous army units across the world are now implementing training modules modeled after Indian Mountain Warfare training systems. These include forces from UK, US, Russia, etc. In 2004, US special forces teams were sent to India to learn from Indian Army experiences of the Kargil War prior to their deployment for operations in Afghanistan. Russian troops also trained at the High Altitude Warfare School in Gulmarg for operations in Chechnya. They also visited Siachen and other Army posts.

ITALY

The Alpini, meaning "the Alpines", are the elite mountain warfare soldiers of the Italian Army. They are currently organised in two main operational brigades, which are subordinated to the Alpini Corps Command. The singular is an Alpino (an "Alpine").

Italian Alpini

On June 7, 1883, the Alpini were awarded the "fiamme verdi" (green flames) collar patch. Also adopted was their distinctive headdress; the "Cappello Alpino" with its black feather, which led to them being nicknamed "Le Penne Nere" or "black feathers".

Originally formed in 1872, their mission was to protect Italy's northern mountainous borders. In 1888 the Alpini were sent to their first mission abroad, in Africa, during the First Italo–Ethiopian War. They distinguished themselves during World War I when they fought against Austro-Hungarian soldiers in what has since been called the "War in snow and ice". During World War II, the Alpini fought together with Axis forces mostly on the Eastern Front being tasked to hold the front in the Don river plains.

In the 1990s, after the end of the Cold War, three of the five Alpini brigades and many support units were disbanded due to the reorganisation process of the Italian Army. Currently, despite having some of the best trained and best equipped mountain troops in the world, the military role of Alpines is seen in terms of peacekeeping missions and minor disputes interventions. The 4th Alpini Regiment is a SOF (Special Operations Forces) unit of elite mountain infantry specialized in the airborne assault role. It originates from the Alpini Paracadutisti platoons of Alpini Brigade founded in the '50s, then merged, on the 1st of april 1964, in the Alpine Paratroopers Company.

The "CENTRO ADDESTRAMENTO ALPINO" Aosta (MOUNTAIN TRAINING CENTRE) is the Army school responsible for the Alpini corp officers training and graduation.

ROMANIA

The Vânători de Munte ("Mountain Hunters/Rangers", Romanian pronunciation: are the elite mountain troops of the Romanian Land Forces. They were first established as an independent Army Corps in 1916 during World War I, and became operational in 1917 under Corpul de Munte designation.

Thought as of being elite troops, the Romanian Vânători de Munte saw action in World War II on the Eastern Front in some of the harshest battles–including the battles of Sevastopol and Stalingrad–where their performance lived up to their reputation: virtually all their commanders from brigade level and up received the Knight's Cross of the Iron Cross. There are currently two brigades operational, one subordinated to the 1st Territorial Army Corps (the 2nd Mountain Troops Brigade), and another one subordinated to the 4th Territorial Army Corps (61st Mountain Troops Brigade). Often, mountain troops units are participating in peacekeeping missions in Iraq and Afghanistan.

PAKISTAN

In the Pakistan Army, mountain training is considered part of overall training and all soldiers and units are expected to be proficient at it. Almost all units of all arms serve tours in Kashmir and Northern Areas, often in active duties on the LOC or Siachin. The Pakistan Army's High-Altitude School, at Rattu in Northern Kashmir, is an ideal location on the confluence of the Hindukush, Himalayas, and Karakorum ranges. The school conducts training throughout the year and includes mountain climbing on peaks ranging from 15,000 to 20,000 feet and survival on glaciated terrain and in snowy and icy conditions.

POLAND

Podhale rifles (Polish: Strzelcy podhalańscy) is a traditional name of the mountain infantry units of the Polish Army. Formed in 1918 out of volunteers of the region of Podhale, in 1919 the smaller detachments of Podhale rifles were pressed into two mountain infantry divisions, the 21st Mountain Infantry and 22nd Mountain Infantry Divisions, as well as into three brigades of mountain infantry. Considered an elite of the Polish Army, the units were roughly equivalent to the German Gebirgsjäger troops.

FORMER SOVIET UNION

The USSR maintained several thousand of mountain troops and used them to good effect in the Caucasus and in Afghanistan.

SPAIN

Spain has a Brigade of Mountain troop:

- Brigada de Cazadores de Montaña "Aragón" I (1st Mountain Brigade)
- Regimiento de Cazadores de Montaña "Galicia" 64 (64th Mountain Regiment)
- Regimiento de Cazadores de Montaña "America" 66 (66th Mountain Regiment)
- Grupo de Artillería de Montaña I (1st Mountain Artillery Battalion)
- Grupo Logístico de Montaña I (1st Mountain Logistic Battalion)

- Batallón de Cuartel General I (1st Headquarters Battalion)
- Unidad de Zapadores de Montaña 1 (1st Mountain Sapper Company)

SWEDEN

Mountains constitute almost half the area of Sweden. Especially its northern border areas are mountainous. Winter and mountain warfare skills were therefore always important to the country. Between 1945 and 2000 Sweden trained and deployed several companies per year at the Army Ranger School and later the Lapland/Arctic Mountain Ranger regiment (I22) in Kiruna (located some 150 KM north of the arctic circle in Lapland). From the start on the school/regiment drew on experiences gained during WW II from guarding and patrolling the mountainous northern borders and uninhabited inland mountain regions as well as from light infantry and ski fighting in Finland in the wars against the Soviet Union. Later the army as a whole benefited from the regiments location for training of not only the regiments own ranger units but also commanding and training officers and complete fighting units from brigades and battalions all over the country as well as from the regiments co-operation and exchange on training and methods development with similar units in for example Finland, Norway, Germany, Austria, Switzerland, France, the UK, and the USA.

In recent years, after massive cut backs in the armed forces, Sweden have deployed troops to the Middle East and due to experiences from there and after having identified it actually lacked the trademark Swedish winter and mountain fighting skills and abilities available to it before the surprising political decision to close the Lapland ranger regiment (I22) in Kiruna and to inactivate its several already trained and equipped battalion and company sized field units in 2000, the army has (faced with its currently very limited resources, few remaining training regiments/locations, and few more than company sized field units of any kind) had to again start up a dedicated mountain platoon. This is, however, nowadays based at Bodens Infantry regiment's (I19/P5) ranger detachment in Arvidsjaur (located 100 KM SOUTH of the arctic circle more in woodland terrain than in harsh northern mountainous terrain). The daunting task for this single platoon is to guide other smaller units in the mountains besides taking on own recon and limited fighting tasks.

UNITED KINGDOM

In the United Kingdom the Royal Marines are the principal regular unit trained in mountain and cold weather warfare and have a specialised instructor cadre: the Mountain Leader Training Cadre. The capability is fielded by 3 Commando Brigade. The British Army also have the Mountain Troops of Special Air Service squadrons.

UNITED STATES

The US has a history in mountain warfare, the 10th Mountain Division served in the Italian Apennine Mountains in WWII. In the United States there are three training facilities dedicated to preparing for mountain and cold weather warfare. The Army Mountain Warfare School located in Jericho Vermont, the Northern Warfare Training Center located in Black Rapids Alaska and most notably the Marine Corps Mountain Warfare Training Center located in Pickel Meadows California. These facilities offer challenging training in the most austere of training environments. The men assigned to these training establishments are extremely fit and highly trained. American experience in mountain warfare continues to the present: see Operation Anaconda.

ARCTIC WARFARE

Arctic Warfare or winter warfare is a term used to describe armed conflict that takes place in an exceptionally cold weather, usually in snowy and icy terrain, sometimes on ice-covered bodies of water. One must note the distinction between alpine and Arctic warfare–Arctic war does not always take place in mountainous terrain, and mountain warfare does not always take place in the cold.

Soviet Offensive in the Battle of Moscow, December 1941

HISTORY

Most winter battles have taken place in northern and eastern Europe. In 1242, the Teutonic Order lost the Battle of the Ice on Lake Peipus to Novgorod. In 1520, the decisive Battle of Bogesund between Sweden and Denmark occurred on the ice of lake Åsunden.

Sweden and Denmark fought several wars during the 16th and 17th centuries. As a great deal of Denmark consists of islands, it was usually safe from invasion, but in January 1658, most of the Danish waters froze. Charles X Gustav of Sweden led his army across the ice of the Belts to besiege Copenhagen. The war ended with the treaty of Roskilde, the most favourable Swedish peace treaty ever.

During the Great Northern War, Swedish king Charles XII set off to invade Moscow, but was eventually defeated at the battle of Poltava after being weakened by cold weather and scorched earth tactics. Sweden suffered more casualties during the same war as Carl Gustaf Armfeldt with 6000 men tried to invade Trondheim, and 3000 of them died in a blizzard on a snowy mountain named Öjfjället.

During the Finnish War, the Russian army unexpectedly crossed the frozen Gulf of Bothnia from Finland to the Åland Islands and, by 19 March 1809, reached the Swedish shore within 70 km from the Swedish capital, Stockholm. This daring manoeuvre decided the outcome of the war.

Another famous example is the use of ski troops by the Finnish Army during the Winter War and the subsequent Continuation War, where the numerically dominant Soviet forces had a hard time fighting mobile ski soldiers.

In Operation Barbarossa in 1941, both Russian and German Soldiers had to endure terrible conditions during the Russian winter. Petsamo-Kirkenes Operation conducted by the Red Army against the Wehrmacht in 1944 in northern Finland and Norway. In the Lapland War, Finland turned against Nazi Germany under the Soviet Union's pressure, their former cobelligerents. While use of ski infantry was prolific in the Red Army, Germany formed only one division for movement on skis.

Operation Rösselsprung and Operation Wunderland were Arctic naval battles in World War II.

The Falklands War in the 1980s had to end in June, as the southern hemisphere winter caused logistical problems.

Some battles during the Yugoslav wars, the war between India and Pakistan at Siachen, as well as the current conflict in Afghanistan fall into this category.

EQUIPMENT

Arctic warfare is very dependent on equipment. For survival, troops need warm clothing and footwear, extra nutritious food, white camouflage, tents with sleeping bags, heaters and fuel.

Weapons can be fitted with an arctic trigger which permits firing while wearing heavy mittens.

Individual mobility can be increased by skis, ice cleats, and snowshoes.

Motorized vehicles are often unfit to stand freezing temperatures. Special procedures can be used to ensure they perform in the cold, such as running them continuously or starting them at regular intervals. Studded tires or tire chains are useful equipment for maintaining traction of wheeled vehicles. It is also possible to design special vehicles for operation specifically in arctic conditions, such as the BvS 10, M29 Weasel or Aerosan.

NAVAL WARFARE

Naval Warfare is combat in and on seas, oceans, or any other major bodies of water such as large lakes and wide rivers.

HISTORY

Mankind has fought battles on the sea for more than 3,000 years. Land warfare would seem, initially, to be irrelevant and entirely removed from warfare on the open ocean, though this is not necessarily true. Land navigation, until the advent of extensive railroads was extremely dependent upon river systems and canals. The latter were crucial in the development of the modern world in the United Kingdom, the Low Countries and northern Germany, for they enabled the bulk movement of goods and raw materials without which the Industrial Revolution would not have occurred. Prior to 1750, things moved by barge or sea, or not much at all. Thus armies, with their exorbitant needs for food, ammunition and fodder, were tied to the river valleys throughout the ages.

The oceanic influences throughout pre-recorded history (Homeric Legends, e.g. Troy), and classical works like the Odyssey underscore the past influences. The Persian Empire — united and strong — couldn't prevail against the might of the Athenian fleet combined with that of lesser city states in several attempts to conquer the Greek city states. Phoenicia's and Egypt's power, Carthage's and even Rome's depended in no mean way upon control of the seas. So too did the Venetian Republic dominate Italy's city states, thwart the Ottoman Empire, and dominate commerce on the Silk Road and the Mediterranean in general for centuries. For three centuries, the Northmen commonly called the Vikings raided and pillaged and went where they willed, far into central Russia and the Ukraine, and even to far off Constantinople (both via the Black Sea tributaries and through the Strait of Gibraltar).

The many sea battles through history also provide a reliable source of shipwrecks for underwater archaeology. A major example, albeit not very commonly known, is the exploration of the wrecks of various battleships in the Pacific Ocean, namely Japanese warships that sank during the Battle of Midway.

OARS PEOPLE OF THE MEDITERRANEAN SEA

The first dateable recorded sea battle occurred about 1210 BC: Suppiluliuma II, king of the Hittites, defeated a fleet from Cyprus, and burned their ships at sea.

An ancient Greek trireme vessel

Assyrian reliefs from the 700s BC show Phoenician fighting ships, with two levels of oars, fighting men on a sort of bridge or deck above the oarsmen, and some sort of ram protruding from the bow. No written mention of strategy or tactics seems to have survived.

The Greeks of Homer just used their ships as transport for land armies, but in 664 BC there is a mention of a battle at sea between Corinth and its colony city Corcyra. The Persian Wars were the first to feature large-scale naval operations, not just sophisticated fleet engagements with dozens of triremes on each side, but combined land-sea operations. It seems unlikely that all this was the product of a single mind or even of a generation; most likely the period of evolution and experimentation was simply not recorded by history. After some initial battles while subjugating the Greeks of the Ionian coast, the Persians determined to invade Greece proper. Themistocles of Athens estimated that the Greeks would be outnumbered by the Persians on land, but that Athens could protect itself by building a fleet (the famous "wooden walls"), using the profits of the silver mines at Laurium to finance them.

The first Persian campaign, in 492 BC, was aborted because the fleet was lost in a storm, but the second, in 490 BC, captured islands in the Aegean Sea before landing on the mainland near Marathon. Attacks by the Greek armies repulsed these.

The third Persian campaign, under Xerxes I of Persia ten years later (480 BC), followed the pattern of the first in marching the army via the Hellespont while the fleet paralleled them offshore. Near Artemisium, in the narrow channel between the mainland and Euboea, the Greek fleet held off multiple assaults by the Persians, the Persians breaking through a first line, but then being flanked by the second line of ships. But the defeat on land at Thermopylae forced a Greek withdrawal, and Athens evacuated its population to nearby Salamis Island.

The ensuing Battle of Salamis was one of the decisive engagements of history. Themistocles trapped the Persians in a channel too narrow for them to bring their greater numbers to bear, and attacked them vigorously, in the end causing the loss of 200 Persian ships vs 40 Greek. At the end, Xerxes still had a fleet stronger than the Greeks, but withdrew anyway, and after losing at Plataea in the following year, returned to Asia Minor, leaving the Greeks their freedom. Nevertheless, the Athenians and Spartans attacked and burned the laid-up Persian fleet at Mycale, and freed many of the Ionian towns.

During the next fifty years, the Greeks commanded the Aegean, but not harmoniously. After several minor wars about which we know little, tensions exploded into the Peloponnesian War (431 B.C.) between Athens' Delian League and the Spartan Peloponnese. Naval strategy was critical; Athens walled itself off from the rest of Greece, leaving only the port at Piraeus open, and trusting in its navy to keep supplies flowing while the Spartan army besieged it. This strategy worked, although the close quarters likely contributed to the plague that killed many Athenians in 429.

There were a number of sea battles between galleys; at Rhium, Naupactus, Pylos, Syracuse, Cynossema, Cyzicus, Notium. But the end came for Athens in 405 at Aegospotami in the Hellespont, where the Athenians had drawn up their fleet on the beach, and were surprised by the Spartan fleet, who landed and burned all the ships. Athens surrendered to Sparta in the following year.

Navies next played a major role in the complicated wars of the successors of Alexander the Great.

The Roman Republic had never been much of a seafaring nation, but it had to learn, and learn fast, in the Punic Wars with Carthage, and developed the technique of grappling and boarding enemy ships with soldiers. The Roman Navy grew gradually as Rome found itself involved in more and more Mediterranean politics; by the time of the Roman Civil War and the Battle of Actium in 31 BC, hundreds of ships were involved, many of them quinqueremes mounting catapults and fighting towers. The Roman Empire however had little use for navies beyond periodic piracy suppression.

ANCIENT CHINA

In ancient China, the first known naval battles took place during the Warring States (481 BC–221 BC), a period where regional kings battled against one another. Chinese naval warfare in this ancient period featured grapple-and-hook, as well as ramming tactics with ships called "stomach strikers" and "colliding swoopers". It was written in the subsequent Han Dynasty that the Warring States era Chinese had employed ge chuan ships (dagger-axe ships, or halberd ships), thought to have a simple description of a ship manned by marines carrying dagger-axe halberds as personal weapons. However, the later 3rd century Three Kingdoms era Chinese writer Zhang Yan asserted in his writing that the Warring States Chinese named the boats this way because halberd blades were actually fixed and attached to the hull of the ship in order to rip into the hull of another ship while ramming, to stab enemies in the water that had fallen overboard and were swimming, or simply to clear any possible dangerous marine animals in the path of the ship (since the ancient Chinese did believe in sea monsters, see Xu Fu for more info).

Qin Shi Huang, the first emperor of the Qin Dynasty (221 BC–207 BC), owed much of his success in unifying China (specifically southern China) to naval power, although an official navy was not yet established (see Medieval Asia section below). Zhou Dynasty era Chinese were known to use temporary pontoon bridges for general means of transportation, but it was during the Qin and later Han Dynasty that large permanent pontoon bridges were assembled, and used for purposes of warfare (first written account of a pontoon bridge in the West being the oversight of the Greek Mandrocles of Samos in aiding a military campaign of Persian Emperor Darius I over the Bosporus).

During the Han Dynasty (202 BC–AD 220), the Chinese discovered the use of the stern-mounted steering rudder, as well as designed a new ship type, the junk. During the late Han Dynasty into the Three Kingdoms period, significantly large naval battles like the Battle of Chibi marked the advancement of naval warfare in the East. In the latter engagement, the Chinese military strategist Zhuge Liang from the Kingdom of Shu is well known for his fire attack upon the massive naval fleet of Prime Minister Cao Cao.

In terms of seafaring abroad, arguably one of the first Chinese to sail into the Indian Ocean and to reach Sri Lanka and India by sea was the Buddhist monk Fa Xian in the early 5th century (although diplomatic ties and land trade to Persia and India was established during the earlier Han Dynasty). However, Chinese naval maritime influence would not present itself in the Indian Ocean until the medieval period.

EUROPE, MIDDLE EAST AND NORTH AFRICA

The barbarian invasions of the 4th century and later mostly occurred by land, but there are mentions of a Vandal fleet fighting with the Romans, and a defeat of an Ostrogothic fleet at Sena Gallica in the Adriatic Sea.

During the Muslim conquests of the 7th century, Arab fleets begin to make an appearance, raiding Sicily in 652 (see History of Islam in southern Italy and Emirate of Sicily), and defeating the Byzantine Navy in 655. Constantinople is saved from a prolonged Arab siege in 678 by the invention of Greek fire, an early form of flamethrower that was devastating to the ships in the besieging fleet. These were just the first of many encounters during the Byzantine-Arab Wars.

The Islamic Caliphate, or Arab Empire, became the dominant naval power in the Mediterranean Sea from the 7th to 13th centuries, during what is known as the Islamic Golden Age. One of the most significant inventions in medieval naval warfare was the torpedo, invented in Syria by the Arab inventor Hasan al-Rammah in 1275. His torpedo ran on water with a rocket system filled with explosive gunpowder materials and had three firing points. It was a very effective weapon against ships.

In the 8th century the Norse Vikings begin to make an appearance, although their usual style is to appear quickly, plunder, and disappear, preferably undefended locations. King Alfred the Great of England built a fleet and was able to stay the Viking incursions, establishing the boundaries of Danelaw in a 884 treaty. The Norse also fought several sea battles among themselves. This was normally done by binding the ships on each side together, thus essentially fighting a land battle on the sea. However the fact that the losing side could not easily escape meant that battles tended to be hard and bloody. The Battle of Svolder is perhaps the most famous of these battles.

As Arab power in the Mediterranean began to wane, the Italian trading towns of Genoa, Pisa, and Venice stepped in to seize the opportunity, setting up commercial networks and building navies to protect them. At first the navies fought with the Arabs (off Bari in 1004, at Messina in 1005), but then they found themselves contending with Normans moving into Sicily, and finally with each other. The Genoese and Venetians fought four naval wars, in 1253–1284, 1293–1299, 1350–1355, and 1378–1381. The last ended with a decisive victory for Venice, which gave them almost a century to enjoy Mediterranean trade domination before other European countries started exploring to the south and west.

In the north of Europe, the near-continuous conflict between England and France rarely entails naval activity more sophisticated than carrying knights across the English Channel, and perhaps trying to attack the transports. The Battle of Dover in 1217, between a French fleet of 80 ships under Eustace the Monk and an English fleet of 40 under Hubert de Burgh, is notable as the first recorded battle using sailing ship tactics.

EAST AND SOUTH ASIA

The Sui Dynasty (581–618) and Tang Dynasty (618–907) of China were involved in several naval affairs over the triple-set of polities ruling medieval Korea (Three Kingdoms of Korea), along with engaging naval bombardments on the peninsula from Asuka period Yamato Kingdom (Japan). A prominent factor in the sudden decline and collapse of the Sui Dynasty was its pouring of state funds into the Goguryeo-Sui Wars, where the Chinese assembled an enormous naval fleet that in the end was unsuccessful. The succeeding Tang Dynasty of China took on a different foreign policy, aiding the Silla Dynasty (see also Unified Silla) in expelling the armies and naval forces of the Japanese (see Battle of Baekgang) and conquering Silla's other Korean rivals, Baekje and Goguryeo by 668. In addition, the Chinese Tang Dynasty had maritime trading, tributary, and diplomatic ties as far as modern-day Sri Lanka, India, Islamic Iran and Arabia, as well as Somalia in East Africa. From the Axumite Kingdom in modern-day Ethiopia, the

Arab traveller Sa'd ibn Abi-Waqqas sailed from there to Tang China during the reign of Emperor Gaozong. Two decades later, he returned with a copy of the Quran, establishing the first Islamic mosque in China, the Mosque of Remembrance in Guangzhou. What followed was a rising rivalry between Arab and Chinese for dominant control of sea lanes of trade in the Indian Ocean. In his book Cultural Flow Between China and the Outside World, Shen Fuwei notes that maritime Chinese merchants in the 9th century were landing regularly at Sufala in East Africa to cut out Arab middle-men traders.

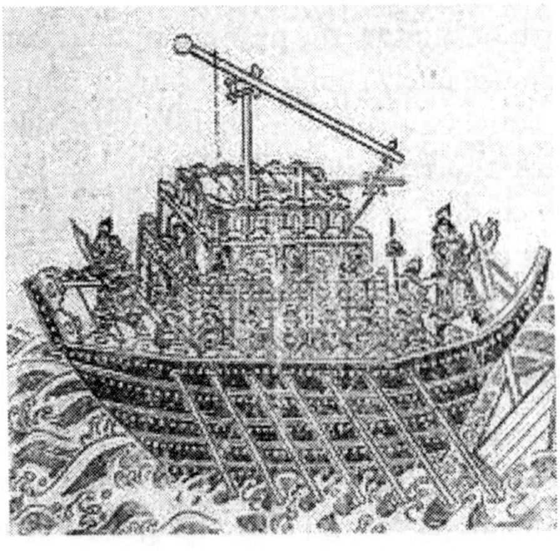

A Chinese Song Dynasty naval river ship with a Xuanfeng traction-trebuchet catapult on its top deck, taken from an illustration of the Wujing Zongyao (1044)

The Chola Dynasty of medieval India was a dominant seapower in the Indian Ocean, an avid maritime trader and diplomatic entity with Song China. Rajaraja Chola I (reigned 985 to 1014) and his son Rajendra Chola I (reigned 1014-42), who were from the Dravidian kingdom in southern India, sent out a great naval expedition that occupied parts of Myanmar, Malaya, and Sumatra. While many believe the Cholas were the first rulers noted to have a naval fleet in the Indian subcontinent, there are at least two evidences to cite use of navies. Narasimhavarman Pallava I transported his troops to Sri Lanka to help Manavarman to reclaim the throne. Shatavahanahas were known to possess a navy that was widely deployed to influence Southeast Asia. What is not known is the extent of use. Some argue that there is no evidence to support naval warfare in a contemporary sense. Others say that ships routinely carried bands of archers to keep pirates at bay. However, since the Arabs were known to use catapults, naptha, and devices attached to ships to prevent boarding parties, one can reasonably conclude that Chola navies not only transported troops but also provided support, protection, and attack capabilities against enemy targets.

In the 12th century, China's first permanent standing navy was established by the Southern Song Dynasty, the headquarters of the Admiralty stationed at Ding-hai. This came about after the conquest of northern China by the Jurchen people (see Jin Dynasty) in 1127, while the Chinese court fled south from Kaifeng to Hangzhou. Equipped with the magnetic compass and knowledge of Shen Kuo's famous treatise (on the concept of true north), the Chinese became proficient experts of navigation in their day. They raised their naval strength from a mere 11 squadrons of 3,000 marines to 20 squadrons of 52,000 marines in a century's time.

A Chinese paddle-wheel driven ship from a Qing Dynasty encyclopedia published in 1726

Employing paddle wheel crafts and trebuchet's throwing gunpowder bombs from the decks of their ships, the Chinese became a formidable foe to the Jin Dynasty during the 12th-13th centuries (see also Battle of Caishi and Battle of Tangdao). With a powerful navy, China dominated maritime trade throughout South East Asia as well.

Until 1279, the Chinese were able to use their naval power to defend against the Jin to the north, until the Mongols finally conquered all of China. After the Song Dynasty, the Mongol-led Yuan Dynasty of China was a powerful maritime force in the Indian Ocean. The Yuan Emperor Kublai Khan attempted to invade Japan twice with enormous fleets (of both Mongols and Chinese), in 1274 and again in 1281, both attempts being unsuccessful (see Mongol invasions of Japan). Building upon the technological achievements of the earlier Chinese Song Dynasty, the Mongols also employed early cannons upon the decks of their ships.

While the Chinese Song Dynasty built its naval strength, the Japanese also had considerable naval prowess. The strength of Japanese naval forces could be seen in the Genpei War, in the large-scale Battle of Dan-no-ura on April 25, 1185. The forces of Minamoto no Yoshitsune were 850 ships strong, while Taira no Munemori had 500 ships under his command.

In the mid 14th century, the rebel leader Zhu Yuanzhang (1328-1398) seized power in the south amongst many other rebel groups. His early success was owed to the aid of capable officials such as Liu Ji and Jiao Yu, and their gunpowder weapons (see Huolongjing). Yet the decisive battle that cemented his success and his founding of the Ming Dynasty (1368-1644) was the Battle of Lake Poyang, considered one of the largest naval battles in history. In the 15th century, the Chinese Ming Dynasty Admiral Zheng He was assigned to assemble a massive fleet for several tributary missions abroad, sailing throughout the waters of the South East Pacific and the Indian Ocean.

During his maritime missions, on several occasions Zheng's fleet came into conflict with pirates. Zheng's fleet also became involved in a conflict in Sri Lanka, where the King of Ceylon traveled back to Ming China afterwards to make a formal apology to the Emperor.

In the late 16th century, Toyotomi Hideyoshi of Momoyama-era Japan gathered an enormous fleet to assault the Joseon Dynasty of Korea when the Korean King Seonjo refused to allow Japanese armies to invade Ming Dynasty China via the Korean Peninsula as a staging ground. During the Japanese invasions of Korea (1592-1598), the Japanese employed clever close-range tactics on land with arquebus rifles, but also relied upon close-range firing of muskets in grapple-and-board style naval engagements.

The Japanese were successful in first capturing the Korean port at Busan, the capital at Hanseong (In modern-day Seoul) fell to their forces, and then proceeded to move far north into the Korean peninsula. Military aid sent by Chinese Wanli Emperor of Ming assisted the Koreans somewhat, but the farther firing range of Korean cannons, along with the brilliant naval strategies of the Korean Admiral Yi Sun-sin, were the main detrimental factors in ultimate Japanese defeats. Admiral Yi is credited Turtle ship (Geobukseon).

Turtle Ships were used mostly to spearhead attacks. They were best used in tight areas and around islands rather than the open sea. Admiral Yi effectively cut off the possible Japanese supply line that would have run through the Yellow Sea to China, as well as severely weakened the Japanese strength and fighting morale in several heated engagements (where many regard the most critical Japanese defeat to be the Battle of Hansan Island).

SAILS AND EMPIRES

The late Middle Ages was important as the time of the development of the cogs, caravels and carracks ships capable of surviving the tough conditions of the open ocean, with enough backup systems and crew expertise to make long voyages routine. In addition, they grew from 100 tons to 300 tons displacement, enough to carry cannons as armament and still have space left over for profitable cargo. One of the largest ships of the time, the Great Harry displaced over 1,500 tons.

The voyages of discovery were fundamentally commercial rather than military in nature, although the line was sometimes blurry in that a country's ruler was not above funding exploration for personal profit, nor was it a problem to use military power to enhance that profit. Later the lines gradually separated, in that the ruler's motivation in using the navy was to protect private enterprise so that they could pay more taxes.

The early 17th century galleon Vasa. on display at the Vasa Museum in Stockholm. Vasa, with its high stern castle and double battery decks, was a transitional design between the preferences for boarding tactics and the line of battle.

Like the Egyptian Shia-Fatimids and Mamluks, the Sunni-Islamic Ottoman Empire centered in modern-day Turkey dominated the eastern Mediterranean Sea. The Ottomans built a powerful navy, rivaling the Italian city-state of Venice during the Ottoman-Venetian Wars (1499-1503). Although they were sorely defeated in the Battle of Lepanto (1571) by the Holy League, the Ottomans quickly rebuilt their naval strength, and afterwards successfully defended the island of Cyprus so that it would stay in Ottoman hands. However, with the concurrent Age of Discovery, Europe had far surpassed the Ottoman Empire, and successfully bypassed their reliance on land-trade by discovering maritime routes around Africa and towards the Americas.

The first naval action in defense of the new colonies was just ten years after Vasco da Gama's epochal landing in India. In March

1508, a combined Gujarati/Egyptian force surprised a Portuguese squadron at Dabul, and only two Portuguese ships escaped. The following February, the Portuguese viceroy destroyed the allied fleet at Diu, thus confirming Portuguese domination of the Indian Ocean.

In 1582, the Battle of Ponta Delgada in the Azores, in which a Spanish fleet defeated a combined Portuguese, French, English and Dutch force, thus suppressing a revolt in the islands, was the first battle fought in mid-Atlantic.

In 1588, Philip II of Spain sent his Spanish Armada to subdue Elizabeth I of England, but Admiral Sir Charles Howard forced its retreat, beginning the rise to prominence of the Royal Navy. However it was unable to follow up with a decisive blow against the Spanish navy, which remained the most important for another half century. After the war's end in 1604 the English fleet went through a time of relative neglect and decline.

In the 16th century, the Barbary Coast|Barbary states of North Africa rose to power and they collectively became a dominant naval power in the Mediterranean Sea due to the Barbary pirates. The coastal villages and towns of Italy, Spain and List of islands in the Mediterranean|Mediterranean islands were frequently attacked by them and long stretches of the Italian and Spanish coasts were almost completely abandoned by their inhabitants; after 1600 Barbary pirates occasionally entered the Atlantic and struck as far north as Iceland. According to Robert Davis between 1 million and 1.25 million Europeans were captured by Barbary pirates and sold as slaves in North Africa and the Ottoman Empire between the 16th and 19th centuries. These slaves were captured mainly from seaside villages in Italy, Spain and Portugal, and from farther places like France, England, the Netherlands, Ireland and even Iceland and North America. The Barbary pirates were also able to successfully defeat and capture many European ships, which was largely due to advances in sailing technology by the Barbary states. The earliest naval trawler, xebec and windward ships were employed by the Barbary pirates from the 16th century.

From the middle of the 17th century competition between the expanding English and Dutch commercial fleets came to a head in the Anglo-Dutch Wars, the first wars to be conducted entirely at sea. Most memorable of these battles was the raid on the Medway, in which the Dutch admiral Michiel de Ruyter sailed up the river Thames, and destroyed most of the British fleet. This remains to date the greatest naval defeat of England and her consecutive countries, and established Dutch supremacy at sea for over half a century. The English and Dutch wars were also known for very few ships being sunk, as it was very difficult to hit ships below the water level; the water surface deflected cannon balls, and the few holes produced could be patched quickly. Naval forces were severely weakened by casualties to the men and damage to the sails more than by loss of ships.

The 1805 Battle of Trafalgar, depicted here in its opening phase, was the climactic battle of the Age of Sail.

The 18th century developed into a period of seemingly continuous world wars, each larger than the last. At sea, the British and French were bitter rivals; the French aided the fledgling United States in the American Revolutionary War, but their strategic purpose was to capture territory in India and the West Indies—which they did not achieve. In the Baltic Sea, the final attempt to revive the Swedish Empire led to Gustav III's Russian War, with its grande finale at the Second Battle of Svensksund. The battle was unrivalled in size until the 20th century, was a decisive Swedish tactical victory but its strategical result was poor (due to poor army performance and previous lack of initiative from the Swedes) and the war ended without any territorial changes.

Even the change of government due to the French Revolution seemed to intensify rather than diminish the rivalry, and the Napoleonic Wars included a series of legendary naval battles, culminating in the Battle of Trafalgar in 1805, by which Admiral Horatio Nelson broke the power of the French and Spanish fleets, but lost his own life in so doing.

FROM WOOD AND WIND TO STEEL AND STEAM

Trafalgar ushered in the Pax Britannica of the 19th century, marked by general peace in the world's oceans, under the ensigns of the Royal Navy. But the period was one of intensive experimentation with new technology; steam power for ships appeared in the 1810s, improved metallurgy and machining technique produced larger and deadlier guns, and the development of explosive shells, capable of demolishing a wooden ship at a single blow, in turn required the addition of iron armour.

Although naval power during the Song, Yuan, and Ming dynasties established China as a major world seapower in the East, the Qing Dynasty lacked an official standing navy. They were more interested in pouring funds into military ventures closer to home (China proper), such as Mongolia, Tibet, and Central Asia (modern Xinjiang). However, there were some considerable naval conflicts during the Qing Dynasty before the Opium Wars (such as the Battle of Penghu, or the conflict against Koxinga). The insignificant naval effort that the Manchus/Chinese pitted against the more advanced British steam-powered ships during the first of the Opium Wars in the 1840s was sorely defeated. This left China open to virtual foreign domination (from European powers and then Japan) via spheres of influence over regions of China for economic gain. Although the Qing Dynasty attempted to modernize the Chinese navy, China's Beiyang Fleet was dealt a severe blow by the Imperial Japanese Navy in the First Sino-Japanese War (1894-1895).

The famous battle of the CSS Virginia and USS Monitor in the American Civil War was the duel of ironclads that symbolized the changing times. The first fleet action between ironclad ships was fought in 1866 at the Battle of Lissa between the navies of Austria and Italy. Because the decisive moment of the battle occurred when the Austrian flagship the Erzherzog Ferdinand Max successfully sank the Italian flagship Re d'Italia by ramming, in subsequent decades every navy in the world largely focused on ramming as the main tactic.

As the century came to a close, the familiar modern battleship began to emerge; a steel-armored ship, entirely dependent on steam, and sporting a number of large shell guns mounted in turrets arranged along the centerline of the main deck. The ultimate design was reached in 1906 with the HMS Dreadnought (1906) which entirely dispensed with smaller guns, her main guns being sufficient to sink any existing ship of the time.

The Russo-Japanese War and particularly the Battle of Tsushima in 1905 was the first test of the new concepts, resulting a stunning Japanese victory and the destruction of most Russian ships.

With the advent of the steamship, it became possible to create massive gun platforms and to provide them with heavy armor protection. The Dreadnought battleships and their successors were the first capital ships that combined technology and firepower with a mobile platform. However, in the first half of the 20th century, the effect of airpower on the effectiveness and usability of large capital ships became clear.

World War I pitted the old Royal Navy against the new navy of Imperial Germany, culminating in the 1916 Battle of Jutland. (The future was heralded when seaplane carrier HMS Campania missed the battle.)

Between wars, the first aircraft carrier, HMS Argus, appeared. Many nations agreed to the Washington Naval Treaty and scrapped many of their battleships and cruisers while still in the shipyards, but the growing tensions of the 1930s restarted the building programmes, with even larger ships than before; Yamato, the largest battleship ever, displaced 72,000 tons and mounted 18.1-inch (460 mm) guns.

ABOVE AND BELOW THE SURFACE

The victory of the Royal Navy at the Battle of Taranto was a pivotal point as this was the first true demonstration of naval air power. Following 7 December 1941 when the United States came into World War II, the sinking of HMS Prince of Wales and HMS Repulse marked the end of the era of the battleship, and the new importance of aircraft and their transportation, the aircraft carrier, came to the fore. During the Pacific War, battleships and cruisers spent most of their time bombarding shore positions, while the carriers were the stars of the key Battle of the Coral Sea, Battle of Midway, Battle of the Philippine Sea, and the climactic Battle of Leyte Gulf. Air power remained key to navies throughout the 20th century, moving to jets launched from ever-larger carriers, and augmented by cruisers armed with guided missiles and cruise missiles.

HMS Tireless. Nuclear submarines proved to be very successful during the Falklands War when HMS Conqueror sank ARA Belgrano with ease.

Roughly parallel to the development of naval aviation was the development of submarines to travel underneath the sea, at first for short dives, then later to be able to spend weeks or months underwater powered by a nuclear reactor. In both World Wars, submarines (U-boats in Germany) primarily exerted their power by using torpedoes to sink merchant ships, as well as other warships. In the 1950s the Cold War inspired the development of ballistic missile submarines, each one loaded with dozens of nuclear-armed missiles and with orders to launch them from sea should the other nation attack.

Against the backdrop of these developments, World War II had seen the United States become by far the largest Naval power in the world. Throughout the rest of the 20th century The United States Navy would maintain a tonnage greater than that of the next 17 largest navies combined.

The only major naval conflict that took place in the second half of the 20th century was the well known Falklands War, pitting Argentina against the United Kingdom. The Falklands showed the vulnerability of modern ships to sea-skimming missiles like the Exocet. One hit from an Exocet sank HMS Sheffield, a modern anti-air warfare destroyer. Important lessons about ship design, damage control and ship construction materials were learnt from the conflict. At the present time, large naval wars seem to be very rare affairs, with the main function of the modern navy being to exploit its control of the seaways to project power ashore. Power projection has been the primary naval feature of conflicts like the Korean War, Suez Crisis, Vietnam War, Konfrontasi, Gulf War, Kosovo War and both campaigns of the War on Terrorism in Afghanistan and Iraq.

Chapter 5

GUERRILLA WARFARE

Guerrilla Warfare is the unconventional warfare and combat in which a small group of combatants use mobile tactics in the form of ambushes and raids to combat a larger and less mobile formal army. The guerrilla army uses ambush and mobility in attacking vulnerable targets in enemy territory.

This term means "little war" in Spanish and was created during the Peninsular War. The concept acknowledges a conflict between armed civilians against a powerful nation state army, either foreign or domestic.

The Spanish guerrillero Juan Martín Díez, known by his nom de guerre, El Empecinado.

The tactics of guerrilla warfare were used successfully in the 20th century by, among others, the People's Liberation Army in the Chinese Civil War, the Irish Republican Army during the Irish War of Independence, Fidel Castro's rebel army in the Cuban Revolution, and by the Viet Cong, and the North Vietnam Army in the Vietnam War. Most factions of the Iraqi Insurgency and groups such as FARC are said to be engaged in some form of guerrilla warfare.

Guerrilla is the diminutive of the Spanish word guerra "war". It derives from the Old High German word Werra or from the middle Dutch word warre; adopted by the Visigoths in A.D. 5th century Hispania. The use of the diminutive evokes the differences in number, scale, and scope between the guerrilla army and the formal, professional army of the state. An early example of this came when General John Burgoyne, who, during the Saratoga campaign of the American War of Independence, noted that in proceeding through dense woodland:

Statue of Juana Galán in Valdepeñas, Spanish woman guerrillere

'The enemy is infinitely inferior to the King's Troop in open space, and hardy combat, is well fitted by disposition and practice, for the stratagems of enterprises of Little War...upon the same principle must be a constant rule, in or near woods to place advanced sentries, where they may have a tree or some other defence to prevent their being taken off by a single marksman.'

So conscious of hidden marksmen was Burgoyne that he asked his men, 'When the Lieut't General visits an outpost, the men are not to stand to their Arms or pay him any compliment', clearly being aware he would be singled out. The word was thus not coined in Spain to describe resistance to Napoleon Bonaparte's French régime during the Peninsula War. Its meaning was however broadened to mean any similar-scale armed resistance. Guerrillero is the Spanish word for guerrilla fighter, while in Spanish-speaking countries the noun guerrilla usually denotes guerrilla army (e.g. la guerrilla de las FARC translates as "the FARC guerrilla group"). Moreover, per the OED, 'the guerrilla' was in English usage (as early as 1809), describing the fighters, not only their tactics (e.g."the town was taken by the guerrillas"). However, in most languages guerrilla still denotes the specific style of warfare.

STRATEGY, TACTICS AND ORGANISATION

The strategy and tactics of guerrilla warfare tend to focus around the use of a small, mobile force competing against a large, unwieldy one. The guerrilla focuses on organising in small units, dependent on the support of the local population. Tactically, the guerrilla army attacks its enemy in small, repetitive attacks from the opponents center of gravity with a view to reducing casualties and becoming an intensive, repetitive strain on the enemies resources, forcing an over-eager response which will both anger their own supporters and increase support for the guerrilla, thus forcing the enemy to withdraw.

HISTORY

Since Classical Antiquity, when many strategies and tactics were used to fight foreign occupation that anticipated the modern guerrilla. An early example was the hit-and-run tactics employed by the nomadic Scythians of Central Asia against Darius the Great's

Persian Achaemenid Empire and later against Alexander the Great's Macedonian Empire.

The Fabian strategy applied by the Roman Republic against Hannibal in the Second Punic War could be considered another early example of guerrilla tactics: After witnessing several disastrous defeats, assassinations and raiding parties, the Romans set aside the typical military doctrine of crushing the enemy in a single battle and initiated a successful, albeit unpopular, war of attrition against the Carthaginians that lasted for 14 years.

In expanding their own Empire, the Romans encountered numerous examples of guerrilla resistance to their legions as well. The success of Judas Maccabeus in his rebellion against Seleucid rule was at least partly due to his mastery of irregular warfare.

The victory of the Basque forces against Charlemagne's army in the Battle of Roncevaux Pass, which gave birth to the Medieval myth of Roland, was due to effective use of a guerrilla principles in the mountain terrain of the Pyrenees. Mongols also faced irregulars composed of armed peasants in Hungary after the Battle of Mohi.

One of the most successful of the guerrilla campaigns was that of Robert the Bruce in the Scottish War of Independence when using strategies of ambushes, avoiding large battles, destroying enemy strongholds and using a scorched earth policy, the Scots forced the English out of Scotland without a single largescale battle until the Battle of Bannockburn eight years after the start of the war.

In the 15th century, Vietnamese leader Le Loi launched a guerrilla war against Chinese. One of the most successful guerrilla wars against the invading Ottomans was led by Gjergj Kastrioti Skanderbeg from 1443 to 1468. In 1443 he rallied Albanian forces and drove the Turks from his homeland. For 25 years Skanderbeg kept the Turks from retaking Albania, which due to its proximity to Italy, could easily have served as a springboard to the rest of Europe. In 1462, the Ottomans were driven back by Wallachian prince Vlad III Dracula. Vlad was unable to stop the Turks from entering Wallachia, so he resorted to guerrilla war, constantly organising small attacks and ambushes on the Turks.

During The Deluge in Poland guerrilla tactics were applied. In the 100 years war between England and France, commander Bertrand du Guesclin used guerrilla tactics to pester the English invaders. The Frisian warlord Pier Gerlofs Donia fought a guerrilla against Philip I of Castile and with co-commander Wijerd Jelckama against Charles V.

During the Dutch Revolt of the 16th century, the Geuzen waged a guerrilla war against the Spanish Empire. During the Scanian War, a pro-Danish guerrilla group known as the Snapphane fought against the Swedes.

In 17th century Ireland, Irish irregulars called tories and rapparees used guerrilla warfare in the Irish Confederate Wars and the Williamite war in Ireland. Finnish guerrillas, sissis, fought against Russian occupation troops in the Great Northern War, 1700-1721. The Russians retaliated brutally against the civilian populace; the period is called Isoviha (Grand Hatred) in Finland.

Many clandestine organisations (often known as resistance movements) operated in the countries occupied by Nazi Germany during the World War II. In the former Yugoslavia, guerrillas under General Dra•a Mihailoviæ, known as Chetniks, engaged in a guerrilla war against the German occupation beginning in 1941. Communist guerrillas under Josip Broz Tito, known as Partisans, also engaged the German troops in a guerrilla war. By 1944 the Polish resistance was thought to number 400,000. The strength of the Soviet partisan units and formations can not be accurately estimated, but in Belarus alone is thought to have been in excess of 300,000.

CURRENT AND RECENT GUERRILLA CONFLICTS

Present ongoing guerrilla wars, and regions facing guerrilla war activity include:

Asia:

- Arab-Israeli Conflict
- India–Communist insurgency
- Taliban insurgency in Afghanistan
- Conflict in Iraq
- Kurdish Unrest in Turkey
- Sri Lankan Civil War
- Islamic and Communist Insurgencies in the Philippines
- South Thailand insurgency in Southern Thailand along the Malaysia-Thailand border

Africa:

- Ivorian Civil War
- Sudan
- Darfur Conflict
- Tuareg Rebellion (2007–present)
- Uganda–Lord's Resistance Army

Latin America:

- Zapatista Army of National Liberation, Mexico–have been relatively non-violent since 1994
- Internal conflict in Peru
- Colombian Armed Conflict
- Peru–Shining Path (Communist)

Europe:

- Kosovo War
- Provisional IRA in Northern Ireland
- Real IRA in Northern Ireland
- Euskadi ta Askatasuna (ETA) in Spain

Russia:

- Second Chechen War

COUNTER-GUERRILLA WARFARE

PRINCIPLES

The guerrilla can be difficult to beat, but certain principles of counter-insurgency warfare are well known since the 1950s and 1960s and have been successfully applied.

CLASSIC GUIDELINES

The widely distributed and influential work of Sir Robert Thompson, counter-insurgency expert of the Malayan Emergency, offers several such guidelines. Thompson's underlying assumption is that of a country minimally committed to the rule of law and better governance.

Some governments, however, give such considerations short shrift, and their counterguerrilla operations have involved mass murder, genocide, starvation and the massive spread of terror, torture and execution. The totalitarian regimes of Hitler are classic examples, as are more modern conflicts in places like Afghanistan.

In Afghanistan's anti-Mujahideen war for example, the Soviets implemented a ruthless policy of wastage and depopulation, driving over one third of the Afghan population into exile (over 5 million people), and carrying out widespread destruction of villages, granaries, crops, herds and irrigation systems, including the deadly and widespread mining of fields and pastures. See Wiki article Soviet war in Afghanistan.

Many modern countries employ manhunting doctrine to seek out and eliminate individual guerrillas. Elements of Thompson's moderate approach are adapted here:

1. **The people are the key base to be secured and defended rather than territory won or enemy bodies counted.** Contrary to the focus of conventional warfare, territory gained, or casualty counts are not of overriding importance in counter-guerrilla warfare. The support of the population is the key variable. Since many insurgents rely on the population for recruits, food, shelter, financing, and other

materials, the counter-insurgent force must focus its efforts on providing physical and economic security for that population and defending it against insurgent attacks and propaganda.

2. **There must be a clear political counter-vision that can overshadow, match or neutralize the guerrilla vision.** This can range from granting political autonomy, to economic development measures in the affected region. The vision must be an integrated approach, involving political, social and economic and media influence measures. A nationalist narrative for example, might be used in one situation, an ethnic autonomy approach in another. An aggressive media campaign must also be mounted in support of the competing vision or the counter-insurgent regime will appear weak or incompetent.
3. **Practical action must be taken at the lower levels to match the competitive political vision.** It may be tempting for the counter-insurgent side to simply declare guerrillas "terrorists" and pursue a harsh liquidation strategy. Brute force however, may not be successful in the long run. Action does not mean capitulation, but sincere steps such as removing corrupt or arbitrary officials, cleaning up fraud, building more infrastructure, collecting taxes honestly, or addressing other legitimate grievances can do much to undermine the guerrillas' appeal.
4. **Economy of force.** The counter-insurgent regime must not overreact to guerrilla provocations, since this may indeed be what they seek to create a crisis in civilian morale. Indiscriminate use of firepower may only serve to alienate the key focus of counterinsurgency- the base of the people. Police level actions should guide the effort and take place in a clear framework of legality, even if under a State of Emergency. Civil liberties and other customs of peacetime may have to be suspended, but again, the counter-insurgent regime must exercise restraint,

and cleave to orderly procedures. In the counter-insurgency context, "boots on the ground" are even more important than technological prowess and massive firepower, although anti-guerrilla forces should take full advantage of modern air, artillery and electronic warfare assets.

5. **Big unit action may sometimes be necessary.** If police action is not sufficient to stop the guerrilla fighters, military sweeps may be necessary. Such "big battalion" operations may be needed to break up significant guerrilla concentrations and split them into small groups where combined civic-police action can control them.
6. **Aggressive mobility.** Mobility and aggressive small unit action is extremely important for the counter-insurgent regime. Heavy formations must be lightened to aggressively locate, pursue and fix insurgent units. Huddling in static strongpoints simply concedes the field to the insurgents. They must be kept on the run constantly with aggressive patrols, raids, ambushes, sweeps, cordons, roadblocks, prisoner snatches, etc.
7. **Ground level embedding and integration.** In tandem with mobility is the embedding of hardcore counter-insurgent units or troops with local security forces and civilian elements. The US Marines in Vietnam also saw some success with this method, under its CAP (Combined Action Programme) where Marines were teamed as both trainers and "stiffeners" of local elements on the ground. US Special Forces in Vietnam like the Green Berets, also caused significant local problems for their opponents by their leadership and integration with mobile tribal and irregular forces. The CIA's Special Activities Division created successful guerrilla forces from the Hmong tribe during the war in Vietnam in the 1960s, from the Northern Alliance against the Taliban during the war in Afghanistan in 2001, and from the Kurdish Peshmerga against Ansar al-Islam and the forces of Saddam Hussein

during the war in Iraq in 2003. In Iraq, the 2007 US "surge" strategy saw the embedding of regular and special forces troops among Iraqi army units. These hardcore groups were also incorporated into local neighborhood outposts in a bid to facilitate intelligence gathering, and to strengthen ground level support among the masses.

8. **Cultural sensitivity.** Counter-insurgent forces require familiarity with the local culture, mores and language or they will experience numerous difficulties. Americans experienced this in Vietnam and during the US Iraqi Freedom invasion and occupation, where shortages of Arabic speaking interpreters and translators hindered both civil and military operations.
9. **Systematic intelligence effort.** Every effort must be made to gather and organize useful intelligence. A systematic process must be set up to do so, from casual questioning of civilians to structured interrogations of prisoners. Creative measures must also be used, including the use of double agents, or even bogus "liberation" or sympathizer groups that help reveal insurgent personnel or operations.
10. **Methodical clear and hold.** An "ink spot" clear and hold strategy must be used by the counter-insurgent regime, dividing the conflict area into sectors, and assigning priorities between them. Control must expand outward like an ink spot on paper, systematically neutralising and eliminating the insurgents in one sector of the grid, before proceeding to the next. It may be necessary to pursue holding or defensive actions elsewhere, while priority areas are cleared and held.
11. **Careful deployment of mass popular forces and special units.** Mass forces include village self-defence groups and citizen militias organized for community defence and can be useful in providing civic mobilisation and local security. Specialist units can be used profitably, including commando squads, long range reconnaissance and "hunter-killer" patrols, defectors who can track or persuade

their former colleagues like the Kit Carson units in Vietnam, and paramilitary style groups. Strict control must be kept over specialist units to prevent the emergence of violent vigilante style reprisal squads that undermine the government's programme.

12. **The limits of foreign assistance must be clearly defined and carefully used.** Such aid should be limited either by time, or as to material and technical, and personnel support, or both. While outside aid or even troops can be helpful, lack of clear limits, in terms of either a realistic plan for victory or exit strategy, may find the foreign helper "taking over" the local war, and being sucked into a lengthy commitment, thus providing the guerrillas with valuable propaganda opportunities as the stream of dead foreigners mounts. Such a scenario occurred with the US in Vietnam, with the American effort creating dependence in South Vietnam, and war weariness and protests back home. Heavy-handed foreign interference may also fail to operate effectively within the local cultural context, setting up conditions for failure.
13. **Time.** A key factor in guerrilla strategy is a drawn-out, protracted conflict, that wears down the will of the opposing counter-insurgent forces. Democracies are especially vulnerable to the factor of time. The counter-insurgent force must allow enough time to get the job done. Impatient demands for victory centered around short-term electoral cycles play into the hands of the guerrillas, though it is equally important to recognize when a cause is lost and the guerrillas have won.

VARIANTS

Some writers on counter-insurgency warfare emphasize the more turbulent nature of today's guerrilla warfare environment, where the clear political goals, parties and structures of such places as Vietnam, Malaysia, or El Salvador are not as prevalent. These writers point to numerous guerrilla conflicts that center around religious, ethnic or even criminal enterprise themes, and that do not lend themselves to the classic "national liberation" template.

The wide availability of the Internet has also cause changes in the tempo and mode of guerrilla operations in such areas as coordination of strikes, leveraging of financing, recruitment, and media manipulation. While the classic guidelines still apply, today's anti-guerrilla forces need to accept a more disruptive, disorderly and ambiguous mode of operation.

> "Insurgents may not be seeking to overthrow the state, may have no coherent strategy or may pursue a faith-based approach difficult to counter with traditional methods. There may be numerous competing insurgencies in one theater, meaning that the counterinsurgent must control the overall environment rather than defeat a specific enemy. The actions of individuals and the propaganda effect of a subjective "single narrative" may far outweigh practical progress, rendering counterinsurgency even more non-linear and unpredictable than before. The counterinsurgent, not the insurgent, may initiate the conflict and represent the forces of revolutionary change. The economic relationship between insurgent and population may be diametrically opposed to classical theory. And insurgent tactics, based on exploiting the propaganda effects of urban bombing, may invalidate some classical tactics and render others, like patrolling, counterproductive under some circumstances. Thus, field evidence suggests, classical theory is necessary but not sufficient for success against contemporary insurgencies..."

INFLUENCE ON THE ARTS

- Che, a 2007 film
- Guerrilla Girls, a feminist artist group
- "Guerrilla Radio", a song by Rage Against the Machine
- Guerrilla burlesque, a style of burlesque performance that involves descending upon audiences, uninvited.
- Tomorrow series A series of books written by John Marsden (writer) about guerrilla warfare during a fictional invasion and occupation of Australia.

- For Whom The Bell Tolls, a novel by Ernest Hemingway telling the story of Robert Jordan, a volunteer American attached to an anti-fascist guerrilla unit during the Spanish Civil War.
- Chetniks! The Fighting Guerrillas (1943), a 20th Century Fox movie on the guerrilla resistance movement of General Draza Mihailovich in German-occupied Yugoslavia during World War II.
- Underground Guerrillas (1943), a movie released by Columbia Pictures in the U.S., which was a re-release of the British movie Undercover (film) produced by Ealing Studios.

Chapter 6

PSYCHOLOGICAL WARFARE

The U.S. Department of Defense defines Psychological Warfare (PSYWAR) as:

> "The planned use of propaganda and other psychological actions having the primary purpose of influencing the opinions, emotions, attitudes, and behaviour of hostile foreign groups in such a way as to support the achievement of national objectives."

During World War II the United States Joint Chiefs of Staff defined psychological warfare more broadly stating "Psychological warfare employs any weapon to influence the mind of the enemy. The weapons are psychological only in the effect they produce and not because of the weapons themselves."

HISTORY

ALEXANDER THE GREAT

Although not always accredited as the first practitioner of psychological warfare, Alexander the Great of Macedon undoubtedly showed himself to be effective in swaying the mindsets of the populaces that were expropriated in his campaigns.

In order to keep the new Macedonian states from revolting against their leader, Alexander the Great would leave a number of his men behind in each city to introduce Greek culture, control it and oppress dissident views as well as interbreed. Since this method of persuasion did indeed influence loyalist and separatist opinions alike, it directly altered the psyches of the occupied people to conform.

THE MONGOLS

Genghis Khan, leader of the Mongols in the 13th century AD, united his people to eventually conquer more territory than any other leader in human history. Defeating the will of the enemy was the top priority.

Before attacking a settlement, the Mongol generals demanded submission to the Khan, and threatened the initial villages with complete destruction if they refused to surrender. After winning the battle, the Mongol generals fulfilled their threats and massacred the survivors.

Examples include the destruction of the nations of Kiev and Khwarizm. Consequently, tales of the encroaching horde spread to the next villages and created an aura of insecurity that undermined the possibility of future resistance.

Subsequent nations were much more likely to surrender to the Mongols without fighting. Often this, as much as the Mongols' tactical prowess, secured quick Mongol victories.

Genghis Khan also employed tactics that made his numbers seem greater than they actually were. During night operations he ordered each soldier to light three torches at dusk in order to deceive and intimidate enemy scouts and give the illusion of an overwhelming army. He also sometimes had objects tied to the tails of his horses, so that when riding on an open and dry field, would raise a cloud of dust that gave the enemy the impression of great numbers.

The Mongols also employed other gruesome terror tactics to weaken the will to resist. One infamous incident occurred during Tamerlane's Indian campaign. Tamerlane, an heir to the Mongol martial tradition, built a pyramid of 90,000 human heads in front of the walls of Delhi, to convince them to surrender.

Other tactics included firing severed human heads from catapults into enemy lines and over city walls to frighten enemy soldiers and citizens, and spread diseases in the close confines of a besieged city. The results were not only psychological: In 1347, the Mongols under Janibeg catapulted corpses infected with plague into the trading city of Kaffa in Crimea. The dismayed Genoese traders withdrew, bringing the plague back with them to Italy and beginning the European phase of the Black Death.

VLAD TEPES

Vlad Tepes would physically and psychologically torture his enemies with brutality. His most well-known psychological tactic was an incident involving impalement (thus earning him the title "Vlad the Impaler"), where the bodies of thousands of Ottoman soldiers were suspended in the air, impaled through the heart or rectum on giant wooden sticks.

This was so effective, it made an Ottoman army cancel their campaign to invade Romania. In a twist of fate, Vlad Tepes was captured and killed by being impaled through a spike. His severed head was paraded around Istanbul for 3 days before being discarded.

WORLD WAR II

One of the first leaders to inexorably gain fanatical support through the use of microphone technology was Nazi Germany's Adolf Hitler. By first creating a speaking environment, designed by Joseph Goebbels, he was able to exaggerate his presence to make him seem almost god-like. Hitler also coupled this with the resonating projections of his orations for effect. British Prime Minister Winston Churchill made similar use of radio for propaganda against the Nazis.

During World War II, psychological warfare was used effectively by the military as well. The enormous success that the invasion of Normandy displayed was a fusion of psychological warfare with military deception.

Before D-Day, Operation Quicksilver created a fictional "First United States Army Group" (FUSAG) commanded by General George Patton that supposedly would invade France at the Pas-de-Calais. American troops used false signals, decoy installations and phony equipment to deceive German observation aircraft and radio interception operators.

This had the desired effect of misleading the German High Command as to the location of the primary invasion, and of keeping reserves away from the actual landings. Erwin Rommel was the primary target of the psychological aspects of this operation.

Convinced that Patton would lead the invasion, Rommel was caught off-guard and unable to react strongly to the Normandy invasion, since Patton's illusory FUSAG had not "yet" landed. Confidence in his own intelligence and judgement rendered the German response to the beachhead ineffectual.

MODERN PSYCHOLOGICAL WARFARE OPERATIONS

In Iraq and Afghanistan, U.S. troops used music, most commonly American heavy metal or rock music to confuse or scare insurgents.

However, most uses of the term psychological warfare refers to military methods, such as:

- Distributing pamphlets, e.g. in the Gulf War, encouraging desertion or (in World War II) supplying instructions on how to surrender.
- Propaganda radio stations, such as Lord Haw-Haw in World War II on the "Germany calling" station
- Renaming cities and other places when captured, such as Ho Chi Minh City
- Shock and awe military strategy
- Projecting repetitive and annoying sounds and music for long periods at high volume towards groups under siege.
- Use of loudspeaker systems to communicate with enemy soldiers.

Most of these techniques were developed during World War II or earlier, and have been used to some degree in every conflict since. Daniel Lerner was in the OSS (the predecessor to the US CIA) and in his book, attempts to analyze how effective the various strategies were.

He concludes that there is little evidence that any of them were dramatically successful, except perhaps surrender instructions over loudspeakers when victory was imminent. It should be noted, though, that measuring the success or failure of psychological warfare is very hard, as the conditions are very far from being a controlled experiment.

BRITISH USE OF PSYCHOLOGICAL WARFARE

The British were one of the first major military powers to use psychological warfare in World War II, especially against the Japanese. The Gurkhas, who are Nepalese soldiers in British service, have always been feared by the enemy due to their use of a curved knife called the kukri.

The British put this fear to great effect, as Gurkhas were used to terrorize Japanese soldiers through nighttime raids on their camps. When the Gurkhas landed on the Falkland Islands, some Argentine troops abandoned their positions and fled.

UNITED STATES USE OF PSYCHOLOGICAL WARFARE

The United States ran an extensive programme of psychological warfare during the Vietnam War. The Phoenix Programme had the dual aim of assassinating Viet Cong personnel and terrorising any potential sympathizers or passive supporters.

When members of the VCI were assassinated, CIA and Special Forces operatives placed playing cards in the mouth of the deceased as a calling card. During the Phoenix Programme, over 19,000 Viet Cong supporters were killed.

The CIA made extensive use of Contra death squads in Nicaragua to destabilize the Sandinista government which the U.S.

claimed was communist. The CIA used psychological warfare techniques against the Panamanians by broadcasting pirate TV broadcasts. The CIA has extensively used propaganda broadcasts against the Cuban government through TV Marti, based in Miami, Florida. However, the Cuban government has been somewhat successful in jamming the signal of TV Marti. In the Iraq War, the United States used the shock and awe campaign to psychologically maim, and break the will of the Iraqi Army to fight.

During the siege of the Branch Davidians in Waco, TX. The FBI played music loudly around the clock along with bright lights in order to disturb them.

LERNER'S CATEGORIES OF PSYCHOLOGICAL WARFARE

Lerner divides psychological warfare operations into three categories:

White [Omissions + Emphasis]

Truthful and not strongly biased, where the source of information is acknowledged.

Grey [Omissions + Emphasis + Racial/Ethnic/Religious Bias]

Largely truthful, containing no information that can be proven wrong; the source may or may not be hidden.

Black [Commissions of falsification]

Intended to deceive the enemy.

Lerner points out that grey and black operations ultimately have a heavy cost, in that the target population will sooner or later recognize them as propaganda and discredit the source. He writes, "This is one of the few dogmas advanced by Sykewarriors that is likely to endure as an axiom of propaganda: Credibility is a condition of persuasion. Before you can make a man do as you say, you must make him believe what you say." Consistent with this idea, the Allied strategy in World War II was predominantly one of truth (with certain exceptions).

Chapter 7

BIOLOGICAL WARFARE

Biological Warfare (BW), also known as Germ Warfare (GW), is the use of pathogens such as viruses, bacteria, other disease-causing biological agents, or the toxins produced by them as biological weapons (or bioweapons).

There is a clear overlap between biological warfare and chemical warfare, as the use of toxins produced by living organisms is considered under the provisions of both the Biological and Toxin Weapons Convention and the Chemical Weapons Convention. (Toxins of organic origin are often called "midspectrum agents".)

A biological weapon may be intended to kill, incapacitate, or seriously impair a person, group of people, or even an entire population. It may also be defined as the material or defense against such employment.

Biological warfare is a military technique that can be used by nation-states or non-national groups. In the latter case, or if a nation-state uses it clandestinely, it may also be considered bioterrorism.

OVERVIEW

The creation and stockpiling of biological weapons ("offensive biological warfare") was outlawed by the 1972 Biological Weapons Convention (BWC), signed by over 100 countries. The BWC remains in force, and it prohibits storage, stockpiling, and usage of these weapons. The rationale behind the agreement is to avoid the devastating impact of a successful biological attack which could conceivably result in millions, possibly even billions of deaths and cause severe disruptions to societies and economies. Many countries currently pursue "defensive BW" research (defensive or protective applications) which are not prohibited by the BWC.

As a tactical weapon, the main military problem with a BW attack is that it would take days to be effective, and therefore, unlike a nuclear or chemical attack, would not immediately stop an opposing force. Some biological agents (especially smallpox, plague, and tularemia) have the capability of person-to-person transmission via aerosolized respiratory droplets, which can be undesirable, especially if they are transmitted to unintended target populations, including neutral or even friendly forces. Containment of transmission is less of a concern for terrorists, but it was very much a concern for post-WWII BW development by major powers.

The consensus among military analysts is that, except in the context of bioterrorism, BW is of little military use.

HISTORY

Biological warfare has been practiced repeatedly throughout history. Before the 20th century, the use of biological agents took three major forms:

- Deliberate poisoning of food and water with infectious material
- Use of microorganisms, toxins or animals, living or dead, in a weapon system
- Use of biologically inoculated fabrics

THE ANCIENT WORLD

The earliest documented incident of the intention to use biological weapons is recorded in Hittite texts of 1500-1200 B.C, in which victims of plague were driven into enemy lands. Although the Assyrians knew of ergot, a parasitic fungus of rye which produces ergotism when ingested, there is no evidence that they poisoned enemy wells with the fungus, as has often been claimed.

According to Homer's Iliad and Odyssey, epic poems about the legendary Trojan War, spears and arrows were tipped with poison. During the First Sacred War in Greece, in about 590 BC, Athens and the Amphictionic League poisoned the water supply of the besieged town of Kirrha (near Delphi) with the toxic plant hellebore. The Roman commander Manius Aquillus poisoned the wells of besieged enemy cities in about 130 BC.

During the 4th century BC Scythian archers tipped their arrow tips with snake venom, human blood, and animal feces to cause wounds to become infected. There are numerous other instances of the use of plant toxins, venoms, and other poisonous substances to create biological weapons in antiquity.

In 184 B.C, Hannibal of Carthage had clay pots filled with venomous snakes and instructed his soldiers to throw the pots onto the decks of Pergamene ships. In about AD 198, the city of Hatra (near Mosul, Iraq) repulsed the Roman army led by Septimius Severus by hurling clay pots filled with live scorpions at them.

MEDIEVAL BIOLOGICAL WARFARE

When the Mongol Empire established commercial and political connections between the Eastern and Western areas of the world, its Mongol armies and merchant caravans probably inadvertently brought bubonic plague from central Asia to the Middle East and Europe. The Black Death swept through Eurasia, killing approximately one third to one half of the population and changing the course of Asian and European history.

During the Middle Ages, victims of the bubonic plague were used for biological attacks, often by flinging corpses and excrement over castle walls using catapults. In 1346, the bodies of Mongol warriors of the Golden Horde who had died of plague were thrown over the walls of the besieged Crimean city of Kaffa (now Theodosia). It has been speculated that this operation may have been responsible for the advent of the Black Death in Europe. At the siege of Thun l'Eveque in 1340, during the Hundred Years'

War, the attackers catapulted decomposing animals into the besieged area.

In 1422, during the siege of Karlstein Castle in Bohemia, Hussite attackers used catapults to throw dead (but not plague-infected) bodies and 2000 carriage-loads of dung over the walls.

The last known incident of using plague corpses for biological warfare occurred in 1710, when Russian forces attacked the Swedes by flinging plague-infected corpses over the city walls of Reval (Tallinn). However, during the 1785 siege of La Calle, Tunisian forces flung diseased clothing into the city. Though not used for warfare, in ancient times (circa 1 bc) one form of execution/torture was attaching a corpse to a live person. The person who carried the corpse would become a social outcast and die from sicknesses in about a week.

MODERN TIMES

The 18th century

The Native American population was decimated after contact with the Old World due to the introduction of many different fatal diseases. There is, however, only one documented case of alleged germ warfare, involving British commander Lord Jeffrey Amherst and Swiss-British officer Colonel Henry Bouquet, whose correspondence included a reference to the idea of giving smallpox-infected blankets to Indians as part of an incident known as Pontiac's Rebellion, which occurred during the Siege of Fort Pitt (1763) late in the French and Indian War.

Any smallpox transmitted by Native American tribes was due to the transfer of the disease to blankets during transportation. Historians have been unable to establish whether or not this plan was implemented, particularly in light of the fact that smallpox was already present in the region, and that scientific knowledge of disease at that time had yet to discover bacteria or develop an understanding of plague vectors.

The roots of diseases that killed millions of indigenous peoples in the Americas can be traced back to Eurasians living for millennia in close proximity with domesticated animals. Without long contact with domesticated animals, indigenous Americans had no resistance to plague, measles, tuberculosis, smallpox or most influenza strains.

As it was well documented that many of European origin wished to exterminate the Native peoples, it has been assumed that there could have been many cases of smallpox being used as a quick way to kill off the locals.

Despite the lack of historical evidence, the belief that British and American soldiers used germ warfare against North American tribes has remained fairly strong in certain oral traditions and in popular culture. Such claims that smallpox infested blankets were used are especially strong in the oral traditions of native nations in the Plains and along the west coast of Canada.

The 19th century

In 1834 Cambridge Diarist Richard Henry Dana (Two Years Before the Mast; available in Project Gutenberg) visited San Francisco on a merchant ship. His ship traded many items including blankets with Mexicans and Russians who had established outposts on the northern side of the San Francisco Bay.

Local histories document that the California smallpox epidemic began at the Russian fort soon after they left. Blankets were a popular trading item, and the cheapest source of them was second-hand blankets which were often contaminated.

During the American Civil War, General Sherman reported that Confederate forces shot farm animals in ponds upon which the Union depended for drinking water. This would have made the water unpleasant to drink, although the actual health risks from dead bodies of humans and animals which did not die of disease are minimal.

Jack London in his story "'Yah! Yah! Yah!'" describes a punitive European expedition to a Pacific island deliberately exposing the

Polynesian population to Measles, of which many of them died. While much of the material for London's South Sea Tales is derived from his personal experience in the region, it is not certain that this particular incident is historical.

The 20th century

During the First World War, Germany pursued an ambitious biological warfare programme. Using diplomatic pouches and couriers, the German General Staff supplied small teams of saboteurs in the Russian Duchy of Finland, and in the then-neutral countries of Romania, the US and Argentina.

In Finland, Scandinavian freedom fighters mounted on reindeer placed ampules of anthrax in stables of Russian horses in 1916. Anthrax was also supplied to the German military attache in Bucharest, as was Glanders, which was employed against livestock destined for Allied service.

German intelligence officer and US citizen Dr. Anton Casimir Dilger established a secret lab in the basement of his sister's home in Chevy Chase, Maryland, that produced Glanders which was used to infect livestock in ports and inland collection points including, at least, Newport News, Norfolk, Baltimore, and New York, and probably St. Louis and Covington, Kentucky. In Argentina, German agents also employed Glanders in the port of Buenos Aires and also tried to ruin wheat harvests with a destructive fungus.

The Geneva Protocol of 1925 prohibited the use of chemical weapons and biological weapons, but said nothing about production, storage or transfer; later treaties did cover these aspects. Twentieth-century advances in microbiology enabled the first pure-culture biological agents to be developed by WWII.

There was a period of development by many nations, and Japanese Unit 731, based primarily at Pingfan in occupied China and commanded by Shirô Ishii, did research on BW, conducted forced human experiments, often fatal, on prisoners, and provided biological weapons for attacks in China..

Biological experiments, often using twins with one subject to the procedure and the other as a control, were carried out by Nazi Germany on concentration camp inmates, particularly by Joseph Mengele.

1937-1945

During the Sino-Japanese War (1937-1945) and World War II, Unit 731 of the Imperial Japanese Army conducted human experimentation on thousands, mostly Chinese, Russian, American prisoners. In military campaigns, the Japanese army used biological weapons on Chinese soldiers and civilians.

For example, in 1940, the Imperial Japanese Army Air Force bombed Ningbo with ceramic bombs full of fleas carrying the bubonic plague. A film showing this operation was seen by the imperial princes Tsuneyoshi Takeda and Takahito Mikasa during a screening made by mastermind Shiro Ishii.

However, some operations were ineffective due to inefficient delivery systems, using disease-bearing insects rather than dispersing the agent as an aerosol cloud. It is estimated that 400,000 Chinese died as a direct result of Japanese field testing of biological weapons.

During the Khabarovsk War Crime Trials the accused, such as Major General Kiyashi Kawashima, testified that as early as 1941 some 40 members of Unit 731 air-dropped plague-contaminated fleas on Changde. These operations caused epidemic plague outbreaks..

Some other firsthand accounts testify the Japanese infected civilians through the distribution of foodstuffs, such as dumplings and vegetables, contaminated with plague. There are also reports of contaminated water supplies. Three veterans of Unit 731 testified, in a 1989 interview to the Asahi Shimbun, that they were part of a mission to contaminate the Horustein river with typhoid near the Soviet troops during the Battle of Khalkhin Gol.

In response to biological weapons development in Japan, and at the time suspected in Germany, the United States, United

Kingdom, and Canada initiated a BW development programme in 1941 that resulted in the weaponisation of tularemia, anthrax, brucellosis, and botulism toxin.

The center for U.S. military BW research was Fort Detrick, Maryland, where USAMRIID is currently based; the first director was pharmaceutical executive George W. Merck. Some biological and chemical weapons research and testing was also conducted at Dugway Proving Grounds" in Utah, at a munition manufacturing complex in Terre Haute, Indiana, and at a tract on Horn Island, Mississippi.

Much of the British work was carried out at Porton Down. Field testing carried out in the United Kingdom during World War II left Gruinard island in Scotland contaminated with anthrax for the next 48 years.

1946 to 1972

During the 1948 Israel War of Independence, Red Cross reports raised suspicion that the Jewish Haganah militia had released Salmonella typhi bacteria into the water supply for the city of Acre, causing an outbreak of typhoid among the inhabitants. Egyptian troops later captured disguised Haganah soldiers near wells in Gaza, whom they executed for allegedly attempting another attack. Israel denies these allegations.

During the Cold War, US conscientious objectors were used as consenting test subjects for biological agents in a programme known as Operation Whitecoat. There were also many unpublicized tests carried out on the public during the Cold War.

Considerable research on the topic was performed by the United States (see US Biological Weapon Testing), the Soviet Union, and probably other major nations throughout the Cold War era, though it is generally believed that biological weapons were never used after World War II. This view was challenged by China and North Korea, who accused the United States of large-scale field testing of biological weapons, including the use of disease-carrying insects against them during the Korean War (1950-1953).

E120 biological bomblet, developed before the U.S. signed the Biological and Toxic Weapons Convention

Cuba also accused the US of spreading human and animal disease on their island. Recently revealed documents indicate that this was disinformation produced by Soviet intelligence.

At the time of the Korean War the US had only weaponized one agent, brucellosis (agent US), which is caused by Brucella suis. The original weaponized form used the M114 bursting bomblet in M33 cluster bombs. While the specific form of the biological bomb was classified until some years after the Korean War, in the various exhibits of biological weapons that Korea alleged were dropped on their country nothing resembled an M114 bomblet. There were ceramic containers that had some similarity to Japanese weapons used against the Chinese in WWII, developed by Unit 731.

Some of the Unit 731 personnel were imprisoned by the Soviets and would have been a potential source of information on Japanese weaponisation. The head of Unit 731, Lieutenant General Shiro Ishii, was granted immunity from war crimes prosecution in exchange for providing information to the United States on the Unit's activities.

The Korean War allegations also stressed the use of disease vectors, such as fleas, which, again, were probably a legacy of Japanese biological warfare efforts. The United States initiated its weaponisation efforts with disease vectors in 1953, focused on Plague-fleas, EEE-mosquitoes, and yellow fever–mosquitoes (OJ-AP). However, US medical scientists in occupied Japan undertook extensive research on insect vectors, with the assistance of former Unit 731 staff, as early as 1946.

The United States Air Force was not satisfied with the operational qualities of the M114/US and labeled it an interim item until the US Army Chemical Corps could deliver a superior weapon. The Air Force also changed its plans and wanted lethal biologicals.

The Chemical Corps then initiated a crash programme to weaponize anthrax (N) in the E61 1/2-lb hour-glass bomblet. Though the programme was successful in meeting its development goals, the lack of validation on the infectivity of anthrax stalled standardisation.

Around 1950 the Chemical Corps also initiated a programme to weaponize tularemia (UL). Shortly after the E61/N failed to make standardisation, tularemia was standardized in the 3.4" M143 bursting spherical bomblet. This was intended for delivery by the MGM-29 Sergeant missile warhead and could produce 50% infection over a 7-square-mile (18 km^2) area.

Unlike anthrax, tularemia had a demonstrated infectivity with human volunteers (Operation Whitecoat). Furthermore, although tularemia is treatable by antibiotics, treatment does not shorten the course of the disease.

In addition to the use of bursting bomblets for creating biological aerosols, the Chemical Corps started investigating aerosol-generating bomblets in the 1950s. The E99 was the first workable design, but was too complex to be manufactured. By the late 1950s the 4.5" E120 spraying spherical bomblet was developed; a B-47 bomber with a SUU-24/A dispenser could infect 50% or more of the population of a 16-square-mile (41 km^2) area with tularemia with the E120. The E120 was later superseded by dry-type agents.

Dry-type biologicals resemble talcum powder, and can be disseminated as aerosols using gas expulsion devices instead of a burster or complex sprayer. The Chemical Corps developed Flettner rotor bomblets and later triangular bomblets for wider coverage due to improved glide angles over Magnus-lift spherical bomblets. Weapons of this type were in advanced development by the time the programme ended. Richard Nixon signed an executive order on November 1969, which stopped production of biological weapons in the U.S. and allowed only scientific research of lethal biological agents and defensive measures such as immunisation and biosafety. The biological munition stockpiles were destroyed, and approximately 2,200 researchers became redundant.

United States special forces and the CIA also had an interest in biological warfare, and a series of special munitions was created for their operations. The covert weapons developed for the military (M1, M2, M4, M5, and M32–or Big Five Weapons) were destroyed in accordance with Nixon's executive order to end the offensive programme. The CIA maintained its collection of biologicals well into 1975 when it became the subject of the senate Church Committee.

THE BIOLOGICAL WEAPONS CONVENTION

In 1972, the U.S. signed the Biological and Toxic Weapons Convention, which banned the "development, production and stockpiling of microbes or their poisonous products except in amounts necessary for protective and peaceful research." By 1996, 137 countries had signed the treaty; however it is believed that since the signing of the Convention the number of countries capable of producing such weapons has increased.

The Soviet Union continued research and production of offensive biological weapons in a programme called biopreparat, despite having signed the convention. The United States was unaware of the programme until Dr. Vladimir Pasechnik defected in 1989, and Dr. Kanatjan Alibekov, the first deputy director of Biopreparat defected in 1992.

After the 1991 Persian Gulf War, Iraq admitted to the United Nations inspection team to having produced 19,000 L of concentrated botulinum toxin, of which approximately 10,000 L were loaded into military weapons; the 19,000 L have never been fully accounted for. This is approximately 3 times the amount needed to kill the entire current human population by inhalation, although in practice it would be impossible to distribute it so efficiently, and, unless it is protected from oxygen, it deteriorates in storage. On September 18, 2001 and for a few days after several letters were received by members of the U.S. Congress and media outlets containing anthrax spores: the attack killed five people. The identity of the perpetrator remained unknown until 2008, when a primary suspect was named. See 2001 anthrax attacks.

BIOLOGICAL AGENTS

Biological warfare is the deliberate use of disease and natural poisons to incapacitate humans. It employs pathogens as weapons. Pathogens are the micro-organism, whether bacterial, viral or protozoic, that cause disease. There are four kinds of biological warfare agents: bacteria, viruses, rickettsiae and fungi. Biological weapons are distinguished by being living organisms, that reproduce within their host victims, who then become contagious with a deadly, if weakening, multiplier effect. Toxins in contrast do not reproduce in the victim and need only the briefest of incubation periods; they kill within a few hours.

BIOLOGICAL WEAPONS CHARACTERISTICS

Anti-personnel Biological Warfare

Ideal characteristics of biological weapons targeting humans are high infectivity, high potency, non-availability of vaccines, and delivery as an aerosol.

Diseases most likely to be considered for use as biological weapons are contenders because of their lethality (if delivered efficiently), and robustness (making aerosol delivery feasible).

The biological agents used in biological weapons can often be manufactured quickly and easily. The primary difficulty is not the production of the biological agent but delivery in an effective form to a vulnerable target.

The international biological hazard symbol.

For example, anthrax is considered an effective agent for several reasons. First, it forms hardy spores, perfect for dispersal aerosols. Second, pneumonic (lung) infections of anthrax usually do not cause secondary infections in other people. Thus, the effect of the agent is usually confined to the target. A pneumonic anthrax infection starts with ordinary "cold" symptoms and quickly becomes lethal, with a fatality rate that is 90% or higher. Finally, friendly personnel can be protected with suitable antibiotics.

A mass attack using anthrax would require the creation of aerosol particles of 1.5 to 5 micrometres. Too large and the aerosol would be filtered out by the respiratory system. Too small and the aerosol would be inhaled and exhaled. Also, at this size, nonconductive powders tend to clump and cling because of electrostatic charges. This hinders dispersion. So the material must be treated to insulate and discharge the charges. The aerosol must be delivered so that rain and sun does not rot it, and yet the human lung can be infected. There are other technological difficulties as well.

Diseases considered for weaponisation, or known to be weaponized include anthrax , ebola, Marburg virus, plague , cholera , tularemia, brucellosis, Q fever, Bolivian hemorrhagic fever, Coccidioides mycosis , Glanders, Melioidosis, Shigella, Rocky Mountain spotted fever, typhus , Psittacosis, yellow fever , Japanese B encephalitis , Rift Valley fever, and smallpox. Naturally-occurring toxins that can be used as weapons include ricin, SEB, botulism toxin, saxitoxin, and many mycotoxins. The organisms causing these diseases are known as select agents. In the United States, their possession, use, and transfer are regulated by the Centers for Disease Control and Prevention's Select Agent Programme.

ANTI-AGRICULTURE BW

Biological warfare can also specifically target plants to destroy crops or defoliate vegetation. The United States and Britain discovered plant growth regulators (i.e., herbicides) during the Second World War, and initiated an herbicidal warfare programme that was eventually used in Malaya and Vietnam in counter insurgency. Though herbicides are chemicals, they are often grouped with biological warfare as bioregulators in a similar manner as biotoxins. Scorched earth tactics or destroying livestock and farmland were carried out in the Vietnam war and Eelam War in Sri Lanka.

The United States developed an anti-crop capability during the Cold War that used plant diseases (bioherbicides, or mycoherbicides) for destroying enemy agriculture. It was believed that destruction of enemy agriculture on a strategic scale could thwart Sino-Soviet aggression in a general war. Diseases such as wheat blast and rice blast were weaponized in aerial spray tanks and cluster bombs for delivery to enemy water sheds in agricultural regions to initiate epiphytotics (epidemics among plants). When the United States renounced its offensive biological warfare programme in 1969 and 1970, the vast majority of its biological arsenal was composed of these plant diseases.

In 1980s Soviet Ministry of Agriculture had successfully developed variants of foot-and-mouth disease and rinderpest against cows, African swine fever for pigs, and psittacosis to kill chicken. These agents were prepared to spray them down from tanks attached to airplanes over hundreds of miles. The secret programme was code-named "Ecology".

Attacking animals is another area of biological warfare intended to eliminate animal resources for transportation and food. In the First World War German agents were arrested attempting to inoculate draft animals with anthrax, and they were believed to be responsible for outbreaks of Glanders in horses and mules. The British tainted small feed cakes with anthrax in the Second World War as a potential means of attacking German cattle for food denial, but never employed the weapon. In the 1950s the United States had a field trial with hog cholera.

Unconnected with inter-human wars, humans have deliberately introduced the rabbit disease Myxomatosis, originating in South America, to Australia and Europe, with the intention of reducing the rabbit population–which had devastating but temporary results, with wild rabbit populations reduced to a fraction of their former size but survivors developing immunity and increasing again.

BIODEFENSE

ROLE OF PUBLIC HEALTH DEPARTMENTS AND DISEASE SURVEILLANCE

It is important to note that all of the classical and modern biological weapons organisms are animal diseases, the only exception being smallpox. Thus, in any use of biological weapons, it is highly likely that animals will become ill either simultaneously with, or perhaps earlier than humans.

Indeed, in the largest biological weapons accident known – the anthrax outbreak in Sverdlovsk (now Yekaterinburg) in the Soviet Union in 1979, sheep became ill with anthrax as far as 200 kilometers from the release point of the organism from a military facility in the southeastern portion of the city (known as Compound

19 and still off limits to visitors today, see Sverdlovsk Anthrax leak).

Thus, a robust surveillance system involving human clinicians and veterinarians may identify a bioweapons attack early in the course of an epidemic, permitting the prophylaxis of disease in the vast majority of people (and/or animals) exposed but not yet ill.

For example in the case of anthrax, it is likely that by 24 – 36 hours after an attack, some small percentage of individuals (those with compromised immune system or who had received a large dose of the organism due to proximity to the release point) will become ill with classical symptoms and signs (including a virtually unique chest X-ray finding, often recognized by public health officials if they receive timely reports). By making these data available to local public health officials in real time, most models of anthrax epidemics indicate that more than 80% of an exposed population can receive antibiotic treatment before becoming symptomatic, and thus avoid the moderately high mortality of the disease.

IDENTIFICATION OF BIOWEAPONS

The goal of biodefense is to integrate the sustained efforts of the national and homeland security, medical, public health, intelligence, diplomatic, and law enforcement communities. Health care providers and public health officers are among the first lines of defense. In some countries private, local, and state (province) capabilities are being augmented by and coordinated with federal assets, to provide layered defenses against biological weapons attacks. During the first Gulf War the United Nations activated a biological and chemical response team, Task Force Scorpio, to respond to any potential use of weapons of mass destruction on civilians.

The traditional approach toward protecting agriculture, food, and water: focusing on the natural or unintentional introduction of a disease is being strengthened by focused efforts to address current and anticipated future biological weapons threats that may be deliberate, multiple, and repetitive.

The growing threat of biowarfare agents and bioterrorism has led to the development of specific field tools that perform on-the-spot analysis and identification of encountered suspect materials. One such technology, being developed by researchers from the Lawrence Livermore National Laboratory (LLNL), employs a "sandwich immunoassay", in which fluorescent dye-labeled antibodies aimed at specific pathogens are attached to silver and gold nanowires.

Researchers at Ben Gurion University in Israel are developing a different device called the BioPen, essentially a "Lab-in-a-Pen", which can detect known biological agents in under 20 minutes using an adaptation of the ELISA, a similar widely employed immunological technique, that in this case incorporates fiber optics.

LIST OF BW INSTITUTIONS AND PROGRAMMES BY COUNTRY

According to the United States Office of Technology Assessment, since disbanded, seventeen countries were believed to possess biological weapons in 1995: Libya, North Korea, South Korea, Iraq, Taiwan, Syria, Israel, Iran, China, Egypt, Vietnam, Laos, Cuba, Bulgaria, India, South Africa, and Russia.

United States

- Fort Detrick, Maryland
    - o U.S. Army Biological Warfare Laboratories (1943-69)
        - Building 470
        - One-Million-Liter Test Sphere
        - Operation Whitecoat
  - o United States Army Medical Unit (1954-69)
    - o U.S. Army Medical Research Institute of Infectious Diseases (USAMRIID; 1969-present)
    - o National Biodefense Analysis and Countermeasures Center (NBACC; Projected: 2008)
- Project Bacchus

- Project Clear Vision
- Project SHAD

United Kingdom

- Porton Down
- Gruinard Island
- Nancekuke

Former Soviet Union and Russia

- Biopreparat (18 labs and production centers)
  - o Stepnagorsk Scientific and Technical Institute for Microbiology, Stepnogorsk, northern Kazakhstan
  - o Institute of Ultra Pure Biochemical Preparations, Leningrad, a weaponized plague center
  - o Vector State Research Center of Virology and Biotechnology (VECTOR), a weaponized smallpox center
  - o Institute of Applied Biochemistry, Omutninsk
  - o Kirov bioweapons production facility, Kirov, Kirov Oblast
  - o Zagorsk smallpox production facility, Zagorsk
  - o Berdsk bioweapons production facility, Berdsk
  - o Sverdlovsk bioweapons production facility (Military Compound 19), Sverdlovsk, a weaponized anthrax center
- Poison laboratory of the Soviet secret services
- Vozrozhdeniya Island

Japan

- Unit 731
- Zhongma Fortress
- Unit 100
- Unit 2646
- Unit 8604
- Unit Ei 1644

Iraq

Iraqi biological weapons programme and Iraq and weapons of mass destruction (passim)

- Al Hakum
- Salman Pak facility
- Al Manal facility

TREATIES BANNING OR RESTRICTING BW

- Geneva Protocol
- Biological Weapons Convention

List of people associated with BW

Bioweaponeers:

- Anton Dilger
- George W. Merck
- Ira Baldwin
- Paul Fildes
- Rihab Rashid Taha
- William C. Patrick III
- Kanatjan Alibekov, known as Ken Alibek
- Yuri Ovchinnikov
- Vladimir Pasechnik

Writers and activists:

- Matthew Meselson
- Jeanne Guillemin
- Richard Preston
- Sheldon H. Harris

Chapter 8

CHEMICAL WARFARE

Chemical Warfare (CW) involves using the toxic properties of chemical substances as weapons to kill, injure, or incapacitate an enemy. This type of warfare is distinct from the use of conventional weapons or nuclear weapons because the destructive effects of chemical weapons are not primarily due to their explosive force.

Chemical weapons are classified as weapons of mass destruction by the United Nations, and their production and stockpiling was outlawed by the Chemical Weapons Convention of 1993. The offensive use of living organisms or their toxic products is not considered chemical warfare but biological warfare.

DEFINITION

Chemical warfare is different from the use of conventional weapons or nuclear weapons because the destructive effects of chemical weapons are not primarily due to any explosive force. The offensive use of living organisms (such as anthrax) is considered biological warfare rather than chemical warfare; however, the use of nonliving toxic products produced by living organisms (e.g. toxins such as botulinum toxin, ricin, and saxitoxin) is considered chemical warfare under the provisions of the Chemical Weapons Convention. Under this Convention, any toxic chemical, regardless of its origin, is considered a chemical weapon unless it is used for purposes that are not prohibited (an important legal definition known as the General Purpose Criterion).

About 70 different chemicals have been used or stockpiled as chemical warfare agents during the 20th century. Chemical weapons are classified as weapons of mass destruction by the United Nations, and their production and stockpiling was outlawed by the Chemical Weapons Convention of 1993.

Under the Convention, chemicals that are toxic enough to be used as chemical weapons, or that may be used to manufacture such chemicals, are divided into three groups according to their purpose and treatment:

- **Schedule 1** – Have few, if any, legitimate uses. These may only be produced or used for research, medical, pharmaceutical or protective purposes (i.e. testing of chemical weapons sensors and protective clothing). Examples include nerve agents, ricin, lewisite and mustard gas. Any production over 100 g must be notified to the OPCW and a country can have a stockpile of no more than one tonne of these chemicals.
- **Schedule 2** – Have no large-scale industrial uses, but may have legitimate small-scale uses. Examples include dimethyl methylphosphonate, a precursor to sarin but which is also used as a flame retardant and Thiodiglycol which is a precursor chemical used in the manufacture of mustard gas but is also widely used as a solvent in inks.
- **Schedule 3** – Have legitimate large-scale industrial uses. Examples include phosgene and chloropicrin. Both have been used as chemical weapons but phosgene is an important precursor in the manufacture of plastics and chloropicrin is used as a fumigant. The OPCW must be notified of, and may inspect, any plant producing more than 30 tonnes per year.

TECHNOLOGY

Although crude chemical warfare has been employed in many parts of the world for thousands of years, "modern" chemical warfare began during World War I–see Poison gas in World War I.

Chemical warfare technology timeline				
	Agents	Dissemination	Protection	Detection
1900s	Chlorine Chloropicrin Phosgene Mustard gas	Wind dispersal	Gas masks, urinated-on gauze	Smell
1910s	Lewisite	Chemical shells	Gas mask Rosin oil clothing	
1920s		Projectiles w/ central bursters	CC-2 clothing	
1930s	G-series nerve agents	Aircraft bombs		Blister agent detectors Color change paper
1940s		Missile warheads Spray tanks	Protective ointment (mustard) Collective protection Gas mask w/ Whetlerite	
1950s				
1960s	V-series nerve agents	Aerodynamic	Gas mask w/ water supply	Nerve gas alarm
1970s				
1980s		Binary munitions	Improved gas masks (protection, fit, comfort)	Laser detection
1990s	Novichok nerve agents			

Initially, only well-known commercially available chemicals and their variants were used. These included chlorine and phosgene gas. The methods used to disperse these agents during battle were relatively unrefined and inefficient. Even so, casualties could be heavy, due to the mainly static troop positions which were characteristic features of trench warfare.

Germany, the first side to employ chemical warfare on the battlefield, simply opened canisters of chlorine upwind of the opposing side and let the prevailing winds do the dissemination. Soon after, the French modified artillery munitions to contain phosgene – a much more effective method that became the principal means of delivery.

Since the development of modern chemical warfare in World War I, nations have pursued research and development on chemical weapons that falls into four major categories: new and more deadly agents; more efficient methods of delivering agents to the target (dissemination); more reliable means of defense against chemical weapons; and more sensitive and accurate means of detecting chemical agents.

A Swedish Army soldier wearing a chemical agent protective suit (C-vätskeskydd) and his protection mask *(skyddsmask 90).*

CHEMICAL WARFARE AGENTS

A chemical used in warfare is called a chemical warfare agent (CWA). About 70 different chemicals have been used or stockpiled as chemical warfare agents during the 20th century and the 21st century. These agents may be in liquid, gas or solid form. Liquid agents are generally designed to evaporate quickly; such liquids are said to be volatile or have a high vapor pressure. Many chemical agents are made volatile so they can be dispersed over a large region quickly.

The earliest target of chemical warfare agent research was not toxicity, but development of agents that can affect a target through the skin and clothing, rendering protective gas masks useless. In

July 1917, the Germans employed mustard gas. Mustard gas easily penetrates leather and fabric to inflict painful burns on the skin.

Chemical warfare agents are divided into lethal and incapacitating categories. A substance is classified as incapacitating if less than 1/100 of the lethal dose causes incapacitation, e.g., through nausea or visual problems. The distinction between lethal and incapacitating substances is not fixed, but relies on a statistical average called the LD_{50}.

PERSISTENCY

One way to classify chemical warfare agents is according to their persistency, a measure of the length of time that a chemical agent remains effective after dissemination. Chemical agents are classified as persistent or nonpersistent.

Agents classified as nonpersistent lose effectiveness after only a few minutes or hours. Purely gaseous agents such as chlorine are nonpersistent, as are highly volatile agents such as sarin and most other nerve agents. Tactically, nonpersistent agents are very useful against targets that are to be taken over and controlled very quickly.

Apart from the agent used, the delivery mode is very important. To achieve a nonpersistent deployment, the agent is dispersed into very small droplets comparable with the mist produced by an aerosol can. In this form not only the gaseous part of the agent (around 50%) but also the fine aerosol can be inhaled or taken up by the skin.

Modern doctrine requires very high concentrations almost instantly in order to be effective (one breath should contain a lethal dose of the agent). To achieve this, the primary weapons used would be rocket artillery or bombs and large ballistic missiles with cluster warheads. The contamination in the target area is only low or not existent and after four hours sarin or similar agents are not detectable anymore.

By contrast, persistent agents tend to remain in the environment for as long as several weeks, complicating decontamination.

Defense against persistent agents requires shielding for extended periods of time. Non-volatile liquid agents, such as blister agents and the oily VX nerve agent, do not easily evaporate into a gas, and therefore present primarily a contact hazard.

The droplet size used for persistent delivery goes up to 1 mm increasing the falling speed and therefore about 80% of the deployed agent reaches the ground, resulting in heavy contamination. This implies, that persistent deployment does not aim at annihilating the enemy but to constrain him.

Possible targets include enemy flank positions (averting possible counter attacks), artillery regiments, commando posts or supply lines. Possible weapons to be used are wide spread, because the fast delivery of high amounts is not a critical factor.

A special form of persistent agents are thickened agents. These comprise a common agent mixed with thickeners to provide gelatinous, sticky agents. Primary targets for this kind of use include airfields, due to the increased persistency and difficulty of decontaminating affected areas.

CLASSES

Chemical weapons are inert agents that come in four categories: choking, blister, blood and nerve. The agents are organized into several categories according to the manner in which they affect the human body. The names and number of categories varies slightly from source to source, but in general, types of chemical warfare agents are as follows:

There are other chemicals used militarily that are not scheduled by the Chemical Weapons Convention, and thus are not controlled under the CWC treaties. These include:

- Defoliants that destroy vegetation, but are not immediately toxic to human beings. Some batches of Agent Orange, for instance, used by the United States in Vietnam, contained dioxins as manufacturing impurities. Dioxins, rather than Agent Orange itself, have long-term cancer effects and for causing genetic damage leading to serious birth deformities.

- Incendiary or explosive chemicals (such as napalm, extensively used by the United States in Vietnam, or dynamite) because their destructive effects are primarily due to fire or explosive force, and not direct chemical action.
- Viruses, bacteria, or other organisms. Their use is classified as biological warfare. Toxins produced by living organisms are considered chemical weapons, although the boundary is blurry. Toxins are covered by the Biological Weapons Convention.

DESIGNATIONS

For more details on this topic, see chemical weapon designation.

Most chemical weapons are assigned a one- to three-letter "NATO weapon designation" in addition to, or in place of, a common name. Binary munitions, in which precursors for chemical warfare agents are automatically mixed in shell to produce the agent just prior to its use, are indicated by a "-2" following the agent's designation (for example, GB-2 and VX-2).

Some examples are given below:

Blood agents:	**Vesicants:**
• Cyanogen chloride: CK • Hydrogen cyanide: AC	• Lewisite: L • Sulfur mustard: H, HD, HS, HT
Pulmonary agents:	**Incapacitating agents:**
• Phosgene: CG	• Quinuclidinyl benzilate: BZ
Lachrymatory agents:	**Nerve agents:**
• Pepper spray: OC • Tear gas: CN, CS, CR	• Sarin: GB • VE, VG, VM, VX

DELIVERY

The most important factor in the effectiveness of chemical weapons is the efficiency of its delivery, or dissemination, to a target. The most common techniques include munitions (such as bombs, projectiles, warheads) that allow dissemination at a distance and spray tanks which disseminate from low-flying aircraft. Developments in the techniques of filling and storage of munitions have also been important.

Although there have been many advances in chemical weapon delivery since World War I, it is still difficult to achieve effective dispersion. The dissemination is highly dependent on atmospheric conditions because many chemical agents act in gaseous form. Thus, weather observations and forecasting are essential to optimize weapon delivery and reduce the risk of injuring friendly forces.

DISPERSION

Dispersion is placing the chemical agent upon or adjacent to a target immediately before dissemination, so that the material is most efficiently used. Dispersion is the simplest technique of delivering an agent to its target. The most common techniques are munitions, bombs, projectiles, spray tanks and warheads.

Dispersion of chlorine in World War I

World War I saw the earliest implementation of this technique. The actual first chemical ammunition was the French 26 mm cartouche suffocante rifle grenade, fired from a flare carbine. It contained 35g of the tear-producer ethylbromacetate, and was used in autumn 1914 – with little effect on the Germans.

The Germans on the other hand tried to increase the effect of 10.5 cm shrapnel shells by adding an irritant – dianisidine chlorosulphonate. Its use went unnoticed by the British when it was used against them at Neuve Chapelle in October 1914. Hans Tappen, a chemist in the Heavy Artillery Department of the War Ministry, suggested to his brother, the Chief of the Operations Branch at German General Headquarters, the use of the tear-gases benzyl bromide or xylyl bromide.

Shells were tested successfully at the Wahn artillery range near Cologne on 9 January, 1915, and an order was placed for 15 cm howitzer shells, designated 'T-shells' after Tappen. A shortage of shells limited the first use against the Russians at Bolimów on 31 January, 1915; the liquid failed to vaporize in the cold weather, and again the experiment went unnoticed by the Allies.

The first effective use were when the German forces at the Second Battle of Ypres simply opened cylinders of chlorine and allowed the wind to carry the gas across enemy lines. While simple, this technique had numerous disadvantages. Moving large numbers of heavy gas cylinders to the front-line positions from where the gas would be released was a lengthy and difficult logistical task.

Stockpiles of cylinders had to be stored at the front line, posing a great risk if hit by artillery shells. Gas delivery depended greatly on wind speed and direction. If the wind was fickle, as at Loos, the gas could blow back, causing friendly casualties.

Gas clouds gave plenty of warning, allowing the enemy time to protect themselves, though many soldiers found the sight of a creeping gas cloud unnerving. This made the gas doubly effective, as, in addition to damaging the enemy physically, it also had a psychological effect on the intended victims.

Another disadvantage was that gas clouds had limited penetration, capable only of affecting the front-line trenches before dissipating. Although it produced limited results in World War I, this technique shows how simple chemical weapon dissemination can be.

Shortly after this "open canister" dissemination, French forces developed a technique for delivery of phosgene in a non-explosive artillery shell. This technique overcame many of the risks of dealing with gas in cylinders. First, gas shells were independent of the wind and increased the effective range of gas, making any target within reach of guns vulnerable. Second, gas shells could be delivered without warning, especially the clear, nearly odorless phosgene – there are numerous accounts of gas shells, landing with a "plop" rather than exploding, being initially dismissed as dud high explosive or shrapnel shells, giving the gas time to work before the soldiers were alerted and took precautions.

The major drawback of artillery delivery was the difficulty of achieving a killing concentration. Each shell had a small gas payload and an area would have to be subjected to saturation bombardment to produce a cloud to match cylinder delivery. A British solution to the problem was the Livens Projector. This was effectively a large-bore mortar, dug into the ground that used the gas cylinders themselves as projectiles–firing a 14 kg cylinder up to 1500 m. This combined the gas volume of cylinders with the range of artillery. Over the years, there were some refinements in this technique. In the 1950s and early 1960s, chemical artillery rockets and cluster bombs contained a multitude of submunitions, so that a large number of small clouds of the chemical agent would form directly on the target.

THERMAL DISSEMINATION

Thermal dissemination is the use of explosives or pyrotechnics to deliver chemical agents. This technique, developed in the 1920s, was a major improvement over earlier dispersal techniques, in that it allowed significant quantities of an agent to be disseminated over a considerable distance. Thermal dissemination remains the principal method of disseminating chemical agents today.

Most thermal dissemination devices consist of a bomb or projectile shell that contains a chemical agent and a central "burster" charge; when the burster detonates, the agent is expelled laterally.

Thermal dissemination devices, though common, are not particularly efficient. First, a percentage of the agent is lost by incineration in the initial blast and by being forced onto the ground. Second, the sizes of the particles vary greatly because explosive dissemination produces a mixture of liquid droplets of variable and difficult to control sizes. The efficacy of thermal detonation is greatly limited by the flammability of some agents. For flammable aerosols, the cloud is sometimes totally or partially ignited by the disseminating explosion in a phenomenon called flashing. Explosively disseminated VX will ignite roughly one third of the time. Despite a great deal of study, flashing is still not fully understood, and a solution to the problem would be a major technological advance.

An American-made MC-1 gas bomb

Despite the limitations of central bursters, most nations use this method in the early stages of chemical weapon development, in part because standard munitions can be adapted to carry the agents.

AERODYNAMIC DISSEMINATION

Aerodynamic dissemination is the non-explosive delivery of a chemical agent from an aircraft, allowing aerodynamic stress to disseminate the agent. This technique is the most recent major development in chemical agent dissemination, originating in the mid-1960s.

Soviet chemical weapons canisters from a stockpile in Albania

This technique eliminates many of the limitations of thermal dissemination by eliminating the flashing effect and theoretically allowing precise control of particle size. In actuality, the altitude of dissemination, wind direction and velocity, and the direction and velocity of the aircraft greatly influence particle size. There are other drawbacks as well; ideal deployment requires precise knowledge of aerodynamics and fluid dynamics, and because the agent must usually be dispersed within the boundary layer (less than 200–300 ft above the ground), it puts pilots at risk.

Significant research is still being applied toward this technique. For example, by modifying the properties of the liquid, its breakup when subjected to aerodynamic stress can be controlled and an idealized particle distribution achieved, even at supersonic speed. Additionally, advances in fluid dynamics, computer modeling, and weather forecasting allow an ideal direction, speed, and altitude to be calculated, such that warfare agent of a predetermined particle size can predictably and reliably hit a target.

PROTECTION AGAINST CHEMICAL WARFARE

Ideal protection begins with nonproliferation treaties such as the Chemical Weapons Convention, and detecting, very early, the signatures of someone building a chemical weapons capability. These include a wide range of intelligence disciplines, such as economic analysis of exports of dual-use chemicals and equipment, human intelligence (HUMINT) such as diplomatic, refugee, and agent reports; photography from satellites, aircraft and drones (IMINT); examination of captured equipment (TECHINT); communications intercepts (COMINT); and detection of chemical manufacturing and chemical agents themselves (MASINT).

If all the preventive measures fail and there is a clear and present danger, then there is a need for detection of chemical attacks, collective protection, and decontamination. Since industrial accidents can cause dangerous chemical releases (e.g., the Bhopal disaster), these activities are things that civilian, as well as military, organisations must be prepared to carry out. In civilian situations in developed countries, these are duties of HAZMAT organisations, which most commonly are part of fire departments.

Detection has been referred to above, as a technical MASINT discipline; specific military procedures, which are usually the model for civilian procedures, depend on the equipment, expertise, and personnel available. When chemical agents are detected, an alarm needs to sound, with specific warnings over emergency broadcasts and the like. There may be a warning to expect an attack.

If, for example, the captain of a US Navy ship believes there is a serious threat of chemical, biological, or radiological attack, the crew may be ordered to set Circle William, which means closing all openings to outside air, running breathing air through filters, and possibly starting a system that continually washes down the exterior surfaces. Civilian authorities dealing with an attack or a toxic chemical accident will invoke the Incident Command System, or local equivalent, to coordinate defensive measures. Individual protection starts with a gas mask and, depending on the nature of the threat, through various levels of protective clothing up to a complete chemical-resistant suit with a self-contained air supply. The US military defines various levels of MOPP (mission-oriented protective posture) from mask to full chemical resistant suits; Hazmat suits are the civilian equivalent, but go farther to include a fully independent air supply, rather than the filters of a gas mask.

Collective protection allows continued functioning of groups of people in buildings or shelters, the latter which may be fixed, mobile, or improvised. With ordinary buildings, this may be as basic as plastic sheeting and tape, although if the protection needs to be continued for any appreciable length of time, there will need to be an air supply, typically a scaled-up version of a gas mask.

Members of the Ukrainian Army's 19th Nuclear, Biological and Chemical Battalion practice decontamination drill, at Camp Arifjan, Kuwait

DECONTAMINATION

Decontamination varies with the particular chemical agent used. Some nonpersistent agents, such as most pulmonary agents such as chlorine and phosgene, blood gases, and nonpersistent nerve gases (e.g., GB) will dissipate from open areas, although powerful exhaust fans may be needed to clear out building where they have accumulated.

In some cases, it might be necessary to neutralize them chemically, as with ammonia as a neutralizer for hydrogen cyanide or chlorine. Riot control agents such as CS will dissipate in an open area, but things contaminated with CS powder need to be aired out, washed by people wearing protective gear, or safely discarded. Mass decontamination is a less common requirement for people than equipment, since people may be immediately affected and treatment is the action required. It is a requirement when people have been contaminated with persistent agents. Treatment and decontamination may need to be simultaneous, with the medical personnel protecting themselves so they can function.

There may need to be immediate intervention to prevent death, such as injection of atropine for nerve agents. Decontamination is especially important for people contaminated with persistent agents; many of the fatalities after the explosion of a WWII US ammunition ship carrying mustard gas, in the harbor of Bari, Italy, after a German bombing on 2 December 1943, came when rescue workers, not knowing of the contamination, bundled cold, wet seamen in tight-fitting blankets.

For decontaminating equipment and buildings exposed to persistent agents, such as blister agents, VX or other agents made persistent by mixing with a thickener, special equipment and materials might be needed. Some type of neutralising agent will be needed; e.g. in the form of a spraying device with neutralising agents such as Chlorine, Fichlor, strong alkaline solutions or enzymes. In other cases, a specific chemical decontaminant will be required.

SOCIOPOLITICAL CLIMATE

The study of chemicals and their military uses was widespread in China and India. The use of toxic materials has historically been viewed with mixed emotions and moral qualms in the West. The practical and ethical problems surrounding poison warfare appeared in ancient Greek myths about Hercules' invention of poison arrows and Odysseus's use of toxic projectiles. There are many instances of the use of chemical weapons in battles documented in Greek and Roman historical texts; the earliest example was the deliberate poisoning of Kirrha's water supply with hellebore in the First Sacred War, Greece, about 590 BC.

One of the earliest reactions to the use of chemical agents was from Rome. Struggling to defend themselves from the Roman legions, Germanic tribes poisoned the wells of their enemies, with Roman jurists having been recorded as declaring "armis bella non venenis geri", meaning "war is fought with weapons, not with poisons." Yet the Romans themselves resorted to poisoning wells of besieged cities in Anatolia in the second century BC.

Before 1915 the use of poisonous chemicals in battle was typically the result of local initiative, and not the result of an active government chemical weapons programme. There are many reports of the isolated use of chemical agents in individual battles or sieges, but there was no true tradition of their use outside of incendiaries and smoke.

Despite this tendency, there have been several attempts to initiate large-scale implementation of poison gas in several wars, but with the notable exception of World War I, the responsible authorities generally rejected the proposals for ethical reasons.

For example, in 1854 Lyon Playfair, a British chemist, proposed using a cyanide-filled artillery shell against enemy ships during the Crimean War. The British Ordnance Department rejected the proposal as "as bad a mode of warfare as poisoning the wells of the enemy."

EFFORTS TO ERADICATE CHEMICAL WEAPONS

Nation	CW Possession	Signed CWC	Ratified CWC
Albania	Known	January 14, 1993	May 11, 1994
Burma (Myanmar)	Possible	January 13, 1993	No
the People's Republic of China	Probable	January 13, 1993	April 4, 1997
Egypt	Probable	No	No
France	Probable	January 13, 1993	March 2, 1995
India	Known	January 14, 1993	September 3, 1996
Iran	Known	January 13, 1993	November 3, 1997
Israel	Probable	January 13, 1993	No
Japan	Probable	January 13, 1993	September 15, 1995
Libya	Known	No	January 6, 2004 (acceded)
North Korea	Known	No	No
Pakistan	Probable	January 13, 1993	October 28, 1997
Russia	Known	January 13, 1993	November 5, 1997

Serbia and Montenegro	Probable	No	April 20, 2000 (acceded)
Sudan	Possible	No	May 24, 1999 (acceded)
Syria	Known	No	No
Taiwan	Possible	n/a	n/a
United States	Known	January 13, 1993	April 25, 1997
Vietnam	Probable	January 13, 1993	September 30, 1998

LIST OF CHEMICAL ARMS CONTROL AGREEMENTS

- August 27, 1874: The Brussels Declaration Concerning the Laws and Customs of War is signed, specifically forbidding the "employment of poison or poisoned weapons."
- September 4, 1900: The Hague Conference, which includes a declaration banning the "use of projectiles the object of which is the diffusion of asphyxiating or deleterious gases," enters into force.
- February 6, 1922: After World War I, the Washington Arms Conference Treaty prohibited the use of asphyxiating, poisonous or other gases. It was signed by the United States, Britain, Japan, France, and Italy, but France objected to other provisions in the treaty and it never went into effect.
- September 7, 1929: The Geneva Protocol enters into force, prohibiting the use of poison gas.

CHEMICAL WEAPON PROLIFERATION

Despite numerous efforts to reduce or eliminate them, some nations continue to research and/or stockpile chemical warfare agents. To the right is a summary of the nations that have either declared weapon stockpiles or are suspected of secretly stockpiling or possessing CW research programmes. Notable examples include United States and Russia.

US Vice President Dick Cheney opposed the signing ratification of a treaty banning the use chemical weapons, a recently unearthed letter shows. In a letter dated April 8, 1997, then Halliburton-CEO Cheney told Sen. Jesse Helms, the chairman of the Senate Foreign Relations Committee, that it would be a mistake for America to join the Convention. "Those nations most likely to comply with the Chemical Weapons Convention are not likely to ever constitute a military threat to the United States. The governments we should be concerned about are likely to cheat on the CWC, even if they do participate," reads the letter, published by the Federation of American Scientists.

The CWC was ratified by the Senate that same month. Since then, Albania, Libya, Russia, the United States, and India have declared over 71,000 metric tons of chemical weapon stockpiles, and destroyed about a third of them. Under the terms of the agreement, the United States and Russia are supposed to eliminate the rest of their supplies of chemical weapons by 2012. But that looks unlikely – the U.S. government estimates remaining stocks will be destroyed by 2017.

HISTORY

ANCIENT TO MEDIEVAL TIMES

Chemical weapons have been used for millennia in the form of poisoned spears and arrows, but evidence can be found for the existence of more advanced forms of chemical weapons in ancient and classical times.

A good example of early chemical warfare was the late Stone Age (10 000 BC) hunter-gatherer societies in Southern Africa, known as the San. They used poisoned arrows, tipping the wood, bone and stone tips of their arrows with poisons obtained from their natural environment. These poisons were mainly derived from scorpion or snake venom, but it is believed that some poisonous plants were also utilized. The arrow was fired into the target of choice, usually an antelope (the favourite being an eland), with the hunter then tracking the doomed animal until the poison caused its collapse.

Ancient Greek myths about Hercules poisoning his arrows with the venom of the Hydra Monster are the earliest references to toxic weapons in western literature. Homer's epics, the Iliad and the Odyssey, allude to poisoned arrows used by both sides in the legendary Trojan War (Bronze Age Greece).

TEXTUAL AND LITERARY EVIDENCE

Some of the earliest surviving references to toxic warfare are may appear in the Indian epics Ramayana and Mahabharata. The "Laws of Manu," a Hindu treatise on statecraft (ca 400 BC) forbids the use of poison and fire arrows, but advises poisoning food and water. Kautilya's "Arthashastra," a statecraft manual of the same era, contains hundreds of recipes for creating poison weapons, toxic smokes, and other chemical weapons. Ancient Greek historians reçount that Alexander the Great encountered poison arrows and fire incendiaries in what is now Pakistan in the fourth century BC.

Sun Tzu's "Art of War" (ca 500 BC) advises the use of fire weapons. In the 4th century BC, writings of the Mohist sect in China describe the use of bellows to pump smoke from burning balls of mustard and other toxic vegetables into tunnels being dug by a besieging army.

Even older Chinese writings dating back to about 1000 BC contain hundreds of recipes for the production of poisonous or irritating smokes for use in war along with numerous accounts of their use. From these accounts we know of the arsenic-containing "soul-hunting fog", and the use of finely divided lime dispersed into the air to suppress a peasant revolt in AD 178.

The earliest recorded use of gas warfare in the West dates back to the 5th century BC, during the Peloponnesian War between Athens and Sparta. Spartan forces besieging an Athenian city placed a lighted mixture of wood, pitch, and sulfur under the walls hoping that the noxious smoke would incapacitate the Athenians, so that they would not be able to resist the assault that followed. Sparta wasn't alone in its use of unconventional tactics during these wars: Solon of Athens is said to have used hellebore roots to poison the water in an aqueduct leading from the Pleistrus River around 590 BC during the siege of Kirrha.

Chemical weapons were known and used in ancient and medieval China. Polish chronicler Jan D³ugosz mentions usage of poisonous gas by the Mongol army in 1241 in the Battle of Legnica.

Historian and philosopher David Hume, in his history of England, recounts how during early in the reign of Henry III (r.1216–1272) the English Navy destroyed an invading French fleet, by blinding the enemy fleet with "quicklime," the old name for calcium oxide. D'Albiney employed a stratagem against them, which is said to have contributed to the victory:

Having gained the wind of the French, he came down upon them with violence; and throwing in their faces a great quantity of quicklime, which he purposely carried on board, he so blinded them, that they were disabled from defending themselves.

ARCHAEOLOGICAL EVIDENCE

There is archaeological evidence that the Sasanians deployed chemical weapons against the Roman army in 3rd century AD/CE. Research carried out on the collapsed tunnels at Dura-Europos in Syria suggests that the Iranians used bitumen and sulphur crystals to get it burning. When ignited, the materials gave off dense clouds of choking gases which killed 20 Roman soldiers in the matter of 2 minutes.

REDISCOVERY

During the Renaissance, people again considered using chemical warfare. One of the earliest such references is from Leonardo da Vinci, who proposed a powder of sulfide of arsenic and verdigris in the 15th century:

> throw poison in the form of powder upon galleys. Chalk, fine sulfide of arsenic, and powdered verdegris may be thrown among enemy ships by means of small mangonels, and all those who, as they breathe, inhale the powder into their lungs will become asphyxiated.

It is unknown whether this powder was ever actually used.

Earlier, in the 13th century, of Henry III the English Navy destroyed an invading French fleet, by blinding the enemy fleet with "quicklime," the old name for calcium oxide. (See Calcium oxide#use as a weapon) In the 17th century during sieges, armies attempted to start fires by launching incendiary shells filled with sulphur, tallow, rosin, turpentine, saltpeter, and/or antimony. Even when fires were not started, the resulting smoke and fumes provided a considerable distraction. Although their primary function was never abandoned, a variety of fills for shells were developed to maximize the effects of the smoke.

In 1672, during his siege of the city of Groningen, Christoph Bernhard van Galen, the Bishop of Münster, employed several different explosive and incendiary devices, some of which had a fill that included belladonna, intended to produce toxic fumes. Just three years later, August 27, 1675, the French and the Germans concluded the Strasbourg Agreement, which included an article banning the use of "perfidious and odious" toxic devices.

In 1854, Lyon Playfair, a British chemist, proposed a cacodyl cyanide artillery shell for use against enemy ships as way to solve the stalemate during the siege of Sevastopol. The proposal was backed by Admiral Thomas Cochrane of the Royal Navy. It was considered by the Prime Minister, Lord Palmerston, but the British Ordnance Department rejected the proposal as "as bad a mode of warfare as poisoning the wells of the enemy." Playfair's response was used to justify chemical warfare into the next century:

> There was no sense in this objection. It is considered a legitimate mode of warfare to fill shells with molten metal which scatters among the enemy, and produced the most frightful modes of death. Why a poisonous vapor which would kill men without suffering is to be considered illegitimate warfare is incomprehensible. War is destruction, and the more destructive it can be made with the least suffering the sooner will be ended that barbarous method of protecting national rights. No doubt in time chemistry will be used to lessen the suffering of combatants, and even of criminals condemned to death.

Later, during the American Civil War, New York school teacher John Doughty proposed the offensive use of chlorine gas, delivered by filling a 10 inch (254 millimeter) artillery shell with 2 to 3 quarts (2 to 3 liters) of liquid chlorine, which could produce many cubic feet (a few cubic meters) of chlorine gas. Doughty's plan was apparently never acted on, as it was probably presented to Brigadier General James Wolfe Ripley, Chief of Ordnance, who was described as being congenitally immune to new ideas.

A general concern over the use of poison gas manifested itself in 1899 at the Hague Conference with a proposal prohibiting shells filled with asphyxiating gas. The proposal was passed, despite a single dissenting vote from the United States. The American representative, Navy Captain Alfred Thayer Mahan, justified voting against the measure on the grounds that "the inventiveness of Americans should not be restricted in the development of new weapons."

WORLD WAR I

The Hague Declaration of 1899 and the Hague Convention of 1907 forbade the use of "poison or poisonous weapons" in warfare, yet more than 124,000 tons of gas were produced by the end of World War I. The French were the first to use chemical weapons during the First World War, using tear gas.

Aerial photograph of a German gas attack on Russian forces circa 1916

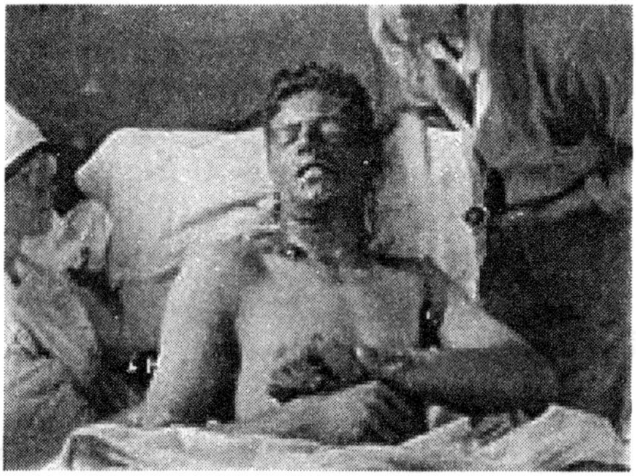

A Canadian soldier with mustard gas burns, ca. 1917–1918.

The German's first use of chemical weapons were shells containing xylyl bromide that were fired at the Russians near the town of Bolimów, Poland in January 1915. The first full-scale deployment of chemical warfare agents was during World War I, originating in the Second Battle of Ypres, April 22, 1915, when the Germans attacked French, Canadian and Algerian troops with chlorine gas. Deaths were light, though casualties relatively heavy.

A total 50,965 tons of pulmonary, lachrymatory, and vesicant agents were deployed by both sides of the conflict, including chlorine, phosgene and mustard gas. Official figures declare about 1,176,500 non-fatal casualties and 85,000 fatalities directly caused by chemical warfare agents during the course of the war.

To this day unexploded WWI-era chemical ammunition is still frequently uncovered when the ground is dug in former battle or depot areas and continues to pose a threat to the civilian population in Belgium and France and less commonly in other countries. The French and Belgian governments have had to launch special programmes for treating discovered ammunition.

After the war, most of the unused German chemical warfare agents were dumped into the Baltic Sea, a common disposal method among all the participants in several bodies of water. Over time, the salt water causes the shell casings to corrode, and mustard gas occasionally leaks from these containers and washes onto shore as a wax-like solid resembling ambergris. Even in this solidified form, the agent is active enough to cause severe contact burns to anybody coming into contact with it.

INTERWAR YEARS

After World War I chemical agents were occasionally used to subdue populations and suppress rebellion.

Following the defeat of the Ottoman Empire in 1917, the Ottoman government collapsed completely, and the former empire was divided amongst the victorious powers in the Treaty of Sèvres. The British occupied Mesopotamia (present-day Iraq) and established a colonial government.

In 1920, the Arab and Kurdish people of Mesopotamia revolted against the British occupation, which cost the British dearly. As the Mesopotamian resistance gained strength, the British resorted to increasingly repressive measures. Much speculation was made about aerial bombardment of major cities with gas in Mesopotamia, with Winston Churchill, then-Secretary of State at the British War Office, arguing in favor of it. In the 1920s generals reported that poison had never won a battle. The soldiers said they hated it and hated the gas masks. Only the chemists spoke out to say it was a good weapon.

In 1925, sixteen of the world's major nations signed the Geneva Protocol, thereby pledging never to use gas in warfare again. Notably, in the United States, the Protocol languished in the Senate until 1975, when it was finally ratified.

The Bolsheviks also employed poison gas in 1921 during the Tambov Rebellion. An order signed by military commanders Tukhachevsky and Vladimir Antonov-Ovseenko stipulated: "The forests where the bandits are hiding are to be cleared by the use of poison gas. This must be carefully calculated, so that the layer of gas penetrates the forests and kills everyone hiding there."

During the Rif War in Spanish Morocco in 1921–1927, combined Spanish and French forces dropped mustard gas bombs in an attempt to put down the Berber rebellion. (See also: Chemical weapons in the Rif War)

In 1935, Fascist Italy used mustard gas during the invasion of Ethiopia in the Second Italo-Abyssinian War. Ignoring the Geneva Protocol, which it signed seven years earlier, the Italian military dropped mustard gas in bombs, sprayed it from airplanes, and spread it in powdered form on the ground. 150,000 chemical casualties were reported, mostly from mustard gas.

WORLD WAR II

Despite article 171 of the Versailles Peace Treaty, article V of the Treaty in Relation to the Use of Submarines and Noxious Gases in Warfare and a resolution adopted against Japan by the League of nations on 14 May 1938, the Imperial Japanese Army frequently used chemical weapons. Because of fear of retaliation however, those weapons were never used against Westerners, but against other Asians judged "inferior" by the imperial propaganda.

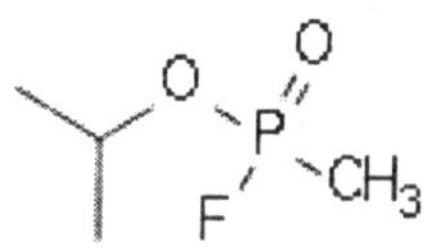

The chemical structure of Sarin nerve gas, developed in Germany (1939)

According to historians Yoshiaki Yoshimi and Seiya Matsuno, the chemical weapons were authorized by specific orders given by Emperor Showa himself, transmitted by the chief of staff of the army. For example, the Emperor authorized the use of toxic gas on 375 separate occasions during the battle of Wuhan from August to October 1938.

They were also profusely used during the invasion of Changde. Those orders were transmitted either by prince Kotohito Kan'in or general Hajime Sugiyama.

The Imperial Japanese Army used mustard gas and the recently-developed blister agent Lewisite against Chinese troops and guerrillas. Experiments involving chemical weapons were conducted on live prisoners (Unit 731 and Unit 516). The Japanese also carried chemical weapons as they swept through Southeast Asia towards Australia.

Some of these items were captured and analyzed by the Allies. Greatly concerned, Australia covertly imported 1,000,000 chemical weapons from the United Kingdom from 1942 onwards.

Shortly after the end of World War I, Germany's General Staff enthusiastically pursued a recapture of their preeminent position in chemical warfare. In 1923, Hans von Seeckt pointed the way, by suggesting that German poison gas research move in the direction of delivery by aircraft in support of mobile warfare. Also in 1923, at the behest of the German army, poison gas expert Dr. Hugo Stolzenberg negotiated with the USSR to built a huge chemical weapons plant at Trotsk, on the Volga river.

Collaboration between Germany and the USSR in poison gas continued on and off through the 1920s. In 1924, German officers debated the use of poison gas versus non-lethal chemical weapons against civilians. Even before World War II, chemical warfare was revolutionized by Nazi Germany's discovery of the nerve agents tabun (in 1937) and sarin (in 1939) by Gerhard Schrader, a chemist of IG Farben. IG Farben was Germany's premier poison gas manufacturer during World War I, so the weaponisation of these agents can not be considered accidental. Both were turned over to the German Army Weapons Office prior to the outbreak of the war.

The nerve agent soman was later discovered by Nobel Prize laureate Richard Kuhn and his collaborator Konrad Henkel at the Kaiser Wilhelm Institute for Medical Research in Heidelberg in spring of 1944. The Nazis developed and manufactured large quantities of several agents, but chemical warfare was not extensively used by either side. Chemical troops were set up (in Germany since 1934) and delivery technology was actively developed.

Recovered Nazi documents suggest that German intelligence incorrectly thought that the Allies also knew of these compounds, interpreting their lack of mention in the Allies' scientific journals as evidence that information about them was being suppressed. Germany ultimately decided not to use the new nerve agents, fearing a potentially devastating Allied retaliatory nerve agent deployment. *Fisk, Robert (December 30, 2000).* "Poison gas from Germany".

William L. Shirer, in The Rise and Fall of the Third Reich, writes that the British high command considered the use of chemical weapons as a last-ditch defensive measure in the event of a Nazi invasion of Britain.

On the night of December 2, 1943, German Ju 88 bombers attacked the port of Bari in Southern Italy, sinking several American ships–among them SS John Harvey, which was carrying mustard gas intended for use in retaliation by the Allies if German forces initiated gas warfare. The presence of the gas was highly classified, and authorities ashore had no knowledge of it – which increased the number of fatalities, since physicians, who had no idea that they were dealing with the effects of mustard gas, prescribed treatment improper for those suffering from exposure and immersion.

The whole affair was kept secret at the time and for many years after the war (in the opinion of some, there was a deliberate and systematic cover-up). According to the U.S. military account, "Sixty-nine deaths were attributed in whole or in part to the mustard gas, most of them American merchant seamen" out of 628 mustard gas military casualties. The large number of civilian casualties among the Italian population were not recorded. Part of the confusion and controversy derives from the fact that the German attack was highly destructive and lethal in itself, also apart from the accidental additional effects of the gas (it was nicknamed "The Little Pearl Harbor"), and attribution of the causes of death between the gas and other causes is far from easy.

Rick Atkinson, in his book The Day of Battle, describes the intelligence that prompted Allied leaders to deploy mustard gas to Italy. This included Italian intelligence that Adolf Hitler had threatened to use gas against Italy if the state changed sides, and prisoner of war interrogations suggesting that preparations were being made to use a "new, egregiously potent gas" if the war turned decisively against Germany. Atkinson concludes that "No commander in 1943 could be cavalier about a manifest threat by Germany to use gas."

The Grand Mufti of Jerusalem, Amin al-Husayni, the senior Islamic religious authority of the Palestinian Arabs and ally of Adolf Hitler was accused of sponsoring an unsuccessful chemical warfare assault on the Jewish community in Tel-Aviv during 1944 by The David S. Wyman Institute for Holocaust Studies. Allegations suggest that five parachutists were supplied with maps of Tel Aviv, canisters of a German–manufactured "fine white powder," and instructions from the Mufti to dump chemicals into the Tel Aviv water system. District police commander Fayiz Bey Idrissi later recalled, "The laboratory report stated that each container held enough poison to kill 25,000 people, and there were at least ten containers."

NORTH YEMEN CIVIL WAR

The first attack took place on June 8, 1963 against Kawma, a village of about 100 inhabitants in northern Yemen, killing about seven people and damaging the eyes and lungs of twenty-five others. This incident is considered to have been experimental, and the bombs were described as "home-made, amateurish and relatively ineffective". The Egyptian authorities suggested that the reported incidents were probably caused by napalm, not gas. The Israeli Foreign Minister, Golda Meir, suggested in an interview that Nasser would not hesitate to use gas against Israel as well.

There were no reports of gas during 1964, and only a few were reported in 1965. The reports grew more frequent in late 1966. On December 11, 1966, fifteen gas bombs killed two people and injured thirty-five. On January 5, 1967, the biggest gas attack came against the village of Kitaf, causing 270 casualties, including 140 fatalities. The target may have been Prince Hassan bin Yahya, who had installed his headquarters nearby. The Egyptian government denied using poison gas, and alleged that Britain and the US were using the reports as psychological warfare against Egypt. On February 12, 1967, it said it would welcome a UN investigation. On March 1, U Thant said he was "powerless" to deal with the matter.

On May 10, the twin villages of Gahar and Gadafa in Wadi Hirran, where Prince Mohamed bin Mohsin was in command, were gas bombed, killing at least seventy-five. The Red Cross was alerted and on June 2, it issued a statement in Geneva expressing concern. The Institute of Forensic Medicine at the University of Berne made a statement, based on a Red Cross report, that the gas was likely to have been halogenous derivatives–phosgene, mustard gas, lewisite, chloride or cyanogen bromide.

The gas attacks stopped for three weeks after the Six-Day War of June, but resumed on July, against all parts of royalist Yemen. Casualty estimates vary, and an assumption, considered conservative, is that the mustard and phosgene-filled aerial bombs caused approximately 1,500 fatalities and 1,500 injuries.

COLD WAR

After World War II, the Allies recovered German artillery shells containing the three German nerve agents of the day (tabun, sarin, and soman), prompting further research into nerve agents by all of the former Allies. Although the threat of global thermonuclear war was foremost in the minds of most during the Cold War, both the Soviet and Western governments put enormous resources into developing chemical and biological weapons.

DEVELOPMENTS BY THE WESTERN GOVERNMENTS

In 1952, researchers in Porton Down, England, invented the VX nerve agent but soon abandoned the project. In 1958 the

British government traded their VX technology with the United States in exchange for information on thermonuclear weapons; by 1961 the U.S. was producing large amounts of VX and performing its own nerve agent research. This research produced at least three more agents; the four agents (VE, VG, VM, VX) are collectively known as the "V-Series" class of nerve agents. Also in 1952 the U.S. Army patented a process for the "Preparation of Toxic Ricin", publishing a method of producing this powerful toxin.

During the 1960s, the U.S. explored the use of anticholinergic deleriant incapacitating agents. One of these agents, assigned the weapon designation BZ, was allegedly used experimentally in the Vietnam War. These allegations inspired the 1990 fictional film Jacob's Ladder.

In 1961 and 62 the Kennedy administration authorized the use of chemicals to destroy vegetation and food crops in South Vietnam. Between 1961 and 1967 the US Air Force sprayed 12 million US gallons of concentrated herbicides, mainly Agent Orange (containing dioxin as an impurity in the manufacturing process) over 6 million acres (24,000 km^2) of foliage and trees, affecting an estimated 13% of South Vietnam's land. In 1965, 42% of all herbicides were sprayed over food crops. Besides destroying vegetation used as cover by the NLF and destroying food crops the herbicide was used to drive civilians into RVN-controlled areas.

In 1997, an article published by the Wall Street Journal reported that up to half a million children were born with dioxin related deformities, and that the birth defects in South Vietnam were fourfold those in the North. The use of Agent Orange may have been contrary to international rules of war at the time. It is also of note that the most likely victims of such an assault would be small children. A 1967 study by the Agronomy Section of the Japanese Science Council concluded that 3.8 million acres (15,000 km^2) of land had been destroyed, killing 1000 peasants and 13,000 livestock.

Between 1967 and 1968, the U.S. decided to dispose of obsolete chemical weapons in an operation called Operation CHASE, which stood for "cut holes and sink 'em." Several shiploads of chemical and conventional weapons were put aboard old Liberty ships and sunk at sea.

In 1969, 23 U.S. servicemen and one U.S. civilian stationed in Okinawa, Japan, were exposed to low levels of the nerve agent sarin while repainting the depots' buildings. The weapons had been kept secret from Japan, sparking a furor in that country and an international incident. These munitions were moved in 1971 to Johnston Atoll under Operation Red Hat.

George H.W. Bush and Mikhail Gorbachev signing the bilateral treaty on 1990-06-01

A UN working group began work on chemical disarmament in 1980. On April 4, 1984, U.S. President Ronald Reagan called for an international ban on chemical weapons. U.S. President George H.W. Bush and Soviet Union leader Mikhail Gorbachev signed a bilateral treaty on June 1, 1990, to end chemical weapon production and start destroying each of their nation's stockpiles. The multilateral Chemical Weapons Convention (CWC) was signed in 1993 and entered into force (EIF) in 1997.

In December, 2001, the United States Department of Health and Human Services, CDC, NIOSH, National Personal Protective

Technology Laboratory (NPPTL), along with the U.S. Army Research, Development Engineering Command Edgewood Chemical/Biological Center (ECBC), and the U.S. Department of Commerce National Institute for Standards and Technology (NIST) published the first of six technical performance standards and test procedures designed to evaluate and certify respirators intended for use by civilian emergency responders to a chemical, biological, radiological, or nuclear weapon release, detonation, or terrorism incident. To date NIOSH/NPPTL has published six new respirator performance standards based on a tiered approach that relies on traditional industrial respirator certification policy, next generation emergency response respirator performance requirements, and special live chemical warfare agent testing requirements of the classes of respirators identified to offer respiratory protection against chemical, biological, radiological, and nuclear (CBRN) agent inhalation hazards. These CBRN respirators are commonly known as open-circuit self-contained breathing apparatus (CBRN SCBA), air-purifying respirator (CBRN APR), air-purifying escape respirator (CBRN APER), self-contained escape respirator (CBRN SCER) and loose or tight fitting powered air-purifying respirators (CBRN PAPR).

UNITED STATES SENATE REPORT

A 1994 United States Senate Report, entitled "Is military research hazardous to veterans health? Lessons spanning a half century," detailed the United States Department of Defense's practice of experimenting on animal and human subjects, often without their knowledge or consent. This included:

- Approximately 60,000 [US] military personnel were used as human subjects in the 1940s to test the chemical agents mustard gas and lewisite. "Mustard" section,
- Between the 1950s through the 1970s, at least 2,200 military personnel were subjected to various biological agents, referred to as Operation Whitecoat. Unlike most of the studies discussed in this report, Operation Whitecoat was truly voluntary. "Seventh" section,

- Between 1951 and 1969, Dugway Proving Ground was the site of testing for various chemical and biological agents, including an open air aerodynamic dissemination test in 1968 that accidentally killed, on neighboring farms, approximately 6,400 sheep by an unspecified nerve agent."Dugway" section.

DEVELOPMENTS BY THE SOVIET GOVERNMENT

Due to the secrecy of the Soviet Union's government, very little information was available about the direction and progress of the Soviet chemical weapons until relatively recently. After the fall of the Soviet Union, Russian chemist Vil Mirzayanov published articles revealing illegal chemical weapons experimentation in Russia.

In 1993, Mirzayanov was imprisoned and fired from his job at the State Research Institute of Organic Chemistry and Technology, where he had worked for 26 years. In March 1994, after a major campaign by U.S. scientists on his behalf, Mirzayanov was released.

Among the information related by Vil Mirzayanov was the direction of Soviet research into the development of even more toxic nerve agents, which saw most of its success during the mid-1980s. Several highly toxic agents were developed during this period; the only unclassified information regarding these agents is that they are known in the open literature only as "Foliant" agents (named after the programme under which they were developed) and by various code designations, such as A-230 and A-232.

According to Mirzayanov, the Soviets also developed weapons that were safer to handle, leading to the development of the binary weapons, in which precursors for the nerve agents are mixed in a munition to produce the agent just prior to its use.

Because the precursors are generally significantly less hazardous than the agents themselves, this technique makes handling and transporting the munitions a great deal simpler.

Additionally, precursors to the agents are usually much easier to stabilize than the agents themselves, so this technique also made it possible to increase the shelf life of the agents a great deal.

During the 1980s and 1990s, binary versions of several Soviet agents were developed and are designated as "Novichok" agents (after the Russian word for "newcomer"). Together with Lev Fedorov, he told the secret Novichok story exposed in the newspaper Moscow News.

IRAN–IRAQ WAR

Chemical weapons employed by Saddam Hussein killed and injured numerous Iranians, and even Iraqis. According to Iraqi documents, assistance in developing chemical weapons was obtained from firms in many countries, including the United States, West Germany, the Netherlands, the United Kingdom, France and China.

Victims of Iraq's poison gas attack in civil area during Iran–Iraq War

The Iran–Iraq War began in 1980 when Iraq attacked Iran. Early in the conflict, Iraq began to employ mustard gas and tabun delivered by bombs dropped from airplanes; approximately 5% of all Iranian casualties are directly attributable to the use of these agents. About 100,000 Iranian soldiers were victims of Iraq's chemical attacks. Many were hit by mustard gas. The official estimate does not include the civilian population contaminated in bordering towns or the children and relatives of veterans, many of whom have developed blood, lung and skin complications, according to the Organisation for Veterans. Nerve gas agents killed about 20,000 Iranian soldiers immediately, according to official reports. Of the 80,000 survivors, some 5,000 seek medical treatment regularly and about 1,000 are still hospitalized with severe, chronic conditions.

Iraq also targeted Iranian civilians with chemical weapons. Many thousands were killed in attacks on populations in villages and towns, as well as front-line hospitals. Many still suffer from the severe effects.

Despite the removal of Saddam and his regime by Coalition forces, there is deep resentment and anger in Iran that it was Western companies based in the Netherlands, West Germany, France, and the U.S. that helped Iraq develop its chemical weapons arsenal in the first place, and that the world did nothing to punish Iraq for its use of chemical weapons throughout the war.

Shortly before war ended in 1988, the Iraqi Kurdish village of Halabja was exposed to multiple chemical agents, killing about 5,000 of the town's 50,000 residents. After the incident, traces of mustard gas and the nerve agents sarin, tabun and VX were discovered.

- During the Persian Gulf War in 1991, Coalition forces began a ground war in Iraq. Despite the fact that they did possess chemical weapons, Iraq did not use any chemical agents against coalition forces. The commander of the Allied Forces, Gen. H. Norman Schwarzkopf, suggested this may have been due to Iraqi fear of retaliation with nuclear weapons.

FALKLANDS WAR

Technically, the reported employment of tear gas by Argentine forces during the 1982 invasion of the Falkland Islands constitutes chemical warfare. However, the tear gas grenades were employed as nonlethal weapons to avoid British casualties. The British claim that more lethal, but legally-justifiable as they are not considered chemical weapons under the Chemical Weapons Convention, white phosphorus grenades were used. The barrack buildings the weapons were used on proved to be deserted in any case.

TERRORISM

For many terrorist organisations, chemical weapons might be considered an ideal choice for a mode of attack, if they are available: they are cheap, relatively accessible, and easy to transport. A skilled chemist can readily synthesize most chemical agents if the precursors are available.

The earliest successful use of chemical agents in a non-combat setting was in 1946, motivated by a desire to obtain revenge on Germans for the Holocaust. Three members of a Jewish group calling themselves Dahm Y'Israel Nokeam ("Avenging Israel's Blood") hid in a bakery in the Stalag 13 prison camp near Nuremberg, Germany, where several thousand SS troops were being detained. The three applied an arsenic-containing mixture to loaves of bread, sickening more than 2,000 prisoners, of whom more than 200 required hospitalisation.

In July 1974, a group calling themselves the Aliens of America successfully firebombed the houses of a judge, two police commissioners, and one of the commissioner's cars, burned down two apartment buildings, and bombed the Pan Am Terminal at Los Angeles International Airport, killing three people and injuring eight. The organisation, which turned out to be a single resident alien named Muharem Kurbegovic, claimed to have developed and possessed a supply of sarin, as well as 4 unique nerve agents named AA1, AA2, AA3, and AA4S. Although no agents were found at the time he was arrested in August 1974, he had reportedly acquired "all but one" of the ingredients required to produce a nerve agent. A search of his apartment turned up a variety of materials, including precursors for phosgene and a drum containing 25 pounds of sodium cyanide.

The first successful use of chemical agents by terrorists against a general civilian population was on March 20, 1995. Aum Shinrikyo, an apocalyptic group based in Japan that believed it necessary to destroy the planet, released sarin into the Tokyo subway system killing 12 and injuring over 5,000. The group had attempted biological and chemical attacks on at least 10 prior occasions, but managed to affect only cult members. The group did manage to successfully release sarin outside an apartment building in Matsumoto in June 1994; this use was directed at a few specific individuals living in the building and was not an attack on the general population. On 29 December, 1999, four days after Russian forces began assault of Grozny, Chechen terrorists exploded two chlor tanks in town. Because of the wind conditions, no Russian soldiers were injured.

In 2001, after carrying out the attacks in New York City on September 11, the organisation Al Qaeda announced that they were attempting to acquire radiological, biological and chemical weapons. This threat was lent a great deal of credibility when a large archive of videotapes was obtained by the cable television network CNN in August 2002 showing, among other things, the killing of three dogs by an apparent nerve agent.

On October 26, 2002, Russian special forces used a chemical agent (presumably KOLOKOL-1, an aerosolized fentanyl derivative), as a precursor to an assault on Chechen terrorists, ending the Moscow theater hostage crisis. All 42 of the terrorists and 120 of the hostages were killed during the raid; all but one hostage, who was killed, died from the effects of the agent.

In early 2007 multiple terrorist bombings have been reported in Iraq using chlorine gas. These attacks have wounded or sickened more than 350 people. Reportedly the bombers are affiliated with Al-Qaeda in Iraq and have used bombs of various sizes up to chlorine tanker trucks. United Nations Secretary-General Ban Ki-moon condemned the attacks as, "clearly intended to cause panic and instability in the country.

Chapter 9

MINE WARFARE

Mine Warfare may refer to:

- Land mine
- Naval mine
- Mining

LAND MINE

A Land Mine is a target (person or vehicle) operated explosive weapon. Their non-explosive predessors (caltrops, stakes and spikes) have been used on the battlefield since ancient times. Landmines were designed to be used to deter, channel, delay and kill an enemy. They have been used, in various formats, for centuries and have featured in all major conflicts. Land mines are force multiplier increasing the efficiency a defending force without requiring more personnel.

From left to right: an M14, Valmara 69, and VS-50

The name originates from the practice of mining, where tunnels were dug under enemy fortifications or forces. These tunnels ("mines") were first collapsed to destroy fortifications above, and later filled with explosives and detonated. Land mines generally refer to devices specifically manufactured for this purpose, as distinguished from improvised explosive devices ("IEDs").

Land mines are controversial because they remain dangerous after the conflict in which they were deployed, killing and injuring civilians and rendering land impassable and unusable for decades.

The International Campaign to Ban Landmines campaigned successfully to prohibit their use, culminating in the 1997 Convention on the Prohibition of the Use, Stockpiling, Production and Transfer of Anti-Personnel Mines and on their Destruction, known informally as the Ottawa Treaty. As of 2007, a total of 158 nations have agreed to the treaty.

Thirty-seven countries have not agreed to the ban, including China, India, Israel, Pakistan, Russia and the United States.

USE

Land mines were designed for two main uses–to create tactical barriers and to act as area-denial weapons. The latter use seeks to deny access to land areas by military and civilian traffic. When used as a tactical barrier, they serve to deter direct attack from or over a defined and marked area. This is the stated reason for their use in the demilitarized zones (DMZs) of warm spots such as Cyprus and Korea.

Anti-personnel land mines or APLs are widely considered to be unethical weapons. Even those that have not joined the emerging global norm against APLs accept that they are unethical when used in the area-denial role, because their victims are commonly civilians, who are often killed or maimed long after a war has ended. According to anti-land mine campaigners, in Cambodia alone, area-denial mines have resulted in 35,000 amputees after the cessation of hostilities. Removal of land mines carries certain risks and can be slow and costly; however, a limited number of countries maintain that land mines are necessary to protect their soldiers in times of war and to suppress hostilities across demilitarized zones.

HISTORY

PREMODERN DEVELOPMENT

Forces in ancient Rome sometimes dug small foot-sized holes, covered and armed with a sharpened spike. In the Middle Ages in Europe, small, four-pronged spiked devices called caltrops or crows' feet could be scattered on the ground to delay the advance of an enemy, but these devices were not explosive.

Some sources report that the 3rd century Prime Minister Zhuge Liang of the Kingdom of Shu in China invented a landmine type device in the third century. This claim was made by Jiao Yu in his Huolongjing Quanzhi (Fire-drake Manual in One Complete Volume), his preface written in 1412 AD (although the book was originally published in the mid 14th century), and that Zhuge had used not only "fire weapons" but landmines in the Battle of Hulugu Valley against the forces of Sima Yi and his son Sima Zhao of the Wei Kingdom. However, this claim is dubious, considering that gunpowder warfare did not exist in China until the advent of the flamethrower (Pen Huo Qi) in the 10th century, while the land mine was not seen in China until the late 13th century.

EXPLOSIVE LANDMINES

The Chinese 'self-tripped trespass land mine' from the Huolongjing, compiled by Jiao Yu and Liu Ji in the mid 14th century.

EAST ASIA

Explosive landmines were being used in 1277 AD by the Song Dynasty Chinese against an assault of the Mongols, who were besieging a city in southern China. The invention of this detonated "enormous bomb" was credited to one Lou Qianxia of the 13th century.

The famous 14th century Chinese text of the Huolongjing, which was the first to describe hollow cast iron cannonball shells filled with gunpowder, was also the first to describe the invention of the landmine in greater detail than references found in texts written beforehand. This mid 14th century work compiled during the late Yuan Dynasty and early Ming Dynasty (before 1375, when its co-editor Liu Ji died) stated that mines were made of cast iron and were spherical in shape, filled with either 'magic gunpowder', 'poison gunpowder', or 'blinding and burning gunpowder', any one of these compositions being suitable for use. The wad of the mine was made of hard wood, carrying three different fuses in case of defective connection to the touch hole. In those days, the Chinese relied upon command signals and carefully timed calculation of enemy movements into the minefield, since a long fuse had to be ignited by hand from the ambushers in a somewhat far-off location lying in wait. However, the Huolongjing also describes landmines that were set off by enemy movement, called the 'ground-thunder explosive camp', one of the 'self-trespassing' (zifan) types, as the text says:

These mines are mostly installed at frontier gates and passes. Pieces of bamboo are sawn into sections nine feet in length, all septa in the bamboo being removed, save only the last; and it is then bandaged round with fresh cow-hide tape. Boiling oil is next poured into (the tube) and left there for some time before being removed. The fuse starts from the bottom (of the tube), and (black powder) is compressed into it to form an explosive mine. The gunpowder fills up eight-tenths of the tube, while lead or iron pellets take up the rest of the space; then the open end is sealed with wax. A trench five feet in depth is dug (for the mines to be concealed). The fuse is connected to a firing device which ignites them when disturbed.

The Huolongjing describes the trigger device used for this as a 'steel wheel', which directed sparks of flame onto the connection of fuses running to the multiple-laid land mines underneath the carefully-hidden trap. However, further description of how this flint device operated was not made until a Chinese text of 1606 AD revealed that a weight drive (common in medieval clockworks) had been used to work the 'steel wheel'. The way in which the Chinese land mine trigger worked was a system of two steel wheels rotated by a falling weight, the chord of which was wound around their axle, and when the enemy stepped onto the disguised boards they released the pins that dropped the weights. In terms of global significance, the first wheellock musket in Europe was sketched by Leonardo da Vinci around 1500 AD, although no use of metal flint for gunpowder weapons were known before that point in Europe.

Besides the use of steel wheels providing sparks for the fuses, there were other methods used as well, such as the 'underground sky-soaring thunder'. The Ming Dynasty (1368-1644) text of the Wubei Zhi (Treatise on Armament Technology), written by Mao Yuanyi in 1628, outlined the use of land mines that were triggered by the heat of a slow-burning incandescent material in an underground bowl placed directly above the train of fuses leading to the mines buried 3 ft beneath. The booby trap of this mine system had a mound where weapons of halberds, pikes, and lances were dug in, meant to entice the enemy to walk up the small mound and claim their stolen prize of war booty. When the weapons were removed from the mound, this movement disturbed the bowl beneath them where the butt ends of the staffs were, which in turn ignited the fuses. According to the Wubei Huolongjing volume of the 17th century, the formula for this slow-burning incandescent material allowed it to burn continuously for 20 to 30 days without going out. This formula included 1 lb of white sandal wood powder, 3 oz of iron rust (ferric oxide), 5 oz of 'white' charcoal powder (from quicklime), 2 oz of willow charcoal powder, 6 oz of dried, ground, and powdered red dates, and 3 oz of bran. The Chinese also employed the use of the naval mine at sea and on the rivers of China and elsewhere in maritime battles.

EUROPE AND THE UNITED STATES

The first land mine in Europe was created by Pedro Navarro (d. 1528), a Spanish soldier, who used it in the settles of the Italian castles, in the beginning of the sixteenth century. At Augsburg in 1573, a German military engineer by the name of Samuel Zimmermann invented an extremely effective mine known as the fladdermine. It consisted of a fougasse (or later, sometimes a shell fougasse, that is, a fougasse loaded not with stones but with early black powder mortar shells, similar to large black powder hand grenades) activated by a snaphance or flintlock mechanism connected to a tripwire on the surface. Combining the effects of a tripwire activated bounding fragmentation mine with a cluster bomb, it was devastating to massed attackers but required high maintenance due to the susceptibility of black powder to dampness. Consequently it was mainly employed in the defenses of major fortifications, in which role it continued to be used until the 1870s.

In Europe in the early eighteenth century, improvised land mines or booby traps were constructed in the form of bombs buried in shallow wells in the earth and covered with scrap metal and/or gravel to serve as shrapnel. Known in French as fougasse, the term is sometimes still used in the present day to describe such devices. This technique was used in several European wars of the eighteenth Century, the American Revolution, and the American Civil War.

The first modern mechanically fused high explosive anti-personnel land mines were created by Confederate troops of Brigadier General Gabriel J. Rains during the Battle of Yorktown in 1862. As a Captain, Rains had earlier employed explosive booby traps during the Seminole Wars in Florida in 1840. Both mechanically and electrically fused "land torpedoes" were employed, although by the end of the war mechanical fuses had been found to be generally more reliable. Many of these designs were improvised in the field, especially from explosive shells, but by the end of the war nearly 2,000 standard pattern "Rains mines" had been deployed.

British troops mining a road to halt the German advance in 1918.

Improved designs of mines were created in Imperial Germany, circa 1912, and were copied and manufactured by all major participants in the First World War. In World War One, land mines were used notably at the start of the Battle of Passchendaele. Well before the war was over, the British were manufacturing land mines that contained poison gas instead of explosives. Poison gas mines were manufactured at least until the 1980s in the Soviet Union. The United States was known to have at least experimented with the concept in the 1950s.

Nuclear mines have also been developed, both land and naval varieties. An example is the British Blue Peacock project, while another was the U.S. Medium Atomic Demolition Munition.

LAND MINES IN THE UK

Landmines occasionally are found, or explode, within the UK, due to the large amount that were used during World War I and World War II, and often buried or abandoned afterwards.

Damage was caused to the 17th-century manor house of Barlow Woodseats Hall in Derbyshire by a land mine in April 1941.

CHARACTERISTICS AND FUNCTIONING

A land mine typically includes the following components:

- firing mechanism or other device (including anti-handling devices)
- detonator or igniter (sets off the booster charge)
- booster charge (may be attached to the fuse, or the igniter, or be part of the main charge)
- main charge (in a container, usually forms the body of the mine)
- casing (contains all of the above parts)

FIRING MECHANISMS AND INITIATING ACTIONS

A land mine can be triggered by a number of things including pressure, movement, sound, magnetism and vibration. Anti-personnel mines commonly use the pressure of a person's foot as a trigger, but tripwires are also frequently employed. Most modern anti-vehicle mines use a magnetic trigger to enable it to detonate even if the tires or tracks did not touch it. Advanced mines are able to sense the difference between friendly and enemy types of vehicles by way of a built-in signature catalog. This will theoretically enable friendly forces to use the mined area while denying the enemy access.

Many mines combine the main trigger with a touch or tilt trigger to prevent enemy engineers from defusing it. Land mine designs tend to use as little metal as possible to make searching with a metal detector more difficult; land mines made mostly of plastic have the added advantage of being very inexpensive.

Some types of modern mines are designed to self-destruct, or chemically render themselves inert after a period of weeks or months to reduce the likelihood of civilian casualties at the conflict's end. However, these self-destruct mechanisms are not absolutely reliable, and most land mines laid historically are not equipped in this manner.

ANTI-HANDLING DEVICES (AHD)

Anti-handling devices detonate the mine if someone attempts to lift, shift or disarm it. The intention is to hinder deminers by discouraging any attempts to clear minefields. There is a degree of overlap between the function of a boobytrap and an anti-handling device insofar as some mines have optional fuze pockets into which standard pull or pressure-release boobytrap firing devices can be screwed. Alternatively, some landmines may mimic a standard design, but actually be specifically intended to kill deminers e.g. the MC-3 and PMN-3 variants of the PMN mine. Anti-handling devices can be found on both anti-personnel mines and anti-tank mines, either as an integral part of their design or as improvised add-ons. For this reason, the standard render-safe procedure for mines is often to destroy them on site without attempting to lift them.

ANTI-TANK (AT) MINES

Anti-tank mines are designed to immobilize or destroy vehicles and their occupants. In U.S. military jargon destroying the vehicles is referred to as a catastrophic kill (k-kill) while only disabling its movement is referred to as a mobility kill (m-kill).

Section of an anti-tank mine. Note the yellow main charge wrapped around a red booster charge, and the secondary fuse well on the side of the mine designed for an anti-handling device.

Anti-tank mines are typically larger than anti-personnel mines and require more pressure to detonate. The high trigger pressure (normally 100 kg (220 lb.)) prevents them from being set off by infantry or smaller vehicles of lesser importance. More modern anti-tank mines use shaped charges to focus and increase the armor penetration of the explosives.

ANTI-PERSONNEL (AP) MINES

Anti-personnel mines are designed to kill or injure enemy combatants as opposed to destroying vehicles. They are often designed to injure rather than kill in order to increase the logistical support (evacuation, medical) burden on the opposing force. Some types of anti-personnel mines can also damage the tracks or wheels of armored vehicles.

Under the Ottawa Treaty, signatory countries undertake not to manufacture, stockpile or use anti-personnel mines. As of 2009, it has been signed/accessioned by 156 countries. Thirty-eight states, including the People's Republic of China, Russian Federation and the United States, are not party to the Convention.

WARFARE

In military science, minefields are considered a defensive or harassing weapon, used to slow the enemy down, to help deny certain terrain to the enemy, to focus enemy movement into kill zones, or to reduce morale by randomly attacking material and personnel. In some engagements during World War II, anti-tank mines accounted for half of all vehicles disabled.

A U.S. Army soldier removing the fuse from a Russian-made mine in order to clear a minefield outside of Fallujah, Iraq.

Since combat engineers with mine-clearing equipment can clear a path through a minefield relatively quickly, mines are usually considered effective only if covered by fire.

The extents of minefields are often marked with warning signs and cloth tape, to prevent friendly troops and non-combatants from entering them. Of course, sometimes terrain can be denied using dummy minefields. Most forces carefully record the location and disposition of their own minefields, because warning signs can be destroyed or removed, and minefields should eventually be cleared. Minefields may also have marked or unmarked safe routes to allow friendly movement through them.

Placing minefields without marking and recording them for later removal is considered uncivilized and is illegal under international conventions.

Artillery and aircraft scatterable mines allow minefields to be placed in front of moving formations of enemy units, including the reinforcement of minefields or other obstacles that have been breached by enemy engineers. They can also be used to cover the retreat of forces disengaging from the enemy, or for interdiction of supporting units to isolate front line units from resupply. In most cases these minefields consist of a combination of anti-tank and anti-personnel mines, with the anti-personnel mines making removal of the anti-tank mines more difficult. Mines of this type used by the United States are designed to self destruct after a preset period of time, reducing the requirement for mine clearing to only those mines whose self destruct system did not function. Some designs of these scatterable mines require an electrical charge (capactior or battery) to detonate. After a certain period of time, the charge dissipates, leaving them effectively inert.

GUERRILLA WARFARE

None of the conventional tactics and norms of mine warfare applies when they are employed in a guerrilla role:

- The mines are not used in a defensive role (for specific position or area).

- Mined areas are not marked.
- Mines are usually placed singly and not in groups covering an area.
- Mines are often left unattended (not covered by fire).

One of the aims of terrorism–and to a certain extent guerrilla warfare is to spread fear and panic. This can be achieved by a single mine left on a civilian road to be detonated by a civilian target which is clearly quite different from the normal military application.

One example where such tactics were in employed is in the various Southern African conflicts during the 1970s and 1980s, specifically Angola, Mozambique, Namibia, South Africa and Zimbabwe.

LAYING MINES

Minefields may be laid by several means. The preferred, but most labour-intensive, way is to have engineers bury the mines, since this will make the mines practically invisible and reduce the number of mines needed to deny the enemy an area. Mines can be laid by specialized mine-laying vehicles. Mine-scattering shells may be fired by artillery from a distance of several tens of kilometers.

Minefield warning on the Golan Heights, still valid more than 40 years after creation of the field by the Syrian army

Mines may be dropped from helicopters or airplanes, or ejected from cluster bombs or cruise missiles.

Anti-tank minefields can be scattered with anti-personnel mines to make clearing them manually more time-consuming; and anti-personnel minefields are scattered with anti-tank mines to prevent the use of armored vehicles to clear them quickly. Some anti-tank mine types are also able to be triggered by infantry, giving them a dual purpose even though their main and official intention is to work as anti-tank weapons. Some minefields are specifically booby-trapped to make clearing them more dangerous. Mixed anti-personnel and anti-tank minefields, double-stacked anti-tank mines, anti-personnel mines under anti-tank mines, and fuses separated from mines have all been used for this purpose.

Another specific use is to mine an aircraft runway immediately after it has been bombed in order to delay or discourage repair. Some cluster bombs combine these functions, one example is the British JP233 cluster bomb which includes munitions to damage (crater) the runway as well as anti-personnel mines in the same cluster bomb.

DEMINING

Whereas the placing and arming of landmines is relatively inexpensive and simple, the process of detecting and removing them is typically expensive, slow, and dangerous. This is especially true of irregular warfare where mines were used on an ad hoc basis in unmarked areas. Anti-personnel mines are most difficult to find, due to their small size and the fact that many are made almost entirely of non-metallic materials specifically to escape detection.

School posters in Karabakh educating children on mines and UXO

Manual clearing remains the most effective technique for clearing mine fields, although hybrid techniques involving the use of animals and robots are being developed. Animals are desirable due to their strong sense of smell, which is more than capable of detecting a land mine. Animals like rats and dogs can also differentiate between other metal objects and land mines because they can be trained to detect the explosive agent itself.

Other techniques involve the use of geo-location technologies. A joint team of researchers at the University of New South Wales and Ohio State University is working to develop a system based on multi-sensor integration.

Ironically, the laying of land mines inadvertently proved a positive development in the Falkland Islands. This is because the mine fields laid by the sea during the Falklands War have become favorite places for penguins, which are too light to detonate the mines, and are therefore able to breed safely in areas where humans do not enter. These odd sanctuaries have proven so popular and lucrative for ecotourism that there has been some effort to prevent having the mines removed by offering to finance mine removal in regions with human populations where mines are a persistent danger, such as in Cambodia.

Norwegian NGO Norwegian People's Aid is one organisation involved in the safe removal of land mines.

EFFORTS TO BAN ANTI-PERSONNEL MINES

The Ottawa Treaty (Convention on the Prohibition of the Use, Stockpiling, Production and Transfer of Anti-Personnel Mines and on their Destruction) came into force on March 1, 1999. The treaty was the result of the leadership of the Government of Canada working with the International Campaign to Ban Landmines, launched in 1992. The campaign and its leader, Jody Williams, won the Nobel Peace Prize in 1997 for its efforts.

The treaty does not include anti-tank mines, cluster bombs or claymore-type mines operated in command mode and focuses specifically on anti-personnel mines, because these pose the greatest long term (post-conflict) risk to humans and animals since they are typically designed to be triggered by any movement or pressure of only a few kilograms, whereas anti-tank mines require much more weight (or a combination of factors that would exclude humans). Existing stocks must be destroyed within four years of signing the treaty.

Party states to the Ottawa Treaty

Argentine minefield at Port William, Falkland Islands created in 1982; clearance inhibited by boggy terrain

Signatories of the Ottawa Treaty agree that they will not use, develop, manufacture, stockpile or trade in anti-personnel land mines. There were originally 122 signatories in 1997; currently[update], it has been signed by 155 countries and ratified by 153. Another 40 have yet to sign on. United States is not one of the signatories, based on lacking an exception for the DMZ of Korea.

There is a clause in the treaty, Article 3, which permits countries to retain land mines for use in training or development of countermeasures. 64 countries have taken this option. As an alternative to an outright ban, 10 countries follow regulations that are contained in a 1996 amendment of Protocol II of the Convention on Conventional Weapons (CCW). The countries are China, Finland, India, Israel, Morocco, Pakistan, South Korea, Sri Lanka, and the United States.

MANUFACTURERS

The ICBL has identified the following countries as manufacturing land mines as of August 2004. None are signatories of the Ottawa Treaty.

- Burma
- China
- Cuba
- India
- Iran
- Iraq (although production had presumably ceased since the invasion of 2003)
- Nepal
- North Korea
- Pakistan
- Russian Federation
- Singapore
- Vietnam

Of other states which are thought to have manufactured landmines recently:

- Egypt has unofficially stated that production ceased in 1988.
- South Korea has stated that no mines have been produced since 2000.
- An official from China stated in September 2003 that production has ceased there, since they have an ample stockpile.
- In March 2004, a Libyan official stated that the country has never produced anti-personnel mines, but is known to have laid landmines in the 1970s and 1980s
- A United Nations assessment mission to Peru reported that production of landmines in the country ceased in January 1999. Peru was one of the original signatories and the treaty came into force for them in March 1999.
- Denmark has officially declared having 6 factories producing landmines in 1995. But production has ceased since ratifying the Ottawa treaty.
- The United States stopped manufacturing landmines in 1997, but has one of the largest stockpiles.

NAVAL MINE

A Naval Mine is a self-contained explosive device placed in water to destroy ships or submarines. Unlike depth charges, mines are deposited and left to wait until they are triggered by the approach of or contact with an enemy ship. Naval mines can be used offensively, to hamper enemy ships or lock them into a harbour; or defensively, to protect friendly ships and create "safe" zones.

Polish wz. 08/39 contact mine. The protuberances around the top of the mine, called Hertz horns, are part of the detonation mechanism.

Mines can be laid in many ways: by purpose-built minelayers, refitted ships, submarines, or aircraft—and even by dropping them into a harbour by hand. They can be inexpensive: some variants can cost as little as a thousand United States dollars (USD), although more sophisticated mines can cost millions of USD, be equipped with several kinds of sensors, and deliver a warhead by rocket or torpedo.

Their flexibility and cost-effectiveness make mines attractive weapons to the less powerful belligerent in asymmetric warfare. The cost of producing and laying a mine is usually anywhere from 0.5% to 10% of the cost of removing it, and it can take up to 200 times as long to clear a minefield as to lay it. Parts of some World

War II naval minefields still exist, because they are too extensive and expensive to clear; some of these mines might remain dangerous for hundreds of years.

There are three main uses of mines: offensive, defensive, and psychological. Offensive mines are placed in enemy waters, outside harbours and in important shipping routes to sink civilian and military ships. Defensive minefields protect a coast from enemy ships and submarines and force them into areas that are easier to defend. Minefields designed for psychological effect are usually placed in trade routes and are used to stop shipping to an enemy nation. They are also spread out thinly, to create a feeling of random minefields in large areas. A single mine along a shipping route can stop shipping for days until the entire area is swept.

International law requires nations to declare when they mine an area, in order to make it easier for civil shipping to avoid the mines. The warnings do not have to be specific; during World War II, Britain declared simply that it had mined the English Channel, North Sea, and French coast.

In 1988, an Iranian M-08 mine made a 25-foot (8 m) hole in the hull of the USS Samuel B. Roberts (FFG-58), forcing the ship to seek temporary repairs in a dry dock in Dubai, UAE.

Closeup of the Roberts' damaged hull.

HISTORY

The precursor to naval mines was first described by the early Ming Dynasty Chinese artillery officer Jiao Yu, in his 14th century military treatise known as the Huolongjing. Chinese records tell of naval explosives in the 16th century, used to fight against Japanese pirates (Wokou). This kind of naval mine was loaded in a wooden box, sealed by putty. General Qi Jiguang made several timed, drifting explosives to harass Japanese pirate ships. However, in the Tiangong Kaiwu ('The Exploitation of the Works of Nature') treatise, written by Song Yingxing in 1637 AD, it describes naval mines with a rip cord pulled by a hidden ambusher located on the nearby shore which rotated a steel wheellock flint mechanism to produce sparks and ignite the fuse of the naval mine. Although this is the rotating steel wheellock's first use with naval mines, Jiao Yu had described their use for land mines back in the 14th century.

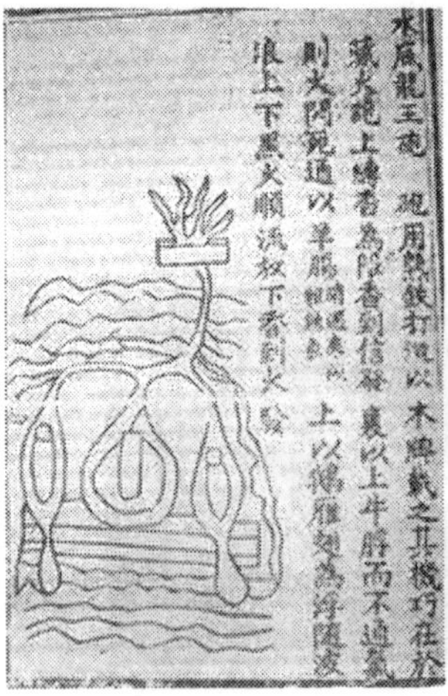

A 14th century drawn illustration of a naval mine and page description from the Huolongjing.

The first plan for a sea mine in the West was by Ralph Rabbards, who presented his design to Queen Elizabeth I of England in 1574. The Dutch inventor Cornelius Drebbel was employed in the Office of Ordnance by King Charles I of England to make weapons, including a "floating petard" which proved a failure. Weapons of this type were apparently tried by the English at the Siege of La Rochelle in 1627.

David Bushnell's mines destroying a British ship in 1777

Infernal machines in the Potomac River in 1861 during the American Civil War, sketch by Alfred Waud.

American David Bushnell invented the first practical mine, for use against the British in the American War of Independence. It was a watertight keg filled with gunpowder that was floated toward the enemy, detonated by a percussion lock if it struck a ship.

In 1812 Russian engineer Pavel Shilling exploded an underwater mine using an electrical circuit. In 1854, during the unsuccessful attempt of the Anglo-French fleet to seize Kronshtadt fortress, British steamships HMS Merlin (9th June 1855, the first successful mining in history), HMS Vulture and HMS Firefly were damaged by underwater explosions of Russian naval mines. More than 1500 naval mines, or infernal machines, designed by Moritz von Jacobi and Alfred Nobel were set by Russian naval specialists in the Gulf of Finland during the Crimean War. The mining of Vulcan led to the worlds first minesweeping operation during the next 72 hours, 33 mines were swept.

The American Civil War also saw the successful use of mines. The first ship sunk by a mine was the USS Cairo in 1862 in the Yazoo River. Rear Admiral David Farragut's famous statement, "Damn the torpedoes, full speed ahead!" refers to a minefield laid at Mobile, Alabama.

In the 19th century, mines were called torpedoes, a name probably conferred by Dennis Fletcher after the torpedo fish, which gives powerful electric shocks. A spar torpedo was a mine attached to a long pole and detonated when the ship carrying it rammed another one. The H. L. Hunley used one to sink the USS Housatonic on February 17, 1864. A Harvey Torpedo was a type of floating mine towed alongside a ship, and was briefly in service in the Royal Navy in the 1870s. Other "torpedoes" attached to ships or propelled themselves. One such weapon, called the Whitehead Torpedo after its inventor, caused the word "torpedo" to be used for self-propelled underwater missiles rather than static devices.

The next major use of mines was in the Russo-Japanese War in 1904, sinking the Russian battleship Petropavlovsk, killing the fleet commander, Admiral Makaroff, and most of the crew. On the other side, two Japanese battleships were sunk by Russian mines in one day. Many early mines were fragile and dangerous to handle, with glass containers filled with nitroglycerin or mechanical devices that activated them upon tipping. Several mine-laying ships were destroyed when their cargo exploded.

The U-boat fleet, which dominated much of the battle of the Atlantic, was small at the beginning of the war and much of the early action by German forces involved mining convoy routes and ports around Britain. The German submarines also operated in the Mediterranean Sea, in the Caribbean Sea, and along the U.S. coast.

Initially contact mines were employed — meaning that a ship had to physically strike a mine to detonate it — usually tethered at the end of a cable just below the surface of the water. By the beginning of World War II most nations had developed mines that could be dropped from aircraft and floated on the surface, making it possible to lay them in enemy harbors. The use of dredging and nets was effective against this type of mine, but this consumed time and resources, and required harbors to be closed. Contact mines usually hole ship's hulls.

Later some ships survived mine blasts, limping into port with buckled plates and broken backs. This appeared to be due to a new type of mine, detecting ships magnetically and detonating at a distance, causing damage with the shock wave of the explosion. Ships that had successfully run the gauntlet of the Atlantic crossing were sometimes destroyed entering freshly cleared British harbors. More shipping was being lost than could be replaced, and Churchill ordered that the intact recovery of one of these new mines was of the highest priority.

The British experienced a stroke of luck in November 1939. A German mine was dropped from an aircraft onto the mud flats of the Thames estuary during low tide. As if this was not sufficiently good fortune, the land belonged to the army, and a base with men and workshops was at hand. Experts were dispatched from London to investigate the mine. They had some idea that the mines used magnetic sensors, so everyone removed all metal, including their buttons, and made tools of non-magnetic brass. They disarmed the mine and rushed it to labs at Portsmouth, where scientists discovered a new type of arming mechanism. A large ferrous object passing through the Earth's magnetic field will concentrate the field through it; the mine's detector was designed to trigger at the mid-point of a steel-hulled ship passing overhead. The mechanism had an adjustable sensitivity, calibrated in milligauss.

From these data, methods were developed to clear the mines. Early methods included the use of large electromagnets dragged behind ships or below low-flying aircraft (a number of older bombers like the Vickers Wellington were used for this). Both of these methods had the disadvantage of "sweeping" only a small strip. A better solution was found in the "Double-L Sweep" using electrical cables dragged behind ships that passed large pulses of current through the seawater. This induced a large magnetic field and swept the entire area between the two ships. The older methods continued to be used in smaller areas. The Suez Canal continued to be swept by aircraft, for instance.

While these methods were useful for clearing mines from local ports, they were of little or no use for enemy-controlled areas. These were typically visited by warships, and the majority of the fleet then underwent a massive degaussing process, where their hulls had a slight "south" bias induced into them which offset the concentration effect almost to zero.

Initially, major warships and large troopships had a copper degaussing coil fitted around the perimeter of the hull, energized by the ship's electrical system whenever in suspected magnetic-mined waters. Some of the first to be so-fitted were the carrier HMS Ark Royal and the liners RMS Queen Mary and RMS Queen Elizabeth, which were used as troopships. This was felt to be impracticable for the myriad of smaller warships and merchant vessels, not least due to the amount of copper that would be required. It was found that "wiping" a current-carrying cable up and down a ship' hull temporarily canceled the ships' magnetic signature sufficiently to nullify the threat. This started in late 1939, and by 1940 merchant vessels and the smaller British warships were largely immune for a few months at a time until they once again built up a field. Many of the boats that sailed to Dunkirk were degaussed in a marathon four day effort by degaussing stations.

The Germans had also developed a pressure-activated mine and planned to deploy it as well, but they saved it for later use when it became clear the British had defeated the magnetic system.

Since World War II, mines have damaged 14 United States Navy ships, whereas air and missile attacks have damaged four. During the Korean War, mines laid by North Korean forces damaged 11 U.S. naval vessels.

During the Iran–Iraq War from 1980 to 1988, the belligerents mined several areas of the Persian Gulf and nearby waters. On April 14, 1988, the USS Samuel B. Roberts (FFG-58) struck an Iranian M-08/39 mine in the central Persian Gulf shipping lane, wounding 10 sailors. During the Gulf War, Iraqi naval mines severely damaged USS Princeton (CG-59) and USS Tripoli (LPH-10).

TYPES

Naval mines may be classified into two major groups.

CONTACT MINES

The earliest mines were usually of this type. They are still used today, as they are extremely low cost compared to any other anti-ship weapon and are effective, both as a terror weapon and to sink enemy ships. Contact mines need to be very close to the target before they detonate, limiting the damage to the direct effects of the explosion and usually affecting only the single vessel that triggers them. (Read the section on damage below for explanation).

Early mines had mechanical mechanisms to detonate them, but these were superseded in the 1870s by the Hertz Horn (or chemical horn), which was found to work reliably even after the mine had been in the sea for several years. The mine's upper half is studded with hollow lead protuberances, each containing a glass vial filled with sulfuric acid. When a ship's hull crushes the metal horn, it cracks the vial inside it, allowing the acid to run down a tube and into a lead-acid battery which until then contains no acid electrolyte. This energises the battery, which detonates the explosive.

Earlier forms of the detonator used a vial filled with sulfuric acid, surrounded by a mixture of potassium perchlorate and sugar.

When the vial was crushed, the acid ignited the perchlorate-sugar mix, and the resulting flame ignited the gunpowder charge.

During World War I the British heavily mined the English Channel and later large areas of the North Sea to prevent German submarines from using it. As the submarine could be at any depth down to the seabed, an American invention, the antenna mine, was widely used. This had a copper wire attached to a buoy that floated above the mine. The top part of the cable connecting the mine to the weight on the seabed was also made of copper. The copper wire was insulated from the steel cable below it. If a submarine's steel hull touched the copper wire, the slight voltage produced because of the contact between two dissimilar metals was amplified and detonated the explosive.

LIMPET MINES

Limpet mines are a special form of contact mine which are attached to the target by magnets and left, and are so named because of the superficial similarity to the limpet, a mollusk.

MOORED CONTACT MINES

Generally, this mine type is set to float just below the surface of the water or as deep as five meters. A steel cable connecting the mine to an anchor on the seabed prevents it from drifting away. The explosive and detonating mechanism is contained in a buoyant metal or plastic shell. The depth below the surface at which the mine floats can be set so that only deep draft vessels such as aircraft carriers, battleships or large cargo ships are at risk, saving the mine from being used on a less valuable target. In littoral waters it is important to ensure that the mine does not become visible when the sea level falls at low tide, so the preset cable length is adjusted to take account of tides. Even at the time of the Second World War there were mines which could be moored in 300-metre-deep water.

Floating mines typically have a mass of around 200 kg, including 80 kg of explosives e.g. TNT, minol or amatol.

A German contact mine laid in Australian waters during World War II

During WWII mine traps were used for blocking port entrances. Two floating mines were anchored some distance apart on either side of a shipping channel, linked by a chain. When a deep draft vessel passed through the trap it would pull the chain along with it, dragging the mines onto the sides of the ship; the resulting double explosion often sank it. This system was not used extensively, but proved effective in blocking ports.

DRIFTING CONTACT MINES

Drifting mines were occasionally used during World War I and World War II. However, they were more feared than effective. Sometimes floating mines break from their moorings and become drifting mines; modern mines are designed to deactivate in this event. After several years at sea, the deactivation mechanism might not function as intended and the mines may remain live. Admiral Jellicoe's British fleet did not pursue and destroy the outnumbered German High Seas Fleet when it turned away at the Battle of Jutland because he thought they were leading him into a trap: he believed it possible that the Germans were either leaving floating mines in their wake, or were drawing him towards submarines, although neither of these was the case.

Churchill promoted "Operation Royal Marine" in 1940 and again in 1944 where floating mines were put into the Rhine in France to float down the river, becoming active after a time calculated to be long enough to reach German territory.

After World War I the drifting contact mine was banned, but was occasionally used during World War II. The drifting mines were much harder to remove than tethered mines after the war, and they caused about the same damage to both sides.

BOTTOM CONTACT MINES

A bottom contact mine is the simplest form of mine. It is merely an explosive charge with some form of fuze fitted lying on the seafloor. They have been used against submarines, as submarines sometimes lie on the seafloor to reduce their acoustic signature. They are also used to prevent landing craft from reaching the shore and were a major obstacle during the D-Day landings. The Germans used antitank mines here with minor modifications to make them more reliable underwater, attaching the mines to the front of many of the obstacles seen in photos of the landing.

These mines usually weighed 2 to 50 kg, including 1 to 40 kg of explosives (TNT or hexatonal).

REMOTELY CONTROLLED MINES

Frequently used in combination with coastal artillery and hydrophones, remote controlled (or command detonation) mines can be in place in peacetime, which is a huge advantage in blocking important shipping routes. The mines can usually be turned into "normal" mines with a switch (which prevents the enemy from simply capturing the controlling station and deactivating the mines), detonated on a signal or be allowed to detonate on their own. The earliest ones were developed around 1812 by Robert Fulton. The first remotely controlled mines were moored mines used in the American Civil War, detonated electrically from shore. They were considered superior to contact mines because they did not put friendly shipping at risk. Modern examples usually weigh 200 kg (440 lb), including 80 kg (175 lb) of explosives (TNT or hexatonal).

INFLUENCE MINES

These mines are triggered by the influence of a ship or

submarine, rather than direct contact. Such mines incorporate electronic sensors designed to detect the presence of a vessel and detonate when it comes within the blast range of the warhead. The fuzes on such mines may incorporate one or more of the following sensors: magnetic, passive acoustic or water pressure displacement caused by the proximity of a vessel.

First used during the Second World War, the sophistication of influence mine fuzes has increased considerably over the years as first transistors and then microprocessors have been incorporated into designs. Simple magnetic sensors have been superseded by total-field magnetometers. Whereas early magnetic mine fuzes would respond only to changes in a single component of a target vessel's magnetic field, a total field magnetometer responds to changes in the magnitude of the total background field (thus enabling it to better detect even degaussed ships). Similarly, the original broadband hydrophones of 1940s acoustic mines (which operate on the integrated volume of all frequencies) have been replaced by narrow-band sensors which are much more sensitive and selective. Mines can now be programmed to listen for highly specific acoustic signatures (e.g. a gas turbine powerplant and/or cavitation sounds from a particular design of propellor) and ignore all others. The sophistication of modern electronic mine fuzes incorporating these Digital Signal Processing capabilities makes it much more difficult to detonate the mine with electronic countermeasures because several sensors working together (e.g. magnetic, passive acoustic and water pressure) allow it to ignore signals which are not recognised as being the unique signature of an intended target vessel.

Modern influence mines such as the BAE Stonefish are computerised, with all the programmability that this implies e.g. the ability to quickly load new acoustic signatures into fuzes, or programme them to detect a single, highly distinctive target signature. In this way, a mine with a passive acoustic fuze can be programmed to ignore all friendly vessels and small enemy vessels, only detonating when a very large enemy target passes over it.

Alternatively, the mine can be programmed specifically to ignore all surface vessels regardless of size and exclusively target submarines.

Even as far back as the Second World War it was possible to incorporate a "ship counter" facility into mine fuzes e.g. set the mine to ignore the first two ships to pass over it (which could be mine-sweepers deliberately trying to trigger mines) but detonate when the third ship passes overhead—which could be a high-value target such as an aircraft carrier or oil tanker. Even though modern mines are generally powered by a long life lithium battery, it is important to conserve power because they may need to remain active for months or even years. For this reason, most influence mines are designed to remain in a semi-dormant state until an unpowered (e.g. deflection of a magnetic compass needle) or low-powered sensor detects the possible presence of a vessel, at which point the mine fuze powers up fully and the passive acoustic sensors will begin to operate for some minutes. It is possible to programme computerised mines to delay activation for days or weeks after being laid; similarly, they can be programmed to self-destruct or render themselves safe after a preset period of time, e.g., 12 days or 12 months. Generally, the more sophisticated the mine design, the more likely it is to have some form of anti-handling device fitted in order to hinder clearance by divers or remotely piloted submersibles.

MOORED MINES

The moored mine is the backbone of modern mine systems. They are deployed where water is too deep for bottom mines. They can use several kinds of instruments to detect an enemy, usually a combination of acoustic, magnetic and pressure sensors, or more sophisticated optical shadows or electro potential sensors. These cost many times more than contact mines. Moored mines are effective against most kinds of ships. As they are cheaper than other anti-ship weapons they can be deployed in large numbers, making them useful area denial or "channelising" weapons. Moored mines usually have lifetimes of more than 10 years, and some almost unlimited. These mines usually weigh 200 kg (440 lb), including 80 kg (175 lb) of explosives (hexatonal). In excess of 150 kg (330 lb) of explosives the mine becomes inefficient, as it becomes too large to handle and the extra explosives add little to the mine's effectiveness.

BOTTOM MINES

Bottom mines are used when the water is no more than 60 meters (180 ft) deep or when mining for submarines down to around 200 meters (660 ft). They are much harder to detect and sweep, and can carry a much larger warhead than a moored mine. Bottom mines commonly use pressure sensitive exploders, which are less sensitive to sweeping.

These mines usually weigh between 150 and 1,500 kilograms (330 to 3,300 pounds), including between 125 and 1,400 kg (275 to 3,090 pounds) of explosives.

UNUSUAL MINES

Several specialized mines have been developed for other purposes than the common minefield.

ANTI SWEEP MINE

The anti sweep mine is a very small mine (40 kg warhead) with as small a floating device as possible. When the wire of a mine sweep hits the mine, it "sinks", letting the sweep wire drag along the anchoring wire of the mine until the sweep hits the mine. That detonates the mine and cuts the sweeping wire.

They are very cheap and usually used in combination with other mines in a minefield to make sweeping more difficult.

ROCKET MINE

A Russian invention, the rocket mine is a bottom distance mine that fires a homing high-speed rocket (not torpedo) upwards towards the target. It is intended to allow a bottom mine to attack surface ships as well as submarines from a greater depth.

TORPEDO MINE

The torpedo mine is a self-propelled variety, able to lie in wait for a target and then pursue it e.g. the CAPTOR mine. Other designs such as the Mk 67 Submarine Launched Mobile Mine (which is based on a Mark 37 torpedo) are capable of swimming as far as 10 miles through or into a channel, harbor, shallow water area and other zones which would normally be inaccessible to craft laying the device.

After reaching the target area they sink to the sea bed and act like conventionally laid influence mines. Generally, torpedo mines incorporate computerised acoustic and magnetic fuzes.

The U.S. Mark 24 "mine", code-named FIDO, was actually an ASW homing torpedo. The mine designation was disinformation to conceal its function.

BOUQUET MINE

The bouquet mine is a single anchor attached to several floating mines. It is designed so that when one mine is swept/detonated, another takes its place. It is a very sensitive construction and lacks reliability.

ASCENDING MINE

The ascending mine is a floating distance mine that may cut its mooring or in some other way float higher when it detects a target. It lets a single floating mine cover a much larger depth range.

NUCLEAR MINE

During the Cold War a number of tests were conducted with navel mines fitted with tactical nuclear warheads. These weapons were experimental and never went into production.

DAISY-CHAINED MINE

This comprises two moored, floating contact mines which are tethered together by a length of steel cable or chain. Typically, each mine is situated approximately 60 feet (18 m) away from its neighbour, and each floats a few metres below the surface of the ocean. When the target ship hits the steel cable, the mines on either side are drawn down the side of the ship's hull, exploding on contact. In this manner it is almost impossible for target ships to pass safely between two individually moored mines. Daisy-chained mines are a very simple concept which was used during the Second World War.

DUMMY MINE

Plastic drums filled with sand or concrete are periodically rolled off the side of ships as real mines are laid in large mine-fields. These inexpensive false targets (designed to be of a similar shape and size as genuine mines) are intended to slow down the process of mine clearance: a mine-hunter is forced to investigate each suspicious sonar contact on the sea bed, whether it is real or not.

MINE LAYING

Historically several methods were used to lay mines. During the First and Second World Wars, the Germans used U-boats to lay mines around the UK. In the Second World War, aircraft came into favour for mine laying with the one of largest such examples being the mining of the Japanese sea routes in Operation Starvation.

Laying a minefield is a relatively fast process with specialized ships, which is still today the most common method. These minelayers can carry several thousand mines and manoeuvre with high precision. The mines are dropped at a predefined interval into the water behind the ship. Each mine is recorded for later clearing, but it is not unusual for these recordings to be lost together with the ships. Therefore many countries demand that all mining operations shall be planned on land and records kept so the mines can later be recovered more easily.

Other methods to lay minefields include:

- Converted merchant ships–rolled or slid down ramps
- Aircraft–descent to the water is slowed by a parachute

- Submarines–launched from torpedo tubes or deployed from specialized mine racks on the sides of the submarine
- Combat boats–rolled off the side of the boat
- Camouflaged boats–masquerading as fishing boats
- Dropping from the shore–typically smaller, shallow-water mines
- Attack divers–smaller shallow-water mines

In some cases, mines are automatically activated upon contact with the water. In others, a safety lanyard is pulled (e.g. one end attached to the rail of a ship, aircraft or torpedo tube) which starts an automatic timer countdown before the arming process is complete. Typically, the automatic safety-arming process takes some minutes to complete. This is in order to give the people laying the mines sufficient time to move out of its activation/blast zone.

AERIAL MINING IN WORLD WAR II

Germany

In the 1930s, Germany had experimented with the laying of mines by aircraft; it became a crucial element in their overall mining strategy. Aircraft had the advantage of speed, and they would never get caught in their own minefields. German mines held a large 1,000 lb. (450 kg) explosive charge. From April to June 1940, the Luftwaffe laid 1,000 mines in British waters. Soviet ports were mined, as was the Arctic convoy route to Murmansk. The Heinkel He 115 could carry two medium or one large mine while the Heinkel He 59, Dornier Do 18, Junkers Ju 88 and Heinkel He 111 could carry more.

Soviet Union

The USSR was relatively ineffective in its use of naval mines in WWII in comparison with its record in previous wars. Small mines were developed for use in rivers and lakes, and special mines for shallow water. A very large chemical mine was designed to sink through ice with the aid of a melting compound. Special aerial mine designs finally arrived in 1943-1944, the AMD-500 and AMD-1000. Various Soviet Naval Aviation torpedo bombers were pressed into the role of aerial mining in the Baltic Sea and the Black Sea, including Ilyushin DB-3s, Il-4s and Lend Lease Douglas Boston IIIs.

United Kingdom

In September 1939, the UK announced the placement of extensive defensive minefields in waters surrounding the Home Islands. Offensive aerial mining operations began in April 1940 when 38 mines were laid at each of these locations: the Elbe River, the port of Lübeck and the German naval base at Kiel. In the next 20 months, mines delivered by aircraft sank or damaged 164 Axis ships with the loss of 94 aircraft. By comparison, direct aerial attacks on Axis shipping had sunk or damaged 105 vessels at a cost of 373 aircraft lost. The advantage of aerial mining became clear. The United Kingdom geared up for mining; a total of 48,000 aerial mines were laid by the Royal Air Force (RAF) in the European Theatre during World War II.

United States

The United States's early aerial mining efforts used smaller aircraft that are unable to carry many mines. Using TBF Avenger torpedo bombers, the US Navy mounted a direct aerial mining attack on enemy shipping in Palau on 30 March 1944 in concert with simultaneous conventional bombing and strafing attacks. The dropping of 78 mines stopped 32 Japanese ships from escaping Koror harbor; the combined operation sank or damaged 36 ships. Two Avengers were lost; their crews were recovered. The mines brought port usage to a halt for 20 days; further mine-laying in the area contributed to the Japanese abandoning Palau as a base.

As early as 1942, American mining experts such as Naval Ordnance Laboratory scientist Dr. Ellis A. Johnson, Commander, Naval Reserve, suggested massive aerial mining operations against Japan's "outer zone" (Korea and northern China) as well as the "inner zone", their home islands. First, aerial mines would have to be developed further and manufactured in large numbers. Second, laying the mines would require a sizable air group. The US Army Air Force had the carrying capacity but considered mining to be the Navy's job. The US Navy lacked suitable aircraft. Johnson set about convincing General Curtis LeMay of the efficacy of very heavy bombers laying aerial mines.

In the meantime, B-24 Liberator, PBY Catalina and other available bomber aircraft took part in localized mining operations in the Southwest Pacific and the China Burma India (CBI) Theaters, beginning with a very successful attack on the Yangon River in February 1943. Aerial minelaying operations involved a coalition of British, Australian and American aircrews, with the RAF and the Royal Australian Air Force (RAAF) carrying out 60% of the sorties and the USAAF and US Navy covering 40%. Both British and American mines were used. Japanese merchant shipping suffered tremendous losses, while Japanese mine sweeping forces were spread too thin attending to far-flung ports and extensive coastlines. Admiral Thomas C. Kinkaid, who directed nearly all RAAF mining operations in CBI, heartily endorsed aerial mining, writing in July 1944 that "aerial mining operations were of the order of 100 times as destructive to the enemy as an equal number of bombing missions against land targets."

Finally, in March 1945, Operation Starvation began in earnest, using 160 of LeMay's B-29 Superfortress bombers to attack Japan's inner zone. Almost half of the mines were the US-built Mark 25 model, carrying 1250 lbs of explosives and weighing about 2,000 lbs. Other mines used included the smaller 1,000 lb Mark 26. 15 B-29s were lost while 293 enemy merchant ships were sunk or damaged. 12,000 aerial mines were laid, a significant barrier to Japan's access to outside resources. Prince Fumimaro Konoe said after the war that the aerial mining by B-29s had been "equally as effective as the B-29 attacks on Japanese industry at the closing stages of the war when all food supplies and critical material were prevented from reaching the Japanese home islands." The United

States Strategic Bombing Survey (Pacific War) concluded that it would have been more efficient to combine the United States's effective anti-shipping submarine effort with land- and carrier-based air power to strike harder against merchant shipping and begin a more extensive aerial mining campaign earlier in the war. Survey analysts projected that this would have starved Japan, forcing an earlier end to the war. After the war, Dr. Johnson looked at the Japan inner zone shipping results, comparing the total economic cost of submarine-delivered mines versus air-dropped mines and found that, though 1 in 12 submarine mines connected with the enemy as opposed to 1 in 21 for aircraft mines, the aerial mining operation was about ten times less expensive per enemy ton sunk.

CLEARING WWII AERIAL MINES

Between 600,000 and 1,000,000 naval mines of all types were laid in World War II. Advancing military forces worked to clear mines from newly-taken areas, but extensive minefields remained in place after the war. Air-dropped mines had an additional problem for mine sweeping operations: they weren't meticulously charted.

In Japan, much of the B-29 mine-laying work had been performed at high altitude, with the drifting on the wind of mines carried by parachute adding a randomising factor to their placement. Generalized danger areas were identified, with only the quantity of mines given in detail. Mines used in Operation Starvation were supposed to be self-sterilising, but the circuit did not always work. Clearing the mines took so many years that the task was eventually given to the Japan Maritime Self-Defense Force.

For the purpose of clearing all types of naval mines, the Royal Navy employed German crews and minesweepers from June 1945 to January 1948, organised in the German Mine Sweeping Administration, the GMSA, which consisted of 27,000 members of the former Kriegsmarine and 300 vessels.

Mine clearing wasn't always successful: a number of ships were damaged or sunk by mines after the war. Two such examples were the Liberty ships Pierre Gibault which was scrapped after hitting a mine in a previously-cleared area off the Greek island of Kythira in June 1945, and Nathaniel Bacon which hit a minefield off Civitavecchia, Italy in December 1945, caught fire, was beached, and broke in two.

DAMAGE

The damage that may be caused by a mine depends on the "shock factor value", a combination of the initial strength of the explosion and of the distance between the target and the detonation. When taken in reference to ship hull plating, the term "Hull Shock Factor" (HSF) is used, while keel damage is termed "Keel Shock Factor" (KSF). If the explosion is directly underneath the keel, then HSF is equal to KSF, but explosions that are not directly underneath the ship will have a lower value of KSF.

DIRECT DAMAGE

Usually only created by contact mines, direct damage is a hole blown in the ship. Among the crew, shrapnel wounds are the most common form of damage. This rarely sinks the ship, but might flood one or two compartments – usually in the bow.

BUBBLE JET EFFECT

The bubble jet effect occurs when a mine detonates in the water some distance away from the ship. The explosion creates a "hole" in the water, and due to the difference in pressure, this sphere will collapse from the bottom. This creates a "pillar" of water that can go over a hundred meters into the air. The damage to the ship is heavy. The water breaks a meter wide hole straight through the ship, flooding one or more compartments, and might break the ship apart. The crew in the areas hit by the pillar are usually killed instantly. Other damage is usually limited.

SHAKING EFFECT

If the mine detonates at a distance from the ship, the change in water pressure causes the ship to resonate. This is frequently the most deadly type of explosion, if it is strong enough. The whole ship is dangerously shaken and everything onboard is tossed around. Engines rip from their beds, cables from their holders, etc. A badly shaken ship usually sinks quickly, with hundreds, or even thousands of small leaks all over the ship and no way to power the pumps. The crew fare no better, as the violent shaking tosses them around. The resulting gas cavitation and shock-front-differential over the width of the human body will stun or kill the divers.

COUNTERMEASURES

Weapons are frequently a few steps ahead of countermeasures, and mines are no exception. In this field the British, with their large seagoing navy, have had the bulk of world experience, and most anti-mine developments, such as de-gaussing and the double-L sweep were British inventions. When on operational missions, such as the recent invasion of Iraq, the US still rely on British and Canadian minesweeping services. The US have worked on some innovative mine hunting countermeasures, such as the use of military dolphins to detect and flag mines. However, they are of questionable effectiveness.

PASSIVE COUNTERMEASURES

Ships can be designed to be difficult for mines to detect, to avoid detonating them. This is especially true for minesweepers and mine hunters that work in minefields, where a minimal signature outweighs the need for armour and speed. These ships have hulls of glass fibre or wood instead of steel to avoid magnetic signatures, they use special propulsion systems, such as Voith-Schneider propellers, to limit the acoustic signature. They are built with hulls that produce a minimal pressure signature. These measures create other problems. They are expensive, slow, and vulnerable to enemy fire. Therefore, they need protection. Many modern ships have a mine-warning sonar—a simple sonar looking forward and warning the crew if it detects possible mines ahead. It is only effective when the ship is moving slowly.

A steel-hulled ship can be degaussed (more correctly, deoerstedted or depermed) using a special degaussing station that contains many large coils and induces a magnetic field in the hull with alternating current to demagnetize the hull. This is a rather problematic solution, as magnetic compasses need recalibration and all metal objects must be kept in exactly the same place. Ships slowly regain their magnetic field as they travel through the Earth's magnetic field, so the process has to be repeated every six months.

A simpler variation of this technique, called wiping, was developed by Charles F. Goodeve which saved time and resources.

Between 1941 and 1943 the US Naval Gun factory (a division of the Naval Ordinance Laboratory) in Washington D.C. built physical models of all US Naval ships. Three kinds of steel were used in shipbuilding: mild steel for bulkheads, a mixture of mild steel and high tensile steel for the hull, and special treatment steel for armor plate. The models were placed within coils which could simulate the Earth's magnetic field at any location. The magnetic signatures were measured with degaussing coils. The objective was to reduce the vertical component of the combination of the Earth's field and the ship's field at the usual depth of German mines. From the measurements, coils were placed and coil currents determined to minimize the chance of detonation for any ship at any heading at any latitude.

Some ships are built with magnetic inductors, large coils placed along the ship to counter the ship's magnetic field. Using magnetic probes in strategic parts of the ship, the strength of the current in the coils can be adjusted to minimize the total magnetic field. This is a heavy and clumsy solution, suited only to smaller ships.

ACTIVE COUNTERMEASURES

Active countermeasures are ways to clear a path through a minefield or remove it completely. This is one of the most important tasks of any mine warfare flotilla.

MINE SWEEPING

A sweep is either a contact sweep, a wire dragged through the water by one or two ships to cut the mooring wire of floating mines, or a distance sweep that mimics a ship to detonate the mines. The sweeps are dragged by minesweepers, either purpose-built military ships or converted trawlers. Each run covers between one and two hundred meters, and the ships must move slowly in a straight line, making them vulnerable to enemy fire. This was exploited by the Turkish army in the Battle of Gallipoli in 1915, when mobile howitzer batteries prevented the British and French from clearing a way through minefields.

An MH-53E from HM-15 tows a minesweeping sled while conducting simulated mine clearing operations

If a contact sweep hits a mine, the wire of the sweep rubs against the mooring wire until it is cut. Sometimes "cutters", explosive devices to cut the mine's wire, are used to lessen the strain on the sweeping wire. Mines cut free are recorded and collected for research or shot with a deck gun.

Minesweepers protect themselves with an oropesa or paravane instead of a second minesweeper. These are torpedo-shaped towed bodies, similar in shape to a Harvey Torpedo, that are streamed from the sweeping vessel thus keeping the sweep at a determined depth and position. Some large warships were routinely equipped with paravane sweeps near the bows in case they inadvertently sailed into minefields — the mine would be deflected towards the paravane by the wire instead of towards the ship by its wake. More recently, heavy-lift helicopters have dragged minesweeping sleds, as in the 1991 Persian Gulf War.

Minesweeper USS Tide (AM-125) after striking a mine off Utah Beach, 7 June 1944. Note her broken back, with smoke pouring from amidships.

The distance sweep mimics the sound and magnetism of a ship and is pulled behind the sweeper. It has floating coils and large underwater drums. It is the only sweep effective against bottom mines.

During the Second World War, RAF Coastal Command used Vickers Wellington bombers fitted with degaussing coils to trigger magnetic mines.

Modern influence mines are designed to discriminate against false inputs and are therefore much harder to sweep. They often contain inherent anti-sweeping mechanisms. For example, they may be programmed to respond to the unique noise of a particular ship-type, its associated magnetic signature and the typical pressure displacement of such a vessel. As a result, a mine-sweeper must accurately guess and mimic the required target signature in order to trigger detonation. The task is complicated by the fact that an influence mine may have one or more of a hundred different potential target signatures programmed into it.

Another anti-sweeping mechanism is a ship-counter in the mine fuze. When enabled, this allows detonation only after the mine fuze has been triggered a pre-set number of times. To further complicate matters, influence mines may be programmed to arm themselves (or disarm automatically—known as self-sterilisation) after a pre-set time. During the pre-set arming delay (which could last days or even weeks) the mine would remain dormant and ignore any target stimulus, whether genuine or faked.

When influence mines are laid in an ocean minefield, they may have various combinations of fuze settings configured. For example, some mines (with the acoustic sensor enabled) may become active within three hours of being laid, others (with the acoustic and magnetic sensors enabled) may become active after two weeks but have the ship-counter mechanism set to ignore the first two trigger events, and still others in the same minefield (with the magnetic and pressure sensors enabled) may not become armed until three weeks have passed. Groups of mines within this mine-field may have different target signatures which may or may not overlap. The fuzes on influence mines allow many different permutations, which complicates the clearance process.

Mines with ship-counters, arming delays and highly specific target signatures in mine fuzes can falsely convince a belligerent that a particular area is clear of mines or has been swept effectively because a succession of vessels have already passed through safely.

MINE HUNTING

Mine hunting is very different from sweeping, although some minehunters can do both tasks. Mines are hunted using sonar, then inspected and destroyed either by divers or ROVs (remote controlled unmanned mini submarines). It is slow, but also the most reliable way to remove mines. Mine hunting started during the Second World War, but it was only after the war that it became truly effective.

Pinguin B3 mine hunting drone, such are operated from Frankenthal class mine hunters of the German Navy

Sea mammals (mainly the Bottlenose Dolphin) have been trained to hunt and mark mines, most famously by the U.S. Navy Marine Mammal Programme. Mine-clearance dolphins were deployed in the Persian Gulf during the Iraq War in 2003. The Navy claims that these dolphins were effective in helping to clear more than 100 antiship mines and underwater booby traps from Umm Qasr Port.

French naval officer Jacques Yves Cousteau's Undersea Research Group was once involved in mine-hunting operations: They removed or detonated a variety of German mines, but one particularly nasty batch—equipped with acutely sensitive pressure, magnetic, and acoustic sensors and wired together so that one explosion would trigger the rest — was simply left undisturbed for years until corrosion would (hopefully) disable the mines.)

MINE BREAKING

A more drastic method is simply to load a cargo ship with cargo that makes her less vulnerable to sinking (wood for example) and drive her through the minefield, letting the ship to be protected follow the same path. This method was employed by the German Kriegsmarine during WWII, using converted ships known as Sperrbrecher ("barrage breaker"). Alternatively, a shallow draught vessel can be steamed through the minefield at high speed to generate a pressure wave sufficient to trigger mines, with the minesweeper moving fast enough to be sufficiently clear of the pressure wave so that triggered mines do not destroy the ship itself. These techniques are the only way to sweep pressure mines. The technique can be simply countered by use of a ship-counter, set to allow a certain number of passes before the mine is actually triggered. Modern doctrine calls for ground mines to be hunted rather than swept.

Seehund ROVs of the German Navy used for minesweeping/breaking

An updated form of mine breaking is the use of small unmanned ROVs that simulate the acoustic and magnetic signatures of larger ships and are built to survive exploding mines. Repeated sweeps would be required in case one or more of the mines had its "ship counter" facility enabled i.e. were programmed to ignore the first 2, 3, or even 6 target activations.

NATIONAL ARSENALS

US MINES

The United States Navy MK56 ASW mine (the oldest still in use by the US) was developed in 1966. More advanced mines include the MK60 CAPTOR (short for "encapsulated torpedo"), the MK62 and MK63 Quickstrike and the MK67 SLMM (Submarine Launched Mobile Mine). Today, most U.S. naval mines are delivered by aircraft.

MK67 SLMM SUBMARINE LAUNCHED MOBILE MINE

The SLMM was developed by the United States as a submarine deployed mine for use in areas inaccessible for other mine deployment techniques or for covert mining of hostile environments. The SLMM is a shallow-water mine and is basically a modified Mark 37 torpedo.

GENERAL CHARACTERISTICS

- Type: Submarine-laid bottom mine
- Detection System: Magnetic/seismic/pressure target detection devices (TDDs)
- Dimensions: 485 mm by 4.09 m (19 by 161 in)
- Depth Range: Shallow water
- Weight: 754 kg (1658 lb)
- Explosives: 230 kg (510 lb) high explosive
- Date Deployed: 1987

MK65 QUICKSTRIKE

The Quickstrike is a family of shallow-water aircraft-laid mines used by the United States, primarily against surface craft. The MK65 is a 2,000-lb (900 kg) dedicated, purpose-built mine. However, other Quickstrike versions (MK62, MK63, and MK64) are converted general-purpose bombs. These latter three mines are actually a single type of electronic fuze fitted to Mk82, Mk83 and Mk84 air-dropped bombs. Because this latter type of Quickstrike fuze only takes up a small amount of storage space compared to a dedicated sea mine, the air-dropped bomb casings have dual purpose i.e. can be fitted with conventional contact fuzes and dropped on land targets, or have a Quickstrike fuze fitted which converts them into sea mines.

GENERAL CHARACTERISTICS

- Type: aircraft-laid bottom mine (with descent to water slowed by a parachute or other mechanism)

- Detection System: Magnetic/seismic/pressure target detection devices (TDDs)
- Dimensions: 740 mm by 3.25 m (29 by 128 in)
- Depth Range: Shallow water
- Weight: 1086 kg (2390 lb)
- Explosives: Various loads
- Date Deployed: 1983

MK56

GENERAL CHARACTERISTICS

- Type: Aircraft laid moored mine
- Detection System: Total field magnetic exploder
- Dimensions: 570 mm by 2.9 m (22.4 by 114.3 in)
- Depth Range: Moderate depths
- Weight: 909 kg (2000 lb)
- Explosives: 164 kg (360 lb) HBX-3
- Date Deployed: 1966

ROYAL NAVY

According to a statement made to the UK Parliament in 2002:

> "...the Royal Navy does not have any mine stocks and has not had since 1992. Notwithstanding this, the United Kingdom retains the capability to lay mines and continues research into mine exploitation. Practice mines, used for exercises, continue to be laid in order to retain the necessary skills".

However, a British company (BAE Systems) does manufacture the Stonefish influence mine for export to friendly countries such as Australia, which has both war stock and training versions of Stonefish, in addition to stocks of smaller Italian MN103 Manta mines. The computerised fuze on a Stonefish mine contains acoustic, magnetic and water pressure displacement target detection sensors. Stonefish can be deployed by fixed-wing aircraft, helicopters, surface vessels and submarines. An optional kit is available to allow Stonefish to be air-dropped, comprising an aerodynamic tail-fin section and parachute pack to retard the weapon's descent. The operating depth of Stonefish ranges between 30 and 200 metres. The mine weighs 990 kilograms and contains a 600 kilogram aluminised PBX explosive warhead. The shelf life of a Stonefish mine is 20 years, and it has an operational lifetime of 700 days after being deployed on the seabed. Stonefish incorporates arming delays, ship counting and self-sterilisation features which can be configured by the user.

Chapter 10

MINING IN THE CONTEXT OF MILITARY

Mining, undermining, or sapping was a siege method used since antiquity against a walled city, fortress or castle.

USE IN ANTIQUITY

The Greek historian Polybius, in his Histories, gives a graphic account of mining and counter mining at the Roman siege of Ambracia:

> The Aetolians [...] offered a gallant resistance to the assault of the siege artillery and [the Romans], therefore, in despair had recourse to mines and underground tunnels. Having safely secured the central one of their three works, and carefully concealed the shaft with wattle screens, they erected in front of it a covered walk or stoa about two hundred feet long, parallel with the wall; and beginning digging from that, they carried it on unceasingly day and night, working in relays. For a considerable number of days the besieged did not discover them carrying the earth away through the shaft; but when the heap of earth thus brought out became too high to be concealed from those inside the city, the commanders of the besieged garrison set to work vigorously digging a trench inside, parallel to the wall and to the stoa which faced the towers. When the trench was made to the required depth, they next placed in a row along the side of the trench nearest the wall a number of brazen vessels made very thin; and, as they walked along the bottom of the trench past these, they listened for the

> noise of the digging outside. Having marked the spot indicated by any of these brazen vessels, which were extraordinarily sensitive and vibrated to the sound outside, they began digging from within, at right angles to the trench, another underground tunnel leading under the wall, so calculated as to exactly hit the enemy's tunnel. This was soon accomplished, for the Romans had not only brought their mine up to the wall, but had under-pinned a considerable length of it on either side of their mine; and thus the two parties found themselves face to face.

According to Polybius, this was the first time poison gas was used.

Another extraordinary usage of siege-mining in the ancient greece, where during Philip V of Macedon's siege of the little town of Prinassos, according to Polybius,"the ground around the town were extremely rocky and hard, making any siege-mining virtually impossible. However, Philip ordered his soldiers during the cover of night collect earth from elsewhere and throw it all down at the fake tunnel's entrance, making it look like the macedonians were almost finished completing the tunnels! Eventually, when Philip V announced that large parts of the town-walls were undermined the citizens surrendered without delay."

Mining was a siege method used in ancient China from at least the Warring States (481–221 BC) period forward. When enemies attempted to dig tunnels under walls for mining or entry into the city, the defenders used large bellows (the type the Chinese commonly used in heating up the blast furnace for smelting cast iron) to pump smoke into the tunnels in order to suffocate the intruders.

USE IN THE MIDDLE AGES

In warfare during the Middle Ages, a "mine" was a tunnel dug to bring down castles and other fortifications. The technique was used when the fortification was not built on solid rock, and was developed as a response to stone built castles that could not be burned like earlier-style wooden forts. A tunnel would be excavated under the outer defenses either to provide access into the fortification or to collapse the walls. These tunnels would normally be supported by temporary wooden props as the digging progressed. Once the excavation was complete, the wall or tower being undermined would be collapsed by filling the excavation with combustible material that, when lit, would burn away the props leaving the structure above unsupported and thus liable to collapse. Later, explosives were used for greater effect.

A tactic related to mining is sapping the wall, where engineers would dig at the base of a wall with crowbars and picks. Peter of les Vaux-de-Cernay recounts how at the battle of Carcassonne, during the Albigensian Crusade, "after the top of the wall had been somewhat weakened by bombardment from petraries, our engineers succeeded with great difficulty in bringing a four-wheeled wagon, covered in oxhides, close to the wall, from which they set to work to sap the wall" (les Vaux-de-Cernay, 53).

As in the siege of Carcassonne, defenders worked to prevent sapping by dumping anything they had down on attackers who tried to dig under the wall. Successful sapping usually ended the battle since either the defenders would no longer be able to defend and surrender, or the attackers would simply charge in and engage the defenders in close combat.

There were several methods to resist under mining. Often the siting of a castle could be such as to make mining difficult. The walls of a castle could be constructed either on solid rock or on sandy or water logged land making it difficult to dig mines. A very deep ditch or moat could be constructed in front of the walls, as was done at Pembroke Castle, or even artificial lakes as was done at Kenilworth Castle. This makes it more difficult to dig a mine and even if a breach is made the ditch or moat makes exploiting the breach difficult. The defenders could also dig counter mines. From these they could then either dig into the attackers tunnels and sortie into them to either kill the miners or to set fire to the pit-props to collapse the attackers tunnel. Alternatively they could under mine the attackers tunnels and create a camouflet to collapse the attacker's tunnels. Finally if the walls were breached they could either place obstacles in the breach for example a chevaux de frise to hinder a forlorn hope, or construct a coupure. The great concentric ringed fortresses like Beaumaris Castle on Anglesey were designed in such a way that the inner walls were ready built coupures so that if an attacker succeeded in breaching the outer walls would have left them in a killing field between the lower outer walls and the higher inner walls.

USE IN THE AMERICAN CIVIL WAR

During the Siege of Vicksburg in 1863 Union troops led by General Ulysses S. Grant tunnelled under the Confederate trenches and detonated the mine beneath the 3rd Louisiana Redan on June 25, 1863. The following assault led by General John A. Logan gained a foothold in the Confederate trenches where the crater was formed but the attackers were eventually forced to withdraw.

A more famous instance occurred during the Siege of Petersburg, Union troops dug a tunnel under the Confederate lines at Elliott's Salient and packed its end with vast amounts of gunpowder. When set off, the resulting explosion killed about 300 soldiers. It might have been decisive if not for the faulty Union tactic of storming into, rather than around, the resulting crater, allowing the defenders to shoot down onto attackers unable to climb the steep crater sides. The combat was accordingly known as the Battle of the Crater. (The horror of this engagement was portrayed in the Charles Frazier novel and subsequent Anthony Minghella movie Cold Mountain.)

USE IN MODERN WARFARE

Mining saw a brief resurgence as a military tactic during the First World War when army engineers would attempt to break the stalemate of trench warfare by tunneling under no man's land and laying large quantities of explosives beneath the enemy's trench. As in siege warfare, mining was possible due to the static nature of the fighting.

A notable example was the Battle of Messines, when 450 tonnes of high explosive were placed in 21 mines after about two years of sapping. Approximately 10,000 German troops were killed when 19 of the mines were simultaneously detonated. One of the explosive caches exploded years later. The 21st cache was never found and there are still several tonnes of high explosive buried somewhere in the Belgian countryside.

Explosion of the mine beneath Hawthorn Ridge Redoubt, July 1 1916

Another example is recorded in Louis Trenker's Berge in Flammen. Whole mountain peaks at the Alps were exploded during the mountain war. Col di Lana, Lagazuoi and Marmolata, were a few of these peaks. Because World War II troop movements were too fluid, and tunneling too slow, mining proved not to be worth the investment of effort.

AERIAL WARFARE

Aerial Warfare is the use of military aircraft and other flying machines in warfare, including military airlift of cargo to further the national interests as was demonstrated in the Berlin Airlift. Developing from unpowered observation hot air balloons in the 18th century and even older kite, aerial warfare has become a high-technology affair that has led to many advances in technology and techniques such as propulsion, radar, and use of composites and engineered materials such as carbon fibers.

KITE WARFARE

The earliest documented aerial warfare took place in ancient China, when a manned Kite was set off to spy for military intelligence and communication. Ancient Chinese soldiers also mounted massive aerial fire arrow attacks from war kites, where they would send a volley of flaming arrows from the war kite onto the ground target, carrying out the world's first-ever air attacks.

BALLOON WARFARE

BALLOON WARFARE IN ANCIENT CHINA

In or around the 2nd or 3rd century, a prototype Hot air balloon, the Kongming lantern was invented in China serving as military communication.

BALLOON WARFARE IN EUROPE

Some minor warfare use was made of balloons in the infancy of aeronautics. The first instance was by the French Aerostatic Corps at the Battle of Fleurus in 1794, who used a tethered balloon, L'entreprenant, to gain a vantage point.

Balloons had disadvantages. They could not fly in bad weather, fog, or high winds. They were at the mercy of the winds and were also very large targets.

AMERICAN CIVIL WAR

Battle of Fair Oaks with one of Lowe's balloons in the background

UNION ARMY BALLOON CORPS

The American Civil War was the first war to witness significant use of aeronautics in support of battle.. Thaddeus Lowe made noteworthy contributions to the Union war effort using a fleet of balloons he created In June 1861 Professor Thaddeus S. C. Lowe left his work in the private sector as a scientist/balloonist and offered his services as an aeronaut to President Lincoln, who took some interest in the idea of an air war. Lowe's demonstration of flying his balloon Enterprise over Washington, DC, and transmitting a telegraph message to the ground was enough to have him introduced to the commanders of the Topographical Engineers; initially it was thought balloons could be used for preparing better maps.

Lowe's first action was at the First Battle of Bull Run in July 1861 with General Irvin McDowell and the Grand Army of the Potomac. Enterprise did a free flight observation of the Confederate positions.

In another demonstration, Lowe was called to Fort Corcoran by artillery General W. F. Smith. Lowe ascended to a given altitude in order to spot rebel encampments at Falls Church, Virginia. With flag signals he directed artillery fire onto the sleeping encampment. As the General put it, "The signals from the balloon have enabled my gunners to hit with a fine degree of accuracy an unseen and dispersed target area."

By October, Lowe had orders in hand to build four balloons with portable hydrogen gas generators for use in aerial reconnaissance. Working with several other prominent American balloonists he formed the Union Army Balloon Corps who never received commissions, working as civilian contractors, This was of great concern should the aeronauts be shot down over enemy lines, as civilian spying is summarily punishable by death. Therefore Lowe instructed on the strict use of tethered (as opposed to free) flight. By attaining altitudes from 1,000 feet (300 m) to as much as 3-1/2 miles, an expansive view of the battle field and beyond could be had.

Lowe built seven balloons: Eagle, his first; Constitution, one of the smaller balloons; its sister, Washington; Intrepid, a larger balloon and his favorite; a sister, Union; Excelsior; and United States, which never came out of storage.

As the Confederates retreated toward Richmond, the War turned into the Peninsular Campaign. Due to the heavy forests on the peninsula, the balloons were unable to follow on land. Lowe was introduced to George Washington Parke Custis, a coal barge converted to operate balloons. The balloons and their gas generators were loaded aboard and taken down the Potomac, where reconnaissance of the peninsula could continue. Custis was taken up the Pawmunkey River, where Lowe was reunited with McClellan's army.

Prof. Lowe ascending in Intrepid to observe the Battle of Fair Oaks

Lowe's most dramatic action came in the Battle of Fair Oaks, where he was able to view the advancing of Lee's army onto the isolated detachment of General Heintzelman. Working from two balloon camps, one at Mechanicsville and one at Gaine's Farm, Lowe galloped six miles (10 km) twice daily to keep up with the reconnaissance reports. McClellan was sure the rebels were feigning an attack, but Lowe could see differently. Heintzelman was left stranded on the other side of the Chickahominy River with the bridges having been taken out overnight by the swollen waters. Lowe sent a dispatch of utmost urgency to have the bridge repaired immediately and reserves sent to Heintzelman's aid. He then sent dispatch from Mechanicsville to Gaine's Farm calling for the immediate inflation of the large balloon Enterprise, which would aid him in overlooking the imminent battle.

When Lowe arrived at Gaine's Farm, Intrepid will still far from being inflated. In a quick work of inventive ingenuity, Lowe had the bottom of a camp kettle cut out and joined the valve ends of the Intrepid and the partially inflated Constitution hooked together, thereby transferring the gas from the latter into the former. Within 15 minutes he was in the air to oversee the battle.

Lowe fell prey to malaria during Fair Oaks and was out of commission for more than a month. On his return he found the Balloon Corps had been stripped of horses and wagons and left out of service for Antietam. Lowe was called back into service at Sharpsburg and later responded to Gen. Burnside's army at Vicksburg.

The ensuing defeat of the Union Army in what was referred to as the "Mud March" led to Gen. Joseph Hooker relieving Burnside. By this time, the Balloon Corps had been assigned to the Engineers Corps, and a newly promoted Captain Comstock cut Lowe's pay dramatically.

Lowe tendered his resignation and was released from military duty in May 1863. The Balloon Corps continued to operate with Lowe's handlers, but Union generals' continuing ignoring and mistrust of ballooning resulted in balloon-intelligence not being utilized. By August, the Union Army Balloon Corps was disbanded.

SILK DRESS BALLOONS

Due to the effectiveness of the Union Army Balloon Corps, the Confederates felt compelled to incorporate balloons as well. As coke gas was not always available in Richmond, the first balloons were made of the Montgolfier rigid style, cotton stretched over wood framing and filled with hot smoke from fires made of oil-soaked pinecones. They were piloted by Captain John R. Bryant for use at Yorktown. Though Bryant's performance was not all that bad, his handlers were poorly experienced and his balloon was left in the air spinning like a top. Another incident had one of the handlers becoming entangled in the ascending tether rope which had to be chopped loose, leaving the Captain free-flying over his own Confederate positions whose troops threatened to shoot him down.

Attempts at making gas-filled silk balloons were hampered by the South's inability to obtain any imports at all. They did fashion a balloon from dress silk (purportedly silk for making dresses, not from silk dresses themselves). The inflated spheres appeared as multi-colored orbs over Richmond and were piloted by Captain Landon Cheeves. Before the first balloon could be used it was captured during transportation on the James River by the crew of the Monitor. A second balloon did see action until summer 1863, when it was blown from its mooring and taken by Union forces only to be divided up as souvenirs for members of the Federal Congress. As the Union Army reduced its use of balloons, so did the Confederates—much to their relief.

ZEPPELINS, AIRSHIPS AND BLIMPS

As powered aircraft with wings dominated military aviation during WWI, rigid dirigibles and zeppelins were used by the Germans to attack cities. After WWI, the United States Navy researched the use of airships, including their use as a base for fighter aircraft, but efforts were cancelled after losses in storms. In WWII, barrage ballons were used as obstacles against aircraft, and blimps were used as observation and radar platforms.

BEFORE WORLD WAR I

The armies of many countries evaluated the use of aircraft for observation purposes. Naval aviation was pursued as well; several tests were made in which floatplanes were launched by catapult from ships at sea, and recovered later by crane.

The U.S. Navy had been interested in naval aviation since the turn of the 20th century. In August 1910 Jacob Earl Fickel did the first experimenting with Glenn Curtiss shooting a gun from an airplane. In 1910–1911, the Navy conducted experiments which proved the practicality of carrier-based aviation. On November 14, 1910, near Hampton Roads, Virginia, civilian pilot Eugene Ely took off from a wooden platform installed on the scout cruiser USS Birmingham (CL-2). He landed safely on shore a few minutes later. Ely proved several months later that it was also possible to land on a ship. On January 18, 1911, he landed on a platform attached to the American cruiser USS Pennsylvania (ACR-4) in San Francisco harbor.

The first use of airplanes in an actual war occurred in the 1911 Italo-Turkish War with the Italian Army Air Corps bombing a Turkish camp at Ain Zara, Libya, and in the 1912 First Balkan War with the Bulgarian Air Force bombing Turkish positions at Adrianople. Airplanes were also used by the U.S. against Pancho Villa. Air reconnaissance was carried out in both wars too. The air-dropped bomb was extensively used during the First Balkan War (including in the first ever night bombing on 7 November 1912), and subsequently shared with the Imperial German Air Service during World War I.

WORLD WAR I

Initially during that war both sides made use of tethered balloons and airplanes for observation purposes, both for information gathering and directing of artillery fire. A desire to prevent enemy observation led to airplane pilots attacking other airplanes and balloons, initially with small arms carried in the cockpit, but due to the technology of the time pilots couldn't have forward facing machine guns

RAF Sopwith Camel during World War I

Although the addition of deflector plates to the back of propellers by French pilot Roland Garros and designer Raymond Saulnier in the Morane-Saulnier monoplane was the first example of an aircraft able to fire through its propeller, it wasn't until the Dutch aircraft designer Anthony Fokker developed the gun synchronizer in 1915 that it became possible to aim the gun and the airplane at the same time, resulting in German Leutnant Kurt Wintgens scoring the first known victory for a synchronized gun-equipped fighter aircraft, on July 1, 1915. Eventually the Allies were able to capture a Fokker Eindecker with a Fokker-designed Stangensteuerung synchronizer mechanism intact and reverse engineer it, leading to the birth of aerial combat, more commonly known as the dogfight. Tactics for dogfighting evolved by trial and error. Eventually the German ace Oswald Boelcke created eight essential rules of dogfighting, the Dicta Boelcke. Both sides also made use of aircraft for bombing, strafing, sea reconnaissance, antisubmarine warfare, and dropping of propaganda. The German military made use of Zeppelins and, later on, bombers such as the Gotha, to drop bombs on Britain.

By the end of the war airplanes had become specialized into bombers, fighters, and observation (reconnaissance) aircraft.

BETWEEN THE WARS

Between 1918 and 1939 aircraft technology developed very rapidly. In 1918 most aircraft were biplanes with wooden frames, canvas skins, wire rigging and air-cooled engines. Biplanes continued to be the mainstay of air forces around the world and were used extensively in conflicts such as the Spanish Civil War. Most industrial countries also created air forces separate from the army and navy. However, by 1939 military biplanes were in the process of being replaced with metal framed monoplanes, often with stressed skins and liquid cooled engines. Top speeds had tripled; altitudes doubled; ranges and payloads of bombers increased enormously.

Some theorists, especially in Britain, considered that aircraft would become the dominant military arm in the future. They imagined that a future war would be won entirely by the destruction of the enemy's military and industrial capability from the air. The Italian general Giulio Douhet, author of The Command of the Air, was a seminal theorist of this school, which has been associated with Stanley Baldwin's statement that "the bomber will always get through"; that is, regardless of air defenses, sufficient raiders will survive to rain destruction on the enemy's cities. This led to what would later be called a strategy of deterrence and a "bomber gap", as nations measured air force power by number of bombers.

Others, such as General Billy Mitchell in the United States, saw the potential of air power to augment the striking power of naval surface fleets. German and British pilots had experimented with aerial bombing of ships and air-dropped torpedoes during World War I with mixed results. The vulnerability of capital ships to aircraft was demonstrated on 21 July 1921 when a squadron of bombers commanded by General Mitchell sank the ex-German battleship SMS Ostfriesland with aerial bombs; although the Ostfriesland was stationary and defenseless during the exercise, its destruction demonstrated the potency of airplanes against ships.

It was during the Banana Wars, while fighting bandits, freedom fighters and insurgents in places like Haiti, the Dominican Republic and Nicaragua, that United States Marine Corps aviators would begin to experiment with air-ground tactics making the support of their fellow Marines on the ground their primary mission. It was in Haiti that Marines began to develop the tactic of dive bombing and in Nicaraugua where they began to perfect it. While other nations and services had tried variations of this technique, Marine aviators were the first to embrace it and make it part of their tactical doctrine

Germany was banned from possessing an air force by the terms of the WWI armistice. The German military continued to train its soldiers as pilots clandestinely until Hitler was ready to openly defy the ban. This was done by forming the Deutscher Luftsportverband, a flying enthusiast's club, and training pilots as civilians, and some German pilots were even sent to the Soviet Union for secret training; a trained air force was thus ready as soon as the word was given. This was the beginning of the Luftwaffe.

WORLD WAR II

Military aviation came into its own during the Second World War. The increased performance, range, and payload of contemporary aircraft meant that air power could move beyond the novelty applications of WWI, becoming a central striking force for all the combatant nations. Over the course of the war, several distinct roles emerged for the application of air power.

STRATEGIC BOMBING

Strategic bombing of civilian targets from the air was first proposed by the Italian theorist General Giulio Douhet. In his book The Command of the Air (1921), Douhet argued future military leaders could avoid falling into bloody World War I–style trench stalemates by using aviation to strike past the enemy's forces directly at their vulnerable civilian populations. Douhet believed such strikes would cause these populations to force their governments to surrender.

Douhet's ideas were paralleled by other military theorists who emerged from World War I, including Sir Hugh Trenchard in Britain. In the interwar period, Britain and the United States became the most enthusiastic supporters of the strategic bombing theory, with each nation building specialized heavy bombers specifically for this task.

Chinese baby crying in the ruins of Shanghai South Railway Station after a bombing by the Imperial Japanese Navy Air Service on 28 August 1937

IMPERIAL JAPANESE AIR SERVICE

Shôwa strategic bombing was independently conducted during the Second Sino-Japanese war and World War II by the Imperial Japanese Navy Air Service and the Imperial Japanese Army Air Service.

Bombing efforts mostly targeted large Chinese cities such as Shanghai, Wuhan and Chonging. The bombing of Nanjing and Canton, which began on 22 and 23 September 1937, called forth widespread protests culminating in a resolution by the Far Eastern Advisory Committee of the League of Nations.

There were also air raids on Philippines and northern Australia (Bombing of Darwin, 19 February 1942). The Imperial Japanese Navy Air Service used tactical bombing against enemy airfields and military positions, as at Pearl Harbor. The Imperial Japanese Army Air Service also attacked enemy ships and military installations.

LUFTWAFFE

In the early days of WWII, the Luftwaffe launched devastating air attacks against the besieged cities of Warsaw and Rotterdam. In the case of Warsaw, the bombings had little effect, but in the case of Rotterdam, the psychological effect of the bombings did have the intended effect—a relatively rapid ending of Dutch resistance (Buckley 129).

During the Battle of Britain, the Luftwaffe, frustrated in its attempts to gain air superiority in preparation for the planned invasion, turned to bombing of London and other large English cities. However, the Luftwaffe found these raids did not have the effect predicted by prewar airpower theorists.

ROYAL AIR FORCE

The British, started in kind–using a strategic bombing campaign in 1940 that was to last for the rest of the war. Early British bombers were all twin-engined designs and were lacking in defensive armament. Therefore, RAF Bomber Command quickly turned to a policy of night bombing, for which the crews were untrained; their inaccuracy meant they were forced to adopt area bombing and were unable to hit specific targets such as factories or power plants until later in the war when pathfinder tactics, radio location plus ground mapping radar (OBOE and H2S) and very low-level bombing such as that used by the Dambusters in Operation Chastise were developed.

SOVIET RED AIR FORCE

Although the rapid industrialisation the Soviet Union experienced in the 1930s had the potential to enable the Voyenno-vozdushnyye sily (VVS) to be effective against the Luftwaffe, Stalin's purges left the organisation intellectually and morally weakened.

However, when Germany invaded in June 1941 (Operation Barbarossa), the massive size of the VVS, in both planes and people, allowed it to absorb "horrendous" casualties and still maintain capability.

The Spitfire played a vital part for British victory in the Battle of Britain.

Like Japan was to do in December of that year, Nazi Germany had awoken a sleeping giant which was too large to destroy despite the Wehrmacht's superior experience and the Luftwaffe's superior training. Despite the near collapse of both the Red Army and Red Air Force, Germany's 1941 assault failed to destroy either one, and as the massive resources of the Soviet Union were reorganized toward war, Germany's impending destruction become ever more apparent.

As during the Battle of Britain, fundamental flaws in the Luftwaffe were exposed during Germany's war with the Soviet Union. Although strategic bombing requires that the enemy's industrial war capacity be neutralized, some Soviet war factories were moved as much as 1,000 miles (1,600 km) east—far out of reach of the Luftwaffe's bombers. And even factories and VVS facilities that were in reach of the Luftwaffe had to be ignored much of the time because the Luftwaffe's resources were needed for more critical duty in supporting the German army. The Luftwaffe became overstretched, and even victorious battles damaged the overall capability of Germany's air force due to attrition.

By 1943, the Soviets had fully rebounded from the defeats of 1941, and they were able to produce considerably more airplanes than their German rivals; for example, at Kursk, the VVS had twice the number of airplanes that the Luftwaffe had. The VVS's fighter-capability rested on the Yakovlev Yak-9 and Lavochkin La-5, and its primary bombers were the Ilyushin 2 Shturmovik and Petlyakov Pe-2. Utilising overwhelming numerical superiority, Soviet forces were able to drive the Germans out of Soviet territory and take the war to Germany.

U.S. ARMY AIR FORCE

When the U.S. Eighth Air Force arrived in England in 1942, the Americans were convinced they could carry out successful daylight raids. The Eighth was equipped with B-17 Flying Fortresses and B-24 Liberators, both high-altitude four-engined designs. The new bombers also featured the strongest defensive armament yet seen–up to 13 .50 caliber machine guns, depending on the version, most of them in power-operated turrets. Flying in daylight in large, close formations, U.S. doctrine held tactical formations of heavy bombers would be sufficient to gain air superiority in the absence of escort fighters. The intended raids would hit hard on chokepoints in the German war economy such as oil refineries or ball bearing factories.

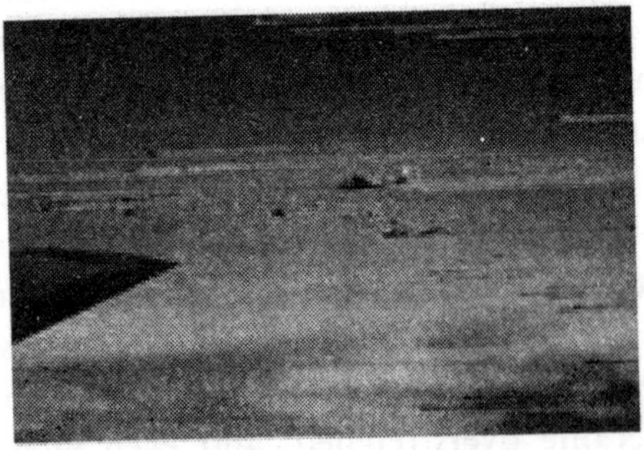

Part of a USAAF stream of over 1,000 B-17 bombers.

The U.S.A.A.F. was compelled to change its doctrine since bombers alone, no matter how heavily armed, could not achieve air superiority against single-engined fighters. Loss rates rose from five to twenty per cent in a series of missions between August 17 and October 14, 1943, when raids against Regensburg and Schweinfurt, penetrating beyond the range of fighter cover, resulted in the loss of 60 bombers on one mission.

AIR SUPERIORITY

During the Battle of Britain, many of the best Luftwaffe pilots had been forced to bail out over British soil, where they were captured. As the quality of the Luftwaffe fighter arm decreased, the Americans introduced the long-range P-38 Lightning and P-51 Mustang escort fighters, carrying drop tanks. Newer, inexperienced German pilots—flying potentially superior aircraft, such as the Focke-Wulf Fw 190, Heinkel He 162, and the Messerschmitt Me 262—gradually became less and less effective at thinning the late-war bomber streams. Adding fighters to the daylight raids gave the bombers much-needed protection and greatly improved the impact of the strategic bombing effort.

Over time, from 1942 to 1944, the Allies' air forces became stronger and stronger while the Luftwaffe became weaker and weaker. During 1944, the Luftwaffe experienced a 78 per cent reduction in its strength, and Germany's air force lost control over Germany's skies. As a result nothing in Germany could be securely protected—not stationary army units, nor moving army units, nor war factories, nor their workers, nor civilians in cities such as Hamburg and Dresden, nor the nation's capital—Berlin. Germans had to watch as their soldiers and civilians began to be slaughtered in the thousands by aerial bombardment—much as the Germans had done to Poland, Rotterdam, Britain, and the Soviet Union.

EFFECTIVENESS

Strategic bombing by non-atomic means did not win the war for the Allies, nor did it succeed in breaking the will to resist of the German (and Japanese) people. But in the words of the German armaments minister Albert Speer, it created "a second front in the air." Speer succeeded in increasing the output of armaments right up to mid-1944 in spite of the bombing. Still, the war against the British and American bombers demanded enormous amounts of resources: antiaircraft guns, day and night fighters, radars, searchlights, manpower, ammunition, and fuel. On the Allied side, strategic bombing diverted material resources, equipment (such as radar) aircraft, and manpower away from the Battle of the Atlantic (where even a couple of squadrons of B-24s could be priceless) and Allied armies. As a result, German army groups in Russia, Italy, and France rarely saw friendly aircraft and constantly ran short of tanks, trucks, and anti-tank weapons. The only option left was to create World War I–style slit trench defenses quite unlike the blitzkriegs of 1939–1941.

US BOMBING OF JAPAN

The long-range Boeing B-29 was used to bomb Japan. On 15 June 1944, 47 B-29s launched from Chengdu, China, bombed the Imperial Iron and Steel Works at Yawata Japan. This was the first attack on Japanese islands since the Doolittle Raid in April 1942. The entire B-29 effort was gradually shifted to the new bases in the Marianas Islands in the Central Pacific The first mission against Japan from bases in the Marianas was flown on 24 November 1944, with 111 B-29s sent to attack Tokyo. From that point, more-and-more intense raids were launched regularly until the end of the war. Tactics evolved from high-altitude to lower altitude attacks, largely removing most defensive guns and switching to incendiary bombs. These attacks succeeded in devastating almost all large Japanese cities. The most famous B-29 was the Enola Gay, which dropped the atomic bomb 'Little Boy' on Hiroshima on 6 August 1945. Bockscar, another B-29, dropped 'Fat Man' on Nagasaki three days later. Although the ethics of nuclear warfare remain controversial, these two actions, along with the Soviet invasion of Manchuria on 9 August 1945, brought about the Japanese surrender, and the official end of World War II.

Enola Gay, a Silverplate version of the Boeing B-29 Superfortress landing after delivering Little boy over Hiroshima

TACTICAL AIR SUPPORT

By contrast with the British strategists, the primary purpose of the Luftwaffe was to support the Army. This accounted for the presence of large numbers of dive bombers on strength and the scarcity of long-range heavy bombers. This 'flying artillery' greatly assisted in the successes of the German Army in the Battle of France (1940). Hitler determined air superiority was essential for the invasion of Britain. When this was not achieved in the Battle of Britain, the invasion was canceled, making this the first major battle whose outcome was determined primarily in the air.

The war in Russia forced the Luftwaffe to devote the majority of its resources to providing tactical air support for the beleaguered German army. In that role, the Luftwaffe used the Junkers Ju 87, Henschel Hs 123 and modified fighters—Bf 109 and FW 190.

The Red Air Force was also primarily used in the tactical support role, and towards the end of the war was very effective in the support of the Red Army in its advance across Eastern Europe. An aircraft of importance to the Soviets was the Ilyushin Il-2 Sturmovik—appropriately called "flying artilery"; the Il-2 was able to make life very difficult for panzer crews, and the Il-2 was an important part of the Soviet victory at Kursk—one of the biggest tank battles in history.

MILITARY TRANSPORT AVIATION AND USE OF AIRBORNE TROOPS

Military transport aviation was invaluable to all sides in maintaining supply and communications of ground troops, and was used on many notable occasions such as resupply of German troops in and around Stalingrad after Operation Uranus, and employment of airborne troops. After the first trials in use of airborne troops by the Red Army displayed in the early 1930s many European nations and Japan also formed the airborne troops, and these saw extensive service on in all Theatres of the Second World War. However their effectiveness as shock troops employed to surprise enemy static troops proved to be of limited success. Most airborne troops served as light infantry by the end of the war despite attempts at massed use in the Western Theatre by US and Britain during the Operation Market Garden.

NAVAL AVIATION

Aircraft and the aircraft carrier first became important in naval battles in World War II. Carrier based aircraft are specialized as dive bombers, torpedo bombers, and fighters, evolving from biplanes such as the Swordfish and fighters such as the F4F Wildcat which were based on biplanes to the F4U Corsair which outperformed many land based types, and the TBF Avenger which had an enclosed gun turret. Surface based aircraft such as the PBY Catalina help find submarines and surface fleets. The aircraft carrier replaces the battleship as the most powerful naval offensive weapons system as battles between fleets are fought entirely out of gun range by aircraft. The Yamato, the most powerful battleship ever built is first turned back by light escort carrier aircraft, and later sunk lacking its own air cover.

In the Doolittle Raid, the US launches normally land-based B-25 Mitchell bombers from carriers in a raid against Tokyo and other Japanese mainland targets. Small escort carriers and light carriers are built in large numbers to escort slow cargo convoys or supplement fast carriers. Aircraft for observation or light raids are also carried by battleships and cruisers, while blimps are used to search for attack submarines.

A Japanese Mitsubishi A6M2 "Zero" fighter

- Battle of the Atlantic, aircraft carried by low-cost escort carriers are used for antisubmarine patrol, defense, and attack
- Battle of Taranto
- Attack of Pearl Harbor First attack on US territory is carried out entirely by carrier based aircraft, destroying or sinking most US battleships, but not finding any US carriers in port.
- Sinking of Prince of Wales and Repulse, the first time a battleship underway was sunk solely by aircraft
- Battle of the Coral Sea, the first where neither fleet was in visual contact with the other and all fighting was carried out by aircraft
- Battle of Midway
- Battle of the Bismarck Sea
- Battle of the Philippine Sea
- Battle of Leyte Gulf, with the first appearance of kamikazes, perhaps the largest naval battle in history. Japan's last carriers and pilots are deliberately sacrificed as a decoy, the super battleship Musashi is sunk by aircraft. The Japanese Navy ceases to be an effective fighting force.

Douglas Dauntless SBD dive-bomber in Battle of Midway

- Battle off Samar A powerful fleet led by the Japanese battleship Yamato catches the light escort carrier "Taffy" task forces within gun range. Although largely unprepared to attack armored ships, aircraft and screening "tin-can" destroyers caused enough damage, sinking or forcing the scuttling of 3 cruisers and 1 destroyer, to turn the Japanese force back.
- Operation Ten-Go The sinking of a fleet with the Yamato and nine other warships with no air cover demonstrated U.S. air supremacy in the Pacific theater by this stage in the war and the vulnerability of surface ships without air cover to aerial attack.

COLD WAR ERA

Military aviation in the post-war years was dominated by the needs of the Cold War. The post-war years saw the almost total conversion of combat aircraft to jet power, which resulted in enormous increases in speeds and altitudes of aircraft. Until the advent of the Intercontinental Ballistic Missile major powers relied on high-altitude bombers to deliver their newly-developed nuclear deterrent; each country strove to develop the technology of bombers and the high-altitude fighters that could intercept them. The concept of air superiority began to play a heavy role in aircraft designs for both the United States and the Soviet Union.

The Americans developed and made extensive use of the high-altitude observation aircraft for intelligence-gathering. The U-2, and later the SR-71 Blackbird were developed in great secrecy. The U-2 at its time was supposed to be invulnerable to defensive measures, due to its extreme altitude. It therefore came as a great shock when the Soviets downed one piloted by Gary Powers with a surface-to-air missile.

Air combat was also transformed through increased use of air-to-air guided missiles with increased sophistication in guidance and increased range.

In the 70s and 80s it became clear that speed and altitude was not enough to protect a bomber against air defences. The emphasis shifted therefore to maneuverable attack aircraft that could fly 'under the radar', at altitudes of a few hundred feet.

KOREAN WAR

The Korean War was best remembered for jet combat, but was one of the last major wars where propeller-powered fighters such as the P-51 Mustang, F4U Corsair and aircraft carrier-based Hawker Sea Fury and Supermarine Seafire were used.[:174] Turbojet fighter aircraft such as F-80s, F-84 Thunderjets and F9F Panthers came to dominate the skies, overwhelming North Korea's propeller-driven Yakovlev Yak-9s and Lavochkin La-9s.[:182]

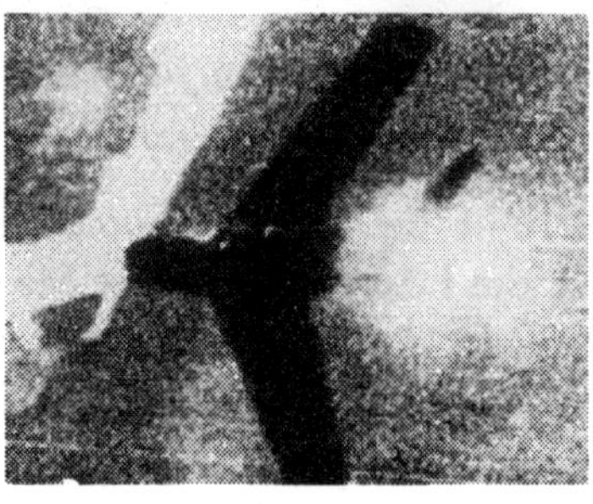

MiG-15 shot down by an F-86 over MiG Alley

From 1950, North Koreans flew the Soviet-made MiG-15 jet fighters which introduced the near-sonic speeds of swept wings to air combat. Though an open secret during the war, the most formidable pilots today now admit that they were experienced Soviet Air Force pilots, a casus belli:[182] deliberately overlooked by the UN allied forces who suspected the use of Russians but were reluctant to engage in open war with the Soviet Union and the People's Republic of China. At first, UN jet fighters, which also included Royal Australian Air Force Gloster Meteors, had some success, but straight winged jets were soon outclassed in daylight by the superior speed of the MiGs. At night, however, radar-equipped Marine Corps F3D Skynight night fighters claimed five MiG kills with no losses of their own, and no B-29s under their escort were lost to enemy fighters.

Over the course of the war, at least 16 B-29 bombers were shot down by communist aircraft.

In December 1950, the U.S. Air Force rushed in their own swept-wing fighter, the F-86 Sabre.:[183] The MiG could fly higher, 50,000 vs. 42,000 feet (12,800 m), offering a distinct advantage at the start of combat. In level flight, their maximum speeds were comparable — about 660 mph (1,060 km/h). The MiG could climb better, while the Sabre could turn and dive better with an all-flying tailplane. For weapons, the MiG carried two 23 mm and one 37 mm cannon, compared to the Sabre's six .50 (12.7 mm) caliber machine guns. The American .50 caliber machine guns, while not packing the same punch, carried many more rounds and were aimed with a more accurate radar-ranging gunsight. The U.S. pilots also had the advantage of G-suits, which were used for the first time in this war.

Even after the Air Force introduced the advanced F-86, its pilots often struggled against the jets piloted by Soviet pilots, dubbed "honchos". The UN gradually gained air superiority over most of Korea that lasted until the end of the war — a decisive factor in helping the UN first advance into the north, and then resist the Chinese invasion of South Korea.

After the war, the USAF claimed 792 MiG-15s and 108 additional aircraft shot down by Sabres for the loss of 78 Sabres, a ratio in excess of 10:1, though some other studies show a gap of close to 2:1 against the best Russian pilots. Some post-war research has been able to confirm only 379 victories, although the USAF continues to maintain its official credits and the debate is possibly irreconcilable.

The Soviets claimed about 1,100 air-to-air victories and 335 combat MiG losses at that time. China's official losses were 231 planes shot down in air-to-air combat (mostly MiG-15) and 168 other losses. The number of losses of the North Korean Air Force was not revealed. It is estimated that it lost about 200 aircraft in the first stage of the war, and another 70 aircraft after Chinese intervention. Soviet claims of 650 victories over the Sabres, and China's claims of another 211 F-86s, are considered to be exaggerated by the USAF. According to a recent U.S. publication, the number of F-86s ever present in the Korean peninsula during the war totaled only 674 and the total F-86 losses from all causes were about 230.

The Korean war was the first time the helicopter was used extensively in a conflict. While helicopters such as the YR-4 were used in World War II, their use was rare, and Jeeps like the Willys MB were the main method of removing an injured soldier. In the Korean war helicopters like the H-19 partially took over in the non combat Medevac area.

®Helicopters like this H-19 were used in the Korean war.

INDIA-PAKISTAN WAR OF 1965

The war saw the Indian Air Force and the Pakistani Air Force being involved in full scale combat for the first time since independence. Though the two forces had previously faced off in the First Kashmir War during the late 1940s, it was limited in scale compared to the '65 conflict.

Both countries hold highly contradictory claims on combat losses during the war and hardly any neutral sources have thoroughly verified the claims of both countries' claim. PAF claimed it had shot down 104 IAF planes losing only 19 in the process. India meanwhile claimed that 35 IAF planes were lost while shooting down 73 PAF aircraft.

Pakistan's main strike force comprised the U.S. made F-86 Sabre jets, which claimed a fair share of Indian planes, though remaining vulnerable to the dimunitive Folland Gnat, nicknamed "Sabre Slayer". The PAF's F-104 Starfighter was by far the fastest fighter on the subcontinent at that time. On the other hand, the Indian Air Force relied largely on the Hawker Hunter for attacks. Unlike the PAF, whose strength largely comprised American craft,

IAF flew an assortment of planes from de Havilland Vampires to Dassault Mysteres, many of which were outdated in comparison to PAF planes, with even Gnats and Hunters being outmatched by Sabres and Starfighters. Some of the fiercest dogfights occurred over Sargodha, which was PAF's main base housing the bulk of its planes; IAF planes attacked the base but PAF was able to repulse the attacks. PAF responded by attacking Indian bases with some success, especially in air to ground attacks but were soon forced to back off, in order to provide cover for its ground troops elsewhere. In one incident, the Gujarat Chief Minister, Balawant Rai Mehta's civilian craft was shot down by PAF Sabres inside Indian territory, killing him and the crew. By the end of the war, neither the numerically larger IAF, nor the PAF which possessed a qualitative advantage, achieved air superiority.

VIETNAM WAR

The South Vietnamese Air Force (VNAF) was originally equipped with helicopters such as the CH-21 and propeller powered aircraft such as the T-28 Trojan when jet aircraft were disallowed by treaty. As US involvement increased, most airpower was directly flown by US forces.

A UH-1D "Huey" seen offloading troops during the Vietnam War.

Large scale use of helicopters by the US Army in Vietnam led to a new class of airmobile troops, and the introduction of "Air Cavalry" in the U.S, culminating in extensive use of the UH-1 Huey helicopter which would become a symbol of that war, while the CH-54 Tarhe "Skycrane" and CH-47 Chinook lifted heavier loads such as vehicles or artillery. Troops were able to land unexpectedly, strike, and leave again, and evacuate wounded. The specialized AH-1 Cobra was developed from the Huey for escort and ground support duties, The later Soviet campaign in Afghanistan would also see widespread use of helicopters as part of the Air Assault brigades and regiments.

US forces provided close support of ground force over South Vietnam, and strategic bombing of targets over North Vietnam. Many types flying close support or COIN (Counter Insurgency Warfare) missions were propeller powered types such as the O-1 and OV-10 Bronco FAC spotters, A-1 Skyraider, B-26 Invader, and AC-47 "Spooky" gunship. C-123 Provider and C-130 Hercules transports flew supplies into battlefields such as Khe Sanh. "Fast movers" included the supersonic F-100 Super Sabre, while the giant B-52 Stratofortress would be modified to unload a massive high explosive payload on enemy troop concentrations. The AC-130 would become the ultimate gunship, while the AX specification to replace the Skyraider would evolve into the A-10 Thunderbolt II.

The USAF F-105 Thunderchiefs flew the bulk of strike missions against North Vietnam in Operation Rolling Thunder, while carrier-based A-4 Skyhawks were flown by the Navy. That first campaign was marred by carefully measured regulations that prohibited attacks against SAM missile sites and fighter bases, and frequent bombing halts, and produced little in political results. Rolling Thunder saw the first combat use of electronic computers aboard PIRAZ ships to display comprehensive real-time aircraft position information for force commanders.

Lessons learned were applied to the later Operation Linebacker which employed Phantoms, B-52s, swing-wing F-111s, A-7

Corsairs and all-weather A-6 Intruders was more successful in bringing North Vietnam to the negotiating table after a massive ground invasion. North Vietnam effectively combined Soviet and Chinese anti-aircraft artillery, SA-2 guided missiles, and MiG fighters to create the most heavily defended airspace up to that time.

US air strikes would combine the use of airbone radar platforms such as the C-121, KC-135s for air refueling, radar jamming aircraft and specialized "Wild Weasel" units to attack SAM missile sites. "Jolly Green Giant" helicopter crews escorted by A-1 "Sandy"s would retrieve downed pilots over hostile territory.With the use of "smart" guided bombs late in the war, this would set the model for future US air operations.

Experts were surprised when advanced F-105s were shot down in its first encounter against the elderly but nimble MiG-17. Dogfights were thought to be obsolete in the age of missiles, but pilots now needed maneuverability. The F-4 Phantom was quickly tasked with protecting against MiGs, but sorely lacked a built-in gun when missiles were often unreliable. Air combat training schools such as TOPGUN would improve kill ratios, but combat experience started programmes that would produce agile air superiority fighters with guns such as the F-15 Eagle by the 1970s.

South Vietnam fell without US air support when faced with a massive assault in 1975. The VNAF South Vietnamese Air Force was never supplied with powerful fighters and bombers such as the Phantom and B-52 which could strike at North Vietnam.

MIDDLE EAST

In the Six-Day War of 1967, the Israeli Air Force launched pre-emptive strikes which destroyed opposing Arab air forces on the ground. The Yom Kippur War of 1973 saw the Arab deployment of mobile SA-6 missiles which proved effective against low-flying Israeli aircraft until they were neutralized by ground forces.

POST COLD WAR

The collapse of the Soviet Union in 1991 forced Western air forces to undergo a shift from the massive numbers felt to be necessary during the Cold War to smaller numbers of multi-role aircraft. The closure of several military bases overseas and the U.S. Base Realignment and Closure programme have served to highlight the effectiveness of aircraft carriers in the absence of dedicated military or air forces bases, as the Falklands war and U.S. operations in the Persian Gulf have highlighted. While the advent of precision-guided munitions have allowed for strikes at arbitrary surface targets once proper reconnaissance is performed (network-centric warfare). In some cases, such as the NATO Operation Allied Force effort against Serbian operations in Kosovo, air power was the deciding factor with ground forces mostly securing the area afterwards. However in most cases the standard military doctrine still applies: wars against third-world regional entities still cannot be won through air power alone.

USS Abraham Lincoln rides out a storm in the Arabian Sea while on station in support of Operation Southern Watch and Operation Enduring Freedom.

OPERATION: DESERT STORM

The role of air power in modern warfare was dramatically demonstrated during the Gulf War in 1991. Behind-the-lines air attacks were made on Iraqi command and control centers, communications facilities, supply depots, and reinforcement forces. Air superiority over Iraq was gained before major ground combat began.

The initial strikes were composed of Tomahawk cruise missiles launched from battleships situated in the Persian Gulf, F-117A Nighthawk stealth bombers with an armament of laser-guided smart bombs, and F-4G Wild Weasel aircraft armed with HARM anti-radar missiles. These first attacks allowed F-14, F-15, F-16, and F/A-18 fighter bombers to gain air superiority over the country and then continue to drop TV and laser-guided bombs. Armed with a gatling gun and heat-seeking or optically guided Maverick missiles, A-10 Thunderbolts bombed and destroyed Iraqi armored forces, supporting the advance of US ground troops. The AH-64 Apache and AH-1 Cobra attack helicopters, fired laser guided Hellfire missiles and TOW missiles which were guided to tanks by ground observers or scout helicopters. The allied air fleet also made use of the E-3A Airborne Warning and Control Systems (AWACS) and a fleet of B-52 bombers.

The aerial strike force was made up of over 2,250 combat aircraft, which included 1,800 US aircraft, which fought against an Iraqi force of about 500 Soviet-built MiG-29 and French-made Mirage F-1 fighters. More than 88,000 combat missions had been flown by allied forces with over 88,000 tons of bombs dropped by the end of the fifth week.

OPERATION: IRAQI FREEDOM

During the 2003 invasion of Iraq led by US and British forces putatively to defeat the regime of Saddam Hussein, aerial warfare continued to be decisive. The US-British alliance began its air campaign on March 19 with limited nighttime bombing on the Iraqi capital of Baghdad. Several days later, intensive bombardment began. About 14,000 sorties were flown, and at a cost of $1 million dollars each, 800 Tomahawk cruise missiles were fired at numerous targets in Iraq from March 19 until mid-April 2003. By this time Iraqi resistance had largely ended.

An F-15E Strike Eagle from the 391st Expeditionary Fighter Squadron at Bagram Air Base, Afghanistan, launches heat decoys during a close-air-support mission over Afghanistan, 15 December 2008.

Iraqi anti-aircraft weapons were unable to open fire on high-altitude US bombers such as the B-52 or stealth aircraft such as the B-2 bomber and the F-117A. US and British aircraft used radar-detecting devices and aerial reconnaissance to locate Iraqi anti-aircraft weapons. Bunker buster bombs, designed to penetrate and destroy underground bunkers, were dropped on Iraqi command and control centers. Iraqi ground forces could not seriously challenge the American ground forces because of their air supremacy. By mid-April 2003, US-British forces controlled all of Iraq's major cities and oil fields.

2006 LEBANON WAR

In the beginning of the 2006 Lebanon War Israel utilized an intensive aerial campaign aimed to eliminate Hezbollah and destroy its military as stated by Israeli prime minister Ehud Olmert. It also aimed to return the kidnapped soldiers. The campaign started by destroying Lebanese infrastructure and Hezbollah targets. This continued during the 33 days of the war. The importance of this war to the history of aerial campaigns lies in the fact that its the first war in the modern history that didn't reach its goals through the use of air force. Taking into consideration the results of 1990 and 2003 wars on Iraq and 1998 war on former Yugoslavia; the Israeli air force, one of the strongest in the world, were unable to accomplish their objectives. This lies on the military doctrine that Hezbollah used in the war which proved effective in facing such kinds of wars. There have also been reports during the conflict that a Hezbollah-manned flying drone penetrated Israeli airspace, and returned to Lebanese territory.

OTHER CONFLICTS

A few other spans of conflicts opened up the use of aerial warfare in recent times. In 1999, India and Pakistan were involved in a brief conflict over Kashmir. The Indian Air Force used Mirage 2000 fighter jet effectively to carry out ground assault sorties against Pakistani positions. The air operations were notable given the high altitude terrain of Kashmir.

Chapter 11

SUBMARINE WARFARE

Naval warfare is divided into three operational areas: surface warfare, air warfare and underwater warfare. The latter may be subdivided into submarine warfare and anti-submarine warfare as well as mine warfare and mine countermeasures. Each area comprises specialized platforms and strategies used to exploit tactical advantages unique and inherent to that area.

Modern submarine warfare consists primarily of diesel and nuclear submarines using weapons (like torpedoes, missiles or nuclear weapons), as well as advanced sensing equipment, to attack other submarines, ships, or land targets. Submarines may also be used for reconnaissance and landing of special forces as well as deterrence. In some navies they may be used for task force screening. The effectiveness of submarine warfare partly depends on the anti-submarine warfare carried out in response.

WORLD WAR I

Submarine warfare in World War I was partly a fight between German U-Boats and Atlantic supply convoys bound for Great Britain. British and Allied submarines conducted wide spread operations in the Baltic, North Sea, Atlantic, Mediterranean and Black Seas. Only a few actions occurred outside of the wider European-Atlantic theatre. German submarine attacks on allied merchant ships gave a direct cause for Americans to enter the war in April 1917.

All participants were supposed to abide by the Hague Conventions of 1899 and 1907 but this was found to be impracticable for submarines. Initially German submarines did attempt to comply with the Prize Rules but then went to unrestricted submarine warfare. American diplomatic pressure forced the Germans to stop this for a while but in January 1917 declared a War Zone around the British Isles and sank up to a quarter of shipping entering it, until escorted convoys were introduced. The sinking of the Pathfinder was the first combat victory of a modern submarine, and the exploits of U-9, which sank three British cruisers in under an hour, establishing the submarine as an important new component of naval warfare.

German submarines were used to lay mines and to attack iron ore shipping in the Baltic. The British submarine flotilla in the Baltic operated in support of the Russians until the Russian-German Pact.

During the war, the British invested effort in developing a submarine that could operate in conjunction with a battleship fleet–the "Fleet Submarine". To achieve the necessary 20 knots (surfaced) the K class submarines were steam powered. In practice the K class were a constant problem and could not operate effectively with a fleet.

INTERWAR PERIOD

Between the wars, navies experimented with submarine cruisers (France, Surcouf), submarines armed with battleship calibre guns (UK, HMS M1) and submarines capable of carrying small aircraft for reconnaissance (HMS M2 and the Surcouf). Germany was denied submarines by the terms of the Treaty of Versailles and secret production was not legitimized until the Anglo-German Naval Agreement of 1935 under which the UK accepted parity in submarine numbers with the Royal Navy.

WORLD WAR II

In World War II, submarine warfare was split into two main areas–the Atlantic and the Pacific. Although the war still waged in

Africa, the Mediterranean Sea was also a very active area for submarine operations. This was particularly true for the British and French as well as the Germans. The Italians were also involved but achieved their greatest success using midget submarines and human torpedoes.

ATLANTIC OCEAN

In the Atlantic, where German submarines again acted against Allied convoys, this part of the war was very reminiscent of the latter part of World War I. Many British submarines were active as well, particularly in the Mediterranean and off Norway, against Axis warships, submarines and merchant shipping.

Initially Hitler ordered his submarines to abide by the Prize Rules but this restriction was withdrawn in December 1939. Although mass attacks by submarine had been carried out in the First World War, the "wolf pack" was mainly a tactic of the Second World War U-boats. The main steps in this tactic were as follows:

- A number of U-boats were dispersed across possible paths of a convoy.
- A boat sighting the convoys would signal its course, speed and composition to German Naval Command.
- The submarine continues to shadow the convoy, reporting any changes.
- The rest of the pack is then ordered to close to the first boat's position.
- When the pack is formed a coordinated attack is made on the surface at night.
- At dawn the pack withdraws leaving a shadower, and resumes the attack at dusk.

With the later increase in warship and aircraft escorts the U-boat losses became unacceptable. Many boats were lost, and the earlier "aces" with them.

PACIFIC OCEAN

In the Pacific, the situation was reversed, with US submarines hunting Japanese shipping, whereas Japanese submarines were few, and often ineffectual. British and Dutch submarines also took part in attacks on Japanese shipping, mostly in coastal waters. A few German and Italian submarines operated in the Pacific Ocean, but never enough to be an important factor.

OTHER AREAS

Indian Ocean

Japanese submarines operated in the Indian Ocean, forcing the British surface fleet to withdraw to the east coast of Africa. Like the Pacific Ocean, a few German and Italian submarines operated in the Indian Ocean, but never enough to be an important factor.See Monsun Gruppe.

POST WORLD WAR II

The advent of the nuclear submarine in the 1950s brought about a major change in submarine warfare. These boats could operate faster, deeper and had much longer endurance. They could be larger and so became missile launching platforms. In response to this the attack submarine became important. The US also used nuclear submarines as radar pickets for a while. Diesel-electric submarines continued to be used as they were better in coastal waters and less expensive. There have also been major advances in sensors and weapons.

Since the Second World War, several wars, such as the Korean War, Indo-Pakistani War of 1971 and the Falklands War, have involved the use of submarines. However, the importance of the submarine has shifted to an even more strategic role than the disruption of merchant shipping, with the advent of the nuclear submarine carrying nuclear weapons to provide second-strike capability. To counter the threat of these submarines, hunter submarines were developed in turn. Later submarine-launched land-attack missiles were employed against Iraq and Afghanistan. The role of the submarine has extended with the use of submarine-launched autonomous unmanned vehicles. The development of new air independent propulsion methods has meant that the submarine's need to surface, making it vulnerable, has been reduced.

At the end of his naval warfare book The Price of Admiralty, military historian John Keegan postulates that eventually, almost all roles of surface warships will be taken over by submarines, as they will be the only naval units capable of evading the increasing intelligence capabilities (space satellites, airplanes etc.) that a fight between evenly matched modern states could bring to bear on them.

MODERN SUBMARINE MISSIONS

A modern submarine is a multi-role platform. It can conduct both overt and covert operations. In peacetime it can act as a deterrent as well as for surveillance operations and information gathering.

In wartime a submarine can carry out a number of missions including:

- Surveillance and information gathering
- Communication of data
- Landing of special operations forces
- Attack of land targets
- Protection of task forces and merchant shipping
- Denial of sea areas to an enemy

Some theorists such as military historian John Keegan have argued that the extreme vulnerability of surface ships (when facing nations of a similar technological level) to aerial and ship-ship missile attacks will eventually lead to a trend for all types of naval vessels to receive submarine versions.

While the United State Navy says that "Submarines require no vulnerable underway logistics chain nor depend on mutual defense from other platforms for survivability."

Chapter 12

SPACE WARFARE

Space Warfare is combat that takes place in outer space, i.e. outside the atmosphere. Technically, as a distinct classification it refers to battles where the targets themselves are in space. Space warfare therefore includes ground-to-space warfare, such as attacking satellites from the Earth, as well as space-to-space warfare, such as satellites attacking satellites. It does not include the use of satellites for espionage, surveillance, or military communications, however useful those activities might be. It does not technically include space-to-ground warfare, where orbital objects attack ground, sea or air targets directly, but the public and media frequently use the term to include any conflict which includes space as a theater of operations, regardless of the intended target. For example, a rapid delivery system in which troops are deployed from orbit might be described as "space warfare," even though the military uses the term as described above.

A film was produced by the U.S. Military in the early 1960s called Space and National Security which depicted space warfare. From 1985 to 2002 there was a United States Space Command, which in 2002 merged with the United States Strategic Command. There is a Russian Space Force, which was established on August 10, 1992, and which became an independent section of the Russian military on June 1, 2001.

Only a few incidents of space warfare have occurred in world history, and all were training missions, as opposed to actions against real opposing forces. In the mid-1980s a USAF pilot in an F-15 successfully shot down the P78-1, a communications satellite in a 345 mile (555 km) orbit. In 2007 the People's Republic of China used a missile system to destroy one of its obsolete satellites (see 2007 Chinese anti-satellite missile test), and in 2008 the United States similarly destroyed its malfunctioning satellite USA 193. To date, there have been no human casualties resulting from conflict in space, nor has any ground target been successfully neutralized from orbit.

International treaties governing space limit or regulate conflicts in space and limit the installation of weapon systems, especially nuclear weapons.

HISTORY

Early efforts to conduct space warfare were directed at space-to-space warfare, as ground-to-space systems were considered to be too slow and too isolated by Earth's atmosphere and gravity to be effective. The history of active space warfare development goes back to the 1960s when the Soviet Union began the Almaz project, a project designed to give them the ability to do on-orbit inspections of satellites and destroy them if needed. Similar planning in the United States took the form of the Blue Gemini project, which consisted of modified Gemini capsules that would be able to deploy weapons and perform surveillance.

An ASAT (anti-satellite) missile being launched in 1985.

One early test of electronic space warfare took place in 1963 when the United States exploded a ground-launched nuclear weapon in space to test the effects of an electromagnetic pulse. The result was a deactivation of many then-orbiting satellites, both American and Soviet. The deleterious and unfocused effects of the EMP test led to the banning of nuclear weapons in space in the Outer Space Treaty of 1968. (See High altitude nuclear explosion.)

Through the 1970s, the Soviet Union continued their project and test-fired a cannon to test space station defense. This was considered too dangerous to do with a crew on board, however, so the test was conducted after the crew had returned to Earth.

Space warfare strongly influenced the final design of the United States Space Shuttle. The distinctive delta wing shape was needed if the shuttle were to launch a military payload towards the Soviet Union and perform an immediate de-orbit after one rotation to avoid being shot down.

Both the Soviets and the United States developed anti-satellite weaponry designed to shoot down satellites. While early efforts paralleled other space-to-space warfare concepts, the United States was able in the 1980s to develop ground-to-space laser anti-satellite weapons. None of these systems is known to be active today; however, a less powerful civilian version of the ground-to-space laser system is commonly used in the astronomical technique of adaptive optics. China successfully tested a ballistic missile-launched anti-satellite weapon on January 11, 2007 (see: 2007 Chinese anti-satellite missile test). This resulted in harsh criticism from the United States of America, Britain, and Japan.

SPACE WARFARE SYSTEM

A space system has three segments, each of which, in principle, offers opportunities for attack to an enemy. The system comprises: (i) the satellite, perhaps the constellation of satellites in orbit; (ii) the up and down links to and from the orbiting vehicle, commands from the ground stations and information flow from the satellite; (iii) and the ground station that controls the behaviour of the satellite and distributes its information to the users."

THEORETICAL SPACE WEAPONRY

BALLISTIC WARFARE

In the late 1970s and through the 1980s the Soviet Union and the United States theorized, designed and in some cases even tested an astonishing variety of bizarre and exotic weaponry designed for warfare in outer space. Space warfare was seen primarily as an extension of nuclear warfare, and so many theoretical systems were based around the destruction or defense of ground and sea-based missiles. Space-based missiles were not a target due to the Outer Space Treaty, which banned the use, testing or storage of nuclear weapons outside the Earth's atmosphere. Systems proposed ranged from measures as simple as ground and space-based anti-missiles to railguns, space based lasers, orbital mines and other such futuristic weaponry. Deployment of these systems was seriously considered in the mid-1980s under the banner of the Strategic Defense Initiative (popularly known as Star Wars). If the Cold War had continued, then many of these systems could have seen deployment: the United States got as far as developing working railguns, and a laser that could destroy missiles at range, though the power requirements of both were phenomenal, and the ranges and firing cycles utterly impractical.

ELECTRONIC WARFARE

With the end of the Cold War and continued development of satellite and electronics technology, attention was focused on space as a supporting theatre for conventional warfare. Currently, military operations in space primarily concern either the vast tactical advantages of satellite-based surveillance, communications, and positioning systems or mechanisms used to deprive an opponent of said tactical advantages. Accordingly, most space-borne proposals which would traditionally be considered "weapons" (a communications or reconnaissance satellite may be useful in warfare but isn't generally classified as a weapon) are designed to jam, sabotage, and outright destroy enemy satellites, and conversely to protect friendly satellites against such attacks. To this end, the US (and presumably other countries) is researching groups of small, highly mobile satellites called "microsats" (about the size of a refrigerator) and "picosats" (approximately 1 cubic foot (H"900 cm^3) in volume) nimble enough to maneuver around and interact with other orbiting objects to repair, sabotage, hijack, or simply collide with them.

KINETIC BOMBARDMENT

Another theorized use involves the extension of conventional weaponry into orbit for deployment against ground targets. Though international treaties bar the deployment of nuclear missiles outside the atmosphere, other categories of weapons are largely unregulated. Traditional ground-based weapons are generally not useful in orbital environments, and few if any would survive re-entry even if they were, but as early as the 1950s, the United States has toyed with kinetic bombardment, i.e. orbiting magazines of non-explosive projectiles to be dropped onto hardened targets from low-earth orbit. Kinetic weapons have always been widespread in conventional warfare—bullets, arrows, swords, clubs, etc.—but the energy a projectile would gain while falling from orbit would make such a weapon rival all but the most powerful explosives. A direct hit would presumably destroy all but the most hardened targets without the need for nuclear weapons. Such a system would involve a 'spotter' satellite, which would identify targets from orbit with high-power sensors, and a nearby 'magazine' satellite to de-orbit a long, needle-like tungsten dart onto it with a small rocket motor or just dropping a very big rock from orbit (such as an asteroid). This would be more useful against a larger but less hardened target (such as a city).Though a common device in science fiction, there is no publicly-available evidence that any such systems have actually been deployed by any nation.

DIRECTED-ENERGY WEAPONS

Weapon systems that fall under this category include lasers, linear particle accelerators or particle-beam based weaponry, microwaves and plasma-based weaponry. Most of these weapons are theoretical or impractical to implement currently, aside from lasers which are starting to be used more widely in terrestrial warfare. Particle beams involve the acceleration of charged or neutral particles in a stream towards a target at extremely high velocities, the impact of which creates a reaction causing immense damage.

PRACTICAL CONSIDERATIONS

Space warfare is likely to be conducted at far greater distances and speeds than terrestrial combat. The vast distances involved pose difficult challenges for targeting and tracking, as even light requires a few seconds to traverse ranges measured in hundreds of thousands of kilometers. For example, if attempting to fire upon a target at the distance of the Moon from the Earth, the image one sees reflects the position of the target slightly more than a second earlier. A projectile weapon will take at least a few seconds to cross that distance, and even a laser will need a measurable amount of time. Additionally, the distance means that an error of even a fraction of a degree in the firing solution could result in a miss by thousands of kilometers. When attempting to hit a target moving at the tremendous speeds involved in space travel—a geostationary satellite moves at a speed of 3.07 km/s whereas objects in low earth orbit can move at up to 8 km/s—the difficulty is magnified.

Regardless of one's reasons for going to war, at present those reasons are not likely to suggest major targets located in space. Most of the main theories which attempt to explain human proclivity for warfare—psychological, sociological, demographic, economic, political, or otherwise—would not indicate space as a likely location of conflict until a significant population is engaged in large-scale activity there· Until then, space warfare is likely to take a supporting role to conventional, terrestrial warfare.

Aside from applications such as communications, reconnaissance, GPS, and the like, which would be difficult or impossible without satellites, there do not appear to be any major advantages to basing weapons systems in space. The main reason is simply cost. Space warfare that involves humans being deployed in space to fight each other is not currently practical because of the difficulty and cost of sustaining human life in space, especially over long periods of time.

Additionally, there are few things that could be accomplished by space warfare that any nation wealthy enough to finance them cannot accomplish far more cheaply through conventional means. Raising any significant mass beyond Earth's gravity will always require a large amount of energy, and the cost increases with mass. For example, though kinetic bombardment potentially offers the ability to strike any target anywhere in the world within minutes, both the United States and Russia, possibly the only nations with the resources and facilities necessary to implement such a system, have sufficiently long-range supersonic bombers that the same target could already be destroyed in a matter of hours at a mere fraction of the cost.

POSSIBLE WARFARE OVER SPACE

Most of the world's communications systems rely heavily on the presence of satellites in orbit around Earth. Protecting these assets might seriously motivate nations dependent upon them to consider deploying more space-based weaponry, especially in conflicts involving advanced countries with access to space. Even without the further militarisation of space, a future conflict conducted largely on the ground through conventional means might well be sparked by actions conducted entirely in space.

Relatedly, though no infrastructure or economic interests exist at the moment to warrant the occupation of terrain on other terrestrial bodies within the Solar system, or to occupy orbital trajectories in outer space, some futurists have predicted[who?] that should such infrastructure be deployed, space-faring nations may go to war for control of extraplanetary resources. Such a conflict could easily involve warfare both within and outside the earth's atmosphere. One suggested point of conflict is the helium-3 resources in the south polar region of the Moon. Russia has already stated its intention of developing this resource, and the Chinese lunar mission is scheduled to land in that area in 2024. However, the high abundance of this isotope would make war quite unlikely.

SPACE WARFARE IN FICTION

Space warfare is a topic often touched upon in science fiction, with a wide range of realism and plausibility, from stories based on anticipated future technology and tactics, to fantasy or historically based scenarios that happen to take place in a science-fiction background. Some portray a space-borne military will be similar to an Air Force, whereas others depict a more naval analog. Still others suggest forces more like marines: highly mobile forces engaged in interplanetary and interstellar warfare but with most of the actual conflict occurring in terrestrial environments.

Both kinetic energy and directed energy weapons are often portrayed, along with various military space vessels. The Lensman series by E. E. Smith is an early example, which also inspired the term Space Opera due to the grandiose scales of the stories. The Ender's Game series by Orson Scott Card is a notable example in that it makes conjecture as to what sort of tactics and training would be required for war in outer space. Other science fiction authors have also delved into the tactics of space combat, such as David Weber in his Honorverse series as well as Larry Niven and Jerry Pournelle in their Mote in God's Eye series. A more recent example would be Alastair Reynolds' Revelation Space universe, which explores combat at relativistic speeds. Robert A. Heinlein's Starship Troopers is perhaps one of the best-known and earliest explorations of the "space marine" idea.

Spaced based vehicular combat is portrayed in many movies and video games, most notably the Halo Series, Star Wars, Descent, Macross and Star Trek. Games such as the Homeworld series provide interesting concepts for space warfare, such as the use of plasma-based projectors that receive their energy from a ships propulsion system, and automated unmanned space combat vehicles.

The fictional worlds in which space warfare occurs are far too numerous to list, but popular examples include Star Trek (in all of its various incarnations), Star Wars, Babylon 5, Buck Rogers, Flash Gordon, Battlestar Galactica, Mass Effect, Stargate SG-1, Atlantis, Halo Series and many comic book franchises. Video games have frequently touched the subject, with the Wing Commander franchise serving as a prototypical example. Note that very few games attempt to simulate an environment with realistic distances and speeds, though Independence War and Frontier: Elite II both do, as does the board game Attack Vector: Tactical.

Chapter 13

ELECTRONIC WARFARE

Electronic Warfare (EW) refers to any action involving the use of the electromagnetic spectrum (EMS) or directed energy (DE) to control the EMS or to attack the enemy.

The purpose of EW is to deny the opponent an advantage in the EMS and ensure friendly unimpeded access to the EM spectrum portion of the information environment. EW can be applied from air, sea, land, and space by manned and unmanned systems. EW includes three major subdivisions: electronic attack (EA), Electronic Protect (EP), and electronic warfare support (ES).

DIVISIONS

ELECTRONIC WARFARE SUPPORT

Electronic Warfare Support (ES), is the subdivision of EW involving actions tasked by, or under direct control of, an operational commander to search for, intercept, identify, and locate or localize sources of intentional and unintentional radiated Electromagnetic (EM) energy for the purpose of immediate threat recognition, targeting, planning, and conduct of future operations.

An overlapping discipline, Signals Intelligence (SIGINT) is the related process of analysing and identifying the intercepted frequencies (e.g. as a cell phone or RADAR). SIGINT is broken into three categories: ELINT, COMINT, and FISINT.

Where these activities are under the control of an operational commander and being applied for the purpose of situational awareness, threat recognition, or EM targeting, they also serve the purpose of Electronic Warfare Support (ES).

Government, law enforcement, and military operational techniques are governed by US Codes for use with intelligence gathering procedures.

ELECTRONIC ATTACK

Electronic attack (EA) or electronic countermeasures (ECM) involves the use of the electromagnetic energy, or anti-radiation weapons to attack personnel, facilities, or equipment with the intent of degrading, neutralising, or destroying enemy combat capability and is considered a form of fires (see Joint Publication [JP] 3-09, Joint Fire Support).

EA operations can be detected by an adversary due to their active transmissions. Many modern EA techniques are considered to be highly classified. Examples of EA include communcations jamming, IADS suppression, DE/LASER attack, expendable decoys (e.g., flares and chaff), and counter radio controlled improvised explosive device (C-RCIED) systems.

ELECTRONIC PROTECTION

Electronic Protection (EP) (also known as electronic protective measures (EPM) or electronic counter countermeasures (ECCM)) involves actions taken to protect personnel, facilities, and equipment from any effects of friendly or enemy use of the electromagnetic spectrum that degrade, neutralize, or destroy friendly combat capability. EP should not be confused with self-protection (jamming).

The use of flare rejection logic on an IR missile to counter an adversary's use of flares is EP. While defensive EA actions and EP both protect personnel, facilities, capabilities, and equipment, EP protects from the EFFECTS of EA (friendly and/or adversary). Other examples of EP include spread-spectrum technologies, use of Joint Restricted Frequency List (JRFL), emissions control (EMCON), and low observability or "stealth".

Chapter 14

CYBER WARFARE

Cyber Warfare, (also known as cyberwar and Cyber Warfare), is the use of computers and the Internet in conducting warfare in cyberspace.

CYBER WARRIOR

A Cyber Warrior is a person who is highly skilled in the art of Cyber Warfare. Governments, their militaries, law enforcement, and the private sector around the world are taking the initiative to train their people in the field of cyber warfare. The necessary skills that a cyber warrior shall possess will vary in magnitude; however, the key skills shall include: information security, hacking, espionage, and computer forensics.

CYBER WARFARE TERRAIN

The cyber warfare terrain includes all aspects of the Internet from the backbones of the web, to the Internet Service Providers, to the varying types of data communication mediums and network equipment. The terrain does not end in a field, mountain range, or a coastline, rather the cyber warfare terrain encompasses the cities, communities, and the world, in which we live. The 21st century battlefield is comprised of many components that include the Internet and all things that connect from a computer to the Internet. This would include: web servers, enterprise information systems, client server systems, datacommunication media [i.e., Cable, DSL, T1-T3, OC12-OC48, frame relay, ATM, varying types of satellites, oceanic cables, etc.], network equipment, and the desktops/laptops that are in our businnesses and homes. The terrain will also encompass information systems like the electrical grids, telecommunication systems, and various corporate and military robotics systems.

CYBER WARFARE TACTICS

There are several methods of attack in cyberwarfare, this list is ranked in order of mildest to most severe

- **Cyber espionage:** Cyber espionage is the act or practice of obtaining secrets (sensitive, proprietary or classified information) from individuals, competitors, rivals, groups, governments and enemies also for military, political, or economic advantage using illegal exploitation methods on internet, networks, software and or computers.
- **Web vandalism:** Attacks that deface web pages, or denial-of-service attacks. This is normally swiftly combated and of little harm.
- **Propaganda:** Political messages can be spread through or to anyone with access to the internet or any device that receives digital transmissions from the Internet to include cell phones, PDAs, etc.
- **Gathering data:** Classified information that is not handled securely can be intercepted and even modified, making espionage possible from the other side of the world. See Titan Rain and Moonlight Maze.
- **Distributed Denial-of-Service Attacks:** Large numbers of computers controlled by one person launch a DoS attack against systems
- **Equipment disruption:** Military activities that use computers and satellites for coordination are at risk from this type of attack. Orders and communications can be intercepted or replaced, putting soldiers at risk.
- **Attacking critical infrastructure:** Power, water, fuel, communications, commercial and transportation are all vulnerable to a cyber attack.

- **Compromised Counterfeit Hardware:** Common hardware used in computers and networks that have malicious software hidden inside the software, firmware or even the micro-processors.

REPORTED CYBER THREATS

The Internet security company McAfee stated in their 2007 annual report that approximately 120 countries have been developing ways to use the Internet as a weapon and target financial markets, government computer systems and utilities.

In activities reminiscent of the Cold War, which caused countries to engage in clandestine activities, intelligence agencies are routinely testing networks looking for weaknesses. These techniques for probing weaknesses in the internet and global networks are growing more sophisticated every year.

Jeff Green, senior vice president of McAfee Avert Labs, was quoted as saying "Cybercrime is now a global issue. It has evolved significantly and is no longer just a threat to industry and individuals but increasingly to national security." They predicted that future attacks will be even more sophisticated. "Attacks have progressed from initial curiosity probes to well-funded and well-organized operations for political, military, economic and technical espionage,"

The report from McAfee says that China is at the forefront of the cyberwar. China has been accused of cyber-attacks on India and Germany and the United States. China denies knowledge of these attacks. Arguments have been expressed regarding China's involvement indicating, in the methods of computer Hackers who use zombie computers, it only indicates that China has the highest number of computers that are vulnerable to be controlled.

In April 2007, Estonia came under cyber attack in the wake of relocation of the Bronze Soldier of Tallinn. Estonian authorities, including Estonian Foreign Minister Urmas Paet accused the Kremlin of direct involvement in the cyber attacks. Estonia's defence minister later admitted he had no evidence linking cyber attacks to Russian authorities

ELECTRICAL POWER GRID

The federal government of the United States admits that the electric power transmission is susceptible to cyberwarfare. The United States Department of Homeland Security works with industry to identify vulnerabilities and to help industry enhance the security of control system networks, the federal government is also working to ensure that security is built in as the next generation of "smart grid" networks are developed. In April 2009, reports surfaced that China and Russia had infiltrated the U.S. electrical grid and left behind software programmes that could be used to disrupt the system, according to current and former national security officials. The North American Electric Reliability Corporation (NERC) has issued a public notice that warns that the electrical grid is not adequately protected from cyber attack. China denies intruding into the U.S. electrical grid. One counter measure would be to disconnect the power grid from the Internet to decrease the likelihood of attack. Massive power outages caused by a cyber attack, could disrupt the economy, distract from a simultaneous military attack, or create a national trauma.

History of Cyber Attacks

- The United States had come under attack from computers and computer networks situated in China and Russia. See Titan Rain and Moonlight Maze.
- On May 17, 2007 Estonia came under cyber attack. The Estonian parliament, ministries, banks, and media were targeted.
- On 14 December 2007 the website of the Kyrgyz Central Election Commission was defaced during its election. The message left on the website read "This site has been hacked by Dream of Estonian organisation". During the election campaigns and riots preceding the election, there were cases of Denial-of-service attacks against the Kyrgyz ISPs.

- Georgian and Azerbaijani sites were attacked by hackers during the 2008 South Ossetia War.
- On March 28, 2009, a cyber spy network using servers mainly based in China has tapped into classified documents from government and private organisations in 103 countries, including the computers of Tibetan exiles, but China denies the claim.
- In July 2009, there were a series of coordinated cyber attacks against major government, news media, and financial websites in South Korea and the United States.

CYBER COUNTERINTELLIGENCE

Cyber counter-intelligence are measures to identify, penetrate, or neutralize foreign operations that use cyber means as the primary tradecraft methodology, as well as foreign intelligence service collection efforts that use traditional methods to gauge cyber capabilities and intentions.

- On April 7, 2009, The Pentagon announced they spent more than $100 million in the last six months responding to and repairing damage from cyber attacks and other computer network problems.
- On April 1, 2009, U.S. lawmakers are pushing for the appointment of a White House cyber security "czar" to dramatically escalate U.S. defenses against cyber attacks, crafting proposals that would empower the government to set and enforce security standards for private industry for the first time.
- On February 9, 2009, the White House announced that it will conduct a review of the nation's cyber security to ensure that the Federal government of the United States cyber security initiatives are appropriately integrated, resourced and coordinated with the United States Congress and the private sector.
- In the wake of the cyberwar of 2007 waged against Estonia, NATO established the Cooperative Cyber Defence Centre

of Excellence (CCD CoE) in Tallinn, Estonia, in order to enhance the organisation's cyber defence capability. The center was formally established on the 14th of May, 2008, and it received full accreditation by NATO and attained the status of International Military Organisation on the 28th of October, 2008. Since Estonia has led international efforts to fight cybercrime, the United States Federal Bureau of Investigation says it will permanently base a computer crime expert in Estonia in 2009 to help fight international threats against computer systems.

PROJECT OF THE INTERNATIONAL CONVENTION ON PROHIBITION OF CYBERWAR

A Ukrainian professor of International Law, Alexander Merezhko, has developed a project called the International Convention on Prohibition of Cyberwar in Internet. According to this project, cyberwar is defined as the use of Internet and related technological means by one state against political, economic, technological and information sovereignty and independence of any other state. Professor Merezhko's project suggests that the Internet ought to remain free from warfare tactics and be treated as an international landmark. He states that the Internet (cyberspace) is a "common heritage of mankind."

DIRECTED-ENERGY WARFARE

Directed-Energy Warfare at the turn of the 21st century is an intelligence operations offensive capability involving actions taken to destroy or damage equipment, facilities, and injure or kill personnel using directed-energy weapons, devices and counter-measures. It applies largely to the hostile use or denial of the electromagnetic spectrum.

Chapter 15

NUCLEAR WARFARE

Not to be confused with nuclear deterrence or nuclear blackmail, i.e. the achievement of military or political ends through the possession of nuclear weapons without their actual use.

The Titan II Intercontinental ballistic missile (ICBM) carried a 9 Mt W53 warhead, one of the most powerful nuclear weapons fielded by the United States during the Cold War.

Nuclear Warfare, or Atomic Warfare, is a military conflict in which nuclear weapons are used. Compared to conventional warfare, nuclear warfare is vastly more destructive in range and extent of damage. A major nuclear exchange could have severe long-term effects, primarily from radiation release but also from possible atmospheric pollution leading to nuclear winter, that could last for decades, centuries, or even millennia after the initial attack. Nuclear war is considered to bear existential risk for civilisation on Earth. The first, and to date only, nuclear war was the atomic bombings of Hiroshima and Nagasaki, Japan by the United States shortly before the end of World War II. At the time of those bombings, the United States was the only country to possess atomic weapons. After World War II, nuclear weapons were also developed by the United Kingdom, France, the Soviet Union, and the People's Republic of China, which contributed to the state of conflict and tension that became known as the Cold War. In the 1970s, India and Pakistan, countries openly hostile to each other, developed nuclear weapons.

After the collapse of the Soviet Union in 1991 and the resultant end of the Cold War, the threat of a major nuclear war between the superpowers was generally thought to have receded. Since then, concern over nuclear weapons has shifted to the prevention of localized nuclear conflicts resulting from nuclear proliferation, and the threat of nuclear terrorism.

TYPES OF NUCLEAR WAR

The possibility of using nuclear weapons in war is usually divided into two subgroups, each with different effects and potentially fought with different types of nuclear armaments.

The first, a limited nuclear war (sometimes attack or exchange), refers to a small scale use of nuclear weapons by one or more parties. A "limited nuclear war" would most likely consist of a limited exchange between two nuclear superpowers targeting each other's military facilities, either as an attempt to pre-emptively cripple the enemy's ability to attack as a defensive measure or as a prelude to an invasion by conventional forces as an offensive measure. It will also refer to a nuclear war between minor nuclear powers, who lack the ability to deliver a decisive strike. This term would apply to any limited use of nuclear weapons, which may involve either military or civilian targets.

The second, a full-scale nuclear war, consists of large numbers of weapons used in an attack aimed at an entire country, including military, economic and civilian targets. Such an attack would seek to destroy the entire economic, social, and military infrastructure of a nation by means of an overwhelming nuclear attack.

Some Cold War strategists argued that a limited nuclear war could be possible between two heavily armed superpowers (such as the United States and the Soviet Union) and if so several predicted that a limited war could "escalate" into an all-out war. Others have called limited nuclear war "global nuclear holocaust in slow motion" arguing that once such a war took place others would be sure to follow over a period of decades, effectively rendering the planet uninhabitable in the same way that a "full-scale nuclear war" between superpowers would, only taking a much longer and more agonising path to achieve the same result.

Even the most optimistic predictions of the effects of a major nuclear exchange foresee the death of a hundred million people within a very short amount of time; more pessimistic predictions argue that a full-scale nuclear war could bring about the extinction of the human race or its near extinction with a handful of survivors (mainly in remote areas) reduced to a pre-medieval quality of life and life expectancy for centuries after and cause permanent damage to most complex life on the planet, Earth's ecosystems, and the global climate, particularly if predictions of nuclear winter are accurate. It is in this latter mode that nuclear warfare is usually alluded to as a doomsday scenario. Such hypothesized civilisation-ending nuclear wars have been a staple of the science fiction literature and film genre for decades.

Either a limited or full-scale nuclear exchange could be an accidental nuclear war, in which a nuclear war is triggered unintentionally. Possible triggers for this scenario have included malfunctioning early warning devices and targeting computers, deliberate malfeasance by rogue military commanders, accidental straying of planes into enemy airspace, reactions to unannounced missile tests during tense diplomatic periods, reactions to military exercises, mistranslated or miscommunicated messages, and so forth. A number of these scenarios did actually occur during the Cold War, though none resulted in a nuclear exchange. Many such scenarios have been depicted in popular culture, such as in the 1962 novel Fail-Safe (released as a film in 1964) and the film Dr. Strangelove or: How I Learned to Stop Worrying and Love the Bomb, also released in 1964.

HISTORY

HIROSHIMA TO SEMIPALATINSK

The United States is the only nation to have ever used nuclear weapons during war, using two atomic bombs on the Japanese cities of Hiroshima and Nagasaki in 1945. For more information, see Atomic bombings of Hiroshima and Nagasaki.

The explosion at Nagasaki, Japan.

Immediately after the bombings of Japan, the status of atomic weapons in international and military relations was unclear. Presumably, the United States hoped atomic weapons could offset the Soviet Union's superior conventional ground forces in Eastern Europe, and possibly be used to pressure Soviet leader Joseph Stalin into concessions. Despite Stalin's palpable fear of the bomb, he was pursuing his own atomic capabilities through scientific research and espionage against the American programme. The Soviets believed that the Americans were unlikely to begin another world war with their limited nuclear arsenal and the Americans were not confident they could prevent a Soviet takeover of Europe, despite their atomic advantage.

Within the United States the authority to produce and develop nuclear weapons was removed from military control and put instead under the civilian control of the United States Atomic Energy Commission. This decision reflected an understanding that nuclear weapons had unique risks and benefits separate from other military technology.

Convair B-36 bomber

For several years after World War II, the US developed and maintained a strategic force based on the Convair B-36 bomber that would be able to attack any potential enemy from bomber bases in the US. It deployed atomic bombs around the world for potential use in conflicts. Over a period of a few years, many in the US defense community became increasingly convinced of the invincibility of the United States to a nuclear attack. Indeed, it became generally believed that the threat of nuclear war would deter any strike against the United States.

Many proposals were suggested to put all US nuclear weapons under international control—for example, by the newly formed United Nations—as an effort to deter both their usage and an arms race. However no terms could be arrived at that made either the United States or the USSR feel secure—the US was not willing to give up its atomic monopoly, and the USSR did not trust UN inspections on its soil.

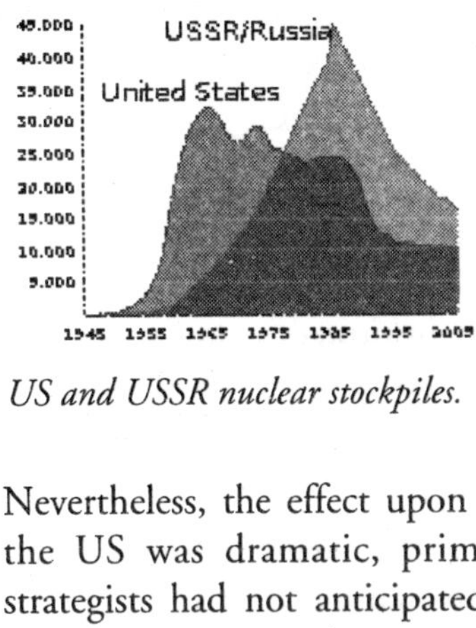

US and USSR nuclear stockpiles.

On August 29, 1949 the USSR tested its first nuclear weapon at Semipalatinsk in Kazakhstan (see also Soviet atomic bomb project). Scientists in the United States from the Manhattan Project had warned that, in time, the Soviet Union would certainly develop nuclear capabilities of its own. Nevertheless, the effect upon military thinking and planning in the US was dramatic, primarily because American military strategists had not anticipated the Soviets would "catch up" so soon. However, at this time, they had not discovered that the Russians had conducted significant espionage of the project from spies at Los Alamos, the most significant of which was done by the theoretical physicist Klaus Fuchs. The first Soviet bomb was more or less a deliberate copy of the Fat Man device.

With the monopoly over nuclear technology broken, world-wide nuclear proliferation accelerated. The United Kingdom tested its first independent atomic bomb in 1952, followed by France in 1960 and then the People's Republic of China in 1964. While much smaller than the arsenals of the USA and the USSR, Western Europe's nuclear reserves were nevertheless a significant factor in strategic planning during the Cold War. A top-secret white paper produced for the British Government in 1959, compiled by the

Royal Air Force, estimated that British atomic bombers were capable of destroying key cities and military targets in the Soviet Union, with an estimated 16 million deaths in the USSR (half of whom were estimated to be killed on impact and the rest fatally injured) before bomber aircraft from the United States' Strategic Air Command reached their targets.

1950s

Though the USSR had nuclear weapon capabilities in the beginning of the Cold War, the US still had an advantage in terms of bombers and weapons. In any exchange of hostilities, the US would have been capable of bombing the USSR, while the USSR would have more difficulties arranging the reverse.

The widespread introduction of jet-powered interceptor aircraft upset this balance somewhat by reducing the effectiveness of the US bomber fleet. In 1949 Curtis LeMay was placed in command of the Strategic Air Command and instituted a programme to update the bomber fleet to one that was all-jet. During the early 1950s the B-47 and B-52 were introduced, providing the ability to bomb the USSR more easily.

Before the development of a capable strategic missile force in the Soviet Union, much of the war-fighting doctrine held by western nations revolved around using a large number of smaller nuclear weapons used in a tactical role. It is debatable whether such use could be considered "limited" however, because it was believed that the US would use their own strategic weapons (mainly bombers at the time) should the USSR deploy any kind of nuclear weapon against civilian targets. Douglas MacArthur, an American general, was fired by President Harry Truman, partially because he persistently requested permission to use his own discretion in deciding whether to use atomic weapons on the People's Republic of China in 1951 (as the Korean War was raging).

Several scares about the increasing ability of the USSR's strategic bomber forces surfaced during the 1950s. The defensive response by the US was to deploy a fairly strong layered defense consisting of interceptor aircraft and anti-aircraft missiles, like the Nike, and guns, like the Skysweeper, near larger cities. However this was a small response compared to the construction of a huge fleet of nuclear bombers. The principal nuclear strategy was to massively penetrate the USSR. Because such a large area could not be defended against this overwhelming attack in any credible way, the USSR would lose any exchange.

This logic became ingrained in US nuclear doctrine and persisted for the duration of the Cold War. As long as the strategic US nuclear forces could overwhelm their USSR counterparts, a Soviet preemptive strike could be averted. Moreover, the USSR could not afford to build any reasonable counterforce as the economic output of the United States was far larger than that of the Soviets, and they would be unable to achieve nuclear parity.

Soviet nuclear doctrine, however, did not match US nuclear doctrine. Soviet planning expected a large-scale nuclear exchange followed by a conventional war which itself would involve heavy use of tactical nuclear weapons. Unfortunately, US doctrine rather assumed that Soviet doctrine was similar—the mutual in Mutually Assured Destruction necessarily requiring that the other side see things in much the same way, rather than believing, as the Soviets did, that they could fight a large-scale, combined nuclear and conventional war.

A revolution in nuclear strategic thought occurred with the introduction of the intercontinental ballistic missile (ICBM), which the USSR first successfully tested in August 1957. In order to deliver a warhead to a target, a missile was more cost-effective than a bomber, and enjoyed a higher survivability due to the enormous difficulty of interception of the ICBMs due to their high altitude and speed. The USSR could now afford to achieve nuclear parity with the US in terms of raw numbers, although for a time they appeared to have chosen not to.

Photos of Soviet missile sites set off a wave of panic in the US military, something the launch of Sputnik would do for the public a few months later. Politicians, notably then-US Senator John

Kennedy suggested a "missile gap" between the Soviets and the US. The US military gave missile development programmes the highest national priority, and several spy aircraft and reconnaissance satellites were designed and deployed to observe Soviet progress.

1960s

Issues came to a head during the Cuban Missile Crisis in 1962. The Soviet Union placed medium range missiles 90 miles (140 km) from the US — a move considered by many as a direct response to American Jupiter missiles placed in Turkey; however, these Jupiter missiles were already somewhat obsolete. After intense negotiation, the Soviets ended up removing the missiles from Cuba and decided to institute a massive building programme of their own.

RF-101 Voodoo reconnaissance photograph of the MRBM launch site in San Cristobal, Cuba (1962).

In exchange, the US dismantled its launch sites in Turkey, although this was done secretly and was not publicly revealed for over two decades. Khrushchev did not even reveal this part of the agreement when he came under fire by political opponents for mishandling the crisis. By the late 1960s, the number of ICBMs and warheads was so high on both sides that either the USA or USSR was capable of completely destroying the other country's infrastructure. Thus a balance of power system known as mutually assured destruction (MAD) came into being. It was thought that any full-scale exchange between the powers could not produce a victorious side and thus neither would risk initiating one. One drawback of this doctrine was the possibility of a nuclear war occurring without either side intentionally striking first. Early warning systems were notoriously error-prone. On 78 occasions in 1979, for example, a "missile display conference" was called to evaluate detections potentially threatening to the North American continent. Some of these were trivial errors, spotted quickly.

But several went to more serious levels. On September 26, 1983, Stanislav Petrov received convincing indications of a US first strike launch against the USSR but positively identified the warning as a false alarm. Though it is unclear what role Petrov's actions played in preventing a nuclear war, he has been honored by the United Nations for his actions.

Similar incidents happened many times in the US, due to failed computer chips flights of geese, test programmes, and bureaucratic failures to notify early warning military personnel of legitimate launches of test or weather missiles. For many years, US strategic bombers were kept airborne on a rotating basis round the clock, until the number and severity of accidents persuaded policymakers it was not worthwhile.

1970s

By the late 1970s, citizens in the US and USSR (and indeed the entire world) had been living with MAD for about a decade. It became deeply ingrained into the popular culture. Such an exchange would have killed many millions of individuals directly and possibly induced a nuclear winter which could have led to the death of a large portion of humanity and, potentially, the collapse of global civilisation.

In May 18, 1974, India conducted its first nuclear test in the Pokhran test range. The name of the operation was Smiling Buddha and India termed the test as a "peaceful nuclear explosion".

According to the 1980 United Nations report General and Complete Disarmament: Comprehensive Study on Nuclear Weapons: Report of the Secretary-General, it was estimated that in total there were approximately 40,000 nuclear warheads in existence at that time with a total yield of approximately 13,000 megatons of TNT. By comparison, when the volcano Mount Tambora erupted in 1815 (turning 1816 into the Year Without A Summer due to the levels of ash expelled), it exploded with a force of roughly 1000 megatons of TNT. Many people believed that a full-scale nuclear war could result in the extinction of the human species, though not all analysts agreed on the assumptions required for these models.

The idea that any nuclear conflict would eventually escalate was a challenge for military strategists. This challenge was particularly severe for the United States and its NATO allies because it was believed until the 1970s that a Soviet tank invasion of Western Europe would quickly overwhelm NATO conventional forces, leading to the necessity of escalating to tactical nuclear weapons.

A number of interesting concepts were developed. Early ICBMs were inaccurate, which led to the concept of countervalue strikes — attacks directly on the enemy population leading to a collapse of the enemy's will to fight. However, it appears that this was the American interpretation of the Soviet stance while the Soviet strategy was never clearly anti-population. During the Cold War the USSR invested in extensive protected civilian infrastructure such as large nuclear-proof bunkers and non-perishable food stores. In the US, by comparison, smaller scale civil defense programmes were instituted starting in the 1950s where schools and other public buildings had basements stocked with non-perishable food supplies, canned water, first aid, dosimeter and Geiger counter radiation measuring devices. Many of the locations were given "Fallout Shelter" designation signs. Also, CONELRAD Radio information systems were adopted, whereby the commercial radio sector would broadcast on two AM frequencies in the event of a CD emergency.

These two frequencies can be seen on 50's vintage radios on online auction sites and museums, with many of these radios still in use on tabletops across America. Also, the occasional backyard fallout shelter was built by private individuals.

The US also made a point during this period of targeting their missiles on Soviet population centers rather than military targets. If the Soviets attacked first, then there would be no point in destroying empty missile silos that had already launched; the only thing left to hit would be cities. By contrast, if the US had gone to great lengths to protect their citizens and targeted the enemy's silos, that might have led the Russians to believe the US was planning a first strike, where they would eliminate Soviet missiles while still in their silos and be able to survive a weakened counter attack in their reinforced bunkers. In this way, both sides were (theoretically) assured that the other would not strike first, and a war without a first strike will not occur.

This strategy had one major and possibly critical flaw, soon realised by military analysts but highly underplayed by the US military: Conventional NATO forces in the European theatre of war were considered to be outnumbered by similar Soviet and Warsaw Pact forces, and while the western countries invested heavily in high-tech conventional weapons to counter this (partly perceived) imbalance, it was assumed that in case of a major Soviet attack (commonly perceived as the "red tanks rolling towards the North Sea" scenario) that NATO, in the face of conventional defeat, would soon have no other choice but to resort to tactical nuclear strikes. Most analysts agreed that once the first nuclear exchange had occurred, escalation to global nuclear war would become almost inevitable.

As missile technology improved, the emphasis moved to counter-force strikes: ones that directly attacked the enemy's means of waging war. This was the predominant doctrine from the late 1960s onwards. Additionally the development of warheads (at least in the US) moved towards delivering a small explosive force more accurately and with a "cleaner" blast (with fewer long-lasting radioactive isotopes). In any conflict therefore, damage would have been initially limited to military targets, there may well have been "withholds" for targets near civilian areas. The argument was that the destruction of a city would be a military advantage to the attacked. The enemy had used up weapons and a threat in the destruction while the attacked was relieved of the need to defend the city and still had their entire military potential untouched.

Only if a nuclear conflict were extended into a number of "spasm" strikes would direct strikes against civilians occur, as the more accurate weapons would be expended early; if one side were "losing", the potential for using less accurate submarine-launched missiles would occur.

The 1980s

In the late seventies and early eighties the balance, in terms of nuclear weapons, shifted towards the Soviets. However, with the ascension to the presidency by Ronald Reagan, the US renewed its commitment to a powerful military, which required large spending on military programmes. These programmes included spending on conventional and nuclear weapons systems, as well as defensive systems like Strategic Defense Initiative.

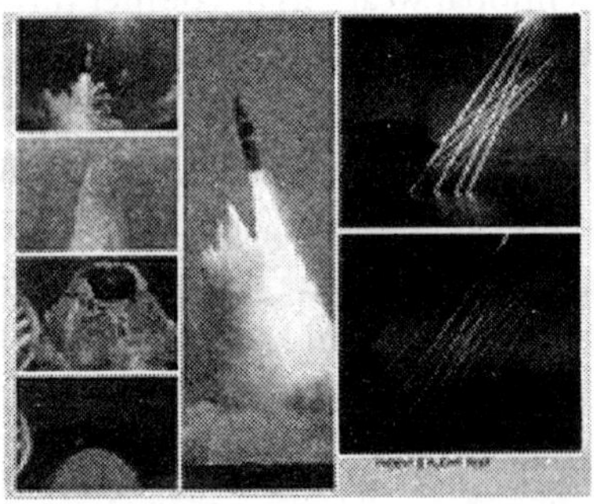

Montage of the launch of a Trident C4 SLBM and the paths of its reentry vehicles.

Another major shift in nuclear doctrine was the development of the submarine-launched ballistic (nuclear) missile, the SLBM.

It was hailed by some military theorists as a weapon that would make nuclear war less likely. SLBMs, which can move with stealth virtually anywhere in the world, give a nation a "second strike" capability. Before the advent of SLBMs, thinkers feared that a nation might be tempted to initiate a first strike if it felt confident that such a strike would incapacitate the nuclear arsenal of its enemy, making retaliation impossible. With the advent of SLBMs, no nation could be certain that a first strike would incapacitate its enemy's entire nuclear arsenal. To the contrary, it would have to fear a retaliatory second strike from SLBMs. Thus a first strike was much less of a feasible option, and nuclear war was held to be less likely.

However, it was soon realized that submarines could "sneak up" close to enemy coastlines and decrease the warning time—the time between detection of the launch and impact of the missile—from as much as half an hour to under three minutes. This effect was especially significant to the United States, Britain, and China, with their capitals all within 100 miles (160 km) of their coasts. Moscow was more secure from this type of threat. This greatly increased the credibility of a "surprise first strike" by one of the factions and theoretically made it possible to knock out or disrupt the chain of command before a counterstrike could be ordered. It strengthened the notion that a nuclear war could be "won", resulting not only in greatly increased tension, and increasing calls for fail-deadly control systems, but also in a dramatic increase in military spending. The submarines and their missile systems were very expensive (one fully equipped nuclear powered nuclear missile submarine could easily cost more than the entire GNP of a third world nation), but the greatest cost came in the development of both sea- and land-based anti-submarine defenses and in improving and strengthening the chain of command. As a result, military spending skyrocketed.

South Africa developed a nuclear weapon during the 1970s and early 1980s. It was operational for a brief period before being dismantled in the early 1990s.

The world came unusually close to nuclear war (although perhaps not as close as during the Cuban Missile Crisis) when the Soviet Union thought the NATO military exercise Able Archer 83 was a cover up to begin a nuclear strike. The Soviets responded by readying their nuclear arsenal. Soviet fears of an attack went away once the exercise concluded without incident.

POST–COLD WAR

Although the dissolution of the Soviet Union ended the Cold War and greatly reduced tensions between the United States and Russia (the Soviet Union's formal successor state), both nations remained in a "nuclear stand-off" due to the continuing presence of a significant number of warheads in both nations. Additionally, the end of the Cold War led the United States to become increasingly concerned with the development of nuclear technology by other nations outside of the former Soviet Union. In 1995, a branch of the US Strategic Command produced an outline of forward-thinking strategies in the document "Essentials of Post-Cold War Deterrence".

The former chair of the United Nations disarmament committee states there are more than 16,000 strategic and tactical nuclear weapons ready for deployment and another 14,000 in storage. The U.S. has nearly 7,000 ready for action and 3,000 in storage and Russia has about 8,500 on hand and 11,000 in storage, he said. China has 400 nuclear weapons, Britain 200, France 350, India 160, and Pakistan 60. North Korea is confirmed as having nuclear weapons, though it is not known how many (a common estimate is between 1 and 10). Israel is also widely believed to have nuclear weapons. NATO has stationed 480 US nuclear weapons in Belgium, the Netherlands, Italy, Germany, and Turkey, with several other countries in pursuit of an arsenal of their own.

A key development in nuclear warfare in the 2000s has been the proliferation of nuclear weapons to the developing world, with India and Pakistan both publicly testing nuclear devices and North Korea conducting an underground nuclear test on October 9,

2006. The US Geological Survey measured a 4.2 magnitude earthquake in the area where the test occurred. A further test was announced by the North Korean government on May 25, 2009. Iran, meanwhile, has embarked on a nuclear programme which, while officially for civilian purposes, has come under scrutiny by the United Nations and individual states.

Recent studies undertaken by the CIA cite the enduring India-Pakistan conflict as the most likely to escalate into nuclear war. During the Kargil War in 1999, Pakistan came close to using their nuclear weapons in case of further deterioration. In fact, Pakistan's foreign minister had even warned that they would "use any weapon in our arsenal", hinting at a nuclear strike against India; the statement was condemned by the international community with Pakistan denying it later on. It remains the only war between two declared nuclear powers. The 2001-2002 India-Pakistan standoff again stoked fears of nuclear war between the two countries.

Despite these very serious threats, relations between India and Pakistan have been improving somewhat over the last few years. A bus line directly linking Indian and Pakistani-administered Kashmir has recently been established. However, with the November 26, 2008 Mumbai terror attacks, India does not rule out war with Pakistan.

Another flashpoint which has analysts worried is a possible conflict between the United States and the People's Republic of China over Taiwan. Although economic forces have decreased the possibility of military conflict, there remains the worry that increasing military buildup and a move toward Taiwan independence could spin out of control.

A third potential flashpoint lies in the Middle East, where Israel is thought to possess between one hundred and four hundred nuclear warheads (this has never been officially confirmed by Israel; however, Mordechai Vanunu, the former nuclear technician on whose 1986 revelations much of the above is based, was kidnapped by Mossad agents from Italy, spent 18 years in detention on charges of "grave espionage", and is still forbidden to leave Israel and is subject to severe restrictions—which tends to lend credence to what he told the British Sunday Times). It has been asserted that the submarines which Israel received from Germany have been adapted to carry missiles with nuclear warheads, so as to give Israel a second strike capacity. Israel has been involved in wars with its neighbours on numerous occasions, and its small geographic size would mean that in the event of future wars the Israeli military might have very little time to react to a future invasion or other major threat; the situation could escalate to nuclear warfare very quickly in some scenarios. In addition, the fact that Iran appears to many observers to be in the process of developing a nuclear weapon has heightened fears of a nuclear conflict in the Middle East, either with Israel or with Iran's Sunni neighbours.

POTENTIAL CONSEQUENCES OF A REGIONAL NUCLEAR WAR

A study presented at the annual meeting of the American Geophysical Union in December 2006 asserted that even a small-scale, regional nuclear war could produce as many direct fatalities as all of World War II and disrupt the global climate for a decade or more. In a regional nuclear conflict scenario where two opposing nations in the subtropics would each use 50 Hiroshima-sized nuclear weapons (ca. 15 kiloton each) on major populated centers, the researchers estimated fatalities from 2.6 million to 16.7 million per country. Also, as much as five million tons of soot would be released, which would produce a cooling of several degrees over large areas of North America and Eurasia, including most of the grain-growing regions. The cooling would last for years and could be "catastrophic" according to the researchers.

SUB-STRATEGIC USE

The above examples envisage nuclear warfare at a strategic level, i.e. total war. However, many nuclear powers are believed to have the ability to launch more limited engagements.

The United Kingdom has reserved the possibility of launching a sub-strategic nuclear strike against an enemy, described by its

Parliamentary Defence Select Committee as "the launch of one or a limited number of missiles against an adversary as a means of conveying a political message, warning or demonstration of resolve". This would see the deployment of strategic nuclear weapons in a very limited role rather than the battlefield exchanges of tactical nuclear weapons. Such a strategy is based on the assumption that an enemy country such as the Russian Federation or the People's Republic of China with a larger stockpile of nuclear weapons would not retaliate with far greater force than had been used by Britain.

British Trident-armed Vanguard class nuclear submarines are believed to carry some missiles for this purpose, potentially allowing a strike as low as one kiloton against a single target. Former Defence Secretary Malcolm Rifkind argued that this capacity offset the reduced credibility of fullscale strategic nuclear attack following the end of the Cold War. Commodore Tim Hare, former Director of Nuclear Policy at the British Ministry of Defence, has described it as offering the Government "an extra option in the escalatory process before it goes for an all-out strategic strike which would deliver unacceptable damage".

However, this sub-strategic capacity has been criticized as potentially increasing the acceptability of using nuclear weapons. The related consideration of new generations of limited-yield nuclear weapons by the United States has also alarmed anti-nuclear groups, who believe it will make the use of nuclear weapons more acceptable.

NUCLEAR TERRORISM

Nuclear terrorism by non-state organisations is an unknown factor in nuclear deterrence thinking, as states possessing nuclear weapons are susceptible to retaliation in kind, but sub- or trans-state actors are not. The collapse of the Soviet Union led to the possibility that former Soviet nuclear weapons might become available on the black market (so-called 'loose nukes'), while no warheads are known to be have been mislaid, it has been alleged that suitcase-size bombs might be unaccounted for. A similar threat may exist via dirty bombs.

Chapter 16

UNDECLARED WAR

An Undeclared War is a conflict that is fought between two or more nations without a formal declaration of war being issued. In the United States, a Declaration of War customarily has to be passed by the legislature. There is no format required for declaration(s) of war. The term "Declaration of War" is not, in fact, mentioned by the United States Constitution. Instead the Constitution says "Congress shall have the power to ... declare War, ..." without defining the form such declarations will take. Therefore, many have argued that congressionally passed authorisations to use military force are "Declarations of War." That concept has never been tested in the US Court system.

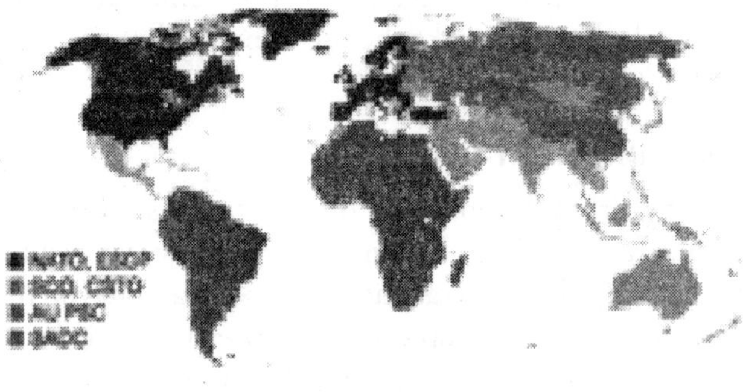

Current Major Military Alliances

After the United Nations action in Korea, a number of democratic governments pursued usually limited warfare by characterising them as something else, such as a "military action" or "armed response." This was most notably used by the United States in its more than decade-long involvement in Vietnam. Nations such as France, which had extensive colonies in which its military provided order, continued to intervene in their former colonies' affairs as police actions since they could no longer be deemed internal conflicts.

Not declaring war provides a way to circumvent constitutional safeguards against the executive declaring war, and also, in some cases, to avoid being bound by the established laws of war. Not using the word "war" is also seen as being more public relations-friendly. For these reasons, they have generally ceased to issue declarations of war, instead describing their actions by euphemisms such as "police action" or "authorized use of force."

Historical examples include the Quasi-War between the United States and France between 1798 and 1800, the Indian Wars of the American Old West and the Anglo-Zulu War.

Boer soldiers during the 1899-1902 Anglo-Boer War, a colonial conflict in what became a province of the British Empire.

COLONIAL WAR

Colonial War is a form of conflict fought between the foreign occupiers of colony and the colony's indigenous population, colonists, or the military forces of a rival colonial power.

The term usually refers to wars fought during the nineteenth century between European armies in Africa, Asia, and the Caribbean, although the term can be used more broadly to describe any war fought in an overseas territory between foreigners and the local population.

VICTORY AGAINST COLONIAL POWER

Although colonial wars usually resulted in a Western victory, local inhabitants were sometimes – though extremely rarely-able to inflict crushing defeats on colonial forces. Perhaps the most famous colonial victory was the American War of Independence, although others include the Battle of Isandhlwana and the Battle of Adowa where native levies commanded by a small force of Europeans were defeated by traditional African soldiery though in overwhelming numbers.

Italian Troops firing on the Turks in Tripoli. 1911

TYPES

BETWEEN OPPOSING COLONIAL POWERS

This is usually the type of conflict referred to be the term colonial war. It was quite a common occurrence from the 15th to 19th centuries for colonial powers to fight for control of lucrative trade routes and colonies that either supplied valuable goods (precious metals, spices) or were vital to the control of these routes. Most often the colonial powers involved were Great Britain, France, Spain, Portugal, Italy, Ottoman Empire and The Netherlands.

BETWEEN COLONIAL POWER AND COLONIST

During the Algerian War of Independence at first the French Government fought with the French settlers against the indigenous people. After Charles de Gaulle agreed to Algerian independence the French government then had to fight elements of the settlers and the French army who did not wish the French government to grant Algeria independence.

EXAMPLES

Examples of colonial wars include the Java War, the American War of Independence, the Indian Rebellion, and various conflicts waged during the Scramble for Africa, such as the Anglo-Zulu War and the Mahdist War. The Anglo-Ashanti Wars of the late 1800s were a typical example of colonial warfare, in which small British armies, equipped with modern artillery and machine guns, repeatedly defeated much larger forces of local warriors.

Chapter 17

RELIGIOUS WAR

A Religious War is a war caused by religious differences. It can involve one state with an established religion against another state with a different religion or a different sect within the same religion, or a religiously motivated group attempting to spread its faith by violence, or to suppress another group because of its religious beliefs or practices. The Muslim Conquests, the French Wars of Religion, the Crusades, and the Reconquista are frequently cited historical examples.

The Muslim concept of jihad, which translates to 'struggle' from Arabic and has a combative aspect, was set down in the 7th Century. Saint Augustine is credited as being the first to detail a "Just War" theory within Christianity, whereby war is justifiable on religious grounds. Saint Thomas Aquinas elaborated on these criteria and his writings were used by the Roman Catholic Church to regulate the actions of European countries.

Many wars that are not religious wars often still include elements of religion, such as priests blessing battleships. Differences in religion can further inflame a war being fought for other reasons. Historically, temples have been destroyed to weaken the morale of the opponent, even when the war itself is not being waged over religious ideals.

Religious designations are sometimes used as shorthand for cultural and historical differences between combatants, giving the often misleading impression that the conflict is primarily about religious differences. For example, there is a common perception of The Troubles in Northern Ireland as a religious conflict, as one side (Nationalists) was predominantly composed of Catholics and the other (Unionists) of Protestants. However, the more fundamental cause is the attachment of Northern Ireland to either the Republic of Ireland or the United Kingdom and while religion played a role as a cultural marker, the conflict was in fact ethnic or nationalistic rather than religious in nature. Since the native Irish were mostly Catholic and the later British-sponsored immigrants were mainly Protestant, the terms become shorthand for the two cultures, but it is inaccurate to describe the conflict as a religious one.

CHRISTIANITY

Those who fought in the name of God were recognized as the Milites Christi, warriors or knights of Christ. Christian fighters believed that victory was achieved through divine intervention or aid from God, and they took great pride in their beliefs. These blessed warriors pursued opposing armies and the heretic religions and cults of the time, and were highly admired by the Church and the State. Often, these enemies would be one and the same, such as the Lombard Legions, which were portrayed as a common enemy of Rome and a satanic Pagan tribe as well.

Usually, the ideals and duties of religion were used as tools to legitimize warfare. Religion essentially gave the armies an excuse for their conquests under the guise of "Christianisation", but their holy conquests turned out to be a long, violent series of raids for territorial expansion, trade and worldwide dominance, in the name of God.

CRUSADES

The Crusades were a series of military campaigns—usually sanctioned by the Papacy—that took place during the 11th through 13th centuries in response to the Muslim Conquests. Originally, the goal was to recapture Jerusalem and the Holy Land from the

Muslims, and support the besieged Christian Byzantine Empire against the Muslim Seljuq expansion into Asia Minor and Europe proper. Later, Crusades were launched against other targets, either for religious reasons, such as the Albigensian Crusade, the Northern Crusades, or because of political conflict, such as the Aragonese Crusade. In 1095, at the Council of Clermont, Pope Urban II raised the level of war from bellum iustum ("just war"), to bellum sacrum.

FRENCH WARS OF RELIGION

In 16th Century France there was a succession of wars between Roman Catholics and Protestants (Hugenots primarily). These series of wars were known as the Wars of Religion.

THIRTY YEARS WAR

In the first half of the 17th century, the German states, Scandinavia (Sweden, primarily) and Poland were beset by religious warfare. Roman Catholicism and Calvinism figured in the opposing sides of this conflict, though Catholic France did take the side of the Protestants but purely for political reasons.

TAIPING REBELLION

Inspired by a formerly illegal Protestant missionary tract in China, the core of the Taiping faith focused on the belief that Shangdi, the high God of classical China, had chosen the Taiping leader, Hong Xiuquan, to establish his Heavenly Kingdom on Earth.

The Taiping rebels, professing this new creed, were able to mount their rebellion and recruit multitudes of followers in their sweep through the empire. The Taiping rebels denounced the divine pretensions of the imperial title and the sacred character of the imperial office as blasphemous usurpations of Shangdi's title and position. In place of the imperial institution, the rebels called for a restoration of the classical system of kingship. Previous rebellions had declared their contemporary dynasties corrupt and therefore in need of revival; the Taiping, by contrast, branded the entire imperial order blasphemous and in need of replacement.

The Bible, in particular a Chinese translation of the Old Testament, profoundly influenced Hong and his followers, leading them to understand the first three of the Ten Commandments as an indictment of the imperial order. The rebels thus sought to destroy imperial culture, along with its institutions and Confucian underpinnings,'all of which they regarded as blasphemous. Strongly iconoclastic, the Taiping followers smashed religious statues and imperially approved icons throughout the lands they conquered.

The Guinness Book of World Records calls this the "bloodiest civil war" with some 20 million estimated dead.

ISLAM

Jihad means "to strive or struggle" in the way of God, and is sometimes referred to as the sixth pillar of Islam, although it has no official status. In the West, Jihad is often understood as "Holy War", but it has a broader meaning in Islamic theology. It can be striving to lead a good Muslim life, praying and fasting regularly, being an attentive and faithful spouse and parent or working hard to spread the message of Islam. Some mujtahids (Islamic scholars) have argued that Jihad is not supposed to include aggressive warfare.

SECOND SUDANESE CIVIL WAR

HINDUISM

From the 11th to the 17th century Hindus fought against the Muslim invasions. Several times during these centuries power swayed from Muslim to Hindu hands. After the loss of power to the Muslims, India was at peace, so long as the Muslim rulers did not attack the faith of the Hindus, but several rulers caused conflicts between them and their Hindu subjects by destroying temples and by giving more power to the Muslim people rather than giving equal power to all Indians. The conflicts in India today between Hindu and Muslim can be traced to these events.

INDO-PAKISTANI PARTITION OF 1947

INDIAN REBELLION OF 1857

In 1813, the East India Company charter was amended in order to allow missionary activity across British India. The missionaries soon spread almost everywhere and started denigrating Hinduism and Islam, besides promoting Christianity, in order to seek converts. Many officers of the British East India Company, such as Herbert Edwardes and Colonel S.G. Wheeler, openly preached to the Sepoys. Such activities caused a great deal of resentment and fear of forced conversions among Indian soldiers of the Company and civilians alike. The perception that the company was trying to convert Hindus and Muslims to Christianity is often cited as one of the causes of the revolt. The revolt is considered by some historians as a semi-national and religious war seeking freedom from English bondage though others question this interpretation. The revolt started, among the Indian soldiers of the British East India Company, when the British introduced new rifle cartridges, rumored to be greased with pig and cow fat– an abhorrent concept to Muslim and Hindu soldiers, respectively, for religious reasons. However, in the aftermath of the revolt, British reprisals were particularly severe with hundreds of thousands being killed. While the death toll is often debated by historians with figures ranging between one hundred thousand and one million, it is usually agreed that several hundred thousand were killed.

FIVE PECKS OF RICE REBELLION

BUDDHISM

A careful examination of the Buddhist texts, particularly The Kalachakra Tantra literature, reveals both external and internal levels of battle that could easily be called "holy wars." Buddhism has not been immune to religious warfare its history, as evidenced by Buddhist conquests of the Cham people, as well as Buddhist war against Tamils in Sri Lanka.

The main ideas of Buddhism emphasized the internal spiritual battle against one's own ignorance and destructive ways and encouraged the principle of Ahinsa(avoidance of violence) and thus most Buddhists remained neutral or tried to resolve wars in non-violent ways. Buddhists have fought against Muslims as well as Hindus, especially from the 8th through the 10th centuries.

SRI LANKAN CIVIL WAR

The Sri Lankan Civil War between the Buddhist Sinhala majority and Hindu and Catholic Tamil ethnic minority has been characterized by outside observers as a "Buddhist holy war" from the viewpoint of the Sinhala Buddhist fundamentalism. The Sinhala hatred for Tamils has been linked to Buddhist religious chauvinism and fundamentalism, and their atrocities on non-Buddhist Tamils been criticized as motivated by a religious-nationalist desire to cleanse the country of non-Buddhist non-Sinhalese ethnics.

JUDAISM

In the Jewish religion, the expression Milhemet Mitzvah (Hebrew: îìçîú îöåää, "commandment war") refers to a war that is both obligatory for all Jews (men and women) and limited to territory within the borders of the land of Israel.

The geographical limits of Israel, and therefore of this religious war, are detailed in the Tanakh, the Hebrew Bible, especially Numbers 34:1-15 and Ezekiel 47:13-20. The relevance of this concept to the contemporary State of Israel is debated. There is no reference to Milhemet Mitzvah in official documents from the Israeli government or defense forces.

JEWISH-ROMAN WAR

The first Jewish-Roman War (66–73), sometimes called The Great Revolt was the first of three major rebellions by the Jews of Iudaea Province against the Roman Empire (the second was the Kitos War in 115–117; the third was Bar Kokhba's revolt, 132–135).

It began in the year 66 initially because of Greek and Jewish religious tensions but grew with anti-taxation protests and attacks upon Roman citizens. It ended when legions under Titus besieged and destroyed the centre of rebel resistance in Jerusalem, and defeated the remaining Jewish strongholds.

FIRST JEWISH SUCCESSES

According to Josephus, the revolt, which began at Caesarea in 66, was provoked by Greeks sacrificing birds in front of a local synagogue.[2] The Roman garrison did not intercede and the long-standing Greek and Jewish religious tensions took a downward spiral. In reaction, the son of Kohen Gadol (High priest) Eliezar ben Hanania ceased prayers and sacrifices for the Roman Emperor at the Temple. Protests over taxation joined the list of grievances and random attacks on Roman citizens and perceived 'traitors' occurred in Jerusalem. Fearing the worst, the pro-Roman king Agrippa II and his sister Berenice fled Jerusalem to Galilee. Cestius Gallus, the legate of Syria, brought a legion, the XII Fulminata, and auxiliary troops as reinforcements to restore order. They were defeated in an ambush at the Battle of Beth Horon, a result that shocked the Roman leadership.

THE ROMAN RESPONSE

Emperor Nero appointed general Vespasian instead of Gallus to crush the rebellion. Vespasian, along with legions X *Fretensis* and V *Macedonica*, landed at Ptolemias in April 67. There he was joined by his son Titus, who arrived from Alexandria at the head Legio XV Apollinaris, as well as by the armies of various local allies including that of king Agrippa II. Fielding more than 60,000 soldiers, Vespasian began operations by subjugating the Galilee[3]. Many towns gave up without a fight, although others had to be taken by force. Of these, Josephus provides detailed accounts of the sieges of Yodfat and Gamla. By the year 68, Jewish resistance in the North had been crushed, and Vespasian made Caesarea Maritima his headquarters and proceeded to methodically clear the coast.

The leaders of the collapsed Northern revolt, John of Giscala and Simon Bar Giora, managed to escape to Jerusalem. Brutal civil war erupted: the Zealots and the fanatical Sicarii executed anyone advocating surrender, and by 68 the entire leadership of the southern revolt was dead, killed by Jewish hands in the infighting.

A NEW EMPEROR

While the war in Judea was being won, great events were occurring in Rome. In the middle of 68 AD, the emperor Nero's increasingly erratic behaviour finally lost him all support for his position. The Roman Senate, the praetorian guard and several prominent army commanders conspired for his removal. When the senate declared Nero an enemy of the people, he fled Rome and committed suicide. The newly installed emperor Galba was murdered after just a few months by a rival, triggering a civil war that came to be known as the Year of the Four Emperors. In 69 AD, though previously uninvolved, the popular Vespasian was also hailed emperor by the legions under his command. He decided, upon gaining further widespread support, to return to Rome to claim the throne from the usurper Vitellius, leaving his son Titus to finish the war in Judea.

FALL OF JERUSALEM

The siege of Jerusalem, the capital city, had begun early in the war, but had turned into a stalemate. Unable to breach the city's defenses, the Roman armies established a permanent camp just outside the city, digging a trench around the circumference of its walls and building a wall as high as the city walls themselves around Jerusalem. Anyone caught in the trench attempting to flee the city would be captured, crucified, and placed in lines on top of the dirt wall facing into Jerusalem. The two Zealot leaders, John of Gischala and Simon Bar Giora, only ceased hostilities and joined forces to defend the city when the Romans began to construct ramparts for the siege. Tens of thousands of crucified bodies encircled Jerusalem by the end of the siege.

Titus Flavius, Vespasian's son, led the final assault and siege of Jerusalem. During the infighting inside the city walls, a stockpiled supply of dry food was intentionally burned by Jewish leaders to induce the defenders to fight against the siege instead of negotiating peace; as a result many city dwellers and soldiers died of starvation during the siege. Zealots under Eleazar ben Simon held the Temple, Sicarii led by Simon Bar Giora held the upper city. Titus eventually wiped out the last remnants of Jewish resistance.

The treasures of Jerusalem (detail from the Arch of Titus).

By the summer of 70, the Romans had breached the walls of Jerusalem, ransacking and burning nearly the entire city. The Romans began by attacking the weakest spot which was the third wall. It was built shortly before the siege so it did not have as much time invested in its protection. They succeeded towards the end of May and shortly afterwards broke through the more important second wall. The Second Temple was destroyed on Tisha B'Av (July 29 or July 30), 70. Tacitus, a historian of the time, notes that those who were besieged in Jerusalem amounted to no fewer than six hundred thousand, that men and women alike and every age engaged in armed resistance, everyone who could pick up a weapon did, both sexes showed equal determination, preferring death to a life that involved expulsion from their country. All three walls were destroyed and in turn so was the Temple, some of whose overturned stones and their place of impact can still be seen. John of Giscala surrendered at Agrippa II's fortress of Jotaphta and was sentenced to life imprisonment. The famous Arch of

Titus still stands in Rome: it depicts Roman legionaries carrying the Temple of Jerusalem's treasuries, including the menorah, during Titus's triumphal procession in Rome.

FALL OF MASADA

During the spring of 71, Titus set sail for Rome. A new military governor was then appointed from Rome, Lucilius Bassus, whose assigned task was to undertake the "mopping-up" operations in Judaea.

Remnants of one of several legionary camps at Masada in Israel, just outside the circumvallation wall which can be seen at the bottom of the image.

He used X *Fretensis* to oppose the few remaining fortresses that still resisted. Bassus took Herodium, and then crossed the Jordan to capture the fortress of Machaerus on the shore of the Dead Sea. Because of illness, Bassus did not live to complete his mission. Lucius Flavius Silva replaced him, and moved against the last Jewish stronghold, Masada, in the autumn of 72. He used Legio X, auxiliary troops, and thousands of Jewish prisoners, for a total of 10,000 soldiers. After his orders for surrender were rejected, Silva established several base camps and circumvallated the fortress. According to Josephus, when the Romans finally broke through the walls of this citadel in 73, they discovered that the 967 defenders had all committed suicide, preferring death over defeat.

THE OUTCOME

The defeat of the Jewish revolt altered the Jewish diaspora, as many of the Jewish rebels were scattered or sold into slavery. Josephus claims that 1,100,000 people were killed during the siege, of which a majority were Jewish. 97,000 were captured and enslaved Many fled to areas around the Mediterranean.

A coin issued by the rebels in 68, note Paleo-Hebrew alphabet. Obverse: "Shekel, Israel.
Year 3". Reverse: "Jerusalem the Holy"

An ancient Roman coin. The inscription reads IVDAEA CAPTA. The coins inscribed Ivdaea Capta (Judea Captured) were issued throughout the Empire in order to demonstrate the futility of possible future rebellions. Judea was represented by a crying woman.

Roman denarius depicting Titus, c. 79. The reverse commemorates his triumph in the Judaean wars, representing a Jewish captive kneeling in front of a trophy of arms.

The Jewish Encyclopedia article on the Hebrew Alphabet states: "Not until the revolts against Nero and against Hadrian did the Jews return to the use of the old Hebrew script on their coins, which they did from similar motives to those which had governed them two or three centuries previously; both times, it is true, only for a brief period."

Titus reportedly refused to accept a wreath of victory, as there is "no merit in vanquishing people forsaken by their own God".

Before Vespasian's departure, the Pharisaic sage and Rabbi Yohanan ben Zakkai obtained his permission to establish a Judaic school at Yavne. Zakkai was smuggled away from Jerusalem in a coffin by his students. Later this school has become a major center of Talmudic study. (See Mishnah)

SOURCES

The main account of the revolt comes from Josephus, the former Jewish commander of Galilee, who after capture by the Romans, attempted to end the rebellion by negotiating with the Judean's on Titus's behalf. Josephus and Titus became quite close friends and later Josephus was granted Roman citizenship and a pension. He was loathed by some of his fellow Jews as a turncoat and Roman apologist and never returned to his homeland after the fall of Jerusalem, living in Rome as an historian under the patronage of Flavius and Titus.

He wrote two works, *The Wars of the Jews* (c. 79) and *Jewish Antiquities* (c. 94), that are frequently contradictory—especially *Jewish Antiquities'* autobiographical appendix. These are the only surviving source materials containing information on specific events that occurred during the fighting. But the material is continually questioned because of claims that cannot be verified by secondary sources. Only since the discovery of the Dead Sea scrolls has some confirmation been given to the events he describes. Often his use of hyperbole, a common trait of ancient historians, has led to his work being used as a guide in archaeology to determine the veracity of certain events.

ARAB–ISRAELI CONFLICT

The Arab–Israeli conflict spans roughly one century of political tensions and open hostilities, though Israel itself only was established in 1948. It involves the establishment of the Zionist movement and the subsequent creation of the modern State of Israel in territory regarded by the Pan-Arab movement as belonging to the Palestinians, be they Muslim, Christian, Druze or other (and in the Pan-Islamic context, in territory regarded as Muslim lands), and by the Jewish people as their historical homeland.

The conflict, which started as a political and nationalist conflict over competing territorial ambitions following the collapse of the Ottoman Empire, has shifted over the years from the large scale regional Arab–Israeli conflict to a more local Israeli-Palestinian conflict, though the Arab World and Israel generally remain at odds with each other over specific territory. The present day issue must be approached with a recognition that neither the Arab-Israel dispute in general nor the Israel-Palestinian conflict in particular is based on or driven forward by *primordial antagonisms* and that it has in fact been less than a century since Jews and Arabs began to view each other as enemies. However, centuries of government sanctioned oppression and persecution of Jews living throughout the Arab countries has been well documented.

RELIGIOUS ASPECTS OF THE CONFLICT

The Land of Canaan or *Eretz Israel* (Land of Israel) was, according to the Torah, promised by God to the Israelites. In his 1896 manifesto *The Jewish State*, Theodor Herzl repeatedly refers to the Biblical Promised land concept (though Herzl was an atheist himself). Biblical records and archaeological evidence indicate that the Jews conquered and began to settle the land of Canaan during the thirteenth century BCE. Moses had given the Israelites political organisation and led them out of Egypt, bringing them to the borders of the promised land. Then, under Joshua, they initiated a prolonged military campaign in which they gradually took control of the territory and made it their home through "a struggle that lasted as much as a century". In the same period, Jewish migration to Palestine (Aliyah) increased in number.

Several studies have argued that beyond the secular motivations, groups on both sides, including Hamas and Gush Emunim, also evoke religious arguments for their uncompromising positions.[5][6] The Likud party is currently the most prominent party which includes the Biblical claim to the Land of Israel in its platform.

Muslims too claim to have religious priority in accordance with the Torah and Quran. Contrary to the Jewish perspective of the land being solely for Israelites, they argue that the Land of Canaan was promised to all descendants of Abraham, with Arabs being the descendants of Abraham's elder son Ishmael. Additionally, Muslims also revere many holy sites which are revered by Jews (such as The Cave of the Patriarchs and the Temple Mount), and have constructed additional sites in the past 1,400 years, such as the Dome of the Rock and the Al-Aqsa Mosque. Muslims also believe that Muhammad passed through Jerusalem on his first journey to heaven.

HISTORY OF THE CONFLICT

End of 19th century–1948

In the late 19th century, under the banner of a movement called Zionism, many European Jews began purchasing swamps and other desert land from the Ottoman sultan and his agents. Theodore Herzl, the founder of the movement, appealed to the Ottomans as a way to raise tax revenues and to modernize the relatively sparsely populated and barren land. At that time, the entire city of Jerusalem was contained in its tiny walled area and only had a few tens of thousands of inhabitants. Under the Zionists, collective farms, known as kibbutzim, were established, and cities were founded, such as Tel Aviv. Generally, at first, the Arabs welcomed the Zionists with their standard of living, education, capital, and jobs. Many Arabs moved into the region, matching the increase in Jews from Europe.

Before World War I, the Middle East, including Palestine, had been under the control of the Ottoman Empire for nearly 500 years. During the closing years of their empire the Ottomans began to espouse their Turkish ethnic identity, asserting the primacy of Turks within the empire, leading to discrimination against the Arabs. The promise of liberation from the Ottomans led many Jews and Arabs to support the allied powers during World War I, leading to the emergence of widespread Arab nationalism.

In 1917, the British government issued the Balfour Declaration, which stated that the government viewed favourably "the establishment in Palestine of a national home for the Jewish people." The Declaration was issued as a result of the belief of key members of the government, including Prime Minister Lloyd George, that Jewish support was essential to winning the war; however, the declaration caused great disquiet in the Arab world. After the war, the area came under British rule as the British Mandate of Palestine. The area mandated to the British, included what is today Israel, Jordan, the West Bank and Gaza.

Jewish immigration to Palestine increased. By 1931, 17 per cent of the population of Palestine were Jews, an increase of six per cent since 1922. Jewish immigration increased soon after the Nazis came to power in Germany, causing the Jewish population in Palestine to double. Palestinian Arabs saw this rapid influx of Jewish immigrants as a threat to their homeland and their identity as a people. Moreover, Jewish policies of purchasing land and prohibiting the employment of Arabs in Jewish-owned industries and farms greatly angered the Palestinian Arab communities. Demonstrations were held as early as 1920, protesting what the Arabs felt were unfair preferences for the Jewish immigrants set forth by the British mandate that governed Palestine at the time. This resentment led to outbreaks of violence. In August 1929, Arabs murdered 67 Jews in the city of Hebron, in what became known as the Hebron Massacre. By 1936, escalating tensions led to the 1936–1939 Arab revolt in Palestine.

By the 1920s, the Jewish and Arab populations had grown hostile to each other and acts of violence persisted from both sides of the conflict. European anti-semitism had spread to the Middle East, and there was great association with the upcoming Nazi movement in Germany. There are notable photos and other documents linking Hitler to leaders like the Grand Mufti in Jerusalem. Similarly, anti-Arab sentiments and prejudices grew steadily among the Jewish population in Palestine. Eventually, violence between Arab and Jews had begun a vicious cycle which continues to this day.

In response to Arab pressure, the British Mandate authorities greatly reduced the number of Jewish immigrants to Palestine (see White Paper of 1939 and the Exodus ship). These restrictions remained in place until the end of the mandate, a period which coincided with the Nazi Holocaust and the flight of Jewish refugees from Europe. As a consequence, most Jewish entrants to Palestine were illegal (see Aliyah Bet), causing further tensions in the region. Following several failed attempts to solve the problem diplomatically, the British asked the newly formed United Nations for help. On 15 May 1947 the UN appointed a committee, the UNSCOP, composed of representatives from eleven states. To make the committee more neutral, none of the Great Powers were represented. After five weeks of in-country study, the commission recommended creating a partitioned state with separate territories for the Jews and the Arabs in Palestine. This "two state solution" was accepted with resolution 181 by the UN General Assembly in November 1947 by 33 votes to 13 with 10 abstentions. The Arab states, which constituted the Arab League, voted against. On the ground, Arab and Jewish Palestinians were fighting openly to control strategic positions in the region. Several major atrocities were committed by both sides.

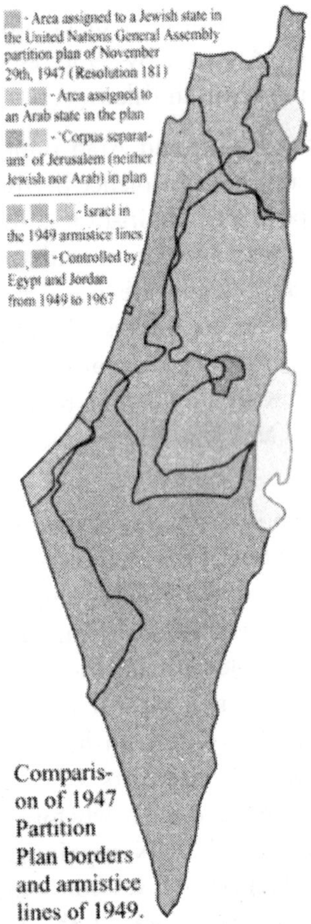

The main differences between the 1947 partition proposal and 1949 armistice lines are highlighted in light red and magenta

In the months prior to the end of the Mandate the Haganah launched a number of offensives in which they gained control over all the territory allocated by the UN to the Jewish State, creating a large number of refugees and capturing the towns of Tiberias, Haifa, Safad, Beisan and, in effect, Jaffa.

On May 14, 1948, one day before the end of the British Mandate of Palestine, Israel declared its independence and sovereignty on the portion partitioned by UNSCOP for the Jewish state. The next day, the Arab League reiterated officially their opposition to the "two-state solution" in a letter to the UN. That day, the armies of Egypt, Lebanon, Syria, Jordan, and Iraq invaded the territory partitioned for the Arab state, thus starting the 1948 Arab-Israeli War. The nascent Israeli Defense Force repulsed the Arab nations from part of the occupied territories, thus extending its borders beyond the original UNSCOP partition. By December 1948, Israel controlled most of the portion of Mandate Palestine west of the Jordan River. The remainder of the Mandate consisted of Jordan, the area that came to be called the West Bank (controlled by Jordan), and the Gaza Strip (controlled by Egypt). Prior to and during this conflict, 711,000. Palestinians Arabs fled their original lands to become Palestinian refugees, in part, due to an alleged promise from Arab leaders that they would be able to return when the war is won.

Many Palestinians fled from the areas that are now present-day Israel as a response to massacres of Arab towns by militant and terrorist Jewish organisations like the Irgun and the Stern Gang. Many historians speculate that these massacres took place with the intention of causing psychological distress amongst the Arab population, giving them ample reason and fear to flee their homes and surrounding areas. The War came to an end with the signing of the 1949 Armistice Agreements between Israel and each of its Arab neighbours. This 1949 armistice line, the so-called green line, is to this day the internationally-recognized border of the state of Israel. It is often referred to as the "pre-1967" border.

David Ben Gurion, Israel's first Prime Minister, accepted the two state solution that the UN established in 1947, but Ben Gurion expressed in a letter to his wife:

> *...a "partial" Jewish State was just a beginning, and [Ben Gurion] planned the organisation of a powerful army, and the use of coercion or force to absorb all the country's extension.*

1949–1967

Following the adoption by the United Nations of Resolution 181 in November 1947 and the declaration of the State of Israel in May 1948, several Arab countries adopted discriminatory measures against their local Jewish populations. There were riots in Yemen and Syria. In Libya, Jews were deprived of citizenship, and in Iraq, their property was seized. As a result, a large number of Jews were forced to emigrate from Arab lands, although many also emigrated for ideological reasons. Over 700,000 Jews emigrated to Israel between 1948 and 1952, with approximately 285,000 of them from Arab countries. Overall, about 850,000 Jews had left the Arab World by the early 1970s (according to official Arab documentation), with many of them leaving their property behind. Today, these displaced Jews and their descendants represent 41% of the total population of Israel. *For details, see Jewish exodus from Arab lands.*

As a result of Israel's victory in its 1948 war of independence, any Arabs caught on the wrong side of the cease-fire line were unable to return to their homes in what became Israel. Likewise, any Jews on the West Bank or in Gaza were exiled from their property and homes to Israel. The main difference between the two is that Arabs were allowed to stay in Israel and gain citizenship post-1948, while Jews were completely removed from Arab-held areas after 1948. Today's Palestinian refugees are the descendants of those who left, either out of fear for their lives or in response to instructions from the Grand Mufti and/or Arab armies to leave their homes, so the Arab armies would have a free-fire range to evict the Jews from the new UN-created State of Israel.

In 1956, Egypt closed the Straits of Tiran to Israeli shipping, and blockaded the Gulf of Aqaba, in contravention of the Constantinople Convention of 1888. Many argued that this was also a violation of the 1949 Armistice Agreements. On July 26, 1956, Egypt nationalized the Suez Canal Company, and closed the canal to Israeli shipping.

Israel responded on October 29, 1956, by invading the Sinai Peninsula with British and French support. During the Suez Canal Crisis, Israel captured the Gaza Strip and Sinai Peninsula. The United States and the United Nations soon pressured it into a ceasefire.[29][30] Israel agreed to withdraw from Egyptian territory. Egypt agreed to freedom of navigation in the region and the demilitarisation of the Sinai. The United Nations Emergency Force (UNEF) was created and deployed to oversee the demilitarisation. The UNEF was only deployed on the Egyptian side of the border, as Israel refused to allow them on its territory.

On May 19, 1967, Egypt expelled UNEF observers, and deployed 100,000 soldiers in the Sinai Peninsula. It again closed the Straits of Tiran to Israeli shipping, returning the region to the way it was in 1956 when Israel was blockaded.

In 1966-67, Egypt's leader, Gamal Abdel Nasser, began a pan-Arab campaign seeking unified support to conquer Israel and expel the Jews. Freshly armed with the latest in Soviet supplied planes, tanks, and other military stocks, Egypt felt, for the first time since 1948, that they were in a position to overrun Israel. Egyptian media began a relentless and supportive jingoist campaign whipping up a fervor of popular support for war. This enthusiasm spilled over to the other Arab capitals.

On May 30, 1967, Jordan entered into the mutual defense pact between Egypt and Syria. Egypt mobilized Sinai units, crossing UN lines (after having expelled the UN border monitors) and mobilized and massed on Israel's southern border. Likewise, armies in Syria, Lebanon, and Jordan also mobilized, encircling Israel for an imminent coordinated attack. In response, on June 5 Israel sent almost all of its planes on a preemptive mission into Egypt. The Israeli Air Force (IAF) destroyed most of the Egyptian Air Force in a surprise attack, then turned east to destroy the Jordanian, Syrian and Iraqi air forces. This strike was the crucial element in Israel's victory in the Six-Day War.[34][36] At the war's end, Israel had gained control of the Sinai Peninsula, the Gaza Strip, the West Bank, eastern Jerusalem, and the Golan Heights. The results of the war affect the geopolitics of the region to this day.

1967–1973

In the summer of 1967, Arab leaders met in Khartoum in response to the war, to discuss the Arab position toward Israel. They reached consensus that there should be no recognition, no peace and no negotiations with the State of Israel, the so-called "three nos".

In 1969, Egypt initiated the War of Attrition, with the goal of exhausting Israel into surrendering the Sinai Peninsula. The war ended following Nasser's death in 1970.

On October 6, 1973, Syria and Egypt staged a surprise attack on Israel on Yom Kippur, overwhelming the Israeli military. The Yom Kippur War accommodated indirect confrontation between the US and the Soviet Union. When Israel had turned the tide of war, the USSR threatened military intervention. The United States, wary of nuclear war, secured a ceasefire on October 25.

1974–2000

EGYPT

Following the Camp David Accords of the late 1970s, Israel and Egypt signed a peace treaty in March, 1979. Under its terms, the Sinai Peninsula returned to Egyptian hands, and the Gaza Strip remained under Israeli control, to be included in a future Palestinian state. The agreement also provided for the free passage of Israeli ships through the Suez Canal and recognition of the Strait of Tiran and the Gulf of Aqaba as international waterways.

JORDAN

In October 1994, Israel and Jordan signed a peace agreement, which stipulated mutual cooperation, an end of hostilities, and a resolution of other issues. The conflict between them had cost roughly 18.3 billion dollars. Its signing is also closely linked with the efforts to create peace between Israel and the Palestinian Liberation Organisation (PLO) representing the Palestinian National Authority (PNA). It was signed at the southern border crossing of Arabah on October 26, 1994 and made Jordan only the second Arab country (after Egypt) to normalize relations with Israel.

IRAQ

In June 1981, Israel attacked and destroyed newly built Iraqi nuclear facilities in Operation Opera.

During the Gulf War, Iraq fired 39 Scud missiles into Israel, in the hopes of uniting the Arab world against the coalition which sought to liberate Kuwait. At the behest of the United States, Israel did not respond to this attack in order to prevent a greater outbreak of war.

LEBANON

In 1970, following an extended civil war, King Hussein expelled the Palestine Liberation Organisation from Jordan. September 1970 is known as the Black September in Arab history and sometimes is referred to as the "era of regrettable events". It was a month when Hashemite King Hussein of Jordan moved to quash the autonomy of Palestinian organisations and restore his monarchy's rule over the country.

The violence resulted in the deaths of tens of thousands of people, the vast majority Palestinians. Armed conflict lasted until July 1971 with the expulsion of the PLO and thousands of Palestinian fighters to Lebanon. The PLO resettled in Lebanon, whence it staged raids into Israel. In 1981, Syria, allied with the

PLO, positioned missiles in Lebanon. In June 1982, Israel invaded Lebanon. Within two months the PLO agreed to withdraw thence.

In March 1983, Israel and Lebanon signed a ceasefire agreement. However, Syria pressured President Amin Gemayel into nullifying the truce in March 1984. By 1985, Israeli forces withdrew to a 15 km wide southern strip of Lebanon, until its complete withdrawal in May 2000, seen by Arab Muslims as the result of painful blows suffered at the hands of Hezbollah. They claim that they had won the war and had forced Israel out.

PALESTINIANS

In December 1987, the First Intifada began. The First Intifada was a mass Palestinian uprising against Israeli rule in the Palestinian Territories. The rebellion began in the Jabalia refugee camp and quickly spread throughout Gaza, the West Bank and East Jerusalem. Palestinian actions ranged from civil disobedience to violence. In addition to general strikes, boycotts on Israeli products, graffiti and barricades, Palestinian demonstrations that included stone-throwing by youths against the Israel Defense Forces brought the Intifada international attention.

The PLO was excluded from peace negotiations until it recognized Israel and renounced terrorism the following year. In mid-1993, Israeli and Palestinian representatives engaged in peace talks in Oslo, Norway. As a result, in September 1993, Israel and the PLO signed the Oslo Accords, known as the Declaration of Principles or Oslo I; in side letters, Israel recognized the PLO as the legitimate representative of the Palestinian people while the PLO recognized the right of the state of Israel to exist and renounced terrorism, violence and its desire for the destruction of Israel. The Oslo II agreement was signed in 1995 and detailed the division of the West Bank into Areas A, B, and C. Area A was land under full Palestinian civilian control. In Area A, Palestinians were also responsible for internal security. The Oslo agreements remain important documents in Israeli-Palestinian relations.

2000–PRESENT

As an attempt to halt the al-Aqsa Intifada, Israel raided facilities in major urban centers in the West Bank in 2002. This included re-taking many parts of land in Area A. Violence again swept through the region. Israeli Prime Minister Ariel Sharon began a policy of unilateral withdrawal from the Gaza Strip in 2003. This policy was fully implemented in August 2005. Sharon's announcement to disengage from Gaza came as a tremendous shock to his critics both on the left and on the right. A year previously, he had commented that the fate of the most far-flung settlements in Gaza, Netzararem and Kfar Darom, was regarded in the same light as that of Tel Aviv. The formal announcements to evacuate seventeen Gaza settlements and another four in the West Bank in February 2004 represented the first reversal for the settler movement since 1968. It divided his party. It was strongly supported by Trade and Industry Minister Ehud Olmert and Tzipi Livni, the Minister for Immigration and Absorption, but Foreign Minister Silvan Shalmon and Finance Minister Bibi Netanyahu equally strongly condemned it. It was also uncertain whether this was simply the beginning of further evacuation.

In June 2006, a cross border raid by Palestinian militants from the Gaza Strip resulted in the capture of Israeli soldier Gilad Shalit; to date, he's been held hostage by Hamas, who barred the International Red Cross from seeing him, and demands the release of 450 Palestinian prisoners. Hamas took over control of the strip in 2007. Due to Hamas holding Shalit, firing rockets at Israeli towns, and refusing to recognize past agreements between the Palestinian National Authority and Israel, the latter has tightened its control over Gaza's borders and restricted the flow of goods and people into and out of the area. Due to this policy, according to the BBC, "there are high levels of poverty, deprivation and unemployment in Gaza City... Only basic humanitarian items have been allowed in [the Gaza Strip], and virtually no exports permitted, paralysing the economy."

In July 2006, Hezbollah fighters crossed the border from Lebanon into Israel, attacked and killed eight Israeli soldiers, and abducted two others as hostages, setting off the 2006 Lebanon War which caused much destruction in Lebanon A UN-sponsored ceasefire went into effect on August 14, 2006, officially ending the conflict. The conflict killed over a thousand people, mostly Lebanese civilians, severely damaged Lebanese civil infrastructure, and displaced approximately one million Lebanese and 300,000–500,000 Israelis, although most were able to return to their homes. After the ceasefire, some parts of Southern Lebanon remained uninhabitable due to Israeli unexploded cluster bomblets.

On September 6, 2007, in Operation Orchard, Israel bombed an eastern Syrian complex which was allegedly a nuclear reactor being built with assistance from North Korea. Israel had also bombed Syria in 2003.

In April 2008, Syrian President Bashar Al Assad told a Qatari newspaper that Syria and Israel had been discussing a peace treaty for a year, with Turkey as a go-between. This was confirmed in May 2008 by a spokesman for Prime Minister Ehud Olmert. As well as a peace treaty, the future of the Golan Heights is being discussed. President Assad was quoted in the The Guardian as telling the Qatari paper:

> ...there would be no direct negotiations with Israel until a new US president takes office. The US was the only party qualified to sponsor any direct talks, President Assad told the paper, but added that the Bush administration "does not have the vision or will for the peace process. It does not have anything."

Speaking in Jerusalem on August 26, 2008, United States Secretary of State Condoleezza Rice criticized Israel's increased settlement construction in the West Bank as detrimental to the peace process. Rice's comments came amid reports that Israeli construction in the disputed territory had increased by a factor of 1.8 over 2007 levels.

A fragile six-month truce between Hamas and Israel expired on December 19, 2008; attempts at extending the truce failed amid accusations of breaches from both sides. Following the expiration, Hamas resumed rocket and mortar attacks on Israeli cities, most notably firing over 60 rockets on December 24. On December 27, 2008, Israel launched Operation Cast Lead — a massive aerial assault and subsequent land invasion — against Hamas, beginning a major battle in Gaza. The Israeli Operation began with an intense bombardment of the Gaza strip, targeting Hamas bases, police training camps, police headquarters and offices.

Civilian infrastructure, including mosques, houses and schools were also attacked with allegations being made by Israel that Hamas fighters were operating out of them. Throughout the conflict, Hamas and other organisations fired hundreds of rockets and mortar shells on Israeli cities. Human Rights groups and aid organisations have accused Hamas and Israel of War Crimes and called for independent investigations and review of arms sales to Israel. The conflict came to an end on January 18 after first Israel and then Hamas announced unilateral ceasefires. In the days following the ceasefire, the BBC reported that, "more than 40,000 Gazans were left without running water and 4,000 homes had been ruined, leaving tens of thousands of people homeless.

COST OF CONFLICT

A report by Strategic Foresight Group has estimated the opportunity cost of conflict for the Middle East from 1991-2010 at $12 trillion. The report's opportunity cost calculates the peace GDP of countries in the Middle East by comparing the current GDP to the potential GDP in times of peace. Israel's share is almost $1 trillion. In other words, had there been peace and cooperation between Israel and Arab nations since 1991, every Israeli citizen would be earning over $44,000 instead of $23,000 in 2010.

In terms of the human cost, estimates range from 51,000 fatalities (from 1950 to 2007) to 92,000 fatalities (from 1945 to 1995).

SIKHISM

In Sikhism, a Holy War is only justifiable when all other means to achieve peace have been tried and failed. The early Sikhs of the 15-1600's fought off many Mughal Islamic Invaders, as well as Hindu Rajputs. Sikhs are only allowed to fight for the well being of righteousness, as stated by their 10th guru, Guru Gobind Singh. “”When all other means have failed, It is then lawful to take to the sword.”

SIKH UPRISING (1982-91)

SAXON WARS

The Saxon Wars have been described as a religious war.

ZOROASTRIANISM

Persian Empires with the state religion of Zoroastrianism did not engage in wars for religion, but rather for conquest and expansion.

Chapter 18

ACTIVE AUTONOMIST AND SECESSIONIST MOVEMENTS

This is a list of currently active autonomist and secessionist movements around the world. Entries on this list meet two criteria: they are active movements with living, active members, and they are seeking greater autonomy or self-determination for a geographic region (as opposed to personal autonomy). What is and is not considered an autonomy or secession movement is, of course, contentious.

Under each region listed is one or more of the following:

- **Proposed State** (proposed name for the seceding State)
- **De facto State** (for regions with de facto autonomy from the Government; also replaces proposed State unless both are of different names, such as Taiwan)
- **Proposed Autonomous Region** (for movements toward greater autonomy but not outright secession; can be used alongside the above fields for the same region)
- **Government-in-Exile** (if a Government with or without control is based outside of the region in question)
- **Political Party/ies** (for organisations involved in a political system to push for autonomy or secession)
- **Rebel Organisation**(s) (for armed organisations; may also be used for political parties that have taken up arms, such as Hamas)

- **Pressure Group(s)** (for non-belligerent non-politically participatory entities)

AFRICA

ALGERIA

- Kabyles
  - o **Proposed State:** Kabylie
  - o **Political Party:** Mouvement pour l'Autonomie de la Kabylie

ANGOLA

- Cabinda (**member of the Unrepresented Nations and Peoples Organisation**)
  - o **Proposed State:** Republic of Cabinda
  - o **Government-in-Exile:** Frente para a Libertação do Enclave de Cabinda (FLEC)
  - o **Political Party:** Frente para a Libertação do Enclave de Cabinda (FLEC)
  - o **Rebel Organisation:** Forças Armadas de Cabinda (FAC)

CAMEROON

- Bakassi Peninsula
  - o **Proposed State:** Democratic Republic of Bakassi
- Southern Cameroons (**member of the Unrepresented Nations and Peoples Organisation**)
  - o **Proposed State:** Federal Republic of Southern Cameroon, Ambazonia
  - o **Political Party:** Southern Cameroons National Council

COMOROS

- Anjouan
  - o **Political Parties:** Anjouan People's Movement, Mouvement Populaire Anjouanais, Mawana
- Mohéli

- o **Proposed State:** Democratic Republic of Mwali

CONGO-KINSHASA

- Bas-Congo
  - o **Pressure Group:** Bundu dia Kongo
  - o **Proposed State:** Kingdom of Kongo
- Katanga
  - o **Political Parties:** Confédération des Associations de Katanga Tribales, Union of Independent Federalists and Republicans
  - o **Rebel Organisations:** Mai-Mai community-based militia groups
  - o **Status:** Sporadic violence
- Kwili, Kivu, Bukavu
  - o **Status:** Confused fighting in progress

CÔTE D'IVOIRE

- Northern Regions
  - o **Proposed State:** Republique des les Regions Nordenses.
  - o **Pressure Groups:** Patriotic Movement of Côte d'Ivoire" (MPCI), Mouvement populaire ivoirien du Grand Ouest (MPIGO), Movement for Justice and Peace (MJP)

EGYPT

- Copts
  - o **Proposed State:** Coptic Pharaonic Republic
  - o **Pressure Group:** Coptic Christians living abroad

EQUATORIAL GUINEA

- Bioko
  - o **Pressure Group:** Movement for the Self-Determination of Bioko Island
  - o **Status:** The indigenous Bubi people are now outnumbered by Fernandinos and Fang immigrants from the mainland.

ETHIOPIA

- Gambela Region
  - o **Rebel Organisation:** Gambella Peoples Liberation Front
- Ogaden (Somali Region)
  - o **Proposed State:** Republic of Ogadenia (**member of the Unrepresented Nations and Peoples Organisation**)
  - o **Political Party:** Ogaden National Liberation Front, Western Somali Liberation Front, Liberation Spiders of Ogaden / The Spiders
  - o **Pressure Group:** Ogaden Youth Association
- Oromia Region
  - o **Rebel Organisations:** Oromo Independence Movement, Oromo Liberation Front, Islamic Front for the Liberation of Oromia, Conference of Oromiya Peoples Liberation Front

FRANCE (AFRICA)

- Réunion

KENYA

- Somalis in Kenya

MAURITIUS

- Rodrigues Island

MOROCCO

- Western Sahara
  - o **Ethnic Group:** Sahrawi people
  - o **De facto State:** Free Zone
  - o **Government-in-exile:** Sahrawi Arab Democratic Republic based in refugee camps in Tindouf Province, Algeria
  - o **Political Party:** Polisario Front
  - o **Rebel Movement:** Polisario Front
- Republic of Rif
  - o **Proposed State:** Republic of Rif

NAMIBIA

- Caprivi
  - o **Ethnic Group:** Lozi
  - o **Proposed State:** Free State of Caprivi Strip/Itenge
  - o **Political Party:** Caprivi African National Union
  - o **Rebel Organisation:** Caprivi Liberation Army

NIGER

- Agadez Department
  - o **Ethnic Group:** Tuareg people
  - o **Rebel Organisation:** Revolutionary Armed Forces of the Sahara
  - o **Political Parties:** Taniminnak Tidot N Tenere, Tidot Union of Tenere.
  - o **Proposed State:** Akal N Tenere, Tenere Republic

NIGERIA

- Bakassi Peninsula
  - o **Proposed state:** Democratic Republic of Bakassi
- Igbo
  - o **Proposed State:** Biafra (defunct)
  - o **Political Party:** Movement for the Actualisation of the Sovereign State of Biafra
- Ijaw
  - o **Proposed State:** Niger Delta Republic
  - o **Rebel Organisation:** Movement for the Emancipation of the Niger Delta, Niger Delta People's Volunteer Force
- Ogoni
  - o **Political Party:** Movement for the Survival of the Ogoni People
- Yoruba
  - o **Proposed State:** Oduduwa Republic of the Yorubas
  - o **Political Party:** Oodua Republic Front

RWANDA

- Batwa (**member of the Unrepresented Nations and Peoples Organisation**)
  - **Political Party:** Association for the Promotion of Batwa

SOMALIA

- Jubaland
  - **Proposed state:** Republic of Jubaland
  - **Rebel Organisation:** Somali Patriotic Movement
- Maakhir
- Puntland
  - **De facto State:** Republic of Puntland State of Somalia
  - **Political Party:** Somali Salvation Democratic Front
- Somaliland
  - **De facto State:** Republic of Somaliland
  - **Political Party:** Somali National Movement
- Southwestern Somalia
  - **Proposed Autonomous Region:** State of Southwestern Somalia
  - **Rebel Organisation:** Rahanwein Resistance Army

SENEGAL

- Casamance
  - **Rebel Organisation:** Movement of Democratic Forces of Casamance

SOUTH AFRICA

- Boere-Afrikaners
  - **Proposed State:** Volkstaat
  - **Pressure Group:** Orania Movement
  - **Rebel Organisation:** Afrikaner Weerstandsbeweging, Boeremag
- Cape Party

SUDAN

- Beja
  - o **Rebel Organisation:** Beja Congress
- Darfur
  - o **Rebel Organisation:** Darfur Liberation Front
- Eastern Sudan
  - o **Rebel Organisation:** Eastern Front (Sudan)
- Southern Sudan
  - o **Proposed State:** Southern Sudan

TANZANIA

- Zanzibar (**member of the Unrepresented Nations and Peoples Organisation**)
  - o **Political Party:** Civic United Front

ZAMBIA

- Barotse
  - o **Ethnic Group:** Lozi
  - o **Proposed State:** Barotseland
  - o **Rebel Organisation:** Barotse Patriotic Front

ASIA

AFGHANISTAN

- Badakhshan (Wakhan Corridor)
  - o **Political Party:** Lali Badakhshon
  - o **Proposed Autonomous Region:** United Badakhshan Peoples Republic
- Pashtunistan

AZERBAIJAN

- Nagorno-Karabakh
  - o **De facto State:** Nagorno-Karabakh Republic
- Talysh-Mughan

- o **Proposed Autonomous Region:** Talysh-Mughan Autonomous Republic

BANGLADESH

- Chittagong Hill Tracts (member of the Unrepresented Nations and Peoples Organisation)
- **Political Party:** Parbatya Chattagram Jana Sanghati Samiti
- **Proposed Autonomous Region:** Jummaland Autonomous Region
- **Rebel orgnaisation:** Banga Sena
- **Proposed State:** Hindu Republic of Bangabhumi

People's Republic of China

Secessionist movements

- Hong Kong
  - o **Pressure Groups:** Hong Konger Front; it is unclear whether this actually exists as an organisation.
  - o **Proposed State:** Republic of Hong Kong
- Inner Mongolia (member of the Unrepresented Nations and Peoples Organisation)
  - o **Political Parties:** Inner Mongolian People's Party, Southern Mongolian Democratic Alliance
- Tibet (**member of the Unrepresented Nations and Peoples Organisation**)
  - o the 14th Dalai Lama, head of the **Government-in-exile:** Tibetan Government in Exile
  - o **Political Party:** International Tibet Independence Movement, National Democratic Party of Tibet, United Liberation Front of Tibet
  - o **Pressure Groups:** Students for a Free Tibet
  - o See also: 2008 unrest in Tibet
- East Turkestan / Uyghuristan / Xinjiang (member of the Unrepresented Nations and Peoples Organisation)
  - o **Rebel Organisation:** East Turkestan Islamic Movement

  - **Political Party:** East Turkestan Government in Exile
  - **Proposed State:** Eastern Turkestan Republic
  - **Pressure Groups:** World Uyghur Congress
- Manchuria
  - **Proposed State:** Manchukuo
  - **Government-in-exile:** Manchukuo Temporary Government

AUTONOMIST MOVEMENTS

- Macau
  - **Political Party:** New Democratic Macau Association

GEORGIA

- Abkhazia (**member of the Unrepresented Nations and Peoples Organisation)**
  - **De facto State:** Republic of Abkhazia
- Armenians in Samtskhe-Javakheti region
  - **Pressure Group:** Javakh, United Javakh-Democratic Alliance, Virk
  - **Proposed Autonomous Region:** Javakh autonomous region
- South Ossetia
  - **De facto State:** Republic of South Ossetia

INDIA

- Andhra Pradesh
  - **Political Party:** Jai Andhra
- Arunachal Pradesh
  - **Rebel Organisation:** Arunachal Dragon Force
  - **Proposed Autonomous Region:** Teola country
- Assam
  - **Rebel Organisation:** United Liberation Front of Assam, Muslim United Liberation Tigers of Assam

- Bodoland
    - o **Political Parties:** National Democratic Front of Bodoland
- Dimasaland
    - o **Political Party:** Dima Halim Daogah (Two factions)
- Garo
    - o **Rebel Organisations:** People's Liberation Front of Meghalaya/Achik National Volunteer Council
    - o **Proposed Autonomous Region:** Achikland
- Kamtapur
    - o **Political Party:** Kamtapur Peoples Party (political wing of KLO)
    - o **Rebel Organisations:** Kamtapur Liberation Organisation, Koch-Rajbongshi Liberation Organisation
    - o **Proposed Autonomous Region:** Kamtapur state curved out of West Bengal
- Karbi
    - o **Rebel Organisation:** Karbi National Volunteers, United People's Democratic Solidarity
    - o **Proposed Autonomous Region:** Karbi-Anglong
- Nagaland
    - o **Rebel Organisation:** National Socialist Council of Nagaland
    - o **Government-in-Exile:** Government of the People's Republic of Nagaland
    - o **Proposed State:** Nagalim, or Peoples Republic of Nagaland
- Manipur
    - o **Rebel Organisations:** Hmar People's Convention–Democrat, Manipur People's Liberation Front, United National Liberation Front, Revolutionary People's Front of Manipur, People's Revolutionary Party of Kangleipak
- Mizoram

- o **Rebel Organisations:** Zomi Revolutionary Organisation· Mizoram Farmers Liberation Force
- o **Proposed State:** Zozam

- Punjab
  - o **Proposed State:** Khalistan
  - o **Rebel Organisations:** Khalistan Commando Force, Babbar Khalsa International, Khalistan Zindabad Force, International Sikh Youth Federation, Khalistan Liberation Force
- Rayalaseema
- Tamil Nadu
  - o **Rebel Organisations:** Tamil National Retrieval Troops, Tamil Nadu Liberation Army
- Tripura
  - o **Rebel Organisations:** National Liberation Front of Tripura (two factions operating), All Tripura Tiger Force
- Vidarbha
  - o **Political Parties:** Vidarbha Rajya Party, Vidarbha Vikas Party, seeking to separate Vidarbha from Maharashtra.
- Zomi
  - o **Political Parties:** Zomi National Congress
  - o Indonesia
- South Moluccas (**member of the Unrepresented Nations and Peoples Organisation**)
  - o **Government-in-exile:** Republik Maluku Selatan
  - o **Pressure Group:** Maluku Sovereignty Front
- West Papua
  - o **Rebel Organisation:** Free Papua Movement
- Riau
- Sulawesi
- Bali
  - o **Proposed State:** Republic of Bali

    - **Pressure Group:** Bali Independence Movement
- Eastern Java
    - **Proposed State:** Republic of East(ern) Java
    - **Pressure Groups:** Local community political activists.

JAPAN

- Ryûkyûs, Ryukyuan people
- **Proposed State:** Republic of the Ryûkyûs
- **Political Party:** Ryukyu independence movement, Kariyushi Club (formerly "Ryûkyû Independent Party")

LAOS

- Hmong

MYANMAR (BURMA)

- Arakan
    - **Pressure Group:** Arakan Independence Alliance
- Chin
    - **Rebel Organisation:** Chin National Front
    - **Proposed State:** Chinland
- Kachin
    - **Political Party:** Kachin National Organisation
    - **Proposed State:** Kachinland
- Karen
    - **Pressure Group:** Karen National Union
    - **Rebel Organisation:** Karen National Liberation Army
    - **Proposed State:** Republic of Kawthoolei
- Karenni (**member of the Unrepresented Nations and Peoples Organisation)**
    - **Pressure Group:** Karenni National Progressive Party
    - **Rebel Organisation:** Karenni Army
    - **Government-in-Exile:** Karenni Provisional Government
    - **Proposed State:** United Karenni Independent States

- Kuki
  - **Pressure Group:** Kuki National Organisation
  - **Rebel Organisation:** Kuki National Army
  - **Proposed State:** Kukiland
- Mon
  - **Political Party:** New Mon State Party
- Nagaland
  - **Rebel organisation:** National Socialist Council of Nagaland
  - **Government-in-exile:** Government of the People's Republic of Nagaland
  - **Proposed state:** Nagalim, or Peoples Republic of Nagaland
- Rakhine people
  - **Pressure Group:** Arakan Rohingya National Organisation
- Shan (**Member of the Unrepresented Nations and Peoples Organisation**)
  - **Political Party:** Shan Democratic Union
  - **Pressure Group:** Restoration Council of Shan State
  - **Rebel Organisation:** Shan State Army
  - **Proposed State:** Federated Shan States
- Wa
  - **Political Party:** United Wa State Party
  - **Rebel Organisation:** United Wa State Army
  - **Proposed state:** Wa State
- Zomi
  - **Political Parties:** Zomi National Congress, Zomi Reunification Organisation
  - **Rebel Organisations:** Zomi National Front/Army, Zomi Revolutionary Army
  - **Proposed State:** Zogam, or Federated State of Zomi

PAKISTAN

- Balochistan
    - o **Rebel Organisation:** Balochistan Liberation Front, Balochistan Liberation Army
- Balawaristan
    - o **Political Party:** Gilgit Baltistan United Movement
    - o **Proposed State:** Republic of Gilgit Baltistan
- Sindh
    - o **Proposed State:** Sindhudesh
    - o **Political Movement:** Jeay Sindh Qaumi Mahaz
- Waziristan
    - o **Political Party:** Taliban, al-Qaeda
    - o **De facto State:** Islamic Emirate of Waziristan
- Pashtunistan

PHILIPPINES

- Bangsamoro
    - o **Political Party:** Moro National Liberation Front
    - o **Rebel Organisation:** Moro Islamic Liberation Front
    - o **Proposed state:** Federal Republic of Mindanao, Bangsamoro Juridical Entity
- Cordillera (**member of the Unrepresented Nations and Peoples Organisation)**
    - o **Political Party:** Cordillera Bodong Association
    - o **Rebel Organisation:** Cordillera People's Liberation Army

Russian Federation (Asia)

- Altai Republic
- Buryatia
    - o **Political Party:** All Buryat Association for the Development of Culture
- Khakassia
- Sakha

- o **Political Party:** Sakha-Amuk
- Tuva
  - o **Political Party:** People's Party of Sovereign Tuva, People's Front "Free Tuva"

SRI LANKA

- Tamil
  - o **Proposed state:** Tamil Eelam
  - o **Rebel organisation:** Liberation Tigers of Tamil Eelam (militarily inactive)

REPUBLIC OF CHINA (TAIWAN)

- Taiwan independence, Political status of Taiwan) (member of the Unrepresented Nations and Peoples Organisation)
  - o **Political Parties:** Pan-Green Coalition (Democratic Progressive Party, Taiwan Solidarity Union, Taiwan Independence Party)
  - o **Proposed State:** Republic of Taiwan
  - o **De facto State:** Republic of China

TAJIKISTAN

- Gorno-Badakhshan Autonomous Region
  - o **Political Party:** Lali Badakhshon

THAILAND

- Patani
  - o **Rebel Organisation:** Patani United Liberation Organisation (PULO) (irredentist)
  - o **Proposed State:** "Greater Patani State" (Negara Patani Raya)

Turkey (Asia)

- Assyrian/Chaldean/Syriac people (politically divided between Iraq, Iran, Lebanon, Syria and Turkey) (Assyria is a **member of the Unrepresented Nations and Peoples Organisation)**

- Kurdish people
    - o **Rebel Organisation:** Kurdistan Workers Party (PKK)
    - o **Proposed State:** Kurdistan

UZBEKISTAN

- Karakalpakstan
- Group: Free Karakalpakstan National Revival Party. (obscure: possibly only exists the Internet)

VIETNAM

- Degar
    - o **Proposed Autonomous Region:** Tây Nguyên
    - o **Pressure Group:** Montagnard Foundation

THE MIDDLE EAST

IRAN

- Assyrian people, Aramean-Syriac people and Chaldean people

See also: Assyrian independence

- Status: Politically divided between Iraq, Iran, Syria and Turkey
- Assyria is a member of the Unrepresented Nations and Peoples Organisation
- Kurdish people
- Political parties: Kurdistan Democratic Party of Iran (KDPI), Kurdistan Independence Party (PSK)
- Rebel organisations: Party for a Free Life in Kurdistan (PJAK), Komalah
- Proposed state: Kurdistan
- Balochistan
- Status: Formal groups not identified, but pressure for independence of Baloch people
- Arabistan (Khuzestan)

- o Rebel organisations: Al-Ahwaz Arab People's Democratic Popular Front, Ahwaz Arab Renaissance Party, Ahwaz Liberation Organisation
- o Pressure group: Democratic Solidarity Party of Al-Ahwaz

- Azerbaijan
- Proposed state: To be a part of Azerbaijan (supported only by a small minority)

IRAQ

- Assyrian people, Aramean-Syriac people and Chaldean people (politically divided between Iraq, Iran, Lebanon, Syria and Turkey; see respective entries) (See also: Assyrian independence) (The Assyrian Universal Alliance is a **member of the Unrepresented Nations and Peoples Organisation**)
  - o **Political Party:** Assyrian Universal Alliance (AUA)
  - o **Proposed Autonomous region:** Assyria
- Kurdish people (the Kurdistan Democratic Party (KDP) and the Patriotic Union of Kurdistan (PUK) are **members of the Unrepresented Nations and Peoples Organisation**)
  - o **Political Parties:** Kurdistan Democratic Party (KDP) and the Patriotic Union of Kurdistan (PUK)
  - o **Proposed State:** Kurdistan
- Shi'a Muslims
  - o **Political** Supreme Islamic Iraqi Council
- Iraqi Turkmen (**The Iraqi National Turkmen Party is a member of the Unrepresented Nations and Peoples Organisation**)
  - o **Political Party:** Iraqi Turkmen Front (ITF) (goal: recognition of Turkmen as a national minority)

ISRAEL

- Palestine
  - o **Rebel Organisations:** al-Aqsa Martyrs Brigade (now officially known as al-Shaid Yasser Arafat Brigades), Hamas, Palestinian Islamic Jihad, Tanzim

- o **Political Parties:** Hamas, Democratic Front for the Liberation of Palestine, Fatah, Palestine Liberation Front, Palestine Liberation Organisation, Palestinian National Authority, Popular Front for the Liberation of Palestine
- Jewish settlers in Judea (and Samaria)
  - o **Proposed State:** State of Judea

SYRIA

- Assyrian people, Aramean-Syriac people and Chaldean people (politically divided between Iraq, Iran, Lebanon, Syria and Turkey;) (Assyria is a **member of the Unrepresented Nations and Peoples Organisation**)
- Kurdish people
  - o **Political Party:** Kurdistan Democratic Party (KDP)
  - o **Rebel Organisation:** Kurdistan Workers Party (PKK)
  - o **Proposed State:** Kurdistan

YEMEN

- Tribal and regional factions call for autonomous rights in the Aden, Yemen and Dhofar regions.

EUROPE

Various ethnic groups in Europe are seeking greater autonomy or independence. In the European Union, several of these groups are members of the European Free Alliance. In some cases, the group seeks union with a neighboring country.

BELGIUM

- Brussels-Capital Region
  - o **Political Parties** (seeking a union with France):
    - Rassemblement Bruxelles-France
  - o **Political Parties** (seeking a union with Flanders):
    - Lijst Dedecker
    - Nieuw-Vlaamse Alliantie member of the European People's Party

    - Vlaamse Progressieven member of the European Free Alliance
    - Vlaams Belang member of the Identity, Tradition, Sovereignty-Group
    - VLOTT
- Flemish Region
  - **Political Parties** (seeking independence or confederation and, in some cases, a certain degree of cooperation with the Netherlands):
    - Lijst Dedecker
    - Nieuw-Vlaamse Alliantie member of the European People's Party
    - Vlaamse Progressieven member of the European Free Alliance
    - Vlaams Belang member of the Identity, Tradition, Sovereignty-Group
    - VLOTT
- German-speaking Community of Belgium
  - **Political Parties:**
    - Partei der deutschsprachigen Belgier member of the European Free Alliance
- Walloon Region
  - **Political Parties** (seeking a union with France):
    - Rassemblement Wallonie-France

BOSNIA AND HERZEGOVINA

- Republika Srpska
  - **Political Parties:** Alliance of Independent Social Democrats, Serbian Democratic Party

CROATIA

- Istria
  - **Political Parties:** Istrian Democratic Assembly, Istrian Democratic Forum

- Krajina:
  - o **Political Party:** Republic of Serbian Krajina Government in Exile

CYPRUS

- Northern Cyprus
  - o **De facto State:** Turkish Republic of Northern Cyprus

CZECH REPUBLIC

- Moravia
  - o **Political Parties:** Moravané member of the European Free Alliance

DENMARK

- Faroe Islands
  - o **Political Party:** Republican Party, People's Party, Centre Party, Self-Government Party

FINLAND

- Åland
- o **Political party:** Future of Åland member of the European Free Alliance
- o **Proposed state:** Åland
- Sami
- o **Proposed autonomous region:** Sápmi

FRANCE (EUROPE)

- Bourgogne
  - o **Political Party:** Mouvement de libération de la Bourgogne
  - o **Rebel Organisation:** GALB
- Alsace-Lorraine
  - o **Political Party:** Alsace d'Abord, Forum Nationaliste d'Alsace-Lorraine, Union du Peuple Alsacien
- Basque Country

- **Political Party**: Abertzaleen Batasuna (AB), Batasuna, Eusko Alkartasuna (EA) member of the European Free Alliance, Parti Nationaliste Basque.
- **Pressure Group**: All local politicians, even those in "French" parties, agree to demand a Basque département and co-officiality of Basque language, a demand that has been rejected by the French government.
- **Rebel Organisation**: Iparretarrak (defunct), ETA
- **Proposed state**: Euskadi or Euskal Herria (Basque Country)

- Brittany
  - **Pressure Groups**: Celtic League
  - **Political party**: Adsav, Breton Party, Union Démocratique Bretonne member of the European Free Alliance, Emgann
  - **Rebel Organisation**: Armée Révolutionnaire Bretonne, Front de Libération de la Bretagne
  - **Proposed state**: Brittany
- Corsica
  - **Political Party**: Corsica Nazione, Partitu di a Nazione Corsa member of the European Free Alliance
  - **Rebel Organisation**: National Front for the Liberation of Corsica
- Normandy
  - **Political Party**: Le Mouvement Normand
- Northern Catalonia
  - **Political Party**: Esquerra Republicana de Catalunya member of the European Free Alliance, Bloc Català
  - **Proposed State**: Països Catalans
- Savoy
  - **Political Party**: Savoy Region Movement (autonomist)
  - **Political Party**: Savoyard League (secessionist)

- Occitania
  - o **Political Party:** Partit de la Nacion Occitana, Partit Occitan member of the European Free Alliance, Iniciativa per Occitània, Anaram au Patac, Hartèra
- French Flanders or French Netherlands
  - o **Political Party:** Le Bloc Représentatif du Nord-France et Flandres Frances
  - o **Proposed State:** Les Pays-Bas français, Les Flandres françaises or Le Parti du Artois et Flandres

GERMANY

- Bavaria
  - o **Political Party:** Bavaria Party member of the European Free Alliance

ITALY

- Padania
  - o **Proposed State:** Padania
  - o **Political Parties:** Lega Nord
- Aosta Valley
  - o **Political Parties:** Valdotanian Union, Edelweiss Aosta Valley, Autonomist Federation, Valdotanian Renewal, Lively Aosta Valley, Lega Nord Valle d'Aosta
- Piedmont
  - o **Political Parties:** Lega Nord Piemont
- Lombardy
  - o **Political Parties:** Lega Lombarda, Lega Alleanza Lombarda, Lombard Independentist Front
  - o **Pressure groups:** Domà Nunch
- Trentino
  - o **Political Parties:** Union for Trentino, Lega Nord Trentino, Trentino Tyrolean Autonomist Party, Autonomist Trentino, Ladin Autonomist Union, United Valleys, Popular Autonomy, Fassa

- South Tyrol
  - o **Political Parties:** South Tyrolean People's Party, Union for South Tyrol, The Libertarians, South Tyrolean Freedom, Political Movement Ladins, Democratic Party of South Tyrol, Lega Nord Sud Tirolo
- Veneto
  - o **Movement:** Venetism
  - o **Political Parties:** Liga Veneta, North-East Project, Liga Veneta Repubblica, Venetians in Movement, Venetian National Party, Venetian People's Unity
- Friuli-Venezia Giulia
  - o **Political Parties:** Lega Nord Friuli-Venezia Giulia, Friuli Movement, Giulian Front
- Liguria
  - o **Political Party:** Lega Nord Liguria, Ligurian Independentist Movement
- Emilia
  - o **Political Parties:** Lega Nord Emilia
- Romagna
  - o **Political Parties:** Lega Nord Romagna
- Tuscany
  - o **Political Parties:** Lega Nord Toscana
- Marche
  - o **Political Parties:** Lega Nord Marche

UMBRIA

  - o **Political Parties:** Lega Nord Umbria
- Sardinia
  - o **Political Parties:** Sardinia Nation, Sardinian Reformers, Sardinian People's Party, Sardinian Democratic Union, Sardinian Action Party, Independence Republic of Sardinia
- Sicily

    - **Political Parties**: Movement for the Independence of Sicily, Sicilian Alliance, Sicilian People's Party, Sicilian National Front
    - **Pressure Groups**: Terra e Liberazione
- Southern Italy

Further information: Southern Italy autonomist movements

- Political parties: Movement for Autonomy, Federalist Alliance, Lega Sud Ausonia, Southern Action League

KOSOVO

- Republic of Kosovo,
    - **de facto state:** Republic of Kosovo
    - Political parties: Democratic League of Kosovo, Alliance for the Future of Kosovo, Democratic Party of Kosovo, National Movement for the Liberation of Kosovo, The People's Movement for Kosovo
    - Rebel organisation: Kosovo Liberation Army (became Kosovo Protection Corps)
    - See also: Kosovo independence precedent and International reaction to the 2008 Kosovo declaration of independence
- North Kosovo
    - **Proposed State:** part of Serbia
    - See also: 2008 unrest in Kosovo, 2004 unrest in Kosovo, and Kosovo Serb enclaves

MACEDONIA

- Illyrida
    - Political party: Democratic Party of Albanians
    - Status: Continued unrest within Albanian-majority areas of Macedonia

MOLDOVA

- Gagauz Yeri
    - Status: Turkic people–autonomous region.

- Transnistria
  - Status: De facto state: Transnistria

NETHERLANDS (EUROPE)

- Frisia
  - Political party: Frisian National Party, member of the European Free Alliance
  - Status: Democratic movement seeking greater autonomy for Frisian-speaking people in Fryslân
- Frisia
  - Political party: Frisian Alliance
  - Status: Democratic and cultural movement seeking independence for Frisian-speaking people in Fryslân, including areas now part of Germany, in addition to the Netherlands

NORWAY

- Sami
  - **Proposed Autonomous region:** Sápmi

POLAND

- Upper Silesia
  - **Political Party:** Silesian Autonomy Movement

ROMANIA

- Székler Land: Székely autonomy initiatives
  - **Political Organisation:** Székler National Council

RUSSIAN FEDERATION (EUROPE)

- Adygea
- Bashkortostan; no autonomist or secessionist movement can be identified as active in 2009
- Chechnya
  - **Rebel Organisation:** Chechen separatists
  - **Proposed State:** Chechen Republic of Ichkeria

- Dagestan
- Ingushetia
- Kabardino-Balkaria
- Karachay-Cherkessia
- Northern Ossetia
- Chechnya, Dagestan, Ingushetia
  - o **Proposed State:** Caucasian Emirate (claimed successor to Ichkeria)
- Chuvashia; no autonomist or secessionist movement can be identified as active in 2009
- Don Cossackia; no autonomist or secessionist movement can be identified as active in 2009
- Kaliningrad Oblast; ; no autonomist or secessionist movement can be identified as active in 2009
- Kalmykia; no autonomist or secessionist movement can be identified as active in 2009
- Karelia; no autonomist or secessionist movement can be identified as active in 2009
- Kuban Cossackia; no autonomist or secessionist movement can be identified as active in 2009
- Mordovia; no autonomist or secessionist movement can be identified as active in 2009
- Tatarstan
  - o **Political Party:** All-Tatar Public Center
  - o **Proposed State:** Tatarstan, Idel-Ural
- Udmurtia
  - o **Movement:** the Udmurt Counsel (sic) is a member of the Unrepresented Nations and Peoples Organisation
  - o **Proposed State:** Udmurtia

SERBIA

- Vojvodina; Hungarian Regional Autonomy
  - o **Political Parties:** Democratic Party of Vojvodina Hungarians, Democratic Community of Vojvodina

Hungarians, Hungarian Civic Alliance, Alliance of Vojvodina Hungarians; see also Hungarians in Vojvodina

SPAIN

- Basque Country and Navarre
  - o **Political Party:** Partido Nacionalista Vasco (member of the European Democratic Party), Eusko Alkartasuna (member of the European Free Alliance), Aralar, Nafarroa Bai, Basque Nationalist Action, Batasuna
  - o **Terrorist Organisation:** Euskadi Ta Askatasuna (ETA)
  - o **Proposed State:** Euskal Herria (Basque Country)
- Catalonia (Catalan independentism), the Valencian Community and the Balearic Islands
  - o **Civil Organisation:** Sobirania i Progrés, Plataforma pel Dret de Decidir, Cercle d'Estudis Sobiranistes
  - o **Pressure Groups:** Catalunya Acció, Free Catalonia, Endavant, Moviment de Defensa de la Terra, Reagrupament
  - o **Youth Pressure Groups:** Maulets, Coordinadora d'Assemblees de Joves de l'Esquerra Independentista, Joventuts d'Esquerra Republicana de Catalunya
  - o **Political Parties (Secessionist):** Candidatura d'Unitat Popular (in the Catalan Countries); Esquerra Republicana de Catalunya (in Catalonia, Balearic Islands, and Northern Catalonia; called Esquerra Republicana del País Valencià in the Valencian Country), member of the European Free Alliance; Estat Català (in Catalonia).
  - o **Political Parties (Autonomist):** Convergència Democràtica de Catalunya, Unió Democràtica de Catalunya (in Catalonia); Partit Socialista de Mallorca-Entesa Nacionalista, Entesa de l'Esquerra de Menorca (in the Balearic Islands); Bloc Nacionalista Valencià (in the Valencian Country).
  - o **Proposed state:** Catalan Countries (united or federated);

Principality of Catalonia, Valencian Community and Balearic Islands.

- Galicia
  - o **Political Party**: Bloque Nacionalista Galego (Galician Nationalist Block)(autonomist), member of the European Free Alliance, NÓS-Unidade Popular (WE-Popular Unity)(independentist), Frente Popular Galego (Galician Popular Front)(independentist), Partido Galeguista (The Galician Party) , Terra Galega Galician Coalition (Centrist nationalist Party)
  - o **Youth Pressure Groups**: Galiza Nova, AGIR, CAF
  - o **Proposed State**: Galiza
  - o Galician nationalism
- Andalusia
  - o **Political Parties (Autonomist)**: Partido Andalucista, Partido Socialista Andaluz, Bloque Andaluz de Izquierdas, Partido Comunista del Pueblo Andaluz
  - o **Political Parties (Secessionist)**: Nación Andaluza, Asamblea Nacional de Andalucia
  - o **Youth Movement**: Jaleo!!!, Juventudes Andalucistas
  - o **Proposed state**: Andalusia
- Aragon
  - o **Political Party (Autonomist)**: Chunta Aragonesista member of the European Free Alliance
  - o **Political Party (Secessionist)**: Estau Aragonés, Tierra Aragonesa
  - o **Pressure Groups**: Puyalón
  - o **Youth Movement**: Astral, Chobenalla Aragonesista, A Enrestida
  - o **Proposed State**: Aragón
- Asturias
  - o **Political Parties (Autonomist)**: Partíu Asturianista, URAS
  - o **Political Parties (Secessionist)**: Unidá Nacionalista

Asturiana member of the European Free Alliance, Bloque por Asturies, Andecha Astur
  - **Youth Movements:** Darréu, UNA-Mocedá , Fai!
  - **Trade Unions:** CSI, SUATEA, Frenti Estudiantil d'Asturies
  - **Other Pro-independence Organisations:** Sofitu
  - **Proposed State:** Socialist Republic of Asturies
  - **Proposed Flag:** Asturina
- Canary Islands
  - **Political Party:** Congreso Nacional de Canarias (MPAIAC Party), Alternativa Nacionalista Canaria, Unidad del Pueblo
  - **Youth Movement:** Inekaren, Azarug
  - **Syndicates:** Intersindical Canaria, Frente Sindical Obrero de Canarias
  - **Terrorist Organisation:** MPAIAC (defunct)
  - **Proposed State:** Canary Islands
- Cantabria
  - **Political Party:** Conceju Nacionaliegu Cántabru
- Castile
  - **Political Parties (autonomist):** Tierra Comunera
  - **Political Parties (secessionist):** Izquierda Castellana, Movimiento Popular Castellano,
  - **Youth Movement:** YESCA
  - **Proposed State:** Castile
  - **Proposed Flag:** Pendón Morado,Pendón Estrellado
- León
  - **Political Parties:** Unión del Pueblo Leonés (UPL or Leonese People's Union),Partido Regionalista del País Leonés (PREPAL),Unión del Pueblo Salmantino (UPS), Partido Carlista del Reino de León (PC)
  - **Proposed State:** País Llïonés–Leonese Country (Conceyu Xoven)

- **Proposed Autonomous Region:** Comunidad Autónoma de León–Autonomous Community of León (UPL, PREPAL, UPS, PC)
- **Civil Organisations:** Ciudadanos del Reino de Leon (CCRRLL), Ciudadanos Zamoranos (CCZZ)
- **Youth Movements:** Conceyu Xoven (Young Council)
- **Principal Article:** Leonese regionalist movement

SWEDEN

- Sami
  - **Proposed Autonomous Region:** Sápmi
- Scania Political or cultural organisation: Stiftelsen Skånsk Framtid (Scanian Future Foundation) (member of the Unrepresented Nations and Peoples Organisation)

SWITZERLAND

- Jura
  - **Political party:** Mouvement Indépendantiste Jurassien (Jurassian Independentist Movement), Mouvement Autonomiste Jurassien (Jurassian Autonomist Movement), Groupe Bélier (Youth activists movement),
- Ticino
  - **Political party:** Lega dei Ticinesi
  - **Pressure groups:** Domà Nunch

UKRAINE

- Crimea (the Mejlis of the Crimean Tatar People is a **member of the Unrepresented Nations and Peoples Organisation)**
- Carpathian Ruthenia: Congress of Carpathian Ruthenians

UNITED KINGDOM AND ASSOCIATED TERRITORIES (EUROPE)

SECESSIONIST MOVEMENTS

- Cornwall: Cornish nationalism

- o **Pressure Groups:** Revived Cornish Stannary Parliament, Tyr Gwyr Gweryn, Celtic League
- o **Political Parties:** Mebyon Kernow–Party for Cornwall member of the European Free Alliance, Cornish Green Party, Cornish National Party
- o **Millitant Organisation:** Cornish National Liberation Army

- England: English nationalism
  - o **Political Party:** Free England Party
- Gibraltar
  - o **Political Party:** Progressive Democrats
- Guernsey
- Northern Ireland ("Six Counties"): Irish nationalism, Irish Republicanism, Ulster nationalism
  - o **Pressure Groups:** Celtic League
  - o **Political Parties:** Sinn Féin, Social Democratic and Labour Party, Republican Sinn Féin, Irish Republican Socialist Party, Ulster Third Way, Ulster Independence Movement
  - o **Militant Organisation:** Provisional Irish Republican Army, Real IRA, Continuity IRA, Irish National Liberation Army
- Isle of Man
  - o **Pressure Groups:** Celtic League
  - o **Political Parties:** Mec Vannin, Liberal Vannin
- Scotland: Scottish independence
  - o **Pressure Groups:** Independence First, Celtic League, SRSM
  - o **Political Parties:** Scottish National Party member of the European Free Alliance, Scottish Green Party, Scottish Socialist Party, Scottish Enterprise Party, Solidarity
- Wales: Welsh independence
  - o **Pressure Groups:** Cymuned, Cymdeithas yr Iaith Gymraeg, Celtic League

- o **Political Parties**: Plaid Cymru member of the European Free Alliance, Forward Wales, Wales Green Party, Cymru Annibynnol

AUTONOMIST MOVEMENTS

- Cornish self-government movement, Constitutional status of Cornwall
  - o **Pressure Groups:** Cornwall 2000, Cornish Solidarity
- England: English nationalism
  - o **Pressure Groups:** Campaign for an English Parliament
  - o **Political Party:** English Democrats Party, Free England Party
- Wessex
  - o **Pressure Groups:** Wessex Constitutional Convention
  - o **Political Parties:** Wessex Regionalist Party, officially registered as a political party.
- Isle of Wight
  - o **Pressure Group/Political Party** : Isle of Wight Party.
- Shetland
  - o Crown Dependency of Forvik, Udal Law groupShetland Independent NewsletterShetland and Orkney Udal Law groupShetland ConversationCrown Dependency of Forvik

NORTH AMERICA, CANADA

SECESSIONIST MOVEMENTS

- Alberta
  - o **Political Party:** Separation Party of Alberta
- British Columbia + Pacific Northwestern US
  - o **Proposed State:** Cascadia
  - o **Pressure Group:** Republic of Cascadia, Cascadian Independence Project
- Quebec

- o **Civil Organisation:** Saint-Jean-Baptiste Society, Mouvement national des Québécois et des Québécoises (MNQ), Rassemblement pour l'indépendance du Québec (RIQ), Les Intellectuels pour la souveraineté (IPSO), Mouvement de libération nationale du Québec (MLNQ), Réseau de Résistance du Québecois (RRQ)
- o **Labour Union:** Confédération des syndicats nationaux (CSN), Centrale des syndicats du Québec (CSQ), Fédération des travailleurs du Québec (FTQ), Union des artistes (UDA)
- o **Political Party:** Parti Québécois, Bloc Québécois, Québec solidaire, Parti indépendantiste
- o **Proposed State:** Quebec

- Saskatchewan
  - o **Political Party:** Western Independence Party of Saskatchewan
- Western Canada
  - o **Political Party:** Western Independence Party, Western Block Party

AUTONOMIST MOVEMENTS

- Nunatsiavut
- Quebec
  - o **Political Party:** Action démocratique du Québec

DENMARK (NORTH AMERICA)

- Greenland
  - o **Political Party:** Inuit Ataqatigiit

MEXICO

- Chiapas
  - o Zapatista autonomous self-governing region and rebel movement

UNITED STATES (NORTH AMERICA)

- Alaska
  - **Political Party:** Alaskan Independence Party
- Black Belt (U.S. region)
  - **Pressure Group(s):** RNA, New Black Panther Party, Black Liberation Army
  - **Proposed State:** Republic of New Afrika
- Lakota Sioux
  - **Pressure Group(s):** Lakotah Oyate
  - **Proposed State:** Republic of Lakotah
- Maine
  - **Proposed State:** Republic of Maine
  - **Pressure Group(s):** Free Maine
- Minnesota
  - **Proposed State:** People's Republic of the North Star
  - **Pressure Group(s):** North Star Republic
- New England
  - **Pressure Group(s):** New England Confederation Alliance
- New Hampshire
  - **Pressure Group(s):** republicofnh.org Free State Project
- New York City
  - **Pressure Groups(s):** Peter Vallone, Free City of Tri-Insula
- New York State
  - **Pressure Group(s):** Joseph Sawiki (Western Long Island), Randy Kuhl (Upstate)
  - **Proposed State:** Independent Long Island
- Northern New England, Newfoundland, Atlantic Northeast, Middle Atlantic States, Ontario, Canadian prairies, Midwest, Northern Western United States, and Pacific Northwest (Areas of North America [excluding The South] primarily inhabited by whites)—Vinland

- **Pressure Group(s):** Various white nationalist, white separatist, and Neo-Nazi groups
- **Proposed State:** Vinland

- Oklahoma
  - **Pressure Group(s):** Indian Nations Republic of Oklahoma represented by the five largest Native American tribes in that state.
- Pacific Northwest + British Columbia, Canada
  - **Proposed State:** Cascadia
  - **Pressure Group(s):** Republic of Cascadia, Cascadian Independence Project
- The South
  - **Pressure Group(s):** League of the South
  - **Political Party:** Southern Party
  - **Proposed State:** Confederate States of America
- South Carolina
  - **Proposed State:** Republic of South Carolina
  - **Pressure Group(s):** SC League of the South , Christian Exodus
- Southwestern United States
  - **Proposed State:** Aztlan
  - **Pressure Group(s):** Nation of Aztlán, MEChA, Raza Unida Party
- Texas
  - **Proposed State:** Republic of Texas
  - **Pressure Group(s):** Texas Secession
- Vermont
  - **Proposed State:** Green Mountain Republic of Vermont
  - **Pressure Group(s):** Second Vermont Republic

CENTRAL AMERICA AND CARIBBEAN

ST. KITTS AND NEVIS

- Nevis

- o **Political Party:** Concerned Citizens' Movement, Nevis Reformation Party

TRINIDAD AND TOBAGO

- Tobago
  - o **Political party:** Democratic Action Congress

UNITED KINGDOM (CARIBBEAN)

- Montserrat
  - o **Political Parties:** New People's Liberation Movement, United National Front
- Turks and Caicos Islands

UNITED STATES (CARIBBEAN)

- Puerto Rico
  - o **Political Party:** Puerto Rican Independence Party (PIP)
  - o **Pressure Group:** Puerto Rican Nationalist Party, Pro-Independence Universitarian Federation (FUPI), Union of Socialist Youth (UJS), Movimiento Independentista Nacional Hostosiano (MINH), Socialist Front (FS), National Congress for the Descolonisations (CONADE)
  - o **Rebel Organisation:** Boricua Popular Army (Macheteros), Fuerzas Armadas de Liberación Nacional (FALN)

U.S. VIRGIN ISLANDS AND BRITISH VIRGIN ISLANDS

- **Political Party:** Caribbean Virgin Islands Independence Party and the Union of Virgin Islands Party

SOUTH AMERICA

ARGENTINA

- Mapuche (politically divided between Argentina and Chile; see respective entries) **(member of the Unrepresented Nations and Peoples Organisation)**
  - o **Pressure Group:** The All Lands Conseil (Consejo de Todas las Tierras)

  - o **Proposed State**: Mapuche Nation

BRAZIL

- Rio-Grandense Republic
  - o **Pressure Group**: Movimento Pampa Livre (Free Pampa Movement)
  - o Status: Looking for separate the Rio Grande do Sul State from Brazil, restoring the Rio-Grandense Republic independence.
- Southern Region
  - o **Pressure Group**: O Sul é Meu País movement ("The south is my country")
  - o **Status**: Group looking for independence of the states of Paraná, Santa Catarina and Rio Grande do Sul.
- State of São Paulo
  - o Pressure group: Movimento São Paulo Independente
  - o Status: Website says that São Paulo could be viable as an independent state. No evidence of any popular support.

CHILE

- Mapuche (politically divided between Argentina and Chile; see respective entries) (member of the Unrepresented Nations and Peoples Organisation)
  - o **Pressure Group**: The All Lands Conseil (Consejo de Todas las Tierras)

PERU

- Aymara (politically divided between Bolivia, Chile and Peru; see respective entries)
  - o **Pressure Group**: Tupac Katari Guerrilla Army
  - o **Proposed State**: Collasuyu

COLOMBIA

- Departament of Chocó
  - o **Proposed State**: Independent Republic of Chocó

  - o **Pressure Group:** Revolutionary Popular Movement for the Independence of the Chocó

OCEANIA

AUSTRALIA

- Australian Aborigines (member of the Unrepresented Nations and Peoples Organisation)
  - o **Pressure group:** Aboriginal Tent Embassy

CHILE

- Rapa Nui (Easter island)

FIJI

- Rotuma

FRANCE (OCEANIA)

- French Polynesia
  - o **Political Party:** Tavini Huiraatira
- New Caledonia
  - o **Political Party:** Kanak Socialist National Liberation Front (Caledonian Union, Party of Kanak Liberation), Kanak Socialist Liberation, Labour Party, Union of Pro-Independence Co-operation Committees, Renewed Caledonian Union
  - o **Proposed State:** New Caledonia

KIRIBATI

- Banaba Island

NEW ZEALAND

- South Island
  - o South Island Independence
  - o **Political Parties:** South Island Party (2008) (doubtful whether 'active')
  - o **Pressure Groups:** Cut the Cable, South Island First, Zealandia Independence Project

- o **Proposed State:** South Zealand, Zealandia
- Cook Islands
- Niue
- Tokelau

PAPUA NEW GUINEA

- Bougainville (**member of the Unrepresented Nations and Peoples Organisation**)
    - o **Political Party:** Bougainville Revolutionary Army

UNITED STATES (OCEANIA)

- Guam
    - o **Pressure Movement:** Chamoru Nation, Organisation of People for Indigenous Rights
    - o **Local Self-Government:** Guam Commission on Self-Determination, now known as the Commission on Decolonisation
- Hawaii
    - o **Pressure Movement:** Hawaiian sovereignty movement
    - o **Political Party:** Nation of Hawai'i and other nationalist groups attempting to reassert the sovereignty of the Kingdom of Hawai'i. The Kingdom of Hawai'i was internationally recognized as an independent country until the Republic of Hawaii was recognized in its place in 1894.
- Northern Marianas
    - o **Pressure Movement:** Taotao Tano

VANUATU

- Malekula
    - o **Proposed State:** N'Makiaute
- Northern islands
    - o **Proposed State:** Federation Na Griamel.

Chapter 19

CASUS BELLI

Casus Belli is a Latin expression meaning the justification for acts of war. Casus means "incident", "rupture" or indeed "case", while belli means "of war". It is usually distinguished from casus foederis, with casus belli being used to refer to offenses or threats directly against a nation, and casus foederis to refer to offenses or threats to another, allied, nation with which the justifying nation is engaged in a mutual defense treaty, such as NATO.

It is sometimes misspelled and mispronounced as "causus belli" since this resembles the English "cause" (and a different Latin word, causa {cause}). "Casus Belli" is sometimes pronounced this way because the term is used with the meaning of "cause for war", instead of "case of war" (notice that "case" comes from Latin "casus"). The OED, however, gives the pronunciation above.

The term came into wide usage in the seventeenth and eighteenth centuries with the writings of Hugo Grotius (1625), Cornelius van Bynkershoek (1737), and Jean-Jacques Burlamaqui (1748), among others, and the rise of the political doctrine of jus ad bellum or "just war theory". Informal usage varies beyond its technical definition to refer to any "just cause" a nation may claim for entering into a conflict. As such, it has been used both retroactively to describe situations in history before the term came into wide usage and in the present day when describing situations when war has not been formally declared.

Formally, a government would lay out its reasons for going to war, as well as its intentions in prosecuting it and the steps that might be taken to avert it. In so doing, the government would attempt to demonstrate that it was going to war only as a last resort (ultima Ratio) and that it in fact possessed "just cause" for doing so. Effectively international law today only allows three situations as legal cause to go to war: out of self-defense, defense of an ally under a mutual defense pact, or sanctioned by the UN. Any war for another cause is considered illegal and those who engage in it subject to prosecution for a war crime.

Proschema (plural proschemata) is the Greek equivalent term. The stated reasons may or may not be the actual reason for waging the war (prophases). The term was first popularized by Thucydides in his History of the Peloponnesian War, who identified fear, honor, and interest as the three primary real reasons that wars are waged, while proschemata commonly play up nationalism or fearmongering (as opposed to rational or reasonable fears).

REASONS FOR USE

Countries need a public justification for attacking another country. This justification is needed to galvanize internal support for the war, as well as gain the support of potential allies. The United States Declaration of Independence is an example of a written casus belli.

In the post World War Two era, the UN Charter prohibits signatory countries from engaging in war except 1) as a means of defending themselves against aggression, or 2) unless the UN as a body has given prior approval to the operation. The UN also reserves the right to ask member nations to intervene against non-signatory countries which embark on wars of aggression. In effect, this means that countries in the modern era must have a plausible casus belli for initiating military action, or risk possible UN sanctions or intervention.

HISTORICAL EXAMPLES

This section outlines a number of the more famous or controversial cases of casus belli which have occurred in modern times.

WORLD WAR I

A political assassination provided the trigger that led to the outbreak of World War I. The assassination in June 1914 of Archduke Franz Ferdinand of Austria at Sarajevo in Austria-Hungary by Gavrilo Princip, a Yugoslav nationalist from Bosnia, Austrian subject and member of Young Bosnia, was used by Austria-Hungary as a casus belli for declaring war on Serbia.

The Russian Empire started to mobilise its troops in defence of its ally Serbia, which resulted in the German Empire declaring war on Russia in support of its ally Austria-Hungary. Very quickly, after the involvement of France, the Ottoman Empire and the British Empire, five of the six great European powers became involved in the first European general war since the Napoleonic Wars.

WORLD WAR II

In his autobiography Mein Kampf, Adolf Hitler had advocated in the 1920s a policy of lebensraum ("living space") for the German people, which in practical terms meant German territorial expansion into Eastern Europe.

In August 1939, in order to implement the first phase of this policy, Germany's Nazi government under Hitler's leadership staged the Gleiwitz incident, which was used as a casus belli for the invasion of Poland the following September. Since Poland's allies Britain and France honoured their alliance and subsequently declared war on Germany, the invasion of Poland marks the start of World War II.

In 1941, acting once again in accordance with the policy of lebensraum, Nazi Germany invaded the Soviet Union, using the casus belli of pre-emptive war to justify the act of aggression.

The Soviet Union also employed a manufactured casus belli during World War II. In November 1939, shortly after the outbreak of hostilities between Germany, Britain and France, the Soviet Union staged the shelling of the Russian village of Mainila, which it blamed on the Finns. This manufactured incident was then used as a casus belli for the invasion of Finland. In 1998, Russian President Boris Yeltsin admitted that the invasion had in fact constituted a Soviet war of aggression.

SIX-DAY WAR

A casus belli played a prominent role during the Six-Day War of 1967. The Israeli government had a short list of casus belli acts, that it would consider provocations justifying armed retaliation. The most important was a blockade of the Straits of Tiran leading into Eilat, Israel's only port to the Red Sea, through which Israel received much of its oil. After several border incidents between Israel and Egypt's allies Syria and Jordan, Egypt expelled UNEF peacekeepers from the Sinai Peninsula, established a military presence at Sharm el-Sheikh, and announced a blockade of the straits, prompting Israel to cite its casus belli in opening hostilities against Egypt.

VIETNAM WAR

Many historians have suggested that the Gulf of Tonkin Incident was a manufactured pretext for the Vietnam War. North Vietnamese Naval officials have publicly stated that the USS Maddox was never fired on by North Vietnamese naval forces. The movie "The Fog of War" contains an admission from former US Defense Secretary at the time Robert McNamara that the Gulf of Tonkin Incident "never happened".

Deniability played favorably into the propaganda efforts of North Vietnam throughout the war, and for some years to follow. However, the PAVN Museum in Hanoi found it irresistable to proudly display "Part of a torpedo boat... which successfully chased away the USS Maddox August, [sic] 2nd 1964".

1982 ISRAELI INVASION OF LEBANON

The casus belli cited by Israel for its June 1982 invasion of Lebanon was the attempted assassination of the Israeli Ambassador in London, which the Israeli government blamed on the PLO (although the attempt had actually been made by the PNLM, a Palestinian splinter group implacably opposed to the PLO). In reality however, the invasion had long been planned by the Israelis, who were concerned about the growing power of the PLO in Lebanon.

TURKEY AND GREECE

In 1995, The Turkish Parliament issued a casus belli against Greece in reaction to an enacted extension of Greek territorial waters from 6 nautical miles (11 km) to 12 nautical miles (22 km) from the coast (See Aegean dispute).

WAR ON TERROR

The casus belli for the Bush administration's conceptual War on Terror, which resulted in the 2001 Afghan war and the 2003 Iraq war, was the September 11, 2001 attacks on the World Trade Center in New York City, The Pentagon in Arlington, Virginia and the apparently intended attack on the United States Capitol in Washington, D.C.

2003 INVASION OF IRAQ

When the United States invaded Iraq in 2003, it cited non-compliance with the terms of cease-fire for the 1990-1991 Gulf War, as well as planning in 1997 the attempted assasinations of former President George Bush and then-sitting President Bill Clinton as its stated casus belli..

Cited by the Bush administration was Saddam Hussein's weapons of mass destruction (WMD) programme. The administration claimed that Iraq had not conformed with its obligation to disarm under past UN Resolutions, and that Saddam Hussein was actively attempting to acquire a nuclear weapons capability as well as enhance an existing arsenal of chemical and biological weapons. Secretary of State Colin Powell addressed a plenary session of the United Nations Security Council on February 5, 2003 citing these reasons as justification for military action.

Subsequent to the invasion, a US government-sponsored report concluded that although Saddam Hussein had intended to resume WMD production once the Gulf War sanctions were lifted, none of the alleged WMD stockpiles were found during or after the subsequent invasion.

CASUS BELLI IN POPULAR CULTURE

- Canadian Bacon was a satirical comedy directed by Michael Moore about a U.S. President who used the CIA to create a phony attack on the United States and blame it on Canada, intentionally creating conflict with Canada.
- In the computer game Europa Universalis and its sequels, casus belli plays a significant role in war. If war is declared on another nation without a casus belli, the aggressor will suffer a stability penalty, causing a general unrest within the country.
- In the computer games Supreme Ruler 2010 and Supreme Ruler 2020, casus belli is affected by several factors during gameplay. The largest increase happens when an unjustified war is declared or triggered.
- In the board game Pax Britannica by Victory Games, players are limited to declaring war if they have a casus belli against the defending nation.
- In Turkish and several other Turkic languages casus means "spy" and belli means "apparent/obvious"; therefore it is often miscomprehended by the Turkish speaking people as the "Spy is apparent" or "Spy is obvious", instead of "acts of war".
- In the CBS Television series Jericho, the nineteenth episode of Season 1 (original airdate 4/18/2007) the title of the episode itself is "Casus Belli". The name stems from the revelation that the town of New Bern, Kansas is building mortars in preparation of a full scale invasion of Jericho while pretending to fly under the flag of truce.

FAULT LINE WAR

A Fault Line War is one that takes place between two or more identity groups (usually religious or ethnic) from different civilisations. It is a communal conflict between states or groups from different civilisations that has become violent. These wars may take place between states, between nongovernmental groups, or between states and nongovernmental groups. Most often, the issue in a fault line war is often territory, but it could also be over the control of people. Such wars within states may involve groups that are predominantly located in different territories or groups that are intermixed. In the latter, violence often erupts periodically.

The issue at stake in a fault line war is very symbolic for at least one of the groups involved. Because the issue is one of fundamental identity, these wars are longer and more difficult to resolve than conventional warfare. And even when agreements are reached, the groups are rarely fully satisfied, and often the hatred is only dissolved through genocide.

Chapter 20

HORSES IN WARFARE

The first use of Horses in Warfare occurred over 5000 years ago. The earliest evidence of horses ridden in warfare dates from Eurasia between 4000 and 3000 BC. A Sumerian illustration of warfare from 2500 BC depicts some type of equine pulling wagons. By 1600 BC, improved harness and chariot designs made chariot warfare common throughout the Ancient Near East, and the earliest written training manual for war horses was a guide for training chariot horses written about 1350 BC. As formal cavalry tactics replaced the chariot, so did new training methods, and by 360 BC, the Greek cavalry officer Xenophon had written an extensive treatise on horsemanship. The effectiveness of horses in battle was also revolutionised by improvements in technology, including the invention of the saddle, the stirrup, and later, the horse collar.

Many different types and sizes of horses were used in war, depending on the form of warfare. The type used varied with whether the horse was being ridden or driven, and whether they were being used for reconnaissance, cavalry charges, raiding, communication, or supply. Throughout history, mules and donkeys as well as horses played a crucial role in providing support to armies in the field.

Horses were well suited to the warfare tactics of the nomadic cultures from the steppes of Central Asia. Several East Asian cultures made extensive use of cavalry and chariots. Muslim warriors relied upon light cavalry in their campaigns throughout North Africa,

Asia, and Europe beginning in the 7th and 8th centuries AD. Europeans used several types of war horses in the Middle Ages, and the best-known heavy cavalry warrior of the period was the armoured knight. With the decline of the knight and rise of gunpowder in warfare, light cavalry again rose to prominence, used in both European warfare and in the conquest of the Americas. In the Americas, the use of horses and development of mounted warfare tactics were learned by several tribes of indigenous people and in turn, highly mobile horse regiments were critical in the American Civil War.

A modern-day joust at a Renaissance Fair, performed in late medieval style plate armour.

Horse cavalry began to be phased out after World War I in favour of tank warfare, though a few horse cavalry units were still used into World War II. By the end of World War II, horses were seldom seen in battle, but were still used extensively for the transport of troops and supplies. Today, formal horse cavalry units have almost disappeared, although horses are still seen in use by organised armed fighters in Third World countries. Many nations still maintain small units of mounted riders for patrol and reconnaissance, and military horse units are also used for ceremonial and educational purposes. Horses are also used for historical reenactment of battles, law enforcement, and in equestrian competitions derived from the riding and training skills once used by the military.

TYPES OF HORSES USED IN WARFARE

A fundamental principle of equine conformation is "form to function". Therefore, the type of horse used for various forms of warfare depended on the work performed, the weight a horse needed to carry or pull, and distance travelled. Weight affects speed and endurance, creating a trade-off: armour added protection, but added weight reduces maximum speed. Therefore, various cultures had different military needs. In some situations, one primary type of horse was favoured over all others. In other places, multiple types were needed; warriors would travel to battle riding a lighter horse of greater speed and endurance, and then switch to a heavier horse, with greater weight-carrying capacity, when wearing heavy armour in actual combat.

The average horse can carry up to approximately 30% of its body weight. While all horses can pull more than they can carry, the weight horses can pull varies widely, depending on the build of the horse, the type of vehicle, road conditions, and other factors. Horses harnessed to a wheeled vehicle on a paved road can pull as much as eight times their weight, but far less if pulling wheelless loads over unpaved terrain. Thus, horses that were driven varied in size and had to make a trade-off between speed and weight, just as did riding animals. Light horses could pull a small war chariot at speed. Heavy supply wagons, artillery, and support vehicles were pulled by heavier horses or a larger number of horses. The method by which a horse was hitched to a vehicle also mattered: horses could pull greater weight with a horse collar than they could with a breast collar, and even less with an ox yoke.

LIGHT-WEIGHT

Light, oriental horses such as the ancestors of the modern Arabian, Barb, and Akhal-Teke were used for warfare that required speed, endurance and agility. Such horses ranged from about 12 hands to just under 15 hands (48 to 60 inches (1.2 to 1.5 m)), weighing approximately 800 to 1,000 pounds (360 to 450 kg). To move quickly, riders had to use lightweight tack and carry relatively light weapons such as bows, light spears, javelins, or, later, rifles. This was the original horse used for early chariot warfare, raiding, and light cavalry.

Relatively light horses were used by many cultures, including the Ancient Egyptians, the Mongols, the Arabs, and the American Indians. Throughout the Ancient Near East, small, light animals were used to pull chariots designed to carry no more than two passengers, a driver and a warrior. In the European Middle Ages, a light weight war horse became known as the rouncey.

MEDIUM-WEIGHT

Medium-weight horses developed as early as the Iron Age with the needs of various civilisations to pull heavier loads, such as chariots capable of holding more than two people, and, as light cavalry evolved into heavy cavalry, to carry heavily-armoured riders. The Scythians were among the earliest cultures to produce taller, heavier horses. Larger horses were also needed to pull supply wagons and, later on, artillery pieces. In Europe, horses were also used to a limited extent to maneouvre cannon on the battlefield as part of dedicated horse artillery units. Medium-weight horses had the greatest range in size, from about 14.2 hands but stocky, to as much as 16 hands (58 to 64 inches (1.5 to 1.6 m)), weighing approximately 1,000 to 1,200 pounds (450 to 540 kg). They generally were quite agile in combat, though they did not have the raw speed or endurance of a lighter horse. By the Middle Ages, larger horses in this class were sometimes called destriers. They may have resembled modern Baroque or heavy warmblood breeds. Later, horses similar to the modern warmblood often carried European cavalry.

Arriving Japanese samurai prepares to man the fortification against invaders of the Mongol invasions of Japan, painted c. 1293 AD. By this time, a medium-weight horse was used.

HEAVY-WEIGHT

Large, heavy horses, weighing from 1,500 to 2,000 pounds (680 to 910 kg), the ancestors of today's draught horses, were used, particularly in Europe, from the Middle Ages onward. They pulled heavy loads, having the power to pull weapons or supply wagons and disposition to remain calm under fire. Some historians believe they may have carried the heaviest-armoured knights of the European Late Middle Ages though others dispute this claim, indicating that the destrier, or knight's battle horse, was a medium-weight animal. It is also disputed whether the destrier class included draught animals or not. Breeds at the smaller end of the heavyweight category may have included the ancestors of the Percheron, agile for their size and physically able to manoeuvre in battle.

OTHER EQUIDS

Horses were not the only equids used to support human warfare. Donkeys have been used as pack animals from antiquity to the present. Mules were also commonly used, especially as pack animals and to pull wagons, but also occasionally for riding. Because mules are often both calmer and hardier than horses, they were particularly useful for strenuous support tasks, such as hauling supplies over difficult terrain. However, under gunfire, they were less cooperative than horses, so were not used to haul artillery on battlefields. The size of a mule and work to which it was put depended largely on the breeding of the mare that produced the mule. Mules could be lightweight, medium weight, or even, when produced from draught horse mares, of moderate heavy weight.

TRAINING AND DEPLOYMENT

The oldest known manual on training horses for chariot warfare was written c. 1350 BC by the Hittite horsemaster, Kikkuli. An ancient manual on the subject of training riding horses, particularly for the Ancient Greek cavalry is Hippike (On Horsemanship) written about 360 BC by the Greek cavalry officer Xenophon. One of the earliest texts from Asia was that of Kautilya, written about 323 BC.

Whether horses were trained to pull chariots, to be ridden as light or heavy cavalry, or to carry the armoured knight, much training was required to overcome the horse's natural instinct to flee from noise, the smell of blood, and the confusion of combat. They also learned to accept any sudden or unusual movements of humans while using a weapon or avoiding one. Horses used in close combat may have been taught, or at least permitted, to kick, strike, and even bite, thus becoming weapons themselves for the warriors they carried.

In most cultures, a war horse used as a riding animal was trained to be controlled with limited use of reins, responding primarily to the rider's legs and weight. The horse became accustomed to any necessary tack and protective armour placed upon it, and learned to balance under a rider who would also be laden with weapons and armour. Developing the balance and agility of the horse was crucial.

The origins of the discipline of dressage came from the need to train horses to be both obedient and manoeuvrable. The Haute ecole or "High School" movements of classical dressage taught today at the Spanish Riding School have their roots in manoeuvres designed for the battlefield. However, the airs above the ground were unlikely to have been used in actual combat, as most would have exposed the unprotected underbelly of the horse to the weapons of foot soldiers.

Horses used for chariot warfare were not only trained for combat conditions, but because many chariots were pulled by a team of two to four horses, they also had to learn to work together with other animals in close quarters under chaotic conditions.

TECHNOLOGICAL INNOVATIONS

Horses were probably ridden in prehistory before they were driven. However, evidence is scant, mostly simple images of human figures on horse-like animals drawn on rock or clay. The earliest tools used to control horses were bridles of various sorts, which were invented nearly as soon as the horse was domesticated. Evidence of bit wear appears on the teeth of horses excavated at the archaeology sites of the Botai culture in northern Kazakhstan, dated 3500–3000 BC.

HARNESS AND VEHICLES

The invention of the wheel was a major technological innovation that gave rise to chariot warfare. At first, equines, both horses and onagers, were hitched to wheeled carts by means of a yoke around their necks in a manner similar to that of oxen. However, such a design is incompatible with equine anatomy, limiting both the strength and mobility of the animal. By the time of the Hyksos invasions of Egypt, c. 1600 BC, horses were pulling chariots with an improved harness design that made use of a breastcollar and breeching, which allowed a horse to move faster and pull more weight.

Even after the chariot had become obsolete as a tool of war, there still was a need for technological innovations in pulling technologies; horses were needed to pull heavy loads of supplies and weapons. The invention of the horse collar in China during the 5th century AD (Southern and Northern Dynasties) allowed horses to pull greater weight than they could when hitched to a vehicle with the ox yokes or breast collars used in earlier times.

The horse collar arrived in Europe during the 9th century, and became widespread by the 12th century.

Chariots and archers were weapons of war in Ancient Egypt.

RIDING EQUIPMENT

Two major innovations that revolutionised the effectiveness of mounted warriors in battle were the saddle and the stirrup. Riders quickly learned to pad their horse's backs to protect themselves from the horse's spine and withers, and fought on horseback for centuries with little more than a blanket or pad on the horse's back and a rudimentary bridle. To help distribute the rider's weight and protect the horse's back, some cultures created stuffed padding that resembles the panels of today's English saddle. Both the Scythians and Assyrians used pads with added felt attached with a surcingle or girth around the horse's barrel for increased security and comfort. Xenophon mentioned the use of a padded cloth on cavalry mounts as early as the 4th century BC.

The saddle with a solid framework, or "tree," provided a bearing surface to protect the horse from the weight of the rider, but was not widespread until the 2nd century AD. However, it made a critical difference, as horses could carry more weight when distributed across a solid saddle tree. A solid tree, the predecessor of today's Western saddle, also allowed a more built-up seat to give the rider greater security in the saddle. The Romans are credited with the invention of the solid-treed saddle.

Haniwa horse statuette, complete with saddle and stirrups, 6th century, Kofun period, Japan. Tokyo National Museum

An invention that made cavalry particularly effective was the stirrup. A toe loop that held the big toe was used in India possibly as early as 500 BC, and later a single stirrup was used as a mounting aid. But the first set of paired stirrups appeared in China about 322 AD during the Jin Dynasty. By the 7th century, thanks primarily to invaders from Central Asia, stirrups spread across Asia to Europe. The stirrup, which allowed a rider greater leverage with weapons, as well as both increased stability and mobility while mounted, gave nomadic groups such as the Mongols a decisive military advantage. Stirrups were known in Europe in the 8th century, but pictorial and literary references to their use date only from the 9th century. Widespread use is credited to the Vikings, who spread the stirrup to other cultures in the 9th and 10th centuries.

TACTICS

The first archaeological evidence of horses used in warfare dates from between 4000 and 3000 BC in the steppes of Eurasia, in what today is Ukraine, Hungary, and Romania. Not long after domestication of the horse, people in these locations began to live together in large fortified towns for protection from the threat of horseback-riding raiders, who could attack and escape faster than people of more sedentary cultures could follow. The use of horses in organised warfare was also documented early in recorded history. One of the first depictions of equids is the "war panel" of the Standard of Ur, in Sumer, dated c. 2500 BC, showing horses (or possibly onagers or mules) pulling a four-wheeled wagon.

CHARIOT WARFARE

Among the earliest evidence of chariot use are the burials of horse and chariot remains by the Andronovo (Sintashta-Petrovka) culture in modern Russia and Kazakhstan, dated to approximately 2000 BC. The oldest documentary evidence of what was probably chariot warfare in the Ancient Near East is the Old Hittite Anitta text, of the 18th century BC, which mentioned 40 teams of horses at the siege of Salatiwara. The Hittites became well known throughout the ancient world for their prowess with the chariot. Widespread use of the chariot in warfare across most of Eurasia coincides approximately with the development of the composite bow, known from c. 1600 BC. Further improvements in wheels and axles, as well as innovations in weaponry, soon resulted in chariots being driven in battle by Bronze Age societies from China to Egypt.

The Hyksos invaders brought the chariot to Ancient Egypt in the 16th century BC and the Egyptians adopted its use from that time forward. The oldest preserved text related to the handling of war horses in the ancient world is the Hittite manual of Kikkuli, which dates to about 1350 BC, and describes the conditioning of chariot horses.

Chariots existed in the Minoan civilisation, as they were inventoried on storage lists from Knossos in Crete, dating to around 1450 BC. Chariots were also used in China as far back as the Shang Dynasty (c. 1600–1050 BC), where they appear in burials. The high point of chariot use in China was in the Spring and

Autumn Period (770–476 BC), although they continued in use up until the 2nd century BC.

Descriptions of the tactical role of chariots in Ancient Greece and Rome are rare. The Iliad, possibly referring to Mycenaen practices used c. 1250 BC, describes the use of chariots for transporting warriors to and from battle, rather than for actual fighting. Later, Julius Caesar, invading Britain in 55 and 54 BC, noted British charioteers throwing javelins, then leaving their chariots to fight on foot.

CAVALRY

Some of the earliest examples of horses being ridden in warfare were horse-mounted archers or spear-throwers, dating to the reigns of the Assyrian rulers Ashurnasirpal II and Shalmaneser III. However, these riders sat far back on their horses, a precarious position for moving quickly, and the horses were held by a handler on the ground, keeping the archer free to use the bow.

Thus, these archers were more a type of mounted infantry than true cavalry. The Assyrians developed cavalry in response to invasions by nomadic people from the north, such as the Cimmerians, who entered Asia Minor in the 8th century BC and took over parts of Urartu during the reign of Sargon II, approximately 721 BC. Mounted warriors such as the Scythians also had an influence on the region in the 7th century BC. By the reign of Ashurbanipal in 669 BC, the Assyrians had learned to sit forward on their horses in the classic riding position still seen today and could be said to be true light cavalry. The ancient Greeks used both light horse scouts and heavy cavalry, although not extensively, possibly due to the cost of keeping horses.

Heavy cavalry was believed to have been developed by the Ancient Persians, although others argue for the Sarmatians. By the time of Darius (558–486 BC), Persian military tactics required horses and riders that were completely armoured, and selectively bred a heavier, more muscled horse to carry the additional weight. The cataphract was a type of heavily armored cavalry with distinct tactics, armour, and weaponry used from the time of the Persians up until the Middle Ages.

In Ancient Greece, Phillip of Macedon is credited with developing tactics allowing massed cavalry charges. The most famous Greek heavy cavalry units were the companion cavalry of Alexander the Great. The Chinese of the 4th century BC during the Warring States Period (403–221 BC) began to use cavalry against rival states. To fight nomadic raiders from the north and west, the Chinese of the Han Dynasty (202 BC – 220 AD) developed effective mounted units.

Cavalry was not used extensively by the Romans during the Roman Republic period, but by the time of the Roman Empire, they made use of heavy cavalry. However, the backbone of the Roman army was the infantry.

HORSE ARTILLERY

Once gunpowder was invented, another major use of horses was as draught animals for heavy artillery, or cannons. In addition to field artillery, where horse-drawn guns were attended by gunners on foot, many armies had artillery batteries where each gunner was provided with a mount. Horse artillery units generally used lighter pieces, pulled by six horses. "9-pounders" were pulled by eight horses, and heavier artillery pieces needed a team of twelve. Congreve rockets, a type of rocket artillery, required about 25 horses. With the individual riding horses required for officers, surgeons and other support staff, as well as those pulling the artillery guns and supply wagons, an artillery battery of six guns could require 160 to 200 horses. Horse artillery usually came under the command of cavalry divisions, but in some battles, such as Waterloo, the horse artillery were used as a rapid response force, repulsing attacks and assisting the infantry. Agility was important; the ideal artillery horse was 15 to 16 hands high, strongly built, but able to move quickly.

A lifesize model of a c. 1850 Swedish horse artillery team towing a light artillery piece.

ASIA

CENTRAL ASIA

Relations between steppe nomads and the settled people in and around Central Asia were often marked by conflict. The nomadic lifestyle was well suited to warfare, and steppe cavalry became some of the most militarily potent forces in the world, only limited by nomads' frequent lack of internal unity. Periodically, strong leaders would organise several tribes into one force, creating an almost unstoppable power.

These unified groups included the Huns, who invaded Europe, and under Attila, conducted campaigns in both eastern France and northern Italy, over 500 miles apart, within two successive campaign seasons. Other unified nomadic forces included the Wu Hu attacks on China, and the Mongol conquest of much of Eurasia.

INDIA

The literature of ancient India describes numerous Central Asian horse nomads. Some of the earliest references to the use of horses in central Asian warfare are Puranic texts, which refer to an invasion of India by the joint cavalry forces of the Sakas, Kambojas,

Yavanas, Pahlavas, and Paradas, called the "five hordes" (pañca.ganah) or "Kœatriya" hordes (Kœatriya ganah). About 1600 BC, they captured the throne of Ayutthaya by dethroning the Vedic king, Bahu. Later texts, such as the Mahâbhârata, c. 950 BC, appear to recognise efforts taken to breed war horses and develop trained mounted warriors, stating that the horses of the Sindhu and Kamboja regions were of the finest quality, and the Kambojas, Gandharas, and Yavanas were expert in fighting from horses.

In technological innovation, the early toe loop stirrup is credited to the cultures of India, and may have been in use as early as 500 BC. Not long after, the cultures of Mesopotamia and Ancient Greece clashed with those of central Asia and India. Herodotus (484–425 BC) wrote that Gandarian mercenaries of the Achaemenid Empire were recruited into the army of emperor Xerxes I of Persia (486–465 BC), which he led against the Greeks. A century later, the "Men of the Mountain Land," from north of Kabul River, served in the army of Darius III of Persia when he fought against Alexander the Great at Arbela in 331 BC. In battle against Alexander at Massaga in 326 BC, the Assakenoi forces included 20,000 cavalry. The Mudra-Rakshasa recounted how cavalry of the Shakas, Yavanas, Kambojas, Kiratas, Parasikas, and Bahlikas helped Chandragupta Maurya (c. 320–298 BC) defeat the ruler of Magadha and take the throne, thus laying the foundations of Mauryan Dynasty in Northern India.

Mughal cavalry used gunpowder weapons, but were slow to replace the traditional composite bow. Under the impact of European military successes in India, some Indian rulers adopted the European system of massed cavalry charges, although others did not. By the 18th century, Indian armies continued to field cavalry, but mainly of the heavy variety.

EAST ASIA

The Chinese used chariots for horse-based warfare until light cavalry forces became common during the Warring States era (402–

221 BC). A major proponent of the change to riding horses from chariots was Wu Ling, c. 320 BC. However, conservative forces in China often opposed change, and cavalry never became as dominant as in Europe. Cavalry in China also did not benefit from the additional cachet attached to being the military branch dominated by the nobility.

Yabusame archers, Edo period.

The Japanese samurai fought as cavalry for many centuries. They were particularly skilled in the art of using archery from horseback. The archery skills of mounted samurai were developed by training such as Yabusame, which originated in 530 AD and reached its peak under Minamoto Yoritomo (1147–1199 AD) in the Kamakura Period. They switched from an emphasis on mounted bowmen to mounted spearmen during the Sengoku period (1467–1615 AD).

MIDDLE EAST

During the period when various Islamic empires controlled much of the Middle East as well as parts of West Africa and the Iberian peninsula, Muslim armies consisted mostly of cavalry, made up of fighters from various local groups, mercenaries and Turkoman tribesmen. The latter were considered particularly skilled as both lancers and mounted archers. In the 9th century the use of Mamluks, slaves raised to be soldiers for various Muslim rulers, became increasingly common. Mobile tactics, advanced breeding of horses, and detailed training manuals made Mamluk cavalry a highly efficient fighting force. The use of armies consisting mostly of cavalry continued among the Turkish people who founded the Ottoman Empire. Their need for large mounted forces lead to an establishment of the sipahi, cavalry soldiers who were granted lands in exchange for providing military service in times of war.

Battle of Higueruela, 1431. Spanish heavy cavalry fighting the light cavalry Moorish forces of Sultan Muhammed IX of Granada.

Mounted Muslim warriors conquered North Africa and the Iberian Peninsula during the 7th and 8th centuries AD following the Hegira, or Hijra, of Muhammad in 622 AD. By 630 AD, their influence expanded across the Middle East and into western North Africa. By 711 AD, the light cavalry of Muslim warriors had reached Spain, and controlled most of the Iberian peninsula by 720. Their mounts were of various oriental types, including the North African Barb. A few Arabian horses may have come with the Ummayads who settled in the Guadalquivir valley. Another strain of horse that came with Islamic invaders was the Turkoman horse. Muslim invaders travelled north from nowadays Spain into France, where they were defeated by the Frankish ruler Charles Martel at the Battle of Tours in 732 AD.

EUROPE

THE MIDDLE AGES

During the European Middle Ages, there were three primary types of war horses: The destrier, the courser, and the rouncey, which differed in size and usage. A generic word used to describe medieval war horses was charger, which appears interchangeable with the other terms. The medieval war horse was of moderate size, rarely exceeding 15.2 hands (62 inches (1.6 m)). Heavy horses were logistically difficult to maintain and less adaptable to varied terrains. The destrier of the early Middle Ages was moderately larger than the courser or rouncey, in part to accommodate heavier armoured knights. However, destriers were not as large as draught horses, averaging between 14.2 hands and 15 hands (58 to 60 inches (1.5 to 1.5 m)). On the European continent, the need to carry more armour against mounted enemies such as the Lombards and Frisians led to the Franks developing heavier, bigger horses. As the amount of armour and equipment increased in the later Middle Ages, the height of the horses increased; some late medieval horse skeletons were of horses over 15 hands.

A re-imagination of Louis III and Carloman's 879 victory over the vikings; Jean Fouquet, Grandes Chroniques de France

Stallions were often used as destriers due to their natural aggression. However, the use of mares by European warriors cannot be discounted from literary references, and mares, who were quieter and less likely to call out and betray their position to the enemy, were the preferred war horse of the Moors, Muslims who invaded various parts of Southern Europe from 700 AD through the 15th century.

USES

The heavy cavalry charge, while it could be effective, was not a common occurrence. Battles were rarely fought on land suitable for heavy cavalry. While mounted riders remained effective for initial attacks, by the end of the 14th century, it was common for knights to dismount to fight, while their horses were sent to the rear, kept ready for pursuit. Pitched battles were avoided if possible, with most offensive warfare in the early Middle Ages taking the form of sieges, and in the later Middle Ages as swift mounted raids called chevauchées, with lightly armed warriors on swift horses.

Jousting is a sport that evolved out of heavy cavalry practice.

The war horse was also seen in hastiludes—martial war games such as the joust, which began in the 11th century both as sport and to provide training for battle. Specialised destriers were bred for the purpose, although the expense of keeping, training, and outfitting them kept the majority of the population from owning one. While some historians suggest that the tournament had become a theatrical event by the fifteenth and sixteenth centuries, others argue that jousting continued to help cavalry train for battle until the Thirty Years' War.

TRANSITION

The decline of the armoured knight was probably linked to changing structures of armies and various economic factors, and not obsolescence due to new technologies. However, some historians attribute the demise of the knight to the invention of gunpowder, or to the English longbow. Some link the decline to both technologies. Others argue these technologies actually contributed to the development of knights: Plate armour was first developed to resist early medieval crossbow bolts, and the full harness worn by the early 15th century developed to resist longbow arrows. From the 14th century on, most plate was made from hardened steel, which resisted early musket ammunition. In addition, stronger designs did not make plate heavier; a full harness of musket-proof plate from the 17th century weighed 70 pounds (32 kg), significantly less than 16th century tournament armour.

The move to predominately infantry-based battles from 1300–1550 was linked to both improved infantry tactics and changes in weaponry. By the 16th century, the concept of a combined-arms professional army had spread throughout Europe. Professional armies emphasized training, and were paid via contracts, a change from the ransom and pillaging which reimbursed knights in the past. When coupled with the rising costs involved in outfitting and maintaining armour and horses, the traditional knightly classes began to abandon their profession. Light horses, or prickers, were still used for scouting and reconnaissance; they also provided a defensive screen for marching armies. Large teams of draught horses or oxen pulled the heavy early cannon. Other horses pulled wagons and carried supplies for the armies.

EARLY MODERN PERIOD

During the early modern period the shift continued from heavy cavalry and the armoured knight to unarmoured light cavalry, including Hussars and Chasseurs à cheval. Light cavalry facilitated better communication, using fast, agile horses to move quickly across battlefields. The ratio of footmen to horsemen also increased over the period as infantry weapons improved and footmen became more mobile and versatile, particularly once the musket bayonet replaced the more cumbersome pike. During the Elizabethan era, mounted units included cuirassiers, heavily armoured and equipped with lances; light cavalry, who wore mail and bore light lances and pistols; and "petronels", who carried a early carbine. As heavy cavalry use declined, armour was increasingly abandoned, and dragoons, whose horses were rarely used in combat, became more common: mounted infantry provided reconnaissance, escort and security. However, many generals still used the heavy mounted charge, from the late 17th and early 18th centuries, where sword-wielding wedge-formation shock troops penetrated enemy lines, to the early 19th century, where armoured heavy cuirassiers were employed.

French cuirassier in 1809

Light cavalry continued to play a major role, particularly after the Seven Years War when Hussars started to play a larger part in battles.. Though some leaders preferred tall horses for their mounted troops, this was as much for prestige as for increased shock ability, and many troops used more typical horses, averaging 15 hands. Cavalry tactics altered, with-fewer mounted charges, more reliance on drilled manoeuvres at the trot, and use of firearms once within range. Ever-more elaborate movements, such as wheeling and caracole, were developed to facilitate the use of firearms from horseback. These tactics were not greatly successful in battle, since pikemen protected by musketeers could deny cavalry room to manoeuvre.

However, the advanced equestrianism required survives into the modern world as dressage. While restricted, cavalry was not rendered obsolete. As infantry formations developed in tactics and skills, artillery became essential to break formations; in turn, cavalry was required to both combat enemy artillery, which was susceptible to cavalry while deploying, and to charge enemy infantry formations broken by artillery fire. Thus, successful warfare depended in a balance of the three arms: cavalry, artillery and infantry.

As regimental structures developed, many units selected horses of uniform type. Some, such as the Royal Scots Greys even specified colour. Trumpeters often rode distinctive horses, so they stood out. Regional armies developed type preferences, such as British hunters, German Hanoverians, and steppe ponies of the Cossacks, but once in the field, the lack of supplies typical of wartime meant that horses of all types were used.

Since horses were such a vital component of most armies in early modern Europe, many instituted state stud farms to breed horses for the military. However, in wartime, supply rarely matched the demand, resulting in some cavalry troops fighting on foot.

19TH CENTURY

In the 19th century, distinctions between heavy and light cavalry became less significant; by the end of the Peninsular War, heavy cavalry were performing the scouting and outpost duties previously undertaken by light cavalry, and by the end of the 19th century the roles had effectively merged. Most armies at the time preferred cavalry horses to stand 15.2 hands (62 inches (160 cm)) and weigh 990 to 1,100 pounds (450 to 500 kg), although cuirassiers frequently had heavier horses. Lighter horses were used for scouting and raiding. Cavalry horses were generally obtained at 5 years of age, and were in service from 10 or 12 years, barring loss. However, losses of 30–40% were common during a campaign, due to conditions of the march as well as enemy action. Mares and geldings were preferred over less-easily managed stallions.

"Napoleon I with his Generals." This painting shows light cavalry horses which come into use as officer's mounts in 18th and 19th century Europe.

During the French Revolutionary Wars and the Napoleonic Wars, the cavalry's main offensive role were as shock troops. In defence, cavalry were used to attack and harass the enemy's infantry flanks as they advanced. Cavalry were frequently used prior to an infantry assault, to force an infantry line to break and reform into formations vulnerable to infantry or artillery. Frequently, infantry followed behind in order to secure any ground won. Conversely, cavalry also broke up enemy lines following successful infantry action.

Mounted charges were carefully managed. A charge's maximum speed was 20 km/h; moving faster resulted in a break in formation and fatigued horses. Charges occurred across clear rising ground, and were effective against infantry both on the march and when deployed in a line or column.

A foot battalion formed in line was vulnerable to cavalry, and could be broken or destroyed by a well-formed charge. Traditional cavalry functions altered by the end of the 19th century. Many cavalry units transferred in title and role to "mounted rifles": troops trained to fight on foot, but retaining mounts for rapid deployment, as well as for patrols, scouting, communications, and defensive screening. These troops differed from mounted infantry, who used horses for transport but did not perform the old cavalry roles of reconnaissance and support.

SUB-SAHARAN AFRICA

Horses were used for warfare in the central Sudan since the 9th century, where they were considered "the most precious commodity following the slave." The first conclusive evidence of horses playing a major role in the warfare of West Africa dates to the 11th century when the region was controlled by the Almoravids, a Muslim Berber dynasty. During the 13th and 14th centuries, cavalry became an important factor in the area. This coincided with the introduction of larger breeds of horses and the widespread adoption of saddles and stirrups. Increased mobility played a part in the formation of new power centers, such as the Oyo Empire in what today is Nigeria.

The authority of many African Islamic states such as the Bornu Empire also rested in large part on their ability to subject neighboring peoples with cavalry. Despite harsh climate conditions, endemic diseases such as trypanosomiasis the African horse sickness and unsuitable terrain that limited the effectiveness of horses in many parts of Africa, horses were continuously imported and were, in some areas, a vital instrument of war. The introduction of horses also intensified existing conflicts, such as those between the Herero and Nama people in Namibia during the 19th century.

Kanem-Bu warriors armed with spears.
The Earth and Its Inhabitants, 1892.

The African slave trade was closely tied to the imports of war horses, and as the prevalence of slaving decreased, fewer horses were needed for raiding. This significantly decreased the amount of mounted warfare seen in West Africa. By the time of the Scramble for Africa and the introduction of modern firearms in the 1880s, the use of horses in African warfare had lost most of its effectiveness. Nonetheless, in South Africa during the Second Boer War (1899-1902), cavalry and other mounted troops were the major combat force for the British, since the horse-mounted Boers moved too quickly for infantry to engage.

The Boers presented a mobile and innovative approach to warfare, drawing on strategies that had first appeared in the American Civil War. The terrain was not well-suited to the British horses, resulting in the loss of over 300,000 animals. As the campaign wore on, losses were replaced by more durable African Basuto ponies, and Waler horses from Australia.

THE AMERICAS

The horse had been extinct in the Western Hemisphere for approximately 10,000 years prior to the arrival of Spanish Conquistadors in the early 16th century. Consequently, the Indigenous peoples of the Americas had no warfare technologies that could overcome the considerable advantage provided by

European horses and gunpowder weapons. In particular this resulted in the conquest of the Aztec and Inca empires. The speed and increased impact of cavalry contributed to a number of early victories by European fighters in open terrain, though their success was limited in more mountainous regions. The Incas' well-maintained roads in the Andes enabled quick mounted raids, such as those undertaken by the Spanish while resisting the siege of Cuzco in 1536–7.

Native Americans quickly adopted the horse and were highly effective light cavalry. Comanche-Osage fight. George Catlin, 1834

Indigenous populations of South America soon learned to use horses. In Chile, the Mapuche began using cavalry in the Arauco War in 1586. They drove the Spanish out of Araucanía at the beginning of the 17th century. Later, the Mapuche conducted mounted raids known as Malónes, first on Spanish, then on Chilean and Argentine settlements until well into the 19th century. In North America, Native Americans also quickly learned to use horses. In particular, the people of the Great Plains, such as the Comanche and the Cheyenne, became renowned horseback fighters. By the 19th century, they presented a formidable force against the United States Army.

During the American Revolutionary War (1775–1783), the Continental Army made relatively little use of cavalry, primarily relying on infantry and a few dragoon regiments. The United States Congress eventually authorized federal horse regiments in

1855. The newly-formed American cavalry adopted tactics based on experiences fighting over vast distances during the Mexican War (1846–1848) and against indigenous peoples on the western frontier, abandoning some European traditions.

Confederate general Robert E. Lee and Traveller. Cavalry played a significant role in the American Civil War.

During the American Civil War (1861–1865), cavalry held the most important and respected role it would ever hold in the American military.[note 4] Field artillery in the American Civil War was also highly mobile. Both horses and mules pulled the guns, though only horses were used on the battlefield. At the beginning of the war, most of the experienced cavalry officers were from the South and thus joined the Confederacy, leading to the Confederate Army's initial battlefield superiority. The tide turned at the 1863 Battle of Brandy Station, part of the Gettysburg campaign, where the Union cavalry, in the largest cavalry battle ever fought on the North American continent,[note 5] ended the dominance of the South. By 1865, Union cavalry were decisive in achieving victory. So important were horses to individual soldiers that the surrender terms at Appomattox allowed every Confederate cavalryman to take his horse home with him.

20TH CENTURY

Although cavalry was used extensively throughout the world during the 19th century, horses became less important to warfare after the beginning of the 1900s. Light cavalry was still seen on the battlefield at the beginning of the 20th century, but formal mounted cavalry began to be phased out for combat during and immediately after World War I, although units that included horses still had military uses well into World War II.

WORLD WAR I

World War I saw great changes in the use of cavalry. Tanks were beginning to take over the role of shock combat. The mode of warfare changed, and the use of trench warfare, barbed wire and machine guns rendered traditional cavalry almost obsolete.

Australian Imperial Force light horsemen, 1914

Early in the War, cavalry skirmishes were common, and horse-mounted troops widely used for reconnaissance. On the Western Front cavalry were an effective flanking force during the "Race to the Sea" in 1914, but were less useful once trench warfare was established. There a few examples of successful shock combat, and cavalry divisions also provided important mobile fire power. Cavalry played a greater role on the Eastern Front, where trench warfare was less common. On the Eastern Front, and also against the Ottomans, the "cavalry was literally indispensable." British Empire cavalry proved adaptable, since they were trained to fight both on foot and while mounted, while other European cavalry relied primarily on shock action.

On both fronts, the horse was also used as a pack animal. Because railway lines could not withstand artillery bombardments, horses carried ammunition and supplies between the railheads and the rear trenches, though the horses generally were not used in the actual trench zone. This role of horses was critical, and thus horse fodder was the single largest commodity shipped to the front by some countries. Following the war, many cavalry regiments were converted to mechanised, armoured divisions, with light tanks developed to perform many of the cavalry's original roles.

WORLD WAR II

Several nations used horse units during World War II. The Polish army used cavalry to defend against the armies of Nazi Germany during the 1939 invasion. Both the Germans and the Soviet Union maintained cavalry units throughout the war, particularly on the Eastern Front. The British Army used horses early in the war, and the final British cavalry charge was on March 21, 1942, when the Burma Frontier Force encountered Japanese infantry in central Burma. The only American cavalry unit during World War II was the 26th Cavalry. They challenged the Japanese invaders of Luzon, holding off armoured and infantry regiments during the invasion of the Philippines, repelled a unit of tanks in Binalonan, and successfully held ground for the Allied armies' retreat to Bataan.

Polish Cavalry during a Polish Army manoeuvre in late 1930s.

Throughout the war, horses and mules were an essential form of transport, especially in by the British in the rough terrain of Italy and the Middle East. The United States Army utilised a few cavalry and supply units during the war, but there were concerns that the Americans did not use horses often enough. In the campaigns in North Africa, generals such as George S. Patton lamented their lack, saying, "had we possessed an American cavalry division with pack artillery in Tunisia and in Sicily, not a German would have escaped."

The German and the Soviet armies used horses until the end of the war for transportation of troops and supplies. The German Army, strapped for motorised transport because its factories were needed to produce tanks and aircraft, used around 2.75 million horses—more than it had used in World War I. One German infantry division in Normandy in 1944 had 5,000 horses. The Soviets used 3.5 million horses. Today, many of the historical military uses of the horse have evolved into peacetime applications, including exhibitions, historical reenactments, work of peace officers, and competitive events. Formal combat units of mounted cavalry are mostly a thing of the past, with horseback units within the modern military used for reconnaissance, ceremonial, or crowd control purposes. With the rise of mechanised technology, horses in formal national militias were displaced by tanks and armored fighting vehicles, sometimes still referred to as "cavalry".

MODERN USES

ACTIVE MILITARY

Organised armed fighters on horseback are occasionally seen. The best-known current examples are the Janjaweed, militia groups seen in the Darfur region of Sudan, who became notorious for their attacks upon unarmed civilian populations in the Darfur conflict. Many nations still maintain small numbers of mounted military units for certain types of patrol and reconnaissance duties in extremely rugged terrain, including the current conflict in Afghanistan. The only remaining operationally-ready, fully horse-mounted regular regiment in the world is the Indian Army's 61st Cavalry.

U.S. special forces troops on horseback in Afghanistan, 2001

LAW ENFORCEMENT AND PUBLIC SAFETY

Mounted police have been used since the 18th century, and still are used worldwide to control traffic and crowds, patrol public parks, keep order in processionals and during ceremonies and perform general street patrol duties. Today, many cities still have mounted police units. In rural areas, horses are used by law enforcement for mounted patrols over rugged terrain, crowd control at religious shrines, and border patrol.

Mounted police in Poznań, Poland.

In rural areas, law enforcement that operates outside of incorporated cities may also have mounted units. These include specially deputised, paid or volunteer mounted search and rescue units sent into roadless areas on horseback to locate missing people. Law enforcement in protected areas may use horses in places where mechanised transport is difficult or prohibited. Horses can be an essential part of an overall team effort as they can move faster on the ground than a human on foot, can transport heavy equipment, and provide a more rested rescue worker when a subject is found.

CEREMONIAL AND EDUCATIONAL USES

Many countries throughout the world maintain traditionally-trained and historically uniformed cavalry units for ceremonial, exhibition, or educational purposes. One example is the Horse Cavalry Detachment of the U.S. Army's 1st Cavalry Division. This unit of active duty soldiers approximates the weapons, tools, equipment and techniques used by the United States Cavalry in the 1880s. It is seen at change of command ceremonies and other public appearances. A similar detachment is the Governor General's Horse Guards, Canada's Household Cavalry regiment, the last remaining mounted cavalry unit in the Canadian Forces. Nepal's King's Household Cavalry is a ceremonial unit with over 100 horses and is the remainder of the Nepalese cavalry that existed since the 19th century. An important ceremonial use is in military funerals, which often have a caparisoned horse as part of the procession, "to symbolize that the warrior will never ride again". Horses are also used in many historical reenactments. Reenactors try to recreate the conditions of the battle or tournament with equipment that is as authentic as possible.

Horse Cavalry Detachment of the U.S. Army's 1st Cavalry Division demonstrating a mock cavalry charge at Fort Bliss, Texas

EQUESTRIAN SPORT

Modern-day Olympic equestrian events are rooted in cavalry skills and classical horsemanship. The first equestrian events at the Olympics were introduced in 1912, and through 1948, competition was restricted to active-duty officers on military horses. Only after 1952, as mechanisation of warfare reduced the number of military riders, were civilian riders allowed to compete. Dressage traces its origins to Xenophon and his works on cavalry training methods, developing further during the Renaissance in response to a need for different tactics in battles where firearms were used. The three-phase competition known as Eventing developed out of cavalry officers' needs for versatile, well-schooled horses. Though show jumping developed largely from fox hunting, the cavalry considered jumping to be good training for their horses, and leaders in the development of modern riding techniques over fences, such as Federico Caprilli, came from military ranks. Beyond the Olympic disciplines are other events with military roots. Competitions with weapons, such as mounted shooting and tent pegging, test the combat skills of mounted riders.

Chapter 21

SUN TZU

Sun is his family name, and Tzu is an honorific in classic Chinese, roughly equivalent to Sir, or the Learned Gentleman. Sun Tzu is traditionally believed to be the author of The Art of War, sometimes called the Sun Tzu, an influential ancient Chinese book on military strategy considered to be a prime example of Taoist strategy. Sun has had a significant impact on Chinese and Asian history and culture, both as an author of the Art of War and as a legendary figure. During the 19th and 20th centuries, Sun's The Art of War grew in popularity and saw practical use in Western society, and his work has continued to influence both Asian and Western culture and politics.

Historians have questioned whether or not Sun was an authentic historical figure. Traditional accounts place him in the Spring and Autumn Period of China (722–481 BC) as a heroic general of the King of Wu who lived c. 544—496 BC. Scholars accepting his historicity place his supposed writing The Art of War in the Warring States Period (476–221 BC), based on the descriptions of warfare in the text. Traditional accounts state that his descendant, Sun Bin, also wrote a master treatise on military tactics.

LIFE

According to traditional sources, such as the 2nd century BC biography written by Sima Qian, Sun was born in Qi during the Spring and Autumn Period of China (722–481 BC) and became a heroic general for the king of Wu, Helü. His victories then inspired him to write The Art of War. The period was a time of constant war among seven nations (Zhao, Qi, Qin, Chu, Han, Wei and Yan) seeking to control all of China.

The king of Wu tested Sun's skills by commanding him to train a harem of 360 concubines into soldiers. Sun divided them into two companies, appointing the two concubines most favored by the king as the company commanders. When Sun first ordered the concubines to face right, they giggled. In response, Sun said that the general, in this case himself, was responsible for ensuring that soldiers understood the commands given to them. Then, he reiterated the command, and again the concubines giggled. Sun then ordered the execution of the king's two favored concubines, to the king's protests.

He explained that if the general's soldiers understood their commands but did not obey, it was the fault of the officers. Sun also said that once a general was appointed, it was their duty to carry out their mission, even if the king protested. After both concubines were killed, new officers were chosen to replace them. Afterwards, both companies performed their maneuvers flawlessly.

Sima's biography claims that Sun later proved on the battlefield that his theories were effective, that he had a successful military career, and that he wrote The Art of War based on his tested expertise. His descendant, Sun Bin, also became a famous scholar of the military arts.

THE ART OF WAR

The Art of War is attributed to Sun, and it was originally called the Sun Tzu Bing Fa (Pinyin: Sunzi Bingfa), or simply the Sun Tzu. It presents a philosophy of war for managing conflicts and winning battles. Contrary to popular belief, it contains not only the writings of the original author, but also commentary and clarifications from later military philosophers, such as Li Quan and Du Mu. It is accepted as a masterpiece on strategy and often referenced by generals and theorists throughout history. Of the texts written before the unification of China in the 2nd century BC, six major works survived, including The Art of War. During the Song Dynasty in the early 1st millenium AD, the six works were combined with a Tang Dynasty text into a collection called the Seven Military Classics. As a central part of that compilation, The Art of War formed the foundations of orthodox military theory in China. Illustrating this point, the book was required reading to pass the tests needed for imperial appointment to military positions.

A bamboo version of The Art of War

Sun viewed the ideal general as an enlightened Taoist master, which has led to The Art of War being considered a prime example of Taoist strategy. For example, the 11th chapter states that a leader must be "serene and inscrutable" and capable of comprehending "unfathomable plans". The Art of War is distinguished from similar Western works, such as Prussian general Carl von Clausewitz's On War, by this spiritual dimension. Awareness of the Taoist viewpoint in The Art of War is essential to understanding its intended meaning. The book is not only popular among military theorists, but it has also become increasingly popular among political leaders and those in business management. Despite its title, The Art of War addresses strategy in a broad fashion, touching upon public administration and planning. The text outlines theories of battle but also advocates diplomacy and cultivating relationships with other nations as essential to the health of a state.

In the early 1970s, scholars uncovered a collection of ancient texts written on unusually well-preserved bamboo slips. Among them were The Art of War and Sun Bin's Military Methods. Although Han Dynasty bibliographies noted the latter publication as extant and written by a descendant of Sun, it had since been lost. The finding of Sun Bin's work was therefore considered to be extremely important, because of Sun Bin's relationship to Sun, and the work's illustration of military thought in late Chinese antiquity. The discovery as a whole expanded the total known Chinese military works by hundreds. However, Sun Bin's treatise is the only known additional text surviving from the ancient period or bearing a close association with Sun Tzu.

HISTORICITY

Scholars have expressed doubt in Sun's historicity and the traditional dating of The Art of War. The scepticism is fuelled by factors that include historical inaccuracies and anachronisms in the text, as well as the unlikelihood of the execution of the king's favorite concubines. Increasing scepticism, which sometimes cause scholars to completely deny the existence of a historical figure named Sun Wu (Sun Tzu), has lead to acrimonious debate between sceptics and traditionalists, especially in China. Attribution of The Art of War's authorship varies among scholars, and have included people and movements including Sun; Chu scholar Wu Zixu; an unknown author; a school of thought in Qi or Wu; and Sun Bin.

Traditionalists attribute the authorship of The Art of War to the historical figure Sun Wu, who is chronicled in the Records of the Grand Historian and the Spring and Autumn Annals. He was reputedly active in the early 6th century BC, beginning c. 512 BC. The appearance of features from The Art of War in other historical texts is considered to be proof of his historicity and authorship. Certain strategic concepts, such as terrain classification, are attributed to Sun Tzu. Their use in other works, such as by the compilers of The Methods of the Sima, is considered proof of Sun Tzu's historical priority.

Scholars that identify issues with the traditionalist view point to anachronisms in The Art of War that include terms, technology, philosophical ideas, events, and military techniques. There is a disparity between the large scale wars and sophisticated techniques detailed in the text, and the more primitive small scale battles that predominated the 6th century BC. There is also a lack of early contemporary evidence supporting the centuries-later accounts of Sun. For example, there is no corroborating support for his role in the wars between Wu and Yue in the Zuo Zhuan, which is considered the authoritative record of the period. Regardless of Sun's historicity and the actual authorship of The Art of War, the figure of Sun and his traditionally attributed work have been influential.

LEGACY

Sun's The Art of War has influenced many notable figures. Traditional histories recount that the first emperor of a unified China, Qin Shi Huang, considered the book invaluable in ending the Age of Warring States. The Art of War was introduced in Japan c. AD 760, and the book quickly became popular among Japanese generals, significantly influencing the unification of Japan. Mastery of its teachings was considered a mark of respect among the samurai, and its teachings were both exhorted and exemplified by influential samurai such as Oda Nobunaga, Toyotomi Hideyoshi, and Tokugawa Ieyasu.

Historians popularly recount how French emperor Napoleon studied Sun's military writings and used them to successfully wage war against the rest of Europe. The emperor's disregard for central principles such as attentiveness to temporal conditions is largely credited for his eventual defeat in Russia. Admiral of the Fleet Tôgô Heihachirô, who led Japan's forces to victory against Russia in the Russo-Japanese War, was a avid reader of The Art of War". Communist Chinese leader Mao Zedong partially credited his victory over Chiang Kai-shek and the Kuomintang in 1949 to

The Art of War. The work strongly influenced Mao's writings about guerrilla warfare, which further influenced communist insurgencies around the world.

During the Gulf War in the 1990s, General Norman Schwarzkopf, Jr. practiced Sun's principles of deception, speed, and attacking the enemy's weakness. However he stated that "The technology of war may change, the sophistication of weapons certainly changes. But those same principles of war that applied to the days of Hannibal apply today."

Mark McNeilly writes in Sun Tzu and the Art of Modern Warfare that a modern interpretation of Sun and his importance throughout Chinese history is critical in understanding China's push to becoming a superpower in the 21st century.

Modern Chinese scholars explicitly rely on historical strategic lessons and The Art of War in developing their theories, seeing a direct relationship between their modern struggles and those of China in Sun's time. There is a great perceived value in Sun's teachings and other traditional Chinese writers, which are used regularly in developing the strategies of the Chinese state and its leaders.

THE ART OF WAR

The Art of War is a Chinese military treatise that was written by Sun Tzu in the 6th century B.C.E., during the Spring and Autumn period. Composed of 13 chapters, each of which is devoted to one aspect of warfare, it has long been praised as the definitive work on military strategies and tactics of its time, and one of the basic texts on the subject.

The Art of War is one of the oldest and most successful books on military strategy in the world. It has had a huge influence on Eastern military thinking, business tactics, and beyond. Sun Tzu recognized the importance of positioning in strategy and that position is affected both by objective conditions in the physical environment and the subjective opinions of competitive actors in that environment. He thought that strategy was not planning in the sense of working through a to-do list, but rather that it requires quick and appropriate responses to changing conditions. Planning works in a controlled environment, but in a competitive environment, competing plans collide, creating unexpected situations.

The book was first translated into the French language in 1772 by French Jesuit Jean Joseph Marie Amiot, and into English by British officer Everard Ferguson Calthrop in 1905. It very likely influenced Napoleon, Leaders as diverse as Mao Zedong, General Vo Nguyen Giap, Baron Antoine-Henri Jomini, and General Douglas MacArthur have claimed to have drawn inspiration from the work. The Art of War has also been applied to business and managerial strategies.

THE 13 CHAPTERS

The Art of War is divided into 13 chapters (or P'ien), and the collection is referred to as being one Ch'üan ("whole" or alternatively "chronicle"). As different translations have used differing titles for each chapter, a selection appears below. Lionel Giles' 1910 translation is considered the standard reference, but the other titles are, given the nature of translation, equally valid.

Chapter	Lionel Giles (1910)	R.L. Wing (1988)	Chow-Hou Wee (2003)
I	Laying Plans	The Calculations	Detail Assessment and Planning
II	Waging War	The Challenge	Waging War
III	Attack by Stratagem	The Plan of Attack	Strategic Attack
IV	Tactical Dispositions	Positioning	Disposition of the Army
V	Energy	Directing	Forces
VI	Weak Points and Strong	Illusion and Reality	Weaknesses and Strengths
VII	Maneuvering	Engaging The Force	Military Maneuvers
VIII	Variation of Tactics	The Nine Variations	Variations and Adaptability
IX	The Army on the March	Moving The Force	Movement and Development of Troops
X	Terrain	Situational Positioning	Terrain
XI	The Nine Situations	The Nine Situations	The Nine Battlegrounds
XII	The Attack by Fire	The Fiery Attack	Attacking with Fire
XIII	The Use of Spies	The Use of Intelligence	Intelligence and Espionage

CHAPTER SUMMARY

1. **Laying Plans** explores the five fundamental factors that define a successful outcome (the Way, seasons, terrain, leadership, and management). By thinking, assessing and comparing these points you can calculate a victory, deviation from them will ensure failure. Remember that war is a very grave matter of state.
2. **Waging War** explains how to understand the economy of war and how success requires making the winning play, which in turn, requires limiting the cost of competition and conflict.
3. **Attack by Stratagem** defines the source of strength as unity, not size, and the five ingredients that you need to succeed in any war.
4. **Tactical Dispositions** explains the importance of defending existing positions until you can advance them and how you must recognize opportunities, not try to create them.
5. **Energy** explains the use of creativity and timing in building your momentum.
6. **Weak Points & Strong** explains how your opportunities come from the openings in the environment caused by the relative weakness of your enemy in a given area.
7. **Maneuvering** explains the dangers of direct conflict and how to win those confrontations when they are forced upon you.
8. **Variation in Tactics** focuses on the need for flexibility in your responses. It explains how to respond to shifting circumstances successfully.
9. **The Army on the March** describes the different situations in which you find yourselves as you move into new enemy territories and how to respond to them. Much of it focuses on evaluating the intentions of others.
10. **Terrain** looks at the three general areas of resistance (distance, dangers, and barriers) and the six types of

ground positions that arise from them. Each of these six field positions offer certain advantages and disadvantages.

11. **The Nine Situations** describe nine common situations (or stages) in a campaign, from scattering to deadly, and the specific focus you need to successfully navigate each of them.
12. **The Attack by Fire** explains the use of weapons generally and the use of the environment as a weapon specifically. It examines the five targets for attack, the five types of environmental attack, and the appropriate responses to such attack.
13. **The Use of Spies** focuses on the importance of developing good information sources, specifically the five types of sources and how to manage them.

ANNOTATIONS

Before the bamboo scroll version was discovered by archaeologists in April 1972, a commonly cited version of The Art of War was the Annotation of Sun Tzu's Strategies by Cao Cao, the founder of the Kingdom of Wei. In the preface, he wrote that previous annotations were not focused on the essential ideas. Other annotations cited in official history books include Shen You (176-204)'s Sun Tzu's Military Strategy, Jia Xu's Copy of Sun Tzu's Military Strategy, Cao Cao and Wang Ling's Sun Tzu's Military Strategy.

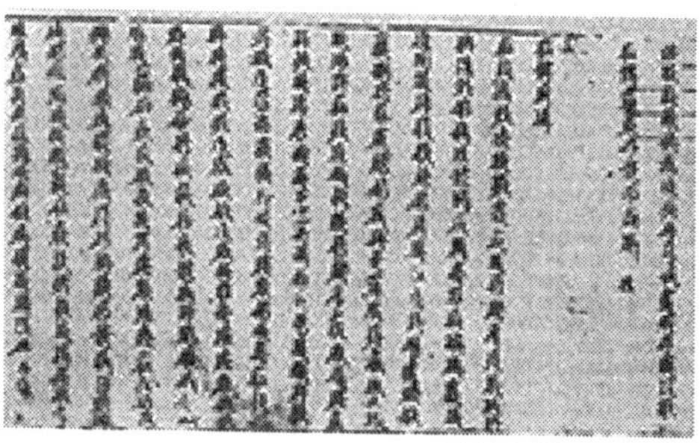

A portion of the Art of War in Tangut script.

The Book of Sui documented seven books named after Sun Tzu. An annotation by Du Mu also includes Cao Cao's annotation. Li Jing's The Art of War is said to be a revision of Master Sun's strategies. Annotations by Cao Cao, Du Mu and Li Quan were translated into the Tangut language before 1040 AD. A book named Ten Schools of The Art of War Annotations was published before 1161 AD.

After the movable type printer was invented, The Art of War (with Cao Cao's annotations) was published as a military text book, known as Seven Military Classics with six other strategy books. As a required reading military textbook since the Song Dynasty, Seven Military Classics has many annotations. More than 30 differently annotated versions of this book exist today.

Vernacular Chinese became increasingly popular in the late 1920s. Annotations in Vernacular Chinese began to appear after this time. Some of these works were translated from other languages, such as Japanese.

The two most common traditional Chinese versions of the Art of War, (the Complete Specialist Focus and Military Bible versions) were the sources for early translation into English and other languages. It was not until the 1970s that these works were compiled with more recent archeological discoveries into a single more complete version in Taipei, Taiwan. The resulting work is known as the Complete Version of Sun Tzu's Art of War for the National Defense Research Investigation Office has been the source for more recent and complete translations.

Quotations

Verses from the book occur in modern daily Chinese idioms and phrases, such as the last verse of Chapter 3:

> So it is said that if you know your enemies and know yourself, you can win a thousand battles without a single loss. If you only know yourself, but not your opponent, you may win or may lose. If you know neither yourself nor your enemy, you will always endanger yourself.

This has been more tersely interpreted and condensed into the modern proverb:

> If you know both yourself and your enemy, you can win a hundred battles without a single loss.

This translation of this sentence 'If you know both sides, you will win a hundred times in one hundred battles.

Furthermore, knowing both sides doesn't guarantee winning. ('If you know both sides, you will win a hundred times in one hundred battles') is untrue since in the beginning paragraph of chapter four, Master Sun wrote 'Hence, we can well predict who would win but there is no strategy guaranteeing winning'. The reason for the uncertainty is chance or luck.

Similar verses have also been borrowed—in a manner construing skillfulness as victory "without fighting" — for example:

> Therefore one hundred victories in one hundred battles is not the most skillful. Seising the enemy without fighting is the most skillful.

Another quotation (chapter 1, paragraph 18) states:

> All warfare is based on deception.

or, alternatively:

> Never will those who wage war tire of deception.

MILITARY APPLICATIONS

In many East Asian countries, The Art of War was part of the syllabus for potential candidates of military service examinations. Various translations are available.

During the Sengoku era in Japan, a daimyo named Takeda Shingen (1521–1573) is said to have become almost invincible in all battles without relying on guns, because he studied The Art of War. The book even gave him the inspiration for his famous battle standard "Fûrinkazan" (Wind, Forest, Fire and Mountain), meaning fast as the wind, silent as a forest, ferocious as fire and immovable as a mountain.

The translator Samuel B. Griffith offers a chapter on "Sun Tzu and Mao Tse-Tung" where The Art of War is cited as influencing Mao's On Guerilla Warfare, On the Protracted War, and Strategic Problems of China's Revolutionary War and includes Mao's quote: "We must not belittle the saying in the book of Sun Wu Tzu, the great military expert of ancient China, 'Know your enemy and know yourself and you can fight a thousand battles without disaster.'"

During the Vietnam War, some Vietcong officers studied The Art of War, and reportedly could recite entire passages from memory. General Vo Nguyen Giap successfully implemented tactics described in The Art of War during the Battle of Dien Bien Phu to end major French involvement in Indochina and led to the accords which partitioned Vietnam into North and South.

The Department of the Army in the United States, through its Command and General Staff College, has directed all units to maintain libraries within their respective headquarters for the continuing education of personnel in the art of war. The Art of War is specifically mentioned by name as an example of works to be maintained at each individual unit, and staff duty officers are obliged to prepare short papers for presentation to other officers on their readings.

The Art of War is listed on the Marine Corps Professional Reading Programme (formerly known as the Commandant's Reading List).

APPLICATION OUTSIDE THE MILITARY

The Art of War has been applied to fields well outside the military. Much of the text is about how to fight wars without actually having to do battle: it gives tips on how to outsmart one's opponent so that physical battle is not necessary. As such, it has found application as a training guide for many competitive endeavors that do not involve actual combat.

The book has gained popularity in corporate culture; there have been a variety of business books written applying its lessons to "office politics" and corporate strategy. Many Japanese companies make the book required reading for their key executives. The book is also popular among Western business management, who have turned to it for inspiration and advice on how to succeed in competitive business situations.

The Art of War has also been the subject of various law books and legal articles on the trial process, including negotiation tactics and trial strategy.

DEPICTION IN MEDIA

"The Art of War" has been frequently mentioned in popular media such as film and television. Below are a few examples of this.

PRINT

- In G I Joe Special Missions # 7 and 8, a small team of Joes is sent to Tibet to retrieve a CIA agent who has gone rogue and is now leading Tibetan freedom fighters in their fight to expel Han Chinese troops. This rogue agent has a copy of The Art of War whose principles he applies. It is passed on to his successor when he dies.

THEATRE

- The Art of War, by Stephen Jeffreys, is a dramatic interpretation incorporating recitations from the text with the telling of two stories: one of a US commander in the Iraq War and the other of a group of Australian company executives. The play was specially commissioned by the Sydney Theatre Company for their resident "Actor's Company" of twelve actors. It was first performed in May 2007.

FILM

- In the 1987 film Wall Street, the main antagonist, Gordon Gekko (played by Michael Douglas), says: "I don't throw darts at a board. I bet on sure things. Read Sun-tzu, The

Art of War. Every battle is won before it is ever fought." His protegé, Bud (played by Charlie Sheen), comes back after reading the text and says: "All warfare is based on deception. If your enemy is superior, evade him. If angry, irritate him. If equally matched, fight and if not: split and re-evaluate," to which Gekko smiles in approval.

- The 2000 Wesley Snipes film The Art of War was named after the book. Snipes is also seen (as a different character) reading the book in his 1992 movie Passenger 57.
- The protagonist, played by Forest Whitaker, in the 1999 film Ghost Dog: The Way of the Samurai makes frequent reference to the text, as well as the Hagakure, upon which he bases his philosophy.
- A passage from the Art of War is recited in the James Bond film Die Another Day by Colonel Tan-Sun Moon and General Moon in the final scenes of the film. The book itself also appears during the fight between Miranda Frost and Jinx.
- The 2003 movie, Gigli, quotes many of the philosophies in this book.

TELEVISION

- In the 2003 animated adaptation of the 'Teen Titans' comic book series, General Immortus quotes the text in the episode 'The Homecoming: Part 2', where he observes the Doom Patrol crossing a vast desert and calls to mind the verse "Strike when your enemy is at his weakest, when he is mired in self-doubt, and your victory will be assured." He also later remarks that Sun Tzu was "one of (his) best students".
- The Art of War is referenced multiple times as a tool for business strategy in Smallville
- The Art of War also figures prominently in the plot resolution of the 1987 Star Trek: The Next Generation episode, "The Last Outpost," wherein the last verse of

Chapter 3 is rendered as "Know your enemy and know yourself and victory will always be yours." It is also said that The Art of War is required reading at Starfleet Academy.

- In the anime 'Grenadier–The Senshi of Smiles', Rushuna and her nation hold the policy of winning by dissolving an enemy's will to fight and thus avoiding combat altogether as the ultimate battle strategy.
- In the five-part GI Joe episode, "Arise Serpentor," one of the DNA's that must be retrieved by Cobra in order to genetically construct Serpentor is that of Sun Tzu.
- In the Family Guy episode, "A Hero Sits Next Door," Stewie Griffin is reading The Art of War, commenting that it is exquisite, until Lois Griffin, Stewie's mother, takes the book away.
- Tony Soprano, the lead character in The Sopranos, praises the utility of The Art of War in a number of episodes.

VIDEO GAMES

- Brøderbund Software published two games based on Sun Tzu's The Art of War. The first, entitled The Ancient Art of War, and the second, The Ancient Art of War at Sea. They are primarily simulation games, incorporating elements of strategy, geography and adventure. They were released on a number of computer platforms including Apple II (First title only), Macintosh, and DOS. The first title was written by Ronald G. Helms.
- In Sid Meier's Civilisation computer game series, "Sun Tsu's Art of War" or "Military Academy" is one of the fictional "World Wonders" that can be created, giving the owner several temporary military advantages.
- A second Sid Meier simulation, Sid Meier's Alpha Centauri, uses an excerpt from The Art of War as a narrative explanation of military intelligence gathering during a cutscene for the construction of a specific secret project.
- In the Total War series computer and video games, by The Creative Assembly, much of the AI in the earlier (and to

some extent, later) games in the series were programmed based on Sun Tzu's stratagems in The Art of War. Passages from the book were also quoted on the Rome: Total War loading screens and were frequently mentioned in Shogun: Total War.

- The MMORPG Eternal Lands has a special day named after Sun Tzu, on which players receive more experience points for attack and defence.

MUSIC

- Bone Thugs-n-Harmony released a double disc album entitled The Art of War with a guest appearance by the late Tupac Shakur
- 30 Seconds to Mars (an American Progressive-Rock band) quotes lines from the book at the end of their debut self-titled CD released 2002 by Virgin Records.
- The War of Art Title of the major label debut album by acclaimed industrial metal act American Head Charge produced by Rick Rubin.
- Chinese American rapper Jin quotes the book in one of his songs.

Chapter 22

WAR CYCLES

The forerunner of the study of war cycles was Edward R Dewey, with Quincy Wright's monumental A Study of War adding impetus to the discipline. The credibility of the study of cycles was frequently questioned, as this type of inquiry attracts persons with marginal credibility and interest in paranormal issues. However, with advent of computer algorithms minimising the dampening effect affecting the abstracted oscillations and facilitating the detection of stochastic drifts, the study of cycles is subject to renewed interest.

INFLECTION POINTS OF WAR CYCLES

In the judgment of the Nuremberg Tribunal, war of aggression is the supreme crime, and there is hardly any other issue that is more relevant to the social sciences than the study of the decision-making process when a person or a group of persons decides that another group of people must face death. Historians speculated about this decision-making process for centuries without reaching consensus, as wars are complex phenomena with multiple determinants. The decision to initiate a war marks an inflection point of the war-peace cycle, and the decision to cease hostilities marks the end of a particular cycle. Comparative studies of war cycles can contribute to explication of facets of this decision-making process. Most relevant of these facets are those that help us to identify the preventable factors influencing the decision to initiate (and to terminate) a war.

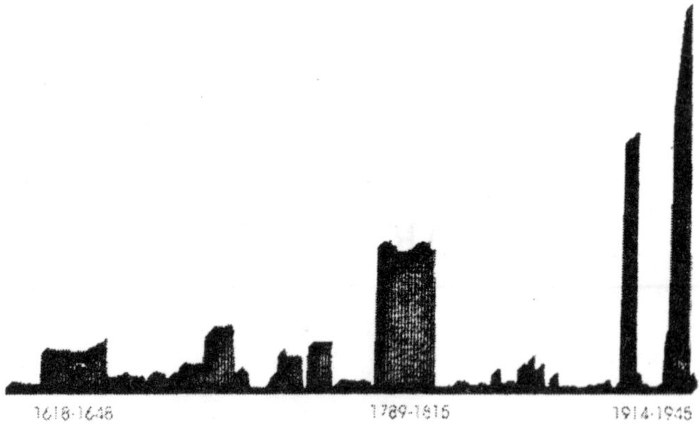

Fig. 1. Frequency and intensity of Western Wars (1600–1945). The 1618-1648 interval marks the Thirty Years 'War, the 1789-1815 interval marks the Wars of the French revolution and the Napoleonic Wars, and the 1914-1945 interval marks World Wars I and II. (From Krus, D.J., Nelsen, E.A. & Webb, J.M. (1998) "Recurrence of war in classical East and West civilisations". Psychological Reports, 83, 139-143).

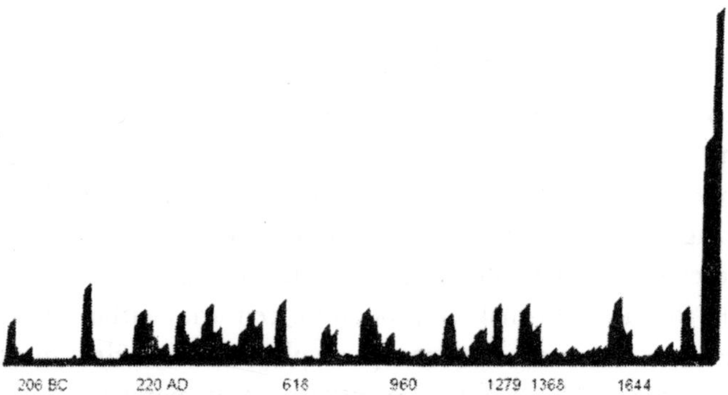

Fig. 2. Frequency and intensity of Chinese Wars (200 BCE–1945). The 220-618 interval marks the "Period of Disunion" (Chinese Dark Ages), during which the Confucian teachings were abandoned. The most intense conflict in recorded history was the Second World War, and both graphs are plotted relative to that conflict. (From Krus, D.J., Nelsen, E.A. & Webb, J.M. (1998) "Recurrence of war in classical East and West civilisations". Psychological Reports, 83, 139-143).

COMPARATIVE STUDIES

Quantitative studies of bellicosity of the Western civilisation and the Confucian civilisation of the East was pioneered by Lewis Fry Richardson. Richardson's studies led him to the conclusion that "Confucian-Taoist-Buddhist religion of China stands out conspicuously as being either itself a pacifier, or else associated with one" and that "it seems probable that the comparative peacefulness of China prior to 1911 was the result of instruction, and in particular of Confucian instruction."

Richardson's findings were based on data spanning about a century. Study by Krus, Nelsen, & Webb (1998) lengthened his perspective for the wars of the Western civilisation by about three centuries (Fig. 1) and for the Eastern Civilisation by about 17 centuries (Fig. 2). In Fig. 2, the 220–618 time interval corresponds to the period in Chinese history called the Period of Disunion (also called the Chinese Dark Ages or six dynasties), when Confucius' teachings were abandoned. Krus et al. (1998) concluded that "In the Empire of China, when the Confucian philosophy was predominant, the peace lasted significantly longer than in the West. When Confucian teachings were abandoned, the frequency of warfare approximated that observed for the Western countries."

For another comparative study that specifies a mathematical model of war cycles and tests it cross-culturally and cross-historically see Secular Cycles and Millennial Trends. Note that this study tries to connect the war cycles with long-term trend dynamics.

ETHICAL CANONS

Pacific ethics of the Western civilisation are based to a degree on ethical teachings of monotheistic religions. These religious canons are quite effective in preventing violence by individuals, but less successful in preventing the collective violence.

Results of the comparative studies of the war cycles support Lewis Richardson's observations of the relative peacefulness of China prior to 1911. Richardson asks the question:

"If China could thus be made peaceable by Confucian instruction in pacific ethics, why not the whole world?"

Richardson's conclusions are echoed by Krus and Webb (2001):

"As the religious factors are paramount in shaping value systems, one may look for the alternatives to the mainstream religions, to systems that erect barriers against the group-sponsored violence: Eastern religions and philosophies as Confucianism, Buddhism and Hinduism, modern Black and Latin American liberation theologies of James H. Cone and Gustavo Gutierrez, and secular value systems perhaps best represented by Noam Chomsky."

Experience of a large segment of humanity over a time interval spanning millennia indicates that a peaceful civilisation can exist without subscribing to religious precepts of monotheistic religions and that a secular ethic system, epitomized by that of Confucius, is likely one of the factors lessening the probability of a decision to initiate a war.

Chapter 23

WATER WAR

A Water War is a colloquial term often used to describe an armed conflict motivated around the use or possession of water resources within a state's boundary or between two or more states. The term is often used by media, but rarely by academics or the security community, who tend to talk about "water-related conflicts" rather than "wars."

A wide range of conflicts over water appear throughout history, though very rarely are these "wars" over water. Instead, access to water has been a source of tensions, a tool during conflicts that start for other reasons, and a target during wars. The only reported example of an actual inter-state conflict over water is the one between the Sumerian states of Lagash and Umma, taking place between 2500 and 2350 B.C.

Water stress can lead to conflicts at local and regional levels.. Increasingly, conflicts over water are occurring at a subnational level rather than between nations. A comprehensive list of water-related conflicts going back 5,000 years can be found at the "Water Conflict Chronology." A more-regularly updated version can be found online at Water Conflict Chronology.

HUMAN CONFLICTS OVER WATER

Some large or small conflicts of the future may be fought over access to water. A worldwide battle for water may well ensue in regard to this limited resource, which is being strained by human population. Water shortages may well result in water wars over this precious resource.

FUTURE WATER CONFLICT

A potential cause for future conflict between India and China is the Yarlung Tsangpo Hydroelectric and Water Diversion Project. It is expected that the construction of a dam would divert large amounts of the waters of the river Brahmaputra as known in India or Yarlung Tsangpo River as known in China away from India's territory. The water would flow through the Shuotian Canal to reach cities in the north of China.

WAR AS METAPHOR

The use of war as metaphor is a literary trope of long-standing. Its currently liveliest metaphoric applications are circulated in the international effort of the "War on Terrorism" and in local efforts, such as the "War on Drugs" or the Culture War in the United States. In Metaphors We Live By, George Lakoff and Mark Johnson describe Jimmy Carter's application of "war" as metaphor for the energy crisis of 1974.

Inter arma enim silent leges is a Latin phrase meaning "In the face of arms, the law falls mute," often rendered as "In time of war, the laws fall silent." This maxim was likely first written in these words by Cicero in his published oration Pro Milone

In a corollary of this usage, the US government restricted American civil liberties in the name of quelling dissent, silencing criticism of political decisions and preserving national security in the American Civil War, when the writ of habeas corpus was suspended by Abraham Lincoln and during World War I.

In discussing the morality of the use of war as a metaphor, James Childress epitomized the dilemma: "In debating social policy through the language of war, we often forget the moral reality of war.

EFFECTS OF WAR

On Soldiers

Based on 1860 census figures, 8% of all white males aged 13 to 43 died in the American Civil War, including 6% in the North and 18% in the South. Of the 60 million European soldiers who were mobilized in World War I, 8 million were killed, 7 million were permanently disabled, and 15 million were seriously injured.

During Napoleon's retreat from Moscow, more French soldiers died of typhus than were killed by the Russians. Felix Markham thinks that 450,000 crossed the Neman on 25 June 1812, of whom less than 40,000 recrossed in anything like a recognizable military formation. More soldiers were killed from 1500-1914 by typhus than from all military action during that time combined. In addition, if it were not for the modern medical advances there would be thousands of more dead from disease and infection.

On Civilians

Many wars have been accompanied by significant depopulations. During the Thirty Years' War in Europe, for example, the population of the German states was reduced by about 30%. The Swedish armies alone may have destroyed up to 2,000 castles, 18,000 villages and 1,500 towns in Germany, one-third of all German towns.

Estimates for the total casualties of World War II vary, but most suggest that some 60 million people died in the war, including about 20 million soldiers and 40 million civilians. The Soviet Union lost around 27 million people during the war, about half of all World War II casualties. The largest number of civilian deaths in a single city was 1.2 million citizens dead during the 872-day Siege of Leningrad.

On the Economy

Once a war has ended, losing nations are sometimes required to pay repartition to the victorious nations. In certain cases, land is ceded to the victorious nations. For example, the territory of Alsace-Lorraine has been traded between France and Germany on three different occasions.

Typically speaking, war becomes very intertwined with the economy and many wars are partially or entirely based on economic reasons such as the American Civil War. In some cases war has stimulated a country's economy (World War II is often credited with bringing America out of the Great Depression) but in many cases, such as the wars of Louis XIV, the Franco-Prussian War, and World War I, warfare serves only to damage the economy of the countries involved. For example, Russia's involvement in World War I took such a toll on the Russian economy that it almost collapsed and greatly contributed to the start of the Russian Revolution of 1917.

WORLD WAR II

One of the starkest illustrations of the effect of war upon economies is the Second World War. The Great Depression of the 1930s ended as nations increased their production of war materials to serve the war effort. The financial cost of the World War II is estimated at about a trillion 1944 U.S. dollars worldwide, making it the most costly war in capital as well as lives.

Property damage in the Soviet Union inflicted by the Axis invasion was estimated to a value of 679 billion rubles. The combined damage consisted of complete or partial destruction of 1,710 cities and towns, 70,000 villages/hamlets, 2,508 church buildings, 31,850 industrial establishments, 40,000 miles of railroad, 4100 railroad stations, 40,000 hospitals, 84,000 schools, and 43,000 public libraries.

MORALITY OF WAR

Throughout history war has been the source of serious moral questions. Although many ancient nations and some modern ones have viewed war as noble, over the sweep of history, concerns about the morality of war have gradually increased. Today, war is seen by some as undesirable and morally problematic. At the same time, many view war, or at least the preparation and readiness and willingness to engage in war, as necessary for the defense of their country and therefore a just war. Pacifists believe that war is inherently immoral and that no war should ever be fought.

The negative view of war has not always been held as widely as it is today. Heinrich von Treitschke saw war as humanity's highest activity where courage, honour, and ability were more necessary than in any other endeavour. Friedrich Nietzsche also saw war as an opportunity for the Übermensch to display heroism, honour, and other virtues.

Another supporter of war, Georg Wilhelm Friedrich Hegel, favoured it as part of the necessary process required for history to unfold and allow society to progress. At the outbreak of World War I, the writer Thomas Mann wrote, "Is not peace an element of civil corruption and war a purification, a liberation, an enormous hope?" This attitude has been embraced by societies from Sparta and Rome in the ancient world to the fascist states of the 1930s.

International law recognises only two cases for a legitimate war:

1. Wars of defense: when one nation is attacked by an aggressor, it is considered legitimate for a nation along with its allies to defend itself against the aggressor.
2. Wars sanctioned by the UN Security Council: when the United Nations as a whole acts as a body against a certain

nation. Examples include various peacekeeping operations around the world.

The subset of international law known as the law of war or international humanitarian law also recognises regulations for the conduct of war, including the Geneva Conventions governing the legitimacy of certain kinds of weapons, and the treatment of prisoners of war. Cases where these conventions are broken are considered war crimes, and since the Nuremberg Trials at the end of World War II the international community has established a number of tribunals to try such cases.

A nation's economy is often stimulated by government war-spending. When countries wage war, more weapons, armor, ammunition, and the like are needed to be created and sold to the armies, thus their economies can enter a boom (or war economy) reducing unemployment. One major depression, the Great Depression, was ended because of World War II.

FACTORS ENDING A WAR

The political and economic circumstances in the peace that follows war usually depends on the "facts on the ground". Where evenly matched adversaries decide that the conflict has resulted in a stalemate, they may cease hostilities to avoid further loss of life and property. They may decide to restore the antebellum territorial boundaries, redraw boundaries at the line of military control, or negotiate to keep or exchange captured territory. Negotiations between parties involved at the end of a war often result in a treaty, such as the Treaty of Versailles of 1919, which ended the First World War.

A warring party that surrenders or capitulates may have little negotiating power, with the victorious side either imposing a settlement or dictating most of the terms of any treaty. A common result is that conquered territory is brought under the dominion of the stronger military power. An unconditional surrender is made in the face of overwhelming military force as an attempt to prevent further harm to life and property. For example, the Empire of

Japan gave an unconditional surrender to the Allies of World War II after the atomic bombings of Hiroshima and Nagasaki (see Surrender of Japan), the preceding massive strategic bombardment of Japan and declaration of war and the immediate invasion of Manchuria by the Soviet Union. A settlement or surrender may also be obtained through deception or bluffing.

Women and priests retrieve the dead bodies of Swabian soldiers just outside the city gates of Constance after the battle of Schwaderloh. (Luzerner Schilling)

Many other wars, however, have ended in complete destruction of the opposing territory, such as the Battle of Carthage of the Third Punic War between the Phoenician city of Carthage and Ancient Rome in 149 BC. In 146 BC the Romans burned the city, enslaved its citizens, and razed the buildings.

Some wars or aggressive actions end when the military objective of the victorious side has been achieved. Others do not, especially in cases where the state structures do not exist, or have collapsed prior to the victory of the conqueror. In such cases, disorganised guerilla warfare may continue for a considerable period. In cases of complete surrender conquered territories may be brought under the permanent dominion of the victorious side. A raid for the purposes of looting may be completed with the successful capture of goods. In other cases an aggressor may decide to end hostilities to avoid continued losses and cease hostilities without obtaining the original objective, such as happened in the Iran–Iraq War.

Some hostilities, such as insurgency or civil war, may persist for long periods of time with only a low level of military activity. In some cases there is no negotiation of any official treaty, but fighting may trail off and eventually stop after the political demands of the belligerent groups have been reconciled, a political settlement has been negotiated, or combatants are gradually killed or decide the conflict is futile.

LIST OF WARS BY DEATH TOLL

These figures include deaths of civilians from diseases, famine, atrocities etc. as well as deaths of soldiers in battle.

- 60,000,000–72,000,000–World War II (1939–1945),
- 36,000,000–An Shi Rebellion (China, 755–763)
- 30,000,000–60,000,000–Mongol Conquests (13th century)
- 25,000,000–Manchu conquest of Ming China (1616–1662)
- 20,000,000–World War I (1914–1918)
- 20,000,000–Taiping Rebellion (China, 1851–1864)
- 20,000,000–Second Sino-Japanese War (1937–1945)
- 10,000,000–Warring States Era (China, 475 BC–221 BC)
- 7,000,000–20,000,000 Conquests of Timur the Lame (1360-1405)
- 5,000,000–9,000,000–Russian Civil War and Foreign Intervention (1917–1921)
- 5,000,000–Conquests of Menelik II of Ethiopia (1882-1898)
- 3,800,000–5,400,000–Second Congo War (1998–2007)
- 3,500,000–6,000,000–Napoleonic Wars (1804–1815)
- 3,000,000–11,500,000–Thirty Years' War (1618–1648)
- 3,000,000–7,000,000–Yellow Turban Rebellion (China, 184–205)

- 2,500,000–3,500,000–Korean War (1950–1953) (see Cold War)
- 2,300,000–3,800,000–Vietnam War (entire war 1945–1975)
    - o 300,000–1,300,000–First Indochina War (1945–1954)
    - o 100,000–300,000–Vietnamese Civil War (1954–1960)
    - o 1,750,000–2,100,000–American phase (1960–1973)
    - o 170,000–Final phase (1973–1975)
    - o 175,000–1,150,000–Secret War (1962–1975)
- 2,000,000–4,000,000–Huguenot Wars
- 2,000,000–Shaka's conquests (1816-1828)
- 2,000,000–Mahmud of Ghazni's invasions of India (1000-1027)
- 300,000–3,000,000–Bangladesh Liberation War (1971)
- 1,500,000–2,000,000–Afghan Civil War (1979-)
    - o 1,000,000–1,500,000 Soviet intervention (1979–1989)
- 1,300,000–6,100,000–Chinese Civil War (1928–1949)
    - o 300,000–3,100,000 before 1937
    - o 1,000,000–3,000,000 after World War II
- 1,000,000–2,000,000–Mexican Revolution (1910–1920)
- 1,000,000–Iran–Iraq War (1980–1988)
- 1,000,000–Japanese invasions of Korea (1592-1598)
- 1,000,000–Second Sudanese Civil War (1983–2005)
- 1,000,000–Nigerian Civil War (1967–1970)
- 618,000–970,000–American Civil War
- 900,000–1,000,000–Mozambique Civil War (1976–1993)
- 868,000–1,400,000–Seven Years' War (1756-1763)
- 800,000–1,000,000–Rwandan Civil War (1990-1994)
- 800,000–Congo Civil War (1991–1997)
- 600,000 to 1,300,000–First Jewish-Roman War
- 580,000–Bar Kokhba's revolt (132–135CE)

- 570,000–Eritrean War of Independence (1961-1991)
- 550,000–Somali Civil War (1988-)
- 500,000–1,000,000–Spanish Civil War (1936–1939)
- 500,000–Angolan Civil War (1975–2002)
- 500,000–Ugandan Civil War (1979–1986)
- 400,000–1,000,000–War of the Triple Alliance in Paraguay (1864–1870)
- 400,000–War of the Spanish Succession (1701-1714)
- 371,000–Continuation War (1941-1944)
- 350,000–Bosnian Genocide (1992–1995) or 100,000 on all sides, as stated in Bosnian Civil War citations of RDC and ICTY Demographic unit.
- 350,000–Great Northern War (1700-1721)
- 315,000–735,000–Wars of the Three Kingdoms (1639-1651) English campaign ~40,000, Scottish 73,000, Irish 200,000-620,000
- 300,000–Russian-Circassian War (1763-1864)
- 300,000–First Burundi Civil War (1972)
- 300,000–Darfur conflict (2003-)
- 270,000–300,000–Crimean War (1854–1856)
- 255,000-1,120,000–Philippine-American War (1898-1913)
- 230,000–1,400,000–Ethiopian Civil War (1974–1991)
- 224,000–Balkan Wars, includes both wars (1912-1913
- 220,000–Liberian Civil War (1989–)
- 217,000–1,124,303–War on Terror (9/11/2001-Present)
- 200,000–1,000,000–Albigensian Crusade (1208-1259)
- 200,000–800,000–Warlord era in China (1917–1928)
- 200,000–Second Punic War (BC218-BC204) (see List of Roman battles)
- 200,000–Sierra Leone Civil War (1991–2000)
- 200,000–Algerian Civil War (1991-)
- 200,000–Guatemalan Civil War (1960–1996)

- 190,000–Franco-Prussian War (1870–1871)
- 180,000–300,000–La Violencia (1948-1958)
- 170,000–Greek War of Independence (1821-1829)
- 150,000–Lebanese Civil War (1975–1990)
- 150,000–North Yemen Civil War (1962–1970)
- 150,000–Russo-Japanese War (1904–1905)
- 148,000-1,000,000–Winter War (1939)
- 125,000–Eritrean-Ethiopian War (1998–2000)
- 120,000–384,000 Great Turkish War (1683-1699)
- 120,000–Third Servile War (BC73-BC71)
- 117,000–500,000–Revolt in the Vendée (1793-1796)
- 103,359+–1,136,920+–Invasion and Occupation of Iraq (2003-Present)
- 102,622–Bosnian War of Independence
- 101,000–115,000–Arab-Israeli conflict (1929-)
- 100,500–Chaco War (1932–1935)
- 100,000–1,000,000–War of the two brothers (1531–1532)
- 100,000–400,000–Western New Guinea (1984–)
- 100,000–200,000–Indonesian invasion of East Timor (1975-1978)
- 100,000–Persian Gulf War (1991)
- 100,000–1,000,000–Algerian War of Independence (1954–1962)
- 100,000–Thousand Days War (1899–1901)
- 100,000–Peasants' War (1524-1525)
- 80,000–Third Punic War (BC149-BC146)
- 75,000–200,000?–Conquests of Alexander the Great (BC336-BC323)
- 75,000–El Salvador Civil War (1980–1992)
- 75,000–Second Boer War (1898–1902)
- 70,000–Boudica's uprising (AD60-AD61)
- 69,000–Internal conflict in Peru (1980-)

- 60,000–Sri Lanka/Tamil conflict (1983-2009)
- 60,000–Nicaraguan Rebellion (1972-91)
- 55,000–War of the Pacific (1879-1885)
- 50,000–200,000–First Chechen War (1994–1996)
- 50,000–100,000–Tajikistan Civil War (1992–1997)
- 50,000–Wars of the Roses (1455-1485)
- 45,000–Greek Civil War (1945-1949)
- 41,000–100,000–Kashmiri insurgency (1989-)
- 36,000–Finnish Civil War (1918)
- 35,000–40,000–War of the Pacific (1879–1884)
- 35,000–45,000–Siege of Malta (1565)
- 30,000–Turkey/PKK conflict (1984-)
- 30,000–Sino-Vietnamese War (1979)
- ~28,000–1982 Lebanon War (1982)
- 25,000–Second Chechen War (1999–present)
- 25,000–American Revolutionary War (1775-1783)
- 23,384–Indo-Pakistani War of 1971 (December 1971)
- 23,000–Nagorno-Karabakh War (1988-1994)
- 20,000–49,600 U.S. Invasion of Afghanistan (2001–2002)
- 19,000+–Mexican–American War (1846-1848)
- 14,000+–Six-Day War (1967)
- 15,000–20,000–Croatian War of Independence (1991–1995)
- 11,053–Malayan Emergency (1948-1960)
- 11,000–Spanish-American War (1898)
- 10,000–Amadu's Jihad (1810-1818)
- 10,000–Halabja poison gas attack (1988)
- 7,264–10,000–Indo-Pakistani War of 1965 (August-September 1965)
- 7,000–24,000–American War of 1812 (1812-1815)
- 7,000–Kosovo War (1996–1999) (disputed)
- 5,000–Turkish invasion of Cyprus (1974)

- 4,588–Sino-Indian War (1962)
- 4,000–Waziristan War (2004-2006)
- 4,000–Irish Civil War (1922-23)
- 3,000–Civil war in Côte d'Ivoire (2002-2007)
- 2,899–New Zealand Land Wars (1845-1872)
- 2,604–7,000–Indo-Pakistani War of 1947 (October 1947-December 1948)
- 2,000–Football War (1969)
- 2,000–Irish War of Independence (1919-21)
- 1,975–4,500+–violence in the Israeli-Palestinian conflict (2000 -)
- 1,724–War of Lapland (1945)
- 1,500–Romanian Revolution (December 1989)
- ~1,500–2006 Lebanon War
- ~1,400–Gaza War (December 2008–January 2009)
- 1,000–Zapatista uprising in Chiapas (1994)
- 907–Falklands War (1982)
- 62–Slovenian Independence War (1991)

Chapter 24

LIST OF ONGOING CONFLICTS

The following is a list of ongoing conflicts that are taking place around the world and which continue to result in violent deaths. This list is for the sole purpose of identifying present-day conflicts and the death toll associated with each conflict. Fatality figures include both civilian and military deaths. Conflicts which no longer produce violent deaths are not listed here, but can be found in the historical list of wars and the list of wars extended by diplomatic irregularity.

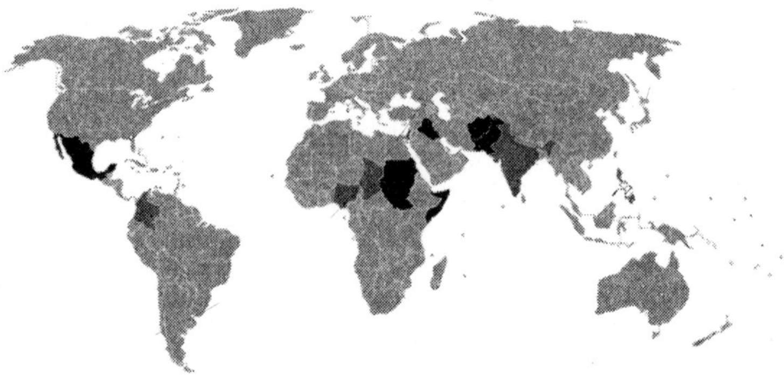

Major wars - 1000+ deaths per year Other conflicts

1000+ DEATHS PER YEAR

Conflicts in the following list are currently causing at least 1000 violent deaths per year, a categorisation used by the Uppsala

Conflict Data Programme and recognised by the United Nations. The UN also use the term "low intensity conflict", which can overlap with the 1000 violent deaths per year categorisation.

Start of Conflict	War/Conflict	Location	Cumulative fatalities
1920	Arab-Israeli Conflict	Egypt, Israel, Jordan, Lebanon, Palestinian Territories, & Syria	50,000 (1950-2006) – 90,000 (1945-1995)
1991	Somali Civil War	Somalia	300,000–400,000
1978	Afghan Civil War	Afghanistan	1,500,000–2,000,000
2003	Kivu conflict	Democratic Republic of the Congo	5,400,000(including previous conflicts)
2003	War in Darfur	Sudan	~450,000
2003	Iraq War	Iraq	100,000–1,000,000 (see: Casualties of the Iraq War)
2004	War in North-West Pakistan	Pakistan	~13,900
2006	Mexican Drug War	Mexico	10,475

OTHER CONFLICTS

There are many other smaller-scale armed conflicts that are currently causing a smaller number of violent fatalities each year.

Start of Conflict	War/Conflict	Location	Cumulative fatalities
1964	Colombian Armed Conflict	Colombia	50,000–200,000
1969	Communist and Islamic Insurgency in the Philippines	Philippines	~120,000
1978	Turkey–Kurdistan Workers' Party conflict	Turkey and Iraqi Kurdistan	~40,000
1989	Insurgency in Jammu and Kashmir	India	~60,000
1967	Naxalite-Maoist insurgency	India	~6,000
2004	Balochistan conflict	Pakistan	~9,000
2004	Conflict in the Niger Delta	Nigeria	unknown
2005	Fourth Civil War of Chad	Chad	~1,400

Chapter 25

WARS AND ARMED CONFLICTS

These figures of one million or more deaths include the deaths of civilians from diseases, famine, etc., as well as deaths of soldiers in battle and possible massacres and genocide.

Where only one estimate is available, it appears in both the low and high estimates. This is a sortable table. Click on the column sort buttons to sort results numerically or alphabetically.

Lowest Estimate	Highest Estimate	Event	Location	From	To	See also
40,000,000	72,000,000	World War II	Worldwide	1939	1945	World War II casualties and Sino-Japanese War
33,000,000	36,000,000	An Shi Rebellion	China	756	763	Medieval warfare
30,000,000	60,000,000	Mongol Conquests	Asia, Europe, Middle East	1207	1472	Mongol invasions and Tatar invasions
25,000,000	25,000,000	Manchu conquest of the Ming Dynasty	China	1616	1662	Qing Dynasty
20,000,000	30,000,000+	Taiping Rebellion	China	1851	1864	Dungan revolt
15,000,000	25,000,000	World War I (High estimate includes Spanish flu deaths)	Worldwide	1914	1918	World War I casualties

10,000,000	20,000,000	Conquests of Timur	Middle East, India, Asia, Russia	1369	1405	List of wars in the Muslim world
8,000,000	12,000,000	Muslim Rebellion	China	1855	1877	Panthay Rebellion
5,000,000	9,000,000	Russian Civil War	Russia	1917	1921	List of civil wars
3,800,000	5,400,000	Second Congo War	Democratic Republic of the Congo	1998	2003	First Congo War
3,500,000	6,500,000	Napoleonic Wars	Europe, Atlantic, Pacific and Indian Ocean	1804	1815	Napoleonic Wars casualties
3,000,000	11,500,000	Thirty Years' War	Holy Roman Empire	1618	1648	
3,000,000	7,000,000	Yellow Turban Rebellion	China	184	205	Part of Three Kingdoms War
2,500,000	3,500,000	Korean War	Korean Peninsula	1950	1953	Cold War
2,495,000	5,020,000	Vietnam War	South East Asia	1959	1975	Indochina War
2,000,000	4,000,000	French Wars of Religion	France	1562	1598	Religious war
2,000,000	2,000,000	Shaka's conquests	Africa	1816	1828	
1,500,000	2,000,000	Afghan Civil War	Afghanistan	1979	present	

GENOCIDES AND ALLEGED GENOCIDES

The CPPCG defines genocide in part as "acts committed with intent to destroy, in whole or in part, a national, ethnical, racial or religious group".

Determining what historical events constitute a genocide and which are merely criminal or inhuman behaviour is not a clear-cut matter. In nearly every case where accusations of genocide have circulated, partisans of various sides have fiercely disputed the interpretation and details of the event, often to the point of promoting wildly different versions of the facts. An accusation of genocide, therefore, will almost always be controversial.

The following list of genocides and alleged genocides should be understood in this context and not necessarily regarded as the final word on the events in question.

Lowest Estimate	Highest Estimate	Event	Location	From	To	Notes
10,000,000	20,000,000	European colonization of the Americas	The Americas	1492	1900	Deaths caused by military conquests, spread of disease and displacement of Native American populations during European settlement of North and South America. The genocidal aspects of this event are entwined with loss of life caused by the lack of immunity of Native Americans to diseases carried by European settlers and their livestock.
5,830,000	11,000,000	Genocides of Nazi Germany	Europe	1941	1945	With around 6 million Jews murdered, many scholars define the Holocaust as a genocide of European Jewry alone. Broader definitions include up to 1,500,000 Romani because, like the European Jewry, the Roma were also targeted for total annihilation due to their race. A broader definition includes political and religious dissenters, 200,000 handicapped, 2 to 3 million Soviet POWs, 5,000 Jehovah's Witnesses, and 15,000 homosexuals, bringing the death toll to around 9 million. The number rises to 11 million if the deaths of 2 million ethnic Poles are included. See Holocaust, Consequences of German Nazism
2,500,000	10,000,000	Holodomor, famine, political repression	Ukrainian SSR	1932	1933	Famine in Ukraine caused by the government of Joseph Stalin, a part of Soviet famine of 1932-1933. Holodomor is claimed by contemporary Ukrainian government to be a genocide of the Ukrainian nation.
1,700,000	3,000,000	Famine, political repression	Cambodia	1975	1979	As of September 2007, no one has been found guilty of participating in this genocide, but on 19 September 2007 Nuon Chea, second in command of the Khmer Rouge and its most senior surviving member, was charged with war crimes and crimes against humanity. He will face Cambodian and United Nations appointed foreign judges at the special genocide tribunal.

26,000	3,000,000	1971 Bangladesh atrocities	East Pakistan (now Bangladesh)	1971	1971	Atrocities in East Pakistan by the Pakistani military, leading to the Bangladesh Liberation War and Indo-Pakistani War of 1971, are widely regarded as a genocide against Bengali people, but to date no one has yet been indicted for such a crime.
800,000	1,000,000	Rwandan genocide	Rwanda	1994	1994	Hutu killed unarmed men, women and children. Some perpetrators of the genocide have been found guilty by the International Criminal Tribunal for Rwanda, but most have not been charged due to no witness accounts.
400,000	1,500,000	Armenian Genocide	Ottoman Empire, early Turkey	1914	1918	Usually called the earliest genocide of the 20th century between half and one and half million were killed in the genocide. The word genocide has been a controversial title and many countries including Turkey refuse to call the incident a genocide, but a handful of countries have deemed it a genocidal act.
500,000	1,500,000	Great Irish Famine	United Kingdom of Great Britain and Ireland	1846	1849	Although blight ravaged potato crops throughout Europe during the 1840s, the impact and human cost in Ireland—where a third of the population was entirely dependent on the potato for food—was exacerbated by a host of political, social and economic factors which remain the subject of historical debate.
275,000	750,000	Assyrian genocide	Ottoman Empire	1915	1918	Disputed, but some consider it a genocide.
270,000	655,000	Ustashe massacres of Serbs, Jews, Roma	Balkans	1941	1945	No academic consensus if this was persecution or genocide during period of Independent State of Croatia
200,000	1,000,000	Greek genocide	Ottoman Empire	1915	1918	Disputed, but some consider it a genocide.
100,000	300,000	Nanking Massacre	Nanking	1937	1938	The Nanking Massacre, commonly known as the Rape of Nanking, was an infamous genocidal war crime committed by the Japanese military in Nanjing, then capital of the Republic of China, after it fell to the Imperial Japanese Army on 13 December 1937.
225,000	650,000	Depopulation of Australian aborigines	Australia	1788	1888	No academic consensus that this was a genocide, see Australian genocide debate
200,000	400,000	Darfur conflict	Sudan	Early 2003	present	See International response to the Darfur conflict
130,000	200,000	Massacres of Mayan Indians	Guatemala	1962	1996	Genocide according to the Historical Clarification Commission.
117,000	500,000	Revolt in the Vendée	France	1793	1796	Described as genocide by some historians. See also French Revolution

150,000	300,000	Political repression of East Timorese	East Timor	1975	1990s	Commonly referred to as genocide by media, scholars.
100,000	400,000	Political repression of West Papuans	Indonesia	1961	present	Genocide according to some sources, see Genocide in West Papua
100,000	200,000	Al-Anfal Campaign	Iraq	1986	1989	Ba'athist Iraq destroys over 2,000 villages and commits genocide on their Kurdish population.
50,000	100,000	Massacres of Hutus	Burundi	1972	1972	Tutsi government massacres of Hutu, see Burundi genocide
50,000	50,000	Massacres of Tutsis	Burundi	1993	1993	Hutu government massacres of Tutsi, see Burundi genocide
24,000	75,000	Herero and Namaqua genocide	Namibia	1904	1908	Generally accepted. See also Imperial Germany
-8,000	-8,000	Srebenica massacre	Srebenica	1995	1995	A genocidal massacre according to the ICTY. See also Bosnia war.

INDIVIDUAL EXTERMINATION CAMPS

- 1,500,000–Auschwitz extermination camp (by Nazi-Germany, located in Oœwiêcim, Poland, 1940-1945)
- 1,000,000–Treblinka extermination camp, (by Nazi Germany, located in Treblinka, Poland, 1942-1943)
- 53,000 -840,000–Jasenovac extermination camp–(by NDH Ustaše Nazi regime in Croatia.)
- 480,000-600,000–Belzec extermination camp, (by Nazi Germany, located in Belzec Poland, 1942-1943)
- 350,000–Majdanek extermination camp, (by Nazi Germany, located in Lublin Poland, 1942-1944)
- 300,000–Chelmno extermination camp, (by Nazi Germany, located in Chelmno Poland, 1941-1943)
- 260,000–Sobibór extermination camp, (by Nazi Germany, located in Sobibor Poland, 1942-1943)
- 55,000–Neuengamme concentration camp, (by Nazi Germany, located by Hamburg, Germany, 1938-1945)

FAMINE

This section includes famines that according to some scholars were caused or exacerbated by the policies of the ruling regime.

Lowest Estimate	Highest Estimate	Event	Location	From	To	Notes
20,000,000	43,000,000	Great Leap Forward famine under the Chinese Communist Party led by Mao Zedong	People's Republic of China	1959	1962	
6,000,000	10,000,000	Famine in the Soviet Union, under the leadership of Joseph Stalin, including Holodomor	Soviet Union	1932	1933	As of November 2006, the Ukraine government was trying to get this mass starvation recognised by the United Nations as an act of genocide, with Russian government and many members of the Ukrainian parliament opposing such a move.
1,250,000	10,000,000	Indian famine of 1899–1900	India	1899	1900	famine in India
5,250,000	10,300,000	Great Famine of 1876–78	India	1876	1878	
4,000,000	4,000,000	Bengal famine in British-ruled India	India	1943	1943	
1,000,000	3,000,000	Iraqi famine in Iraq, UN economic sanctions	Iraq	1990	2003	
500,000	2,000,000	Great Irish Famine	United Kingdom of Great Britain and Ireland	1846	1849	

HUMAN SACRIFICE AND RITUAL SUICIDE

This section lists deaths from the systematic practice of human sacrifice or suicide.

Lowest Estimate	Highest Estimate	Description	Group	Location	From	To	Notes
300,000	unknown	Human sacrifice	Aztecs	Mexico	14th century	1521	Human sacrifice in Aztec culture
13,000	13,000	Human sacrifice	Shang dynasty	China	BC1300	BC1050	Last 250 years of rule
3,912	3,912	Kamikaze suicide pilots, see note	Imperial Japanese air forces	Pacific theatre	1944	1945	
7,941	7,941	Ritual suicides	Sati	Bengal, India	1815	1828	
913	913	Jonestown Revolutionary Suicide	Followers of The Peoples Temple cult	Jonestown	November 18 1978	November 19 1978	The Event was the largest loss of American civilian life until the September 11th 2001 attacks.

Chapter 26

WAR CRIMES

Let us summarize some of the war crimes committed since the Hague Convention of 1907. In addition, those incidents which have been judged in a court of justice to be Crimes Against Peace that have been committed since these crimes were first defined are also included.

Since many war crimes are not ultimately prosecuted (due to lack of political will, lack of effective procedures, or other practical and political reasons), historians and lawyers will often make a serious case that war crimes occurred, even if there was no formal investigations or prosecution of the alleged crimes or an investigation cleared the alleged perpetrators.

War crimes under international law were firmly established by international trials such as the 1945 Nuremberg Major War Crimes Trials and the Tokyo trial of 1946, in which German and Japanese leaders were prosecuted for war crimes committed during World War II. For purpose of selectivity, only war crimes since the customary laws of war were clarified in the Hague Conventions of 1907 are included, because in the judgment at the Major War Crimes Trial in Nuremberg in 1945, it was stated that "*by 1939 these rules laid down in the Hague Convention of 1907 were recognised by all civilised nations, and were regarded as being declaratory of the laws and customs of war*".

1914-1918: WORLD WAR I

World War I was the first major international conflict to take place following the codification of war crimes at the Hague Convention of 1907, including derived war crimes, such as the use of poisons as weapons, as well as crimes against humanity, and derivative crimes against humanity, such as torture, and genocide.

Armed conflict		Perpetrator	
World War I		All belligerents	
Incident	Type of crime	Persons responsible	Notes
Invention and employment of poison gas	Use of poisons as weapons (All major belligerents used poisonous gasses against enemy personnel in combat.)	No prosecutions	Poison gas was introduced by Imperial Germany, and was subsequently used by all major belligerents in the war against enemy soldiers, in violation of the customary law of war, adhered to by all civilized nations and armed groups, thereby constituting the Use of poisons as weapons.
World War I		Ottoman Empire	
Armenian Genocide	War crimes, Crimes against humanity, Crime of genocide (Extermination of Armenians in Anatolia)	The Turkish Courts-Martial of 1919-20 as well as the incomplete Malta Tribunals were trials of certain of the alleged perpetrators.	The Sublime Porte ordered the wholesale extermination of Armenians living within Anatolia. This was carried out by certain elements of their military forces, who either massacred Armenians outright, or deported them to Syria and then massacred them. Nearly one million Armenians perished. The Republic of Turkey, the successor state of the Ottoman Empire, does not accept the word genocide as an accurate description of the events surrounding this matter.

AFTERMATH OF WORLD WAR I

The political reorganisation that followed from World War I led to several events that could possibly considered War crimes or crimes against humanity, with forced displacements of large groups of population mainly based on ethnic criteria.

1936-1939: SPANISH CIVIL WAR

At least 50,000 people were executed during the Spanish Civil War. In his updated history of the Spanish Civil War, Antony Beevor writes, "Franco's ensuing 'white terror' claimed 200,000 lives. The 'red terror' had already killed 38,000." Julius Ruiz concludes that "although the figures remain disputed, a minimum of 37,843 executions were carried out in the Republican zone with a maximum of 150,000 executions (including 50,000 after the war) in Nationalist Spain." César Vidal puts the number of Republican victims at 110,965.

In 2008 a Spanish judge, Socialist Baltasar Garzon, opened an investigation into the executions and disappearances of 114,266 people between 17 July 1936 and December 1951. Among the executions investigated was that of the poet and dramatist Federico García Lorca.

1937-1945: SECOND SINO-JAPANESE WAR

This section includes war crimes up to and through December 6, 1941 when the Second Sino-Japanese War became the Asian Theater of World War II, due to certain events of December 7, 1941. For war crimes after this date see the section called World War II: Japan perpetrated crimes.

AXIS POWERS (LISTED BY COUNTRY)

The Axis Powers (particularly Germany and Japan) were perhaps the most systematic perpetrators of war crimes in modern

Armed conflict		Perpetrator	
Second Sino-Japanese War		Japan	
Incident	Type of crime	Persons responsible	Notes
Attack on China in 1937	Crimes against peace (Waging unprovoked war against China	Sadao Araki, Kenji Doihara, Kingoro Hashimoto, Shunroku Hata, Kiichiro Hiranuma, Koki Hirota, Naoki Hoshino, Seishiro Itagaki, Okinori Kaya, Koichi Kido, Heitaro Kimura, Kuniaki Koiso, Jiro Minami, Akira Muto,	

	(count 27 at the Tokyo Trials))	Takazumi Oka, Hiroshi Oshima, Kenryo Sato, Mamoru Shigemitsu, Shigetaro Shimada, Teiichi Suzuki, Toshio Shiratori, Shigenori Togo, Hideki Tojo, Yoshijiro Umezu	
Nanking Massacre, China, 1937-38	Crimes against humanity; War crimes (Mass murder of civilian population & POWs, rape, looting)	General Asaka Yasuhiko, commander, Japanese Shanghai Expeditionary Force, Imperial Japanese Army. General Iwane Matsui, Commanding general of Japanese forces in China, Imperial Japanese Army. Chief of staff of the Army Kotohito Kan'in, Minister of War Hajime Sugiyama. Debate still is ongoing as to the culpability of Emperor Hirohito in the events.	After the Battle of Nanking, on 13 December 1937, Japanese entered the city virtually resistance free. From then for a period of about 6 weeks after, until early February 1938, widespread war crimes were committed including mass rape, looting, arson, the killing of civilians and prisoners of war. Most estimates put deaths at between 150,000 and 300,000 with newly declassified US government documents estimating an additional 500,000 outside Nanking before its fall.
Hankow massacre,China, 1938	War crimes (Mass execution of POWs)	General Shunroku Hata, commander, China Expeditionary Army , Imperial Japanese Army.	War crimes were committed including the killing of civilians and prisoners of war.

history. Contributing factors included Nazi race theory, a desire for "living space" that justified the eradication of native populations, and militaristic indoctrination that encouraged the terrorisation of conquered peoples and prisoners of war. The Holocaust, the German attack on Russia and occupation of Western Europe, and the Japanese occupation of Manchuria and attack on China contributed to well over half of the civilian deaths in World War II and the conflicts that led up to the war.

CROATIAN PERPETRATED CRIMES

Numerous concentration camps were built in Croatia, most notably Jasenovac, the largest, where hundreds of thousands of Serbs, Gypsies (Roma), Jews and Croatian dissidents died. It was established by the Ustaša regime of the Independent State of Croatia in August 1941 and not dismantled until April 1945, shortly before the end of the war. Other concentration camps were in Gospiæ, Pag, Đakovo, Jastrebarsko and Lepoglava.

According to the Simon Wiesenthal Center (citing the *Encyclopedia of the Holocaust*), "Ustasa terrorists killed 500,000 Serbs, expelled 250,000 and forced 250,000 to convert to Roman Catholicism. They murdered thousands of Jews and Gypsies."

Jasenovac was a complex of five subcamps and three smaller camps spread out over 240 square kilometers (93 square miles), in relatively close proximity to each other, on the bank of the Sava river. Most of the camp was at Jasenovac, about 100 km (62 miles) southeast of Zagreb. The complex also included large grounds at Donja Gradina directly across the Sava River, a camp for children in Sisak to the northwest, and a women's camp in Stara Gradiška to the southeast.

Ante Paveliæ, leader of the Ustasha, fled to Argentina and Spain which gave him protection, and was never extradited to stand trial for his war crimes.

GERMAN PERPETRATED CRIMES

According to the Nuremberg Trials, there were four major war crimes that were alleged against German military (and Waffen-SS and NSDAP) men and officers, each with individual events that made up the major charges.

1. Participation in a common plan of conspiracy for the accomplishment of crimes against peace.

2. Planning, initiating and waging wars of aggression and other crimes against peace.

- Planning and executing a campaign of invasion of its European neighbors, as well as the conspiracy to violate the Treaty of Versailles and the Treaty of Saint-Germain through the remilitarisation of the Rhineland, and the annexations of Austria and Czechoslovakia.

3. **War Crimes.** These were limited to atrocities against

combatants or conventional crimes committed by military units (see War crimes of the Wehrmacht), and include:

- Invasion of Poland, in the period of 1 September–25 October 1939 German Wehrmacht during its military actions engaged in executions of Polish POWs, bombed hospitals, murdered civilians, shot refugees, executed wounded soldiers. The cautious estimates give a number of at least 16,000 murdered victims
- Pacification Operations in German occupied Poland, during the occupation of Poland by German Reich, Wehrmacht forces took part in several pacification actions in rural areas, that resulted in murder of at least 20,000 Polish villagers
- Le Paradis massacre, May 1940, British soldiers of the Royal Norfolk Regiment, captured by the SS and subsequently murdered. Fritz Knoechlein tried, found guilty and hanged.
- Wormhoudt massacre, May 1940, British and French soldiers captured by the SS and subsequently murdered. No one found guilty of the crime.
- d'Ardenne Massacres, June 1944 Canadian soldiers captured by the SS and murdered by 12th SS Panzer Division Hitlerjugend. SS General Kurt Meyer (Panzermeyer) sentenced to be shot 1946; sentence commuted; released 1954
- Malmedy massacre, December 1944, United States POWs captured by *Kampfgruppe Peiper* were murdered outside of Malmedy, Belgium.
- Gardelegen (war crime)
- Marzabotto massacre
- Sant'Anna di Stazzema
- Cefalonia Massacre
- Oradour-sur-Glane
- The annihilation of the Czech city of Lidice. As an act of vengeance for the murder of Reinhard Heydrich.
- Massacre of Kalavryta

- Distomo massacre
- The suppression of the 1944 Warsaw Uprising and subsequent leveling of the whole city
- The treatment of Soviet POWs throughout the war, who were not given the protections and guarantees of the Geneva Convention
- Unrestricted submarine warfare against merchant shipping
- Vinkt Massacre
- Heusden; town hall massacre (November 1944).

4. **Crimes against Humanity.** These were crimes that were committed well away from the lines of battle and were unconnected in any way to military activity.

- The major crime was the Holocaust, including:
    - o The construction and use of *Vernichtungslagern*, most prominently at Auschwitz, Buchenwald, Treblinka, Majdanek, Belzec, Sobibór, and Che³mno
        - ▪ The employment of other camps across Europe, including Dachau, Sachsenhausen, Mauthausen and Bergen-Belsen which served unofficially as death camps to a degree
    - o Death marches of prisoners, particularly in the last months of the war when the aforementioned camps were being overrun by the Allies
    - o The widespread use of slave labor and forced/unfree labor by the Nazi regime, including the use of concentration camp and extermination camp prisoners as slaves
    - o The establishment of Jewish Ghettos in Eastern Europe
    - o The use of SS Einsatzgruppen, mobile extermination squads
    - o Babi Yar
    - o Rumbula
    - o Dnepropetrovsk
    - o Ninth Fort

- o Simferopol
- o The massacre of 100,000 Jews and Poles at Paneriai
- o The suppression of the 1943 Warsaw Ghetto Uprising which erupted when the SS came to clear the ghetto and send all of the occupants to extermination camps
- o Izieu Massacre

Other crimes against humanity included:

- The Porajmos, the Nazi pogrom against the Romany peoples of Europe
- The £apanka or "Catching Game," – Nazi roundups of Poles in the major cities for slave labor and other purposes
- Nikolaev Massacre
- Operation Tannenberg, the AB Action and the Massacre of Lwów professors, all Nazi actions in Poland meant to mass murder the Polish intelligentsia and other potential leaders of resistance.
- The Nazi T-4 Euthanasia Programme, an aborted eugenics programme meant to kill German children who were mentally or physically handicapped. 200,000 people were gassed to death due to this programme.
- The Nazi crimes against Soviet POWs, resulted in some 3.3 million to 3.5 million deaths, about 60% of all Soviet POWs.

At least 10 million, and perhaps over 20 million innocent non-combatants were systematically murdered by the Nazi regime in the commission of crimes against humanity, of which the Holocaust lives on in particular infamy, since the largest number of deaths happened among Jewish citizens of states invaded or controlled by the Nazi regime. At least 5 to 6 million Jews were murdered by the Nazis, although a complete count may never be known. Though much of Continental Europe suffered from the Nazi murders, Poland and Russia, in particular, were the states most devastated by these crimes, with many of their Jewish and a good number of their Christian citizens slaughtered by the Nazi aggressor. After the war, from 1945 to 1949, the Nazi regime was put on trial in two tribunals in Nuremberg, Germany by the victorious Allied powers. The first tribunal indicted 24 major Nazi war criminals, and resulted in 19 convictions (of which 12 led to death sentences) and 3 acquittals, 2 of the accused died before a verdict was rendered. The second tribunal indicted 185 members of the military, economic, and political leadership of Nazi Germany, of which 142 were convicted and 35 were acquitted. In subsequent decades, approximately 20 additional war criminals who escaped capture in the immediate aftermath of World War II were tried in West Germany and Israel. In Germany and many other European nations, the Nazi Party is outlawed.

ITALIAN PERPETRATED CRIMES

- Invasion of Abyssinia: Waging a war of aggression for territorial aggrandizement, War crimes, Use of poisons as weapons, Crimes against humanity; in violation of the Kellogg-Briand Pact, and the customary law of nations, Italy invaded the Kingdom of Abyssinia in 1936 without cause cognizable by the law of nations, and waged a war of annihilation against Ethiopian resistance, using poisons against military forces and civilian persons alike, not giving quarter to POWs who had surrendered, and massacring civilians.
- Invasion of Albania: Waging a war of aggression for territorial aggrandizement; Italy invaded the Kingdom of Albania in 1939 without cause cognizable by the law of nations in a brief but bloody affair that saw King Zog deposed and an Italian proconsul installed in his place. Italy subsequently acted as the suzerain of Albania until its ultimate liberation later in World War II.
- War crimes in the Balkans, in France, Italy and on the Eastern Front
- No one has been brought to trial for war crimes, although in 1950 the former Italian defense minister was convicted for collaboration with Nazi Germany.

JAPANESE PERPETRATED CRIMES

This section includes war crimes from 7 December 1941 when the United States was attacked by Japan so entering World War II. For war crimes before this date which took place during the Second Sino-Japanese War please see the section above called 1937-1945: Second Sino-Japanese War.

Incident	Type of crime	Persons responsible	Notes
World War II	Crimes against peace (Overall waging and/or conspiracy to wage a war of aggression for territorial aggrandizement, as established by the Tokyo Trials)	General Doihara Kenji, Baron Hirota Koki, General Itagaki Seishiro, General Kimura Heitaro, General Matsui Iwane, General Muto Akira, General Hideki Tojo, General Araki Sadao, Colonel Hashimoto Kingoro, Field Marshal Hata Shunroku, Baron Hiranuma Kiichiro, Hoshino Naoki, Kaya Okinori, Marquis Kido Koichi, General Koiso Kuniaki, General Minami Jiro, Admiral Oka Takasumi, General Oshima Hiroshi, General Sato Kenryo, Admiral Shimada Shigetaro, Shiratori Toshio, General Suzuki Teiichi, General Umezu Yoshijiro, Togo Shigenori, Shigemitsu Mamoru	Were tried by the International Military Tribunal for the Far East
Attack on the United States in 1941	Crimes against Peace (Waging aggressive war against the United States (count 29 at the Tokyo Trials)))	Kenji Doihara, Shunroku Hata, Kiichiro Hiranuma, Naoki Hoshino, Seishiro Itagaki, Okinori Kaya, Koichi Kido, Heitaro Kimura, Kuniaki Koiso, Akira Muto, Takasumi Oka, Kenryo Sato, Mamoru Shigemitsu, Shigetaro Shimada, Teiichi Suzuki, Shigenori Togo, Hideki Tojo, Yoshijiro Umezu	Admiral Isoroku Yamamoto, Commander-in-Chief of the Japanese Combined Fleet was ordered by his Militarist superiors to start the war with a bloody sneak attack on a U.S. Naval Base in Pearl Harbor, Hawaii, on December 7, 1941.
War started with attacks on Hong Kong and Malaya	Crimes against peace (Waging aggressive war against the British Commonwealth (count 31 at the Tokyo Trials))	Kenji Doihara, Shunroku Hata, Kiichiro Hiranuma, Naoki Hoshino, Seishiro Itagaki, Okinori Kaya, Koichi Kido, Heitaro Kimura, Kuniaki Koiso, Akira Muto, Takasumi Oka, Kenryo Sato, Mamoru Shigemitsu, Shigetaro Shimada,Teiichi Suzuki, Shigenori Togo, Hideki Tojo, Yoshijiro Umezu	

	Crimes against peace (Waging aggressive war against the Netherlands (count 32 at the Tokyo Trials))	Kenji Doihara, Shunroku Hata, Kiichiro Hiranuma, Naoki Hoshino, Seishiro Itagaki, Okinori Kaya, Koichi Kido, Heitaro Kimura, Kuniaki Koiso, Akira Muto, Takasumi Oka, Kenryo Sato, Mamoru Shigemitsu, Shigetaro Shimada,Teiichi Suzuki, Shigenori Togo, Hideki Tojo, Yoshijiro Umezu	
	Crimes against peace (Waging aggressive war against France in Indochina (count 33 at the Tokyo Trials))	Mamoru Shigemitsu, Hideki Tojo	
	Crimes against peace (Waging aggressive war against the USSR (counts 35 and 36 or both at the Tokyo Trials))	Kenji Doihara, Kiichiro Hiranuma, Seishiro Itagaki	
Nanjing Massacre; Narcotics Trafficking; Bacteriological Warfare	War crimes ("ordered, authorized, and permitted" inhumane treatment of Prisoners of War (POWs) and others (count 54 at the Tokyo Trials))	Kenji Doihara, Seishiro Itagaki, Heitaro Kimura, Akira Muto, Hideki Tojo	
Nanjing Massacre; Narcotics Trafficking; Bacteriological Warfare	War crimes, Crimes against humanity, Crime of torture ("deliberately and recklessly disregarded their duty" to take adequate steps to prevent atrocities (count 55 at the Tokyo Trials))	Shunroku Hata, Koki Hirota, Heitaro Kimura, Kuniaki Koiso, Iwane Matsui, Akira Muto, Mamoru Shigemitsu	
"Black Christmas", Hong Kong, December 25, 1941,	Crimes against humanity (Murder of civilians; mass rape, looting)	no specific prosecutions, although the conviction and execution of Takashi Sakai included some activities in Hong Kong during the time frame	On the day of the British surrender of Hong Kong to the Japanese, Japanese soldiers also terrorised the local population by murdering many, raping an estimated 10,000 women, and looting.

Banka Island Massacre, Dutch East Indies, 1942	Crimes against humanity (Murder of civilians)	no prosecutions	The merchant ship Vyner Brooke was sunk by Japanese aircraft. The survivors who made it to Banka Island were all shot or bayonetted, including 22 nurses ordered into the sea and machine-gunned. One nurse Vivian Bullwinkel survived the massacre and later testified at a war crimes trial in Tokyo in 1947
Bataan Death March, Philippines, 1942	Crime of torture, war crimes (Torture and murder of POWs)	General Masaharu Homma was convicted by an Allied commission of war crimes, including the atrocities of the death march out of Bataan, and the atrocities at Camp O'Donnell and Cabanatuan that followed. He was executed on April 3, 1946 outside Manila.	Approximately 75,000 Filipino and US soldiers, commanded by Major General Edward P. King, Jr. formally surrendered to the Japanese, under General Masaharu Homma, on April 9, 1942, which forced Japan to accept emaciated captives outnumbering them. Captives were forced to march, beginning the next day, about 100 kilometers north to Nueva Ecija to Camp O'Donnell, a prison camp. Prisoners of war were beaten randomly and denied food and water for several days. Those who fell behind were executed through various means: shot, beheaded or bayoneted. Deaths estimated at 650-1,500 U.S. and 2,000 to over 5,000 Filipino-,

Operation Sanko (Three Alls Policy)	Crime of genocide, Crimes against humanity (Extermination of civilians)	General Yasuji Okamura	Authorized in December 1941 to implement a scorched earth policy in North China by Imperial General Headquarters. According to historian Mitsuyoshi Himeta, "more than 2.7 million" civilians were killed in this operation that began in May 1942.
Parit Sulong massacre, Malaysia, 1942	War crimes (Murder of POWs)	Lieutenant General Takuma Nishimura, was convicted for this crime by an Australian Military Court and hanged on June 11, 1951.	Recently captured Australian and Indian POWs, who had been too badly wounded to escape through the jungle, were murdered by Japanese soldiers. Accounts differ on how they were killed. Two wounded Australians managed to escape the massacre and provide eyewitness accounts of the Japanese treatment of wounded prisoners of war, as did locals who witnessed the massacre. Official records indicate that 150 wounded men were killed.
Laha massacre, 1942	War crimes (Murder of POWs)	In 1946, the Laha massacre and other incidents which followed the fall of Ambon became the subject of the largest ever war crimes trial, when 93 Japanese personnel were tried by an Australian tribunal, at Ambon. Among other convictions, four men were executed as a result. Commander Kunito Hatakeyama, who was in direct command of the four massacres, was hanged; Rear Admiral Koichiro Hatakeyama, who was found to have ordered the killings, died before he could be tried.	After the battle Battle of Ambon, more than 300 Australian and Dutch prisoners of war were chosen at random and summarily executed, at or near Laha airfield in four separate massacres. "The Laha massacre was the largest of the atrocities committed against captured Allied troops in 1942.".

Alexandra Hospital massacre, Battle of Singapore, 1942	Crimes against humanity (Murder of civilians)	no prosecutions	At about 1pm on February 14, Japanese soldiers approached Alexandra Barracks Hospital. Although no resistance was offered, some of them shot or bayoneted staff members and patients. The remaining staff and patients were murdered over the next two days, 200 in all.
Sook Ching Massacre, 1942	Crimes against humanity (Murder of civilians)	In 1947, the British Colonial authorities in Singapore held a war crimes trial to bring the perpetrators to justice. Seven officers, were charged with carrying out the massacre. While Lieutenant General Saburo Kawamura, Lieutenant Colonel Masayuki Oishi received the death penalty, the other five received life sentences	The massacre (estimated at 25,000-50,000) was a systematic extermination of perceived hostile elements among the Chinese in Singapore by the Japanese military administration during the Japanese Occupation of Singapore, after the British colony surrendered in the Battle of Singapore on 15 February 1942.
Changjiao massacre,China, 1943	Crimes against humanity, War crimes (Mass murder of civilian population & POWs, rape, looting)	General Shunroku Hata, commander, China Expeditionary Army , Imperial Japanese Army.	War crimes were committed including mass rape, looting, arson, the killing of civilians and prisoners of war.

Manila Massacre	Crimes against humanity (Murder of civilians)	Tomoyuki Yamashita commander, Akira Muto chief of staff	As commander of the 14th Area Army in the Philippines, Gen. Yamashita failed to stop his troops from killing over 100,000 Filipino citizens of Manila while fighting with both native resistance forces and elements of the Sixth U.S. Army during the capture of the city in February, 1945. Yamashita pleaded inability to act and lack of knowledge of the massacre, due to his commanding other operations int the area. The defense failed, establishing the Yamashita Standard, which holds that a commander who makes no meaningful effort to uncover and stop atrocities is as culpable as if he had ordered them. His chief of staff Akira Muto was condemned by the Tokyo tribunal.
Wake Island Massacre	Crimes against humanity (Murder of civilians)	98 US Civilians killed on Wake Island October 5, 1943 by order of Rear Admiral Shigematsu Sakaibara	Shigematsu Sakaibara executed June 18, 1947; subordinate, Lieutenant-Commander Tachibana sentenced to death-later commuted to Life
Unit 100	Crimes against humanity; Use of poisons as weapons (biological warfare experiments on humans)	no prosecutions	

Unit 731	Crimes against humanity; War crimes; Crime of torture; Use of poisons as weapons (biological warfare testing, manufacturing, and use)	12 members of the Kantogun were found guilty for the manufacture and use of biological weapons. Including: General Yamada Otsuzo, former Commander-in-Chief of the Kwantung Army and Major General Kawashima Kiyoshi, former Chief of Unit 731.	During this biological and chemical weapons' program over 10,000 were experimented on without anesthetic and as many as 200,000 died throughout China. The Soviet Union tried some members of Unit 731 at the Khabarovsk War Crime Trials. However, those who surrendered to the Americans were never brought to trial as General Douglas MacArthur, Supreme Commander of the Allied Powers, secretly granted immunity to the physicians of Unit 731 in exchange for providing the United States with their research on biological weapons .
Unit 8604	Crimes against humanity; Use of poisons as weapons (biological warfare experiments on humans)	no prosecutions	
Unit 9420	Crimes against humanity; Use of poisons as weapons (biological warfare experiments on humans)	no prosecutions	
Unit Ei 1644	War crimes, Crimes against humanity; Use of poisons as weapons; Crime of torture (Human vivisection & chemical and biological weapon testing on humans)	no prosecutions	Unit 1644 conducted tests to determine human susceptibility to a variety of harmful stimuli ranging from infectious diseases to poison gas. It was the largest germ experimentation center in China. Unit 1644 regularly carried out human vivisections as well as infecting humans with cholera, typhus, and bubonic plague.

Construction of Burma-Thai Railway, the "Death Railway"	War crimes; Crimes against humanity (POWs and civilian labourers forced to support war effort; massive death toll.)	no prosecutions	The estimated total number of civilian labourers and POWs who died during construction is about 160,000.
Comfort Women	Crimes against humanity (Sexual enslavement of captured Allied women; mass rape.)	no prosecutions	Up to around 200,000 women were forced to work in Japanese military brothels.
Sandakan Death Marches.	Crimes against humanity, War crimes (Murder of civilian slave laborers and POWs)	Three Allied POWs survived to give evidence at war crimes trials in Tokyo and Rabaul. Hokijima was found guilty and hanged on April 6, 1946	Over 6,000 Indonesian civilian slave laborers and POWs died.
War Crimes in Manchukuo	Crimes against humanity; Crime of slaving (Slave labor)	Koa-in	According to historian Zhifen Ju, more than 10 million Chinese civilians were mobilized by the Imperial Japanese Army for slave labor in Manchukuo under the supervision of the Koa-in.
Kaimingye germ weapon attack	Crimes against humanity; War crimes, Use of poisons as weapons (Use of biological weapons)	no prosecutions	These bubonic plague attacks killing hundreds were a joint Unit 731 and Unit Ei 1644 endeavor.
Alleged Changde Bacteriological Weapon Attack April and May, 1943	Crimes against humanity; War crimes; Use of poisons as weapons (Use of chemical and biological weapons in massacre of civilians)	Prosecutions at the Khabarovsk War Crimes Trials	Chemical weapons supplied by Unit 516. Bubonic plague and poison gas were used against civilians in Chengde, followed by further massacres and burning of the city. Witold Urbanowicz, a Polish pilot fighting in China, estimated that nearly 300,000 civilians alone died in the battle.

ROMANIAN PERPETRATED CRIMES

Incident	type of crime	Persons responsible	Notes
Iasi pogrom	Crimes against humanity; Crime of genocide (murder of civilians, ethnic cleansing)	no prosecutions	
Odessa massacre	Crimes against humanity; Crime of genocide (murder of civilians, ethnic cleansing)	no prosecutions	
Aita Seaca massacre	Crimes against humanity (first, Hungarians killed 40 to 100 Romanian soldiers; a few months later, Romanian retaliations left 11 Hungarians dead)	no procecutions	

ALLIED POWERS (LISTED BY COUNTRY)

Soviet Union Perpetrated Crimes

Concurrent with World War II			
Incident	type of crime	Persons responsible	Notes
Katyo massacre	War crimes (Murder of Polish POWs)	Lavrenty Beria, Joseph Stalin	An NKVD-committed massacre of tens of thousands of Polish officers and intelligentsia throughout the spring of 1940. Originally believed to have been committed by the Nazis in 1941 (after the invasion of eastern Poland and the USSR), it was finally admitted by Mikhail Gorbachev in 1990 that it had been a Soviet operation.
Invasion of Lithuania, Estonia, and Latvia	Crimes against humanity (Deportation and murder of civilian population)	Vladimir Dekanozov, Andrey Vyshinsky, Andrei Zhdanov, Ivan Serov, Joseph Stalin	An NKVD-committed deportation of hundreds of thousands of Baltic intelligentsia, land holders and their families in June 1941 and again in January 1949.

Nemmersdorf, East Prussia	War crimes, Crimes against humanity (Pillaging, and rape and murder of civilians, in contravention of Hague Conventions of 1907 "IV - The Laws and Customs of War on Land" Articles: 28,43,46,47,50)	No prosecutions	Nemmersdorf (today Mayakovskoye in Kaliningrad) was one of the first German settlements to fall to the advancing Red Army on October 22, 1944. It was recaptured by the Germans soon afterwards and the German authorities reported that the Red Army killed civilians there. Nazi propaganda widely disseminated the description of the event with horrible details, supposedly to boost the determination of German soldiers to resist the general Soviet advance. Because the incident was investigated by the Nazis and reports were disseminated as Nazi propaganda, discerning the facts from the fiction of the incident is difficult.
Invasion of East Prussia	War crimes, Crimes against humanity, Crime of genocide — spec. ethnic cleansing; in contravention of Hague Conventions of 1907 "IV - The Laws and Customs of War on Land"		War crimes committed by Soviet troops in the areas of Germany occupied by the Red Army. Estimated number of civilian victims in the years 1944-46: at least 300.000 (but not all of them victims of war crimes, many died through starvation, the cold climate and diseases

Treuenbrietzen	Crimes against humanity (Murder of German civilians)	Following the capture of the German city of Treuenbrietzen after fierce fighting. Over a period of several days at the end of April and beginning of May roughly 1000 inhabitants of the city, most of them men, were executed by Soviet troops.
Battle of Berlin	Crimes against humanity (Mass rape)	
Flight and expulsion of Germans from Poland during and after World War II, Expulsion of Germans after World War II	War crimes, Crimes against humanity, Crime of genocide (ethnic cleansing/forced deportation of Germans from their homes in Prussia, Pomerania, Silesia; means used include mass murder, forced rape, other human rights violations)	War crimes committed by Soviet troops in the areas of Germany occupied by the Red Army. Estimated number of civilian victims in the years 1944-46: at least 300,000 (but not all of them victims of war crimes, many died through starvation, the cold climate and diseases

UNITED KINGDOM PERPETRATED CRIMES

Incident	Type of crime	Persons responsible	Notes
Unrestricted submarine warfare against merchant shipping	Breach of London Naval Treaty (1930)	no prosecutions; Allied representatives admitted responsibility at Nuremberg Trials; questionable whether war crime or a breach of a treaty.	It was the conclusion of the Nuremberg Trials of Karl Dönitz that Britain had been in breach of the Treaty "in particular of an order of the British Admiralty announced on 8 May 1940, according to which all vessels should be sunk at sight in the Skagerrak"

The firebombing of the German city of Dresden is considered by many to have been a war crime due to the high number of civilian casualties.

UNITED STATES PERPETRATED CRIMES

Incident	Type of crime	Persons responsible	Notes
Unrestricted submarine warfare against merchant shipping	Breach of London Naval Treaty (1930)	no prosecutions: Chester Nimitz admitted responsibility at Nuremberg Trials: questionable whether war crime or a breach of a treaty.	During the post war Nuremberg Trials, in evidence presented at the trial of Karl Dönitz on his orders to the U-boat fleet to breach the London Rules, Admiral Chester Nimitz stated that unrestricted submarine warfare was carried on in the Pacific Ocean by the United States from the first day that nation entered the war.
Canicattì massacre	Crimes against humanity (Murder of civilians)	no prosecutions	During the Allied invasion of Sicily, eight civilians, including an eleven year old girl, were killed, though the exact number of casualties is uncertain. The incident was covered up fearing that it would lead to reprisals from the civilian population.
Biscari massacre	War crimes (Murder of POWs)	Sergeant Horace T. West: court-martialed and was found guilty, stripped of rank and sentenced to life in prison, though he was later released as a private. Captain John T. Compton was court-martialed for killing 40 POWs in his charge. He claimed to be following orders. The investigating officer and the Judge Advocate declared that Compton's actions were unlawful, but he was acquitted.	Following the capture of Biscari Airfield in Sicily on July 14, 1943, seventy-six German and Italian POWs were shot by American troops of the 180th Regimental Combat Team, 45th Division during the Allied invasion of Sicily. These killings occurred in two separate incidents between July and August 1943.
Dachau massacre	War crimes (Murder of POWs)	Investigated by U.S. forces, found lack of evidence to charge any individual, and a lack of evidence of any practice or policy; however, did find that SS guards were separated from Wehrmacht (regular German Army) prisoners before their deaths.	Some Death's Head SS guards of the Dachau concentration camp attempted to escape, and were shot.
Salina, Utah POW massacre	War crimes (Murder of POWs)	Private Clarence V. Bertucci determined to be insane and confined to a mental institution	Private Clarence V. Bertucci fired a machine gun from one of the guard towers into the tents that were being used to accommodate the German prisoners of war. Nine were killed and 20 were injured.
Rheinwiesenlager	War crimes (Deaths of POWs from starvation and exposure)	no prosecutions	The Rheinwiesenlager (Rhine meadow camps) were transit camps for millions of German POWs after World War II; there were at least thousands and potentially tens of thousands of deaths from starvation and exposure. Estimates range from just over 3,000 to as many as 71,000.

American Mutilation of Japanese War Dead	War crimes (Abuse of Remains)	Though there are no known prosecutions, the occasional mutilation of Japanese remains were recognized to have been conducted by U.S. forces, declared to be atrocities, and explicitly forbidden by order of the U.S. Judge Advocate General in 1943-1944.	Many dead Japanese were desecrated and/or mutilated, for example by urinating on them, shooting corpses, or taking Japanese body parts (such as skulls) as souvenirs or trophies. This is in violation of the law and custom of war, as well as the 1929 Third Geneva Convention, which provided that: "After every engagement, the belligerent who remains in possession of the field shall take measures to search for wounded and the dead and to protect them from robbery and ill treatment.""

The firebombing of Tokyo, as well as the atomic bombings of Hiroshima and Nagasaki, are considered by many to be war crimes because most of the victims were civilians.

YUGOSLAVIAN PARTISANS PERPETRATED CRIMES

Armed conflict		Perpetrator	
Yugoslavia campaign		Yugoslavian partisans	
Incident	Type of crime	Persons responsible	Notes
Foibe massacres	War crimes, crimes against humanity (murder of prisoners of war and civilians).	No prosecutions.	Following Italy's 1943 armistice with the Allied powers, Yugoslavian resistance forces executed an estimated 1,300-1,600 Italian troops and ethnic Italians living in Slovenian/Croatian territories adjacent to Italy.
Bleiburg massacre	War crimes, crimes against humanity (murder of prisoners of war and civilians).	No prosecutions.	The victims were Croatian soldiers and civilians (as well as a number of Chetniks), executed without trial as an act of vengeance for the crimes committed by the pro-Axis Ustaše regime controlled territories during World War II. Estimates vary, from 30,000 to 55,000.

1944-1945 killings in Ba?ka	War crimes, crimes against humanity (murder of prisoners of war and civilians).	No prosecutions.	1944-1945 ethnic cleansing in Ba?ka of thousands of ethnic Hungarians. Estimates vary from 5,000 to 50,000.

UNITED STATES PERPETRATED CRIMES

Armed conflict		Perpetrator	
Vietnam War		United States	
Incident	**Type of crime**	**Persons responsible**	**Notes**
My Lai Massacre	War crimes, Crimes against humanity (Murder of civilians)	Lt. William Calley convicted in 1971 of premeditated murder of 22 civilians for his role in the massacre and sentenced to life in prison. He served 3½ years under house arrest. Others were indicted but not convicted.	In March, 1968, a US army platoon led by Lt. William Calley killed (and in some cases beat, raped, tortured, or maimed) 347 to 504 unarmed civilians – primarily women, children, and old men – in the hamlets of My Lai and My Khe of Son Mo. The My Lai Massacre was allegedly an operation of the Phoenix Program. 26 US soldiers, including 14 officers, were charged with crimes related to the My Lai massacre and its coverup. Most of the charges were eventually dropped, and only Lt. Calley was convicted.

Operation Ranch Hand (Disputed)	Use of defoliant weapons that were (unintentionally) contaminated with poisonous pollutants.	No prosecution for war crimes. A class action law suit by Vietnamese victims at several U.S. courts was dismissed in 2005 and 2007. A further review by the whole panel of judges of the Court of Appeals confirmed this decision. In contrast, veterans of several nations have received in settlements compensations from the producers of the herbicides.	It is not doubted that the defoliants in question were used for their defoliant effects, and at the time of use, their long-term poisonous effects were not known to the U.S. military. There was no intention to poison whatsoever. However, their use did probably cause incredible human suffering to Vietnamese civilians, according to Vietnamese sources, 4.8 million Vietnamese people were exposed to Agent Orange, resulting in 400,000 deaths and disabilities, 500,000 children born with birth defects, and a further two million people have suffered cancers or other illnesses.

- "Vietnam War Crimes Working Group Files"—Briefly declassified (1994) and subsequently reclassified (2002) documentary evidence compiled by a Pentagon task force detailing endemic war crimes. Substantiating 320 incidents by Army investigators, including seven massacres from 1967 through 1971 in which at least 137 civilians died (not including My Lai). Seventy-eight other attacks on noncombatants in which at least 57 were killed, 56 wounded and 15 sexually assaulted. One hundred forty-one instances in which U.S. soldiers tortured civilian detainees or prisoners of war.

NORTH VIETNAMESE PERPETRATED CRIMES

North Vietnam:

- North Vietnamese troops executed 2500(disputed) civilians while occupying the city of Hue in 1968; thus constituting Crimes against humanity. An additional 3500 people are suspected to have been executed, but never found.

1971: BANGLADESH WAR

Armed conflict		Perpetrator	
1971 Bangladesh War		Pakistan	
Incident	Type of crime	Persons responsible	Notes
1971	War crimes, Crimes against humanity,	Allegedly the Pakistan Government, and the Pakistan Army and its local collaborators. A case was filed in the	During the Bangladesh War of 1971, widespread atrocities were committed against the Bengali population of East Pakistan (now Bangladesh), at a level that within Bangladesh, 'genocide' is the term that is still used to describe the event in almost every major publication and newspaper. Although the word 'genocide' was and is still used

Bangladesh atrocities	Crime of genocide (murder of civilians; genocide)	Federal Court of Australia on September 20, 2006 for crimes of Genocide, war crimes and crimes against humanity.	frequently amongst observers and scholars of the events that transpired during the 1971 war, the allegations that a genocide took place during the Bangladesh War of 1971 were never investigated by an international tribunal set up under the auspices of the United Nations, so the alleged genocide is not recognised as a genocide under international law.
Civilian Casualties	Crimes against humanity (murder of civilians)	no prosecutions	The number of civilians that died in the liberation war of Bangladesh is not known in any reliable accuracy. There has been a great disparity in the casualty figures put forth by Pakistan on one hand (26,000, as reported in the Hamoodur Rahman Commission) and India and Bangladesh on the other hand (From 1972 to 1975 the first post-war prime minister of Bangladesh, Sheikh Mujibur Rahman, mentioned that 3 million died on a dozen occasions).
Atrocities on women and minorities	Crimes against humanity; Crime of genocide; Crime of torture (torture, rape and murder of civilians)	no prosecutions	The minorities of Bangladesh, especially the Hindus, were specific targets of the Pakistan army. Numerous East Pakistani women were tortured, raped and killed during the war. The exact numbers are not known and are a subject of debate. Bangladeshi sources cite a figure of 200,000 women raped, giving birth to thousands of war-babies. Some other sources, for example Susan Brownmiller, refer to an even higher number of over 400,000. Pakistani sources claim the number is much lower, though having not completely denied rape incidents.

Killing of intellectuals	Crimes against humanity (murder of civilians)	no prosecutions	During the war, the Pakistan Army and its local supporters carried out a systematic execution of the leading Bengali intellectuals. A number of university professors from Dhaka University were killed during the first few days of the war. However, the most extreme cases of targeted killing of intellectuals took place during the last few days of the war. On December 14, 1971, only two days before surrendering to the Indian military and the Mukhti Bahini forces, the Pakistani army -- with the assistance of the Al Badr and Al Shams – systematically executed well over 200 of East Pakistan's intellectuals and scholars.

CAMBODIAN CIVIL WAR 1970-1994

The Extraordinary Chambers in the Courts of Cambodia for the Prosecution of Crimes Committed During the Period of Democratic Kampuchea, commonly known as the Cambodia Tribunal, is a joint court established by the Royal Government of Cambodia and the United Nations to try senior members of the Khmer Rouge for crimes against humanity committed during the Cambodian Civil War. The Khmer Rouge killed many people due to their political affiliation, education, class origin, occupation, or ethnicity.

CIVIL WAR IN AFGHANISTAN 1978–PRESENT

This war has ravaged the country for over 30 years now, with several foreign actors playing important roles during different periods. Since 2001 U.S. and NATO troops have been fighting in Afghanistan in the "War on Terrorism" that is also treated in the corresponding section below.

Armed conflict		Perpetrator	
Civil war in Afghanistan		Al Qaeda, Islamic Emirate of Afghanistan	
Incident	Type of crime	Persons responsible	Notes
Executions and torture after fall of Mazar-i-Sharif on August 8, 1998	War crimes (Murder, cruel or degrading treatment and torture; Summary execution)	Taliban	Mass killing of the locals; 4,000 to 5,000 civilians were executed, and many more reported tortured.
Assassination of Iranian diplomats	Crimes against humanity (murder of civilians), offenses against the customary law of nations (outrages upon diplomatic plenipotentiaries and agents)	Taliban	8 Iranian diplomats were assassinated and an Iranian press correspondent was murdered by the Taliban.
Murder of Ahmed Shah Massoud	War crimes (Perfidious use of suicide bombers disguised as journalists (who are protected persons) in murder.)	Islamic Emirate of Afghanistan, Al Qaeda	Perfidiously used suicide bombers disguised as television journalists to murder Ahmed Shah Massoud, leader of the Northern Alliance, the leader of the only remaining military opponent of the Taliban, days before the September 11th Attacks, constituting a failure to bear arms openly, and misuse of the status of protected persons, to wit, journalists in war zones.
Civil war in Afghanistan		Northern Alliance	
Incident	Type of crime	Persons responsible	Notes
Atrocities against Taliban prisoners of war	War crimes (Maltreatment leading to death of Islamic Emirate of Afghanistan POWs (Taliban))	Northern Alliance partisans	Allegedly did place captured Taliban POWs in cargo containers, and did seal them, leading to deaths of those within due to suffocation and excessive heat, thereby constituting war crimes.

1980-1988: IRAN – IRAQ WAR

Armed conflict		Perpetrator	
Iran–Iraq War		Iraq	
Incident	Type of crime	Persons responsible	Notes
Iran – Iraq War	Crimes against peace (Waging a war of aggression)	no prosecutions	In 1980, Iraq invaded neighboring Iran, allegedly to capture Iraqi territory held by Iran.
Use of chemical weapons	War crimes, Use of poisons as weapons (Violation of 1925 Geneva Protocol)	No prosecutions	Iraq made extensive use of chemical weapons, including mustard gas and nerve agents such as tabun. Iraqi chemical weapons were responsible for over 100,000 Iranian casualties (including 20,000 deaths).
Attacks on neutral shipping	Crime against peace (Attacks against parties not involved in a war)	No prosecutions	Iraq attacked oil tankers from neutral nations in an attempt to disrupt enemy trade
Halabja poison gas attack	Dutch court has ruled that the incident involved War Crimes and Genocide; also may involve the Use of poisons as weapons and Crimes against humanity.	Ali Hassan Abd al-Majid al-Tikriti, officially titled Secretary General of the Northern Bureau of the Ba'ath Party from March 1987 to April 1989, and advisor to Saddam Hussein, was convicted in June 2007 of war crimes and was sentenced to death by an Iraqi court, along with accomplices Sultan Hashem Ahmed and Hussein Rashid Mohammed. Frans van Anraat war crime.	Iraq also used chemical weapons against their own Kurdish population causing casualties estimated between several hundred up to 5,000 deaths. On December 23, 2005 a Dutch court ruled in a case brought against Frans van Anraat for supplying chemicals to Iraq, that "[it] thinks and considers legally and convincingly proven that the Kurdish population meets the requirement under the genocide conventions as an ethnic group. The court has no other conclusion that these attacks were committed with the intent to destroy the Kurdish population of Iraq." and because he supplied the chemicals before 16 March 1988, the date of the Halabja attack, he is guilty of a war crime but not guilty of complicity in genocide.

Armed conflict		Perpetrator	
Iran – Iraq War		Iran	
Incident	Type of crime	Persons responsible	Notes
Attacks on neutral shipping	Crime against peace (Attacks against parties not involved in the war)	no prosecutions	Iran attacked oil tankers from neutral nations in an attempt to disrupt enemy trade.
Using child soldiers in suicide missions	War crimes (Using child soldiers)	no prosecutions	Iran allegedly used volunteers (among them children) in high risk operations for example in clearing mine fields within hours to allow the advancement of regular troops.
Laid mines in international waters		no prosecutions	Mines damaged the US frigate USS Samuel B. Roberts

UGANDA 1985-PRESENT

- 20 years warfare
- The Times reports (November 26, 2005 p.27):

  Almost 20 years of fighting... has killed half a million people. Many of the dead are children... The LRA [a cannibalism cult] kidnaps children and forces them to join its ranks. And so, incredibly, children are not only the main victims of this war, but also its unwilling perpetrators... The girls told me they had been given to rebel commanders as "wives" and forced to bear them children. The boys said they had been forced to walk for days knowing they would be killed if they showed any weakness, and in some cases forced even to murder their family members... every night up to 10,000 children walk into the centre of Kitgum... because they are not safe in their own beds... more than 25,000 children have been kidnapped ...this year an average of 20 children have been abducted every week.
- The International Criminal Court has launched an investigation and has issued indictments against LRA leaders.

SABRA AND SHATILA MASSACRE 1982

Perpetrators were Lebanese Christian Phalangists, who entered the Sabra and Shatilla refugee camps in question to hunt for "terrorists" and subsequently massacred between upwards of five hundred to several thousand Palestinian civilians, constituting Crimes against humanity. There exists a question of whether the Israeli armed forces either had advanced knowledge that the hunt for "terrorists" by the Phalangists was planned to be a massacre, or, upon hearing reports of the atrocities, failed to stop their Phalangist allies from further killings of civilians. No Phalangists were prosecuted; Ariel Sharon, at the time the Israeli Defense Minister, was found by the Israeli non-judicial Kahan Commission to be indirectly responsible for not restraining the Phalangist forces in question, indirectly resulting in either the massacre, or its continuance after discovery; he was forced to resign from his post.

YUGOSLAV WARS 1991-1999

Croatian War of Independence 1991-1995

Armed conflict		**Perpetrator**	
Croatian War of Independence		**Yugoslav People's Army, Army of Serbian Krajina and paramilitary units.**	
Incident	**Type of crime**	**Persons responsible**	**Notes**
Borovo Selo killings	Crimes against humanity (Murder of 12 and wounding of 20 policemen)	Serb paramilitary units commanded by Vojislav Šešelj. Šešelj is on trial at ICTY.	2 May 1991
Ovčara massacre	Crimes against humanity, War crimes (Over 264 civilians and wounded POWs executed after Battle of Vukovar)	Serb Territorial Defense and paramilitary units. Mile Mrkšić sentenced to 20 years, Veselin Šljivančanin sentenced to 5 years. Miroslav Radić acquitted.	18 November - 21 November 1991; bodies buried in a mass grave
Dalj killings	War crimes (Execution of 11 detainees)	Territorial Defense of SAO SBWS under Željko Ražnatović. Dalj was also one of the charges on the Slobodan Milošević ICTY indictment.	21 September 1991; bodies buried in a mass grave in the village of Celija

Dalj massacre	War crimes (Massacre of 28 detainees)	Territorial Defense of SAO SBWS under Željko Ražnatović. Dalj was also one of the charges on the Slobodan Milošević ICTY indictment.	4 October 1991
Lovas massacre	War crimes; Crimes against humanity (Massacre of 70-75 detainees, most of whom were civilians.)	Yugoslav People's Army. Territorial Defense of SAO SBWS and Dušan Silni paramilitary unit. Ljuban Devetak and 17 individuals are being tried by Croatian Courts. Lovas was also one of the charges on the Slobodan Milošević ICTY indictment.	10 October 1991
Široka Kula massacre	Crimes against humanity (Massacre of 40 civilians.)	JNA and Krajina Serb Territorial Defense.	Široka Kula near Gospić. On October 13, 1991.
Baćin massacre	Crimes against humanity (Massacre of approximately 110 civilians.)	Serb Territorial Defense forces and SAO Krajina militia. Milan Babić and Milan Martić convicted by ICTY. Baćin was also one of the charges on the Slobodan Milošević ICTY indictment.	On 21 October 1991.
Ethnic cleansing of Lipovaca, Vukovići and Saborsko	Crimes against humanity (Massacre of 10 civilians.)	Serb-led JNA and TO forces. Milan Babić and Milan Martić convicted.	On November 7, 1991.
Saborsko massacre	Crimes against humanity (Massacre of 29 civilians.)	Serb-led JNA (special JNA unit from Niš) and rebel Serbs militia. Milan Babić and Milan Martić convicted.	On November 12, 1991.
Škabrnja massacre	Crimes against humanity, War crimes (Massacre of 86 civilians and POWs.)	Serb forces. Milan Babić and Milan Martić convicted.	On November 18, 1991.
Siege of Dubrovnik	Crimes against humanity (Shelling of civilian targets that killed almost 90 civilians)	JNA and Montenegrin territorial forces. Several JNA commanders sentenced.	Shelling of UNESCO protected World Heritage site. October 1991.

Voćin massacre	Crimes against humanity (Massacre of 32 civilians.)	White Eagles paramilitary group under Vojislav Šešelj, indicted by ICTY. Voćin was also one of the charges on the Slobodan Milošević ICTY indictment.	13 December 1991.
Bruška massacre	Crimes against humanity (Massacre of civilians)	Serb forces. Milan Babić and Milan Martić convicted.	On December 21, 1991
Zagreb rocket attack	Crimes against humanity (Shelling of civilian targets in 1995 that killed 7 and wounded at least 175)	RSK Serb forces. Leader Milan Martić bragged on Television about ordering the assault, the videotape being used against him at ICTY, convicted.	Rocket attack was started as revenge for Serb military defeat in Operation Flash.
Ethnic cleansing in Serb Krajina	Crime of genocide (Expulsion of almost 78,000 non-Serbs (mostly Croats))	JNA and Serb paramilitaries. Many people, including leaders Milan Babić and Milan Martić, convicted at ICTY and Croatian courts.	June-December 1991
Armed conflict		Perpetrator	
Croatian War of Independence		Croatian Army and paramilitary units	
Incident	Type of crime	Persons responsible	Notes
Lora prison camp	Crime of torture, War crimes (Torture of POWs)	Croatian army. Several people convicted by Croatian courts.	Croatian internment camp for Serb soldiers and civilians between 1992 and 1997
Borovo Selo killings	Crimes against humanity (Murder of 20 civilians)	Croatian police forces. No prosecutions	2 May 1991; started the ethnic conflict in Baranya, Eastern Slavonia and Western Syrmia
Gospić massacre	Crimes against humanity (Massacre of 50-100 civilians)	Croatian army. Commander Mirko Norac and others convicted by Croatian courts.	16 - 18 October 1991
Operation Otkos 10	Crimes against humanity; Crime of genocide (Killings of numerous individuals and expulsion of thousands of civilians from over 20 villages)	Croatian army. No prosecutions	31 October - 4 November 1991

Miljevci plateau incident	War crimes (Killings of 40 militiamen)	Croatian army. No prosecutions	21 June 1992; invasion and permanent occupation of territory under international protection; bodies buried in mass graves nearby
Battle for Maslenica Bridge	Crimes against humanity, War crimes (Killings of 490 or 491 individuals, including civilians)	Croatian army. No prosecutions	22 January - 1 February 1993; invasion of territory under international protection
Mirlovic Polje incident	Crimes against humanity (Murder of 7 elderly civilians)	Croatian paramilitaries. No prosecutions	6 September 1993; 5 men and 2 women, four were executed and three burned alive at the stake
Operation Medak Pocket	Crimes against humanity, War crimes, Crime against peace (Killings of at least 100 civilians; wounding 4 UN peacekeepers)	Croatian army. Commanders Janko Bobetko and Rahim Ademi. Ademi is on trial at ICTY; Bobetko died in the meantime	9 September - 17 September 1993; invasion of territory under international protection and assault on UN peacekeeping forces
Operation Flash	Crimes against humanity, Crime of genocide (Killings of at least 83 civilians and causing an exodus of 30,000)	Croatian army. No prosecutions	1 May - 3 May 1995; Western Slavonia fully taken from RSK; 53 were killed in their own homes, while 30 during the Croatian raids of the refugee colons; invasion and permanent occupation of territory under international protection

BOSNIAN WAR 1992-1995

Armed conflict		**Perpetrator**	
Bosnian War		Army of Republika Srpska, Paramilitary units from Serbia, local Serb police and civilians.	
Incident	**Type of crime**	**Persons responsible**	**Notes**
Srebrenica Massacre	Crime of genocide, Crimes against humanity (Murder of over 7,000 Bosnian Muslim men and boys)	Army of Republika Srpska. President Radovan Karadžić and General Ratko Mladić charged.	Following the fall of the eastern Bosnian enclave of Srebrenica the men were separated from the women and executed over a period of several days in July 1995.

Markale massacre	Crimes against humanity (Murder of 68 civilians and wounding 144)	Army of Republika Srpska. No prosecutions	The victims were civilians who were shopping in an open air market in Sarajevo when Serb forces shelled the market. Two separate incidents. February 1994; 68 killed and 144 wounded and August 1995; 37 killed and 90 wounded.
Tuzla massacre	Crimes against humanity (Murder of 72 and wounding of more than 200 individuals)	Army of Republika Srpska. ARS Officer Novak Đukić on trial.	On May 25, 1995 the Serb army shelled the city of Tuzla and killed 72 people with a single shell.
Korićani Cliffs massacre	Crimes against humanity, War crimes (More than 200 men executed.)	Serbian reserve police. Darko Mrđa was convicted.	
Ahatovići massacre	Crimes against humanity, Crime of torture (64 men and boys tortured, 56 killed.)	Serb forces. No prosecutions.	Rounded up in an attack on a village, they were tortured. Claiming they were going to be exchanged, Serb forces put them on a bus, which they attacked with machine guns and grenades on June 14, 1992. 8 survived by hiding under bodies of the dead.

Armed conflict		**Perpetrator**	
Bosnian War		**Croat forces HVO.**	
Incident	**Type of crime**	**Persons responsible**	-
Ahmići	Crimes against humanity according to ICTY; Murder of 116 civilians in the village of Ahmići	Croatian Defence Council No prosecutions	On April 16, 1993, the Croatian Defence Council attacked the village of Ahmići and killed 116 Bosniaks.
Stupni Do	Crimes against humanity according to ICTY; Murder of 37 civilians in the village of Stupni Do	Croatian Defence Council. No prosecutions.	On October 23, 1993, the Croatian Defence Council attacked the village of Stupni do and killed 37 Bosniaks.
Armed conflict		perpetrator	
Bosnian War		HVO and Konjic Territorial Defence (TO)	
Incident	type of crime	Persons responsible	-
Čelebići prison camp	Crime of torture	Konjic defence forces. The commander of the camp Zdravko Mucić and the deputy commander Hazim Delić were sentenced to 9 and 18 years.	

KOSOVO WAR 1998-1999

Armed conflict		Perpetrator	
Kosovo War		**KLA**	
Incident	**type of crime**	**Persons responsible**	**Notes**
Llapushnik prison camp	War crimes; Crimes against humanity; Crime of torture (inhumane treatment and torture of Serb and Albanian detainees; murder of 11 Albanian prisoners and execution of 21 detainees)	KLA prison guard Haradin Bala sentenced to 13 years by the ICTY. Fatmir Limaj and Isak Musliu acquitted	a 1998 internment camp for Serbs. Roms and Albanians who wouldn't submit to the KLA; 25-26 July 1998 detainees were thrown off the Berisha mountain
Metohija ethnic cleansing	Crimes against humanity (persecution of non-Albanians: at least 39 Serb and Roma civilians)	ex KLA Commander and Kosovo Prime Minister Ramush Haradinaj, commander of the Black Eagles Idriz Balaj and KLA Deputy Commander Lahi Brahimaj at trial in ICTY	1997-1998; wide-scale ethnic cleansing of western Kosovo, attacks on refugee camps and removal of Serbs, Roms and opposing Albanians
Kosovo War		NATO	
Incident	type of crime	Persons responsible	Notes
Operation Allied Force	Waging war without legal standing (Not crimes against peace, because not a war of aggression; e.g. did not seek territory by conquest.)	NATO countries; no prosecution: allegation controversial.	Entry into the Kosovo War without Article 51 self-defense justification or Resolution of the Security Council. Humanitarian intervention/alleged humanitarian bombing.
Operation Allied Force	War crimes (killing 500 - 3,500 civilians to airbombing)	NATO air forces under Wesley Clark. No prosecutions.	24-10 June 1999

1990-2000: LIBERIA / SIERRA LEONE

"Charles Taylor, the former Liberian President who is one of Africas most wanted men, has gone into hiding in Nigeria to avoid extradition to a UN war crimes tribunal... The UN war crimes tribunal in Sierra Leone holds Mr Taylor responsible for about 250,000 deaths. Throughout the 1990s, his armies and supporters, made up of child soldiers orphaned by the conflict wreaked havoc through a swath of West Africa. In Sierra Leone he supported the

Revolutionary United Front (R.U.F) whose rebel fighters were notorious for hacking off the limbs of civilians.

- Current action–Indicted on 17 counts of war crimes and crimes against humanity by the UN, which has issued an international warrant for his arrest. As of April 2006 located, extradited, and facing trial in Sierra Leone but then transferred to The Netherlands as requested by the Liberian government.

1990: INVASION OF KUWAIT

Armed conflict		Perpetrator	
1990:Invasion of Kuwait		Iraq	
Incident	**Type of crime**	**Persons responsible**	**Notes**
Invasion of Kuwait	Crimes against peace (waging a war of aggression for territorial aggrandizement; "breach of international peace and security" (UN Security Council Resolution 660))	no prosecutions	Did conspire to levy and did levy a war of aggression against Kuwait, a sovereign state, took it by force of arms, did occupy it, and did annex it, by right of conquest, a right utterly alien, hostile, and repugnant to all extant international law, being a grave breach of the Charter of the United Nations, and the customary international law, adhered to by all civilized nations and armed groups, thus constituting Crimes against peace.
Invasion of Kuwait	War crimes, Crimes against humanity, Crime of torture, Criminal environmental modification (Destruction of resources; murder, persecution, and torture of civilians and soldiers; willful environmental devastation and modification)	no prosecutions	Country devastated, resources intentionally and wantonly destroyed for no militarily necessitous purpose, murder of civilians, torture of residents and citizens of Kuwait, attempted criminal environmental modification on a global scale through intentional oil spills and soot from intentional oil well fires.

1998-2006: SECOND CONGO WAR

- Civil war 1998-2002, est. 5 million deaths; war "sucked in" Rwanda, Uganda, Angola, Zimbabwe and Namibia, as well as 17,000 United Nations peacekeepers, its "largest and most costly" peace mission and "the bloodiest conflict since the end of the Second World War."
- Fighting involves Mai-Mai militia and Congolese government soldiers. The Government originally armed the Mai-Mai as civil defence against external invaders, who then turned to banditry.
- 100,000 refugees living in remote disease ridden areas to avoid both sides
- Estimated 1000 deaths a day according to Oxfam:

  "The army attacks the local population as it passes through, often raping and pillaging like the militias. Those who resist are branded Mai-mai supporters and face detention or death. The Mai-mai accuse the villagers of collaborating with the army, they return to the villages at night and extract revenge. Sometimes they march the villagers into the bush to work as human mules."
- In 2003, Sinafasi Makelo, a representative of Mbuti Pygmies, told the UN's Indigenous People's Forum that during the Congo Civil War, his people were hunted down and eaten as though they were game animals. Both sides of the war regarded them as "subhuman". Makelo asked the UN Security Council to recognise cannibalism as a crime against humanity and an act of genocide.

2001-PRESENT: SEPTEMBER 11TH, AND THE "WAR ON TERRORISM"

Part of this section overlaps with the section Afghan Civil War listed above.

Armed conflict		Perpetrator	
September 11th Attacks		**Al Qaeda**	
Incident	**Type of crime**	**Persons responsible**	**Notes**
September 11th Attacks	Crimes against peace (waging a war of aggression against the United States)	Al Qaeda, as an entity, and personal responsibility of the principals thereof, including, but not limited to, "Shaikh" Osama bin Laden, Ayman al-Zawahiri, Khalid Shaikh Mohammed; Yamashita standard/Medina standard command responsibility of the Islamic Emirate of Afghanistan as an entity, including personal command responsibility of "Mullah" Omar of the Taliban/Islamic Emirate of Afghanistan; potentially other indicted or unindicted co-conspirators.	Allegedly ordered, incited, counseled, controlled, directed, and/or waged a common plan and conspiracy to levy a war of aggression upon the United States, being a grave breach of the customary international law, adhered to by all civilized nations and armed groups, thereby constituting crimes against peace.
September 11th Attacks/Attack on the World Trade Center	Crimes against humanity (Willful attacks directed upon civilian targets, to include the World Trade Center; the taking of hostages on board a civil transport aircraft, and their murder)	See previous entry; in addition, the actual perpetrators/attemptors of the attack include Zacharias Moussasoui, Mohammed Atta, et al.	Although carried out by a non-government agency, and actually non-state terrorism, by some are alleged to be war crimes. Perpetrator allegedly ordered, incited, counseled, controlled, directed, participated, and/or waged a common plan and conspiracy to commit and engage in unlawful attacks directed towards and with the express purpose of the destruction of civilian targets and devised so as to kill as many civilian persons as possible, did use a civil transport aircraft transporting non-combatants as a weapon, did take the civilians on board as hostages, and did willfully kill those same hostages, being a grave breach of the customary international law, adhered to by all civilized nations and armed groups, thereby constituting crimes against humanity.

September 11th Attacks/Attack on the Pentagon, Attempted attack upon the U.S. Capitol Building	War crimes, crimes against humanity (Perfidious attacks against C^4ISTAR targets of the U.S. military and government & the taking of civilian hostages and their murder.)	Although carried out by a non-government agency, and actually non-state terrorism, by some are alleged to be war crimes. Perpetrator allegedly ordered, incited, counseled, controlled, directed, participated, and/or waged a common plan and conspiracy to wage perfidious warfare against military and command and control targets of United States, being a grave breach of the customary law of war, adhered to by all civilized nations and armed groups, thereby constituting war crimes. These war crimes did consist, but were not limited to, the following acts of perfidy: 1. Failure to bear arms openly, 2. The use of civilian transport aircraft as a weapon, constituting violation of a flag of truce, and of occupying a protected place while engaged in combat, and the use of a protected place as a weapon, 3. The use of civilians on board civilian transport aircraft as human shields; Also: Allegedly ordered, incited, counseled, controlled, directed, participated, and/or waged a common plan and conspiracy to willfully take civilian hostages, and did murder them, being a grave breach of the customary international law, adhered to by all civilized nations and armed groups, thereby constituting crimes against humanity.

Armed conflict		**Perpetrator**	
War in Afghanistan (2001–present)		**United States**	
Incident	**Type of crime**	**Persons responsible**	**Notes**
Mistreatment of partisans as "unlawful enemy combatants"	War crimes (Deemed Islamic Emirate of Afghanistan (Taliban) POWs who obeyed law of war as "unlawful enemy combatants" and denied treatment due under 3rd Geneva due to fighting for unrecognized state)	Alleged perpetrators are suspected to include John Yoo, David Addington, perhaps other political figures; potential command responsibility of certain forces in the field.	During the initial, 2001-02 period of combat operations, allegedly deemed or conspired to deem Islamic Emirate of Afghanistan (Taliban) partisans who obeyed the law of war, including wearing a fixed distinguishing mark visible at a distance, bore arms openly, had a command structure, and obeyed the law and custom of war, as "unlawful enemy combatants", not subject to the rights of prisoners of war, thereby constituting a violation of 3rd Geneva, and thus, war crimes.

Interrogation and detention atrocities against IEA (Taliban) POWs, al-Qaeda enemy combatants, and al-Qaeda terrorists	War crimes, Crimes against humanity, Crime of torture (Detention of Islamic Emirate of Afghanistan (Taliban) POWs in inhumane conditions contrary to 3rd Geneva; detention of al-Qaeda enemy combatants and al-Qaeda terrorists, including several innocent non-combatants with mistaken identities, in outrageous and depraved conditions, contrary to 4th Geneva, Common Article 3; torture of persons captured in Afghan theater of war or elsewhere, including POWs, enemy combatants, and terrorists.)	Perpetrators, conspirators, and/or other responsible parties: 1. Alleged direct responsibility for ordering, counseling, advising, planning, establishing sham legal rationales, and/or inciting atrocities: John Yoo, Jay Bybee, William Haynes, Douglas Feith, Alberto Gonzalez, and, allegedly, at the apex, David Addington; 2. Alleged direct responsibility for aiding and abetting atrocities: SERE staff and attached psychologists/psychiatrists; 3. Alleged direct responsibility for actual commission of atrocities: Various U.S. lawful and unlawful combatants, including, but not limited to, SOCOM operators (lawful) and CIA paramilitaries (unlawful), potential involvement of regular military personnel; 4. Alleged Yamashita standard (willful blindness to action of own forces under direct command) command responsibility for atrocities: Donald Rumsfeld, various Polish military and intelligence entities (on whose territory atrocities were committed), SOCOM command staff, CIA supervisory staff; 5. Alleged Medina standard (knowledge of, but no action against) command responsibility for atrocities: potentially the high Constitutional officers of the United States, such as George W. Bush and Dick Cheney, depending on how much they knew, and when they knew it.	Alleged participation in or development of a common plan or conspiracy to detain prisoners of war in cruel, inhuman, and degrading conditions at various locations, including the Salt Pit at Bagram Air Base, a Polish "black site", and Guantanamo Bay; this conduct being unlawful under, alien to, and in direct breach of the Third Geneva Convention; alleged participation in or development of a common plan or conspiracy to detain protected persons in cruel, inhuman, and degrading conditions at various locations, including the Salt Pit at Bagram Air Base, a Polish "black site", and Guantanamo Bay; this conduct being unlawful under, alien to, and in direct breach of the Fourth Geneva Convention, Common Article 3. Alleged participation in or development of a common plan or conspiracy to aid, abet, incite, counsel, plan, accessorize, enable, suborn, levy, control, direct, instigate, and/or commit the Crime of torture, as well as other atrocities, against prisoners of war and/or protected persons (to include "unlawful" combatants and terrorists), or did act as accessories after the fact, thereby constituting War crimes, Crimes against humanity, and the Crime of torture.

2003-PRESENT: IRAQ WAR

- (prior to invasion) murders of civilians by Iraqi government forces, including alleged use of chemical weapons.
- abuse and torture of prisoners by U.S. forces at Abu Ghraib detention facility; some soldiers prosecuted, but persons with command responsibility not charged.
- numerous suicide bombings of civilians by unknown parties.
- destruction of Fallujah by U.S. troops.
- ethnic cleansing (forcible removals or murders of civilian members of ethnic groups by armed marauders; various organisations with some members captured and/or prosecuted).
- Haditha killings by U.S. troops.
- Mahmudiyah killings involving the rape and murder of a 14 year old girl and the murder of her family by U.S. troops.
- Mukaradeeb killings also known as the Wedding Party massacre, by U.S. troops.
- 2006 al-Askari Mosque bombing.

2003-PRESENT: DARFUR CONFLICT, WAR IN CHAD (2005–PRESENT)

- The entire conflict is allegedly a genocide perpetrated by the involved combatants in Darfur.

Sudanese authorities claim a death toll of roughly 19,500 civilians while many non-governmental organisations, such as the Coalition for International Justice, claim over 400,000 people have been killed. In September 2004, the World Health Organisation estimated there had been 50,000 deaths in Darfur since the beginning of the conflict, an 18-month period, mostly due to starvation. An updated estimate the following month put the number of deaths for the 6-month period from March to October 2004 due to starvation and disease at 70,000; These figures were criticized, because they only considered short periods and did not include deaths from violence. A more recent British Parliamentary Report has estimated that over 300,000 people have died, and others have estimated even more.

2007–2009 MAY: SRI LANKAN CIVIL WAR, EELAM WAR IV

- By the name of 'War On Terror' Sri Lankan government forces started offensive attack against Tamil Tigers, since 2007. A UN's unconfirm number report says more then 20,000 would have been died. 20,000 killed.

BIBLIOGRAPHY

Adams, James, *The Next World War: Computers are the Weapons and the Front line is Everywhere*, Simon and Schuster, 1998.

Alibek, K. and S. Handelman. *Biohazard: The Chilling True Story of the Largest Covert Biological Weapons Programme in the World–Told from Inside by the Man Who Ran it.* Delta, 2000.

Anthony Joes, James, *Resisting Rebellion: The History and Politics of Counterinsurgency*, Lexington, KY: University Press of Kentucky, 2004.

Armistead, Leigh, *Information Operations: The Hard Reality of Soft Power,* Joint Forces Staff College and the National Security Agency, 2004.

Broad, William J. and David Johnston. "Report Linking Anthrax and Hijackers Is Investigated," *The New York Times*, March 23, 2002, p. A9.

Brophy, L. P., W. D. Miles and C. C. Cochrane, *The Chemical Warfare Service: From Laboratory to Field*, 1959.

Callwell, C.E., *Small Wars: Their Principles & Practice*, Lincoln, Nebraska: Bison Books, 1996.

Catignani, Sergio, *Israeli Counter-Insurgency and the two Intifadas: Dilemmas of a Conventional Army*, London: Routledge, 2008.

Cohen, Fred. *Frauds, Spies, and Lies–and How to Defeat Them*, 2006.

Cohen, Fred. *World War 3 ... Information Warfare Basics*, ASP Press, 2006.

Coleman, Kim (2005). *A History of Chemical Warfare*. Palgrave MacMillan.

Croddy, Eric; Perez-Armendariz, Clarissa; Hart, John (2002). *Chemical and Biological Warfare: A Comprehensive Survey for the Concerned Citizen.* Copernicus Books.

Denning, Dorothy, *Information Warfare and Security*, Addison-Wesley, 1998.

Giuseppe Gagliano-Maurizio Boni, *Sicurezza internazionale e controllo degli armamenti*, New Press 2001.

Gordon, M. Burck and Charles C. Flowerree; *International Handbook on Chemical Weapons Proliferation* 1991

Gregory, J. Rattray, *Strategic Warfare in Cyberspace*, MIT Press, 2001.

Haber, L. F. *The Poisonous Cloud: Chemical Warfare in the First World War* Oxford University Press: 1986

Ivan, Arreguín-Toft, "How to Lose a War on Terror: A Comparative Analysis of a Counterinsurgency Success and Failure," in Jan Ångström and Isabelle Duyvesteyn, Eds., *Understanding Victory and Defeat in Contemporary War*, London: Frank Cass, 2007.

Ivan, Arreguín-Toft, "Tunnel at the End of the Light: A Critique of U.S. Counter-terrorist Grand Strategy," *Cambridge Review of International Affairs*, Vol. 15, No. 3, 2002, pp. 549–563.

Ivan, Arreguín-Toft, *How the Weak Win Wars: A Theory of Asymmetric Conflict*, New York: Cambridge University Press, 2005.

James, W. Hammond Jr.; *Poison Gas: The Myths Versus Reality* Greenwood Press, 1999

Jiri, Janata, Role of Analytical Chemistry in Defense Strategies Against Chemical and Biological Attack, *Annual Review of Analytical Chemistry,* 2009

John, Arquilla and David Ronfeldt, *In Athena's Camp*, RAND, 1997.

John, Arquilla and David Ronfeldt, *Networks and Netwars: The Future of Terror, Crime, and Militancy*, RAND, 2001.

John, H. Jr. Cushman "Rattling New Sabers," *The New York Times*, March 10, 2002, p. A1.

Jonathan, B. Tucker. *Chemical Warfare from World War I to Al-Qaeda*, 2006.

Joseph, Cirincione. "A Much Less Explosive Trend," *The Washington Post*, March 10, 2002, p. B3.

Kitson, Frank. *Low Intensity Operations: Subversion, Insurgency and Peacekeeping*, 1971.

Kleber, B.E. and D. Birdsell, *The Chemical Warfare Service in Combat*, 1966.

Knollenberg, Bernhard, "General Amherst and Germ Warfare," Mississippi Valley Historical Review 41, 1954-1955, 489-494.

Leo, P. Brophy and George J. B. Fisher; *The Chemical Warfare Service: Organizing for War* Office of the Chief of Military History, 1959.

Linebarger, Paul M. A. *Psychological Warfare*. International Propaganda and Communications, ASP Press, 1948.

Merom, Gil, *How Democracies Lose Small Wars: State, Society, and the Failures of France in Algeria, Israel in Lebanon, and the United States in Vietnam*, New York: Cambridge University Press, 2003.

Michael, L. Burgoyne and Albert J. Marckwardt, 2009. *The Defense of Jisr al-Doreaa With E. D. Swinton's "The Defence of Duffer's Drift"*. University of Chicago Press.

Michael, R. Gordon "Nuclear Arms: For Deterrence or Fighting?" *The New York Times*, March 11, 2002, p. A1.

Morel, Benoit and Kyle Olson; *Shadows and Substance: The Chemical Weapons Convention* Westview Press, 1993

Plunkett, Geoff, *Chemical Warfare in Australia*, Australian Military History Publications, 2007

Rid, Thomas, *War and Media Operations: The US Military and the Press from Vietnam to Iraq*], Routledge, 2007.

Schwartau, Winn ed, *Information Warfare: Cyberterrorism: Protecting your personal security in the electronic age*, Thunder's Mouth Press, 2nd ed, 1996.

Ventre, Daniel, *Information Warfare*, Wiley–ISTE, 2009.

Waltz, Edward, *Information Warfare Principles and Operations*, Artech House, 1998.

Wheeler-Bennett, Sir John. *Disarmament and security since Locarno 1925-1931; being the political and technical background of the general disarmament conference, 1932*, New York, Howard Fertig, 1973.

Wines, Michael. "Russia Assails U.S. Stance on Arms Reduction," *The Washington Times*, March 12, 2002, p. A4.

INDEX

A

B

C

D

E

G

H

I

J

K

L

M

N